SRA Reading Mastery

Signature Edition

Presentation Book B
Grade 5

Siegfried Engelmann
Jean Osborn
Steve Osborn
Leslie Zoref

McGraw Hill SRA

Columbus, Ohio

SRAonline.com

 SRA

Send all inquiries to this address:
SRA/McGraw-Hill
4400 Easton Commons
Columbus, OH 43219

ISBN: 978-0-07-612652-1
MHID: 0-07-612652-8

2 3 4 5 6 7 8 9 10 BCM 13 12 11 10 09 08 07

The McGraw-Hill Companies

Table of Contents

Curriculum Map *following final lesson*

Lessons 61–65 • Planning Page

	Lesson 61	**Lesson 62**	**Lesson 63**	**Lesson 64**	**Lesson 65**
BEFORE READING	Hard words Word practice New vocabulary Vocabulary definitions Accents	Hard words New vocabulary Vocabulary definitions	Word practice New vocabulary Vocabulary definitions	Word practice New vocabulary Vocabulary definitions Deductions	Word practice New vocabulary Vocabulary definitions Conversations
NEW VOCABULARY	rebel smirk suppress pirate oyster	forecastle skiff loot	hoist collide churn	bungle puny outwit harsh tow naval surge principal	quarantine station stir mar keg bait
READING	"Pirates on the Bay"	*The Cruise of the Dazzler* (Chapter 1)	*The Cruise of the Dazzler* (Chapter 2)	*The Cruise of the Dazzler* (Chapter 3)	*The Cruise of the Dazzler* (Chapter 4)
INDEPENDENT WORK	Maps Relevant information Sarcasm Deductions Accents Comprehension Writing	Story details Vocabulary Perspectives Deductions Accents Vocabulary review Sarcasm Similes Comprehension Writing	Story details Vocabulary Poem review Character traits Drawing conclusions Perspectives Inference Comprehension Writing	Story details Vocabulary Cause and effect Story review Perspectives Deductions Main idea Vocabulary review Comprehension Writing	Story details Vocabulary Contradictions Perspectives Conversations Vocabulary review Comprehension Writing
SUPPLEMENTS	*Spelling*	*Spelling*	*Spelling*	*Spelling*	*Spelling* *Activities across the Curriculum*

Comprehension Questions Abbreviations Guide

Access Prior Knowledge = (APK)   Author's Point of View = (APoV)   Author's Purpose = (AP)   Cause/Effect = (C/E)   Charts/Graphs/Diagrams/Visual Aids = (VA)

Classify and Categorize = (C+C)   Compare/Contrast = (C/C)   Determine Character Emotions, Motivation = (DCE)   Drawing Conclusions = (DC)   Drawing Inferences = (DI)

Fact and Opinion = (F/O)   Hypothesizing = (H)   Main Idea = (MI)   Making Connections = (MC)   Making Deductions = (MD)   Making Judgements = (MJ)

Narrative Elements = (NE)   Noting Details = (ND)   Predict = (P)   Reality/Fantasy = (R/F)   Recall Facts/Rules = (RF/R)   Retell = (R)   Sequence = (Seq)

Steps in a Process = (SP)   Story Structure = (SS)   Summarize = (Sum)   Understanding Dialogue = (UD)   Using Context to Confirm Meaning(s) = (UCCM)   Visualize = (V)

BEFORE READING

(Have students find lesson 61, part A, in their textbooks.)

Hard Words

1. Look at column 1.
- These are hard words from your textbook stories.

1. rebel	4. San Francisco
2. Farallon Islands	5. Santa Cruz
3. San Jose	6. Yukon

2. Word 1 can be pronounced in two different ways. One way is **REH bull.** Everybody, say that pronunciation. (Signal.) *REH bull.*
- The second pronunciation is **ree BELL.** Everybody, say that pronunciation. (Signal.) *Ree BELL.*
- You will be learning the meaning of the second pronunciation.
3. Line 2 is **Farallon** [FAIR uh lawn] **Islands.** Everybody, what words? (Signal.) *Farallon Islands.*
- (Repeat this procedure for every word in the column.)
4. Let's read the words again.
5. Word 1. Everybody, say the first pronunciation. (Signal.) *REH bull.*
- Say the second pronunciation. (Signal.) *Ree BELL.*
6. Line 2. Everybody, what words? (Signal.) *Farallon Islands.*
- (Repeat this procedure for every word in the column.)
7. (Repeat the column until firm.)

Word Practice

1. Look at column 2.
- We're going to practice these words.

1. cruise	4. experience
2. patrol	5. valuable
3. amusement	

2. Word 1. Everybody, what word? (Signal.) *Cruise.*
- (Repeat this procedure for every word in the column.)
3. (Repeat the column until firm.)

New Vocabulary

1. Look at column 3.
- First we'll read the words in this column. Then we'll read their definitions.

1. rebel	4. pirate
2. smirk	5. oyster
3. suppress	

2. Word 1. Everybody, say the second pronunciation. (Signal.) *Ree BELL.*
3. Word 2. Everybody, what word? (Signal.) *Smirk.*
- (Repeat this procedure for every word in the column.)
4. (Repeat the column until firm.)

Vocabulary Definitions

1. Everybody, find part B. ✔
- These are definitions for the words you just read.
2. (For each word, call on a student to read the definition and the item. Then ask the student to complete the item.)

1. **rebel**—When you *rebel,* you resist doing something you're expected to do. When you resist doing the dishes, you rebel against doing the dishes.
- What's another way of saying *She resisted cleaning her room*?

- What's the answer? (Response: *She rebelled against cleaning her room.*)

2. **smirk**—A *smirk* is a mocking smile.
- What's another way of saying *Wipe that mocking smile off your face*?

- What's the answer? (Response: *Wipe that smirk off your face.*)

3. **suppress**—When you *suppress* something, you hold it back.
- What are you doing when you try to hold back laughter?

- What's the answer? (Idea: *Suppressing laughter.*)

4. **pirate**—A *pirate* is a person who uses a ship or a boat to commit crimes.
- What kinds of crimes do pirates commit?

- What's the answer? (Ideas: *Robbing other ships; stealing cargo from docks; kidnapping people.*)

5. **oyster**—An *oyster* is a small shellfish that people eat. Gems called pearls grow in some types of oysters.
- What's an oyster?

- What's the answer? (Idea: *A small shellfish that people eat.*)

EXERCISE 5
Accents

1. Everybody, turn to part D at the end of today's story. ✔
- (Call on individual students to read several sentences each.)
- (At the end of each section, present the questions for that section.)

You will be reading about a character named Pete, who comes from France. Pete has trouble pronouncing English words such as *the* and *this*.
   Here are statements Pete might make. Rewrite each statement using correct English spelling.
1. "Dis is ze new sailor."

- What's the answer? (Response: *This is the new sailor.*)

2. "His name is Mistaire Joe Díaz."

- What's the answer? (Response: *His name is Mister Joe Díaz.*)
- You'll write the answers later.

READING

EXERCISE 6
Focus Question

1. Everybody, find part C. ✔
2. What's the focus question for today's lesson? (Response: *In what ways is* The Cruise of the Dazzler *a true story?*)

Note: The "Reading Aloud" exercise is recommended for this lesson.

EXERCISE 7
Reading Aloud

1. We're going to read aloud to the diamond.
- (Call on individual students to read several sentences each.)
- (At the end of each section, present the questions for that section.)

Pirates on the Bay
Focus Question: In what ways is *The Cruise of the Dazzler* a true story?

   In the next lesson, you will begin reading *The Cruise of the Dazzler,* a novel by Jack London. The novel tells about the adventures of Frisco Kid and Joe Díaz, two boys who cruise around San Francisco Bay in a pirate ship called the *Dazzler.*
   The story takes place during the 1890s. At that time, many different types of ships sailed around San Francisco Bay. Some of these ships carried passengers, some carried cargo—and some carried pirates. Pirate ships such as the Dazzler were often fast sailboats called sloops. These sloops could outrace many of the police ships and other patrol boats on the bay.

- One character is named Frisco Kid. What city does his name sound like? (Response: *San Francisco.*) **APK**
- About how many years ago does the novel take place? (Idea: *About a hundred.*) **ND**

- Why do you think the pirates used sailboats instead of boats with motors? (Idea: *Motorboats hadn't been invented yet*.) (DI)

The Bay Area

The map shows the San Francisco Bay Area. Three large cities—Oakland, San Francisco, and San José—are located on the eastern, western, and southern sides of the bay. Near the middle of the bay is Angel Island, one of several small islands scattered throughout the bay.

A narrow channel called the Golden Gate connects the bay to the Pacific Ocean. In the 1930s, the Golden Gate Bridge was built across the channel. Before that time, the only way to get across the channel—or any other part of the bay—was by boat. Now tunnels and bridges cross the bay at several locations.

About thirty miles west of the Golden Gate is a small group of rocky islands called the Farallon Islands. A lighthouse on these islands helps guide ships through fog and storms. During the 1890s, several people lived on the islands to take care of the lighthouse. Nowadays, however, the lighthouse is run by machines, so people no longer live on the islands.

Several towns are located on the shores of the Pacific Ocean south of San Francisco. One of these towns is Santa Cruz, which has a small harbor and a famous amusement park. Santa Cruz is about seventy miles south of the Golden Gate. ♦

- Everybody, look at the map.

- Which city is on the eastern side of the bay? (Response: *Oakland*.) (VA)
- Which city is on the western side of the bay? (Response: *San Francisco*.) (VA)
- Which two bodies of water are connected by the Golden Gate? (Idea: *San Francisco Bay and the Pacific Ocean*.) (VA)
- Which islands are straight west from the Golden Gate? (Response: *Farallon Islands*.) (VA)
- Which town is about seventy miles south of the Golden Gate? (Response: *Santa Cruz*.) (VA)

EXERCISE 8

Silent Reading

1. Read the rest of the lesson to yourselves and be ready to answer some questions.

The Oyster Pirate

Jack London, who lived from 1876 to 1916, is one of America's most famous and most popular writers. His novels and short stories have been translated into dozens of foreign languages, and he has millions of fans all over the world. His best-known novel is *The Call of the Wild* (published in 1903), an exciting story about a sled dog's adventures during the Yukon Gold Rush. London's other important novels include *The Sea Wolf* (1904), *White Fang* (1906), and *The Iron Heel* (1908).

London was born in San Francisco but grew up across the bay in Oakland. His family was poor, so he quit school at age fourteen and tried earning a living as a fisherman. Fishing didn't pay very well, but London soon discovered he could make money by stealing oysters.

At that time, oyster farming was big business in the Bay Area. Farmers raised oysters in shallow places along the shore of the bay. London and other pirates would sail up to these oyster beds at night, steal the oysters, and sell them in town the next day.

When he was fifteen, London bought a sloop called the *Razzle-Dazzle*. The sloop—whose name is very much like the *Dazzler*—was so fast that the patrol boats didn't even try to catch it. After a few months, however, London got tired of running from the law. He turned his life around and started working for the California Fish and Game Patrol, capturing some of the very same pirates who used to steal oysters with him. ★

The Writer

One day, London walked into the Oakland library and read a story called "The Cruise of the Pirate-Ship Moonraker." The experience changed his life, and he decided to become a writer.

In the next few years, London finished high school and went on to college, but then he quit school again to join the Yukon Gold Rush in 1897. When he returned to Oakland in 1898, he started writing in earnest.

The Cruise of the Dazzler (1902) was one of London's first novels, and it's the only book he ever wrote for young readers. Many of the events in the book are based on London's experiences as a pirate in San Francisco Bay. He changed one important element, however. Instead of just stealing oysters, the pirates go after more valuable cargo.

As you read the novel, try to figure out which character might be Jack London in disguise. Also think about what the characters learn and what it's like to be a pirate.

- Explain what oyster pirates did. (Idea: *Sailed up to oyster beds, stole the oysters, and sold them in town.*) Ⓡ
- Why did London become an oyster pirate? (Idea: *He needed the money.*) ⒹⒸⒺ
- Why do you think London stopped being an oyster pirate? (Ideas: *He was tired of running from the law; he knew stealing was wrong; he was afraid of getting caught.*) ⒹⒸⒺ
- In what ways is *The Cruise of the Dazzler* a true story? (Ideas: *It's based on London's experiences as an oyster pirate; it takes place in a real location.*) ⓇⒻ
- Why do you think London changed the story so it isn't completely true? (Ideas: *To make it more exciting; to cover up his own criminal activities.*) ⒶⓅ

Paired Practice (Optional)

1. Now you'll read in pairs.
- Whoever read second the last time will read first today.
- Remember to start at the diamond and switch at the star.
2. (Observe students and answer questions as needed.)

AFTER READING

EXERCISE 10

Independent Work

1. Do all the items in your workbook and textbook for this lesson.
2. (The independent work in this lesson includes the following activities.)
- Maps
- Relevant information
- Sarcasm
- Deductions
- Accents
- Comprehension
- Writing

EXERCISE 11

Workcheck

1. (Using the Answer Key, read the questions and answers for the workbook.)
2. (Have students read their answers for the textbook activities.)
3. (Have two or three students read their writing assignments aloud. Comment on each assignment.)
4. (Have students correct and turn in their work.)

SPELLING

(Present Spelling lesson 61 after completing Reading lesson 61. See *Spelling Presentation Book*.)

LESSON 62

BEFORE READING

(Have students find lesson 62, part A, in their textbooks.)

EXERCISE 1

Hard Words

1. Look at column 1.
- These are hard words from your textbook stories.

1. Le Maire	**3. hoist**
2. forecastle	**4. vessel**

2. Line 1 is **Le Maire** [luh MEHR]. Everybody, what words? (Signal.) *Le Maire.*
3. Word 2 is **forecastle** [FOLK sull]. Everybody, what word? (Signal.) *Forecastle.*
- (Repeat this procedure for every word in the column.)
4. Let's read the words again.
5. Line 1. Everybody, what words? (Signal.) *Le Maire.*
- (Repeat this procedure for every word in the column.)
6. (Repeat the column until firm.)

EXERCISE 2

New Vocabulary

1. Look at column 2.
- First we'll read the words in this column. Then we'll read their definitions.

1. forecastle	**3. loot**
2. skiff	

2. Word 1. Everybody, what word? (Signal.) *Forecastle.*
- (Repeat this procedure for every word in the column.)
3. (Repeat the column until firm.)

EXERCISE 3

Vocabulary Definitions

1. Everybody, find part B. ✔
- These are definitions for the words you just read.
2. (For each word, call on a student to read the definition and the item. Then ask the student to complete the item.)

1. **forecastle**—The *forecastle* is a ship's cabin where sailors sleep. It is usually near the front of a ship.
- What do we call a ship's cabin where sailors sleep?

- What's the answer? (Response: *Forecastle.*)

2. **skiff**—A *skiff* is a small rowboat.
- What is a skiff?

- What's the answer? (Response: *A small rowboat.*)

3. **loot**—*Loot* is material that is stolen.
- What do we call material that is stolen?

- What's the answer? (Response: *Loot.*)

READING

EXERCISE 4

Focus Question

1. Everybody, find part C. ✔
2. What's the focus question for today's lesson? (Response: *Why did Joe Díaz decide to start a new life?*)

Note: The "Reading Aloud" exercise is recommended for this lesson.

EXERCISE 5

Reading Aloud

1. We're going to read aloud to the diamond.

- (Call on individual students to read several sentences each.)

Chapter 1
The New Boy

Focus Question: Why did Joe Díaz decide to start a new life?

Frisco Kid was discontented—discontented and disgusted. He frowned, got up from where he had been sunning himself on top of the *Dazzler*'s cabin, and kicked off his heavy rubber boots. Then he stretched himself on the narrow side deck and dangled his feet in the cool salt water.

Frisco Kid was discontented because he had to do more work than usual. He did not mind the cooking nor washing down the decks. But when it came to the paint scrubbing and dishwashing, he rebelled. He felt he should not have to do that kind of work. After all, he knew how to handle the sails, lift anchor, steer, and make landings. That other work was for someone with less experience.

Suddenly, Frisco Kid heard a familiar voice ring out, "Stand out from under!" Pete Le Maire, captain of the *Dazzler,* threw a bundle on deck and jumped aboard.

Then Pete shouted to the boy who owned that bundle. "Come! Queeck!" The boy hesitated on the dock. It was a good fifteen feet to the deck of the ship.

Pete smiled and said to the boy, "When I count three, jump on board. One, two, three!"

The boy threw his body into space, and a moment later, he struck the deck.

Pete addressed Frisco Kid. "Kid, dis is ze new sailor. I make your acquaintance." Pete smirked and bowed and stood aside. "His name is Mistaire Joe Díaz," Pete said.

The two boys regarded each other silently for a moment. They were about the same age. Joe seemed to be the heartiest and strongest. Frisco Kid and Joe shook hands.

"So you're thinking of tackling the water, eh?" the Kid asked.

Joe Díaz nodded and glanced around before answering. "Yes, I think the bay life will suit me for a while. When I've become used to it, I'm going to sea in the forecastle."

"In the what? In the what, did you say?"

"In the forecastle—the place where the sailors live," Joe explained, flushing and feeling unsure of his pronunciation.

"Oh, the foc'sle. Know anything about going to sea?"

"Yes . . . no . . . that is, except what I've read."

Frisco Kid whistled, turned on his heel in a lordly manner, and went into the cabin.

"Going to sea!" Frisco Kid remarked to himself as he built the fire and set about cooking supper. "In the 'forecastle,' too—and thinks he'll like it!" ♦

EXERCISE 6
Silent Reading

1. Read the rest of the lesson to yourselves and be ready to answer some questions.

Meanwhile, Pete Le Maire was showing the newcomer around the sloop as though he were a guest. Pete displayed such charm that Frisco Kid nearly choked trying to suppress a grin.

Joe Díaz enjoyed Frisco Kid's supper. The food was rough but good, and the smack of the salt air around him gave zest to his appetite. The cabin was clean and snug. Every bit of space was used. The table swung up on hinges so it occupied almost no room at all when it was not in use. On either side, and partly under the deck, were two bunks. The blankets were rolled back, and the crew sat on the well-scrubbed bunk boards while they ate. A swinging sea-lamp of brightly polished brass gave them light. In the daytime, light came through the small round portholes in the walls of the cabin. On one side of the door were the stove and woodbox; on the other, the cupboard.

It all seemed like a dream to Joe. He had often imagined scenes like this; but here he was, right in the middle of it, and already it seemed as though he had known his two companions for years. Pete was smiling at him across the table. Pete's face was really quite vicious, but to Joe it seemed only "weather-beaten." Frisco Kid was describing the last storm the *Dazzler* had survived. Joe began to admire the Kid, who had lived so long on the water and knew so much about it.

Pete, however, ignored Frisco Kid's story. When Pete had finished dinner, he stretched out on top of his blankets and was soon snoring loudly.

"Better turn in and get a couple hours' sleep," Frisco Kid said kindly, pointing to Joe's bunk. "We'll most likely be up the rest of the night."

Joe obeyed, but he could not fall asleep. He lay with his eyes wide open, watching the hands of the alarm clock that hung in the cabin. He thought about how quickly things had changed in the last twelve hours. Only that morning, he had been a schoolboy. Now he was a sailor on the *Dazzler* and did not know where the sloop was headed. He was only fifteen, but he felt every inch a man. He wished his friends could see him now. He could almost hear them talking about him as other boys crowded around. "Who?" "What—Joe Díaz?" "Yes, he's run away to sea. Used to be friends with us, you know." ★

Joe pictured the scene proudly. Then his feelings softened at the thought of his mother worrying. But his feelings hardened when he thought of his father. His father did not understand boys, Joe thought. That was where the trouble lay. Only that morning, his father had said that the world wasn't a playground and that boys who thought it was a playground were likely to make mistakes. Well, Joe knew there was plenty of hard work in the world, but he also thought boys had some rights and should be able to do things besides work.

He'd show his father that he could take care of himself. In any case, he could write home after he settled down to his new life.

A skiff nudged the side of the *Dazzler* and interrupted Joe's thoughts. He wondered why he had not heard the sound of the oars. Then two men jumped over the railing and came into the cabin.

One of the men said, "Look at that, Bill. They're asleep!" Then he rolled Frisco Kid out of the blankets with one hand.

Pete put his head up. His eyes were heavy with sleep, but he said, "So it's Bill and Nick. It's about time you two got here."

"Who's this?" asked Nick as he rolled Joe out onto the floor. "A passenger?"

"No, no," Pete answered. "Ze new sailor man. Very good boy."

"Good boy or not, he's got to keep his tongue between his teeth," growled Bill, who had not spoken until now. He glared fiercely at Joe.

"I say," said Nick, "how much of the loot is that new kid going to get? He better not get any of the loot that Bill and I are supposed to get."

Pete said quickly, "Ze *Dazzler,* she take one share—what you call—one third. Den we split ze rest in five shares. Five men, five shares. Very good."

Nick objected, "No, there were only four men and four shares. That's what we agreed on."

Pete said, "Now there are five men and five shares."

This conversation was a mystery to Joe, but he sensed that he was the cause of it. In the end, Pete had his way, and Nick gave in after much grumbling. Then the three men went on deck.

"Just keep out of their way," Frisco Kid whispered to Joe. "I'll teach you everything when we ain't in a hurry."

Joe was grateful to Frisco Kid. He had the strange feeling that Frisco Kid was the only person on board he could trust.

After a while, Joe and Frisco Kid followed the men onto the deck.

- Why did Joe Díaz decide to start a new life? (Ideas: *He didn't want to do the work his father expected; he wanted to prove he could live on his own.*) ⓄCE
- Why was Frisco Kid discontented at the beginning of the chapter? (Ideas: *He didn't want to scrub paint or wash dishes; he thought somebody else should do that work.*) ⓄCE
- How could Frisco Kid tell that Joe didn't have much experience at sea? (Ideas: *Joe didn't know how to pronounce forecastle; Joe had only read about going to sea.*) ⓂJ
- What did Joe want to prove to his father? (Idea: *That he could take care of himself.*) ⓃE
- What do you think Pete and the other men plan to do with the *Dazzler* that evening? Explain your answer. (Idea: *Rob something, because they were talking about splitting up the loot.*) Ⓟ

EXERCISE 7

Paired Practice (Optional)

1. Now you'll read in pairs.
- Whoever read second the last time will read first today.
- Remember to start at the diamond and switch at the star.
2. (Observe students and answer questions as needed.)

AFTER READING

EXERCISE 8

Independent Work

1. Do all the items in your workbook and textbook for this lesson.
2. (The independent work in this lesson includes the following activities.)
- Story details
- Vocabulary
- Perspectives
- Deductions
- Accents
- Vocabulary review
- Sarcasm
- Similes
- Comprehension
- Writing

EXERCISE 9

Workcheck

1. (Using the Answer Key, read the questions and answers for the workbook.)
2. (Have students read their answers for the textbook activities.)
3. (Have two or three students read their writing assignments aloud. Comment on each assignment.)
4. (Have students correct and turn in their work.)

SPELLING

(Present Spelling lesson 62 after completing Reading lesson 62. See *Spelling Presentation Book.*)

LESSON 63

BEFORE READING

(Have students find lesson 63, part A, in their textbooks.)

EXERCISE 1

Word Practice

1. Look at column 1.
* We're going to practice these words.

1. Frisco Kid	4. mainsail
2. private	5. jutted
3. Farallons	

2. Line 1. Everybody, what words? (Signal.) *Frisco Kid.*
* (Repeat this procedure for every word in the column.)
3. (Repeat the column until firm.)

EXERCISE 2

New Vocabulary

1. Look at column 2.
* First we'll read the words in this column. Then we'll read their definitions.

1. hoist	3. churn
2. collide	

2. Word 1. Everybody, what word? (Signal.) *Hoist.*
* (Repeat this procedure for every word in the column.)
3. (Repeat the column until firm.)

EXERCISE 3

Vocabulary Definitions

1. Everybody, find part B. ✔
* These are definitions for the words you just read.
2. (For each word, call on a student to read the definition and the item. Then ask the student to complete the item.)

1. **hoist**—When you *hoist* something, you raise it with ropes.
* What's another way of saying *They raised the mainsail with ropes*?
* What's the answer? (Response: *They hoisted the mainsail.*)

2. **collide**—When two things *collide,* they run into each other.
* What's another way of saying *The bumper cars kept running into each other*?
* What's the answer? (Response: *The bumper cars kept colliding.*)

3. **churn**—When a boat *churns* water, it stirs up the water.
* What's another way of saying *The speedboat stirred up the water into giant waves*?
* What's the answer? (Response: *The speedboat churned the water into giant waves.*)

READING

EXERCISE 4

Focus Question

1. Everybody, find part C. ✔
2. What's the focus question for today's lesson? (Response: *What did Joe discover about his companions?*)

EXERCISE 5

Reading Aloud (Optional)

1. We're going to read aloud to the diamond.
* (Call on individual students to read several sentences each.)

Chapter 2
The Piles of Steel

Focus Question: What did Joe discover about his companions?

Joe heard a creaking noise in the night and saw the men hoisting the huge mainsail above him. Then Bill and Nick untied the *Dazzler* from the dock. The sloop soon caught the breeze and headed out into the bay, pulling a lifeboat and the skiff. Joe heard some talking in low tones. He heard someone say something about turning off the lights and keeping a sharp lookout, but he didn't know what to make of it.

The waterfront lights of Oakland began to slip by. A gentle north wind was blowing the sloop south, and the *Dazzler* sailed noiselessly through the water.

"Where are we going?" Joe asked Nick in a friendly tone.

"Oh, we're going to take a cargo from Bill's factory," Nick replied. Then Bill laughed as if he and Nick had a private joke. Joe didn't think Bill looked like a factory owner, but he said nothing.

Joe was sent into the cabin to blow out the cabin lamp. The *Dazzler* turned around and began to move toward the shore. Everybody kept silent except for occasional questions and answers between Bill and Pete. Finally, the sails were lowered cautiously.

Pete whispered to Frisco Kid, who went forward and dropped the anchor. Nick pulled the *Dazzler*'s lifeboat and his skiff alongside the sloop. Bill and Nick got into the skiff, and Bill said, "Make sure you keep quiet."

Then Frisco Kid motioned Joe to get into the *Dazzler's* lifeboat. "Can you row?" Frisco Kid asked. Joe nodded his head yes. "Then take these oars," Frisco Kid continued, "and don't make a racket."

Frisco Kid moved to the front of the lifeboat, and Pete got into the back. Joe noticed that ropes were wrapped around the oar blades. It was impossible for the oars to make a noise in the water.

Joe rowed the lifeboat and followed the skiff. He glanced to one side and saw that they were nearing a pier that jutted out from the land. A couple of brightly lit ships were docked at the pier, but the lifeboat and the skiff kept just beyond the edge of the ships' light. At last, Frisco Kid commanded Joe to stop rowing. The two boats pulled up on a tiny beach, and the men slipped out. ♦

Silent Reading

1. Read the rest of the lesson to yourselves and be ready to answer some questions.

Frisco Kid stayed in the lifeboat while Joe followed the men, who picked their way carefully up a twenty-foot bank. At the top of the bank, Joe found himself on a narrow railway track that ran between huge piles of valuable steel. Separated by the tracks, these piles extended in every direction. In the distance, Joe could see the vague outlines of a large factory.

The men began to carry loads of the steel down to the beach. Pete gripped Joe by the arm and warned him not to make any noise. Then he handed Joe some steel to carry.

At the beach, the men and Joe turned their loads over to Frisco Kid, who placed them in the two boats. As Joe walked back up the bank toward the steel piles, he began to wonder what the men were doing. Why should there be such a mystery about it, and why did they keep so silent? He had just begun to ask himself these questions when he heard the hoot of an owl from the direction of the beach. Suddenly, a man sprang out from behind a pile of steel and flashed a lantern at Joe. Joe was blinded by the light, and he staggered back. Then the man blew a whistle.

Joe ran toward the beach. He soon collided with another man who came running around the end of one of the piles of steel. The man was knocked over but he quickly got back to his feet and chased Joe to the beach.

Joe dashed into the water for the lifeboat. Pete and Frisco Kid had the boat's nose pointed out to sea and were calmly awaiting Joe's arrival. They had their oars all ready for the start, but they held them quietly at rest. The other skiff was still on the beach. Bill was trying to shove it off and was calling on Nick to lend a hand. But Nick had lost his head completely and came floundering through the water toward the lifeboat.

Joe climbed into the heavily loaded lifeboat, and Nick followed him. Nick's extra weight nearly sank the lifeboat. In the meantime, the two men on the beach had pulled out pistols and opened fire. The alarm had spread. Voices and cries could be heard from the ships on the pier. In the distance, a police siren blew frantically. ★

"Get out!" Frisco Kid shouted at Nick. "You ain't going to sink us. Go and help your partner!"

But Nick's teeth were chattering with fright, and he did not move or speak.

"Throw the crazy man out!" Pete ordered. At this moment, a bullet shattered Pete's oar, and he coolly proceeded to look for a spare one.

"Give us a hand, Joe," Frisco Kid commanded.

Joe understood, and together they seized Nick and flung him overboard. Two or three bullets splashed about him as he came to the surface just in time to be picked up by Bill, who had at last succeeded in getting the skiff into the water. A few oar strokes into the darkness quickly took them out of range of the pistols.

The lifeboat had so much water and steel in it that it was in danger of sinking at any moment. While the other two rowed, Joe began to throw out the steel. This saved them for the time being, but just as they neared the *Dazzler,* the lifeboat lurched and turned over. Joe and Frisco Kid came up side by side, and together they swam toward the *Dazzler.* Pete had already arrived, and he helped them aboard.

Pete began to haul the lifeboat toward the *Dazzler.* Then Bill and Nick appeared on the scene. All the men worked rapidly, and almost before Joe knew it, the mainsail had been hoisted and the anchor lifted. The *Dazzler* began to move rapidly out into the dark bay, pulling the lifeboat and the skiff behind it.

A little while later, Bill and Nick said goodbye and left in their skiff. Pete, in the cabin, moaned about their bad luck and then fell asleep.

The wind picked up, and soon the *Dazzler* was churning through the water. Frisco Kid was steering. Joe sat by his side, pondering the events of the night.

Joe could no longer blind himself to the facts. His mind was in a whirl of confusion. He had done something wrong, but he had done it through ignorance. He had a great fear of the future. His companions were thieves and robbers—the bay pirates. And here he was, working with them. He already had enough information to send them to prison. He knew they wouldn't give him a chance to do that. They would keep a sharp watch on him and not let him escape. But he would still try to escape at the very first opportunity.

- What did Joe discover about his companions? (Ideas: *They were pirates; they were thieves and robbers.*) ⓃⒹ
- What did Nick mean when he said, "We're going to take a cargo from Bill's factory"? (Ideas: *They were going to rob the factory; they were going to steal the steel.*) ⓊⒸⒸⓂ
- Why were ropes wrapped around the oar blades? (Idea: *So the oars wouldn't make any noise.*) Ⓒ/Ⓔ
- Why do you think Nick panicked when the guards appeared? (Ideas: *He was afraid of being caught; he was really just a coward.*) ⒹⒸⒺ
- Why did Joe throw the steel out of the boat? (Ideas: *He was trying to lighten the load; he was trying to keep the boat from sinking.*) ⒹⒸⒺ
- Do you think Joe regrets his decision to go to sea? Explain your answer. (Ideas: *Yes, because he ended up with a group of pirates and his life is in danger; no, because he might escape from the pirates and get a job on another ship.*) ⓂⒿ

Paired Practice (Optional)

1. Now you'll read in pairs.
- Whoever read second the last time will read first today.
- Remember to start at the diamond and switch at the star.
2. (Observe students and answer questions as needed.)

AFTER READING

Independent Work

1. Do all the items in your workbook and textbook for this lesson.
2. (The independent work in this lesson includes the following activities.)
- Story details
- Vocabulary
- Poem review
- Character traits
- Drawing conclusions
- Perspectives
- Inference
- Comprehension
- Writing

Workcheck

1. (Using the Answer Key, read the questions and answers for the workbook.)
2. (Have students read their answers for the textbook activities.)
3. (Have two or three students read their writing assignments aloud. Comment on each assignment.)
4. (Have students correct and turn in their work.)

(Present Spelling lesson 63 after completing Reading lesson 63. See *Spelling Presentation Book.*)

LESSON 64

BEFORE READING

(Have students find lesson 64, part A, in their textbooks.)

EXERCISE 1

Word Practice

1. Look at column 1.
   - We're going to practice these words.

1. naval	5. sardines
2. puny	6. defy
3. quarantine	7. bungle
4. Alcatraz	8. marred

2. Word 1. Everybody, what word? (Signal.) *Naval.*
   - (Repeat this procedure for every word in the column.)
3. (Repeat the column until firm.)

EXERCISE 2

New Vocabulary

1. Look at column 2.
   - First we'll read the words in this column. Then we'll read their definitions.

1. bungle	5. tow
2. puny	6. naval
3. outwit	7. surge
4. harsh	8. principal

2. Word 1. Everybody, what word? (Signal.) *Bungle.*
   - (Repeat this procedure for every word in the column.)
3. (Repeat the column until firm.)

EXERCISE 3

Vocabulary Definitions

1. Everybody, find part B. ✔
   - These are definitions for the words you just read.

2. (For each word, call on a student to read the definition and the item. Then ask the student to complete the item.)

1. **bungle**—When a person *bungles,* that person does something awkwardly. If you do a job awkwardly, you bungle the job.
   - What's another way of saying *She did the haircut awkwardly*?
   - What's the answer? (Response: *She bungled the haircut.*)

2. **puny**—When something is *puny,* it is small and weak.
   - What's another way of saying *She had a small and weak voice*?
   - What's the answer? (Response: *She had a puny voice.*)

3. **outwit**—*Outwit* is another word for *outsmart.*
   - What's another way of saying *The duke outsmarted the knight*?
   - What's the answer? (Response: *The duke outwitted the knight.*)

4. **harsh**—When something is *harsh,* it is rough or unpleasant.
   - What's another way of saying *He tried to get out of the rough wind*?
   - What's the answer? (Response: *He tried to get out of the harsh wind.*)

5. **tow**—When you *tow* something, you pull it along, often with a chain or a rope.
   - What's another way of saying *The truck pulled the car along*?
   - What's the answer? (Response: *The truck towed the car.*)

6. **naval**—When something is *naval,* it belongs to the navy.
   - What's another way of saying *a plane that belongs to the navy*?

- What's the answer? (Response: *A naval plane.*)

7. **surge**—When something *surges,* it rises and falls.
- What's another way of saying *The boat rose and fell through the waves*?

- What's the answer? (Response: *The boat surged through the waves.*)

8. **principal**—The *principal* things are the most important things.
- What's another way of saying *the most important places in a city*?

- What's the answer? (Response: *The principal places in a city.*)

EXERCISE 4

Deductions

1. Everybody, turn to part E at the end of today's story. ✔
- (Call on individual students to read several sentences each.)
- (At the end of each section, present the questions for that section.)

Complete each deduction.
Here's the evidence: *Every newspaper has an editor. The* Press-Herald *is a newspaper.*
1. What's the conclusion about the *Press-Herald?*

- What's the answer? (Response: *The* Press-Herald *has an editor.*)
- Listen to the whole deduction: **Every newspaper has an editor. The *Press-Herald* is a newspaper. Therefore, the *Press-Herald* has an editor.**
- Everybody, say the whole deduction. (Signal.) *Every newspaper has an editor. The* Press-Herald *is a newspaper. Therefore, the* Press-Herald *has an editor.*

Here's the evidence: *Some substances are hard. Silicon is a substance.*
2. What's the conclusion about silicon?

- What's the answer? (Response: *Maybe silicon is a hard substance.*)

- Listen to the whole deduction: **Some substances are hard. Silicon is a substance. Therefore, maybe silicon is a hard substance.**
- Everybody, say the whole deduction. (Signal.) *Some substances are hard. Silicon is a substance. Therefore, maybe silicon is a hard substance.*
- You'll write the answers later.

READING

EXERCISE 5

Story Background

1. Everybody, turn back to part C. ✔
- (Call on individual students to read several sentences each.)

A tiller is a handle at the back of a boat. The tiller is connected to a large paddle that goes into the water. By pushing the tiller to one side or the other, you can make the boat turn.

When the tiller is pushed to the left, the boat turns to the right.

When the tiller is pushed to the right, the boat turns to the left.

When the tiller is straight, the boat continues to move straight ahead.

- Which part is the handle? (Response: *The tiller.*) (ND)
- Which part goes into the water? (Response: *The paddle.*) (ND)

- Look at boat A. (VA)
- Is the tiller pushed to the left, to the right, or straight ahead? (Response: *To the right.*) (VA)

Lesson 64 **15**

- So which way will the boat move? (Response: *To the left.*) (MD)

B

- Look at boat B. (VA)
- Is the tiller pushed to the left, to the right, or straight ahead? (Response: *Straight ahead.*) (VA)
- So which way will the boat move? (Response: *Straight ahead.*) (MD)

C

- Look at boat C. (VA)
- Is the tiller to the left, to the right, or straight ahead? (Response: *To the left.*) (VA)
- So which way will the boat move? (Response: *To the right.*) (MD)

EXERCISE 6

Focus Question

1. Everybody, find part D. ✔
2. What's the focus question for today's lesson? (Response: *How did Joe feel about Frisco Kid?*)

EXERCISE 7

Reading Aloud (Optional)

1. We're going to read aloud to the diamond.
- (Call on individual students to read several sentences each.)

Chapter 3

The Tow Rope

Focus Question: How did Joe feel about Frisco Kid?

The wind began to rise, and soon blasts of air out of the east were shrieking down on the *Dazzler.* The mainsail slapped and thrashed about until it seemed it would tear itself to pieces. The *Dazzler* was rolling wildly. Everything was in confusion, but Joe sensed it was an orderly confusion.

Joe could see that Frisco Kid knew just what to do and how to do it. There was no need to wake Pete, who was still sleeping soundly in his bunk. Frisco Kid had confidence in himself. He was cool and in control. He worked quickly but not carelessly. There was no bungling.

Frisco Kid called Joe forward to help lower the mainsail halfway so the wind would not tear it. It was a struggle, but they were soon finished. The excitement of the struggle chased all the unpleasant thoughts from Joe's mind. He remained calm. He carried out his orders without fumbling. Together the two boys used their puny strength against violent nature, and together they outwitted nature.

Joe followed Frisco Kid to the tiller at the back of the ship. He felt proud of himself. When he saw the unspoken praise in Frisco Kid's eyes, he blushed. But the next instant, the thought flashed across his mind that this boy was a thief, a common thief. Joe's whole life had been sheltered from the harsher things of the world, and he had learned to fear criminals. So he stepped away from Frisco Kid and remained silent. Meanwhile, Frisco Kid was devoting all his energy to handling the sloop. He had no time to notice Joe's sudden change of feeling.

Even though Frisco Kid was a thief, he seemed kind. Instead of feeling afraid of Frisco Kid, Joe was drawn to him. Joe could not help liking him. The Kid's good qualities appealed to Joe—his coolness, his bravery, and his kind face. Joe felt ashamed, for he could not help liking this common thief. ♦

EXERCISE 8

Silent Reading

1. Read the rest of the lesson to yourselves and be ready to answer some questions.

"Let's pull the lifeboat a little closer," commanded Frisco Kid, who had his eye on everything.

The lifeboat was behaving badly. Every once in a while, it would hold back until the towrope tightened. Then it would come leaping ahead and shove its nose under the huge waves that were roaring by. Joe climbed over the railing to the slippery lower deck. Then he grabbed the towrope, which was fastened to the railing.

"Be careful," Frisco Kid warned, as a blast of wind struck the *Dazzler* and made her lean dangerously on her side.

It was ticklish work for a beginner. Joe held on to the railing with one hand while attempting to pull in the towrope with the other. At that instant, the towrope tightened with a tremendous jerk as the lifeboat crashed sharply into the crest of a large wave. The towrope slipped from Joe's hand and began to fly out. He clutched it frantically and was dragged over the slippery deck.

"Let her go! Let her go!" Frisco Kid roared.

Joe let go just as he was about to go overboard. The towrope broke, and the lifeboat dropped rapidly behind. Joe glanced at Frisco Kid with shame. He expected a sharp insult for his awkwardness. But Frisco Kid only smiled.

"That's all right," Frisco Kid said. "No bones broken and nobody overboard. Better to lose a boat than a man any day. That's what I say. Besides, I shouldn't have sent you out there. And there's no harm done. We can pick it up all right. Just do what I tell you. But don't be in a hurry. Take it easy."

Frisco Kid grasped the tiller. "Hard left," he cried, pushing the tiller and following it with his body. "That's good! Now lend me a hand with the sails."

Together, hand over hand, they crawled up the mast. Frisco Kid adjusted the sails so the *Dazzler* could go into the wind, and the sloop began to turn around. As she swept into the wind, her sails began to snarl loudly.

The boys went over the same ground they had just covered. At last, Joe discovered the lifeboat bobbing up and down in the starlit darkness.

"Plenty of time," Frisco Kid said. He turned the *Dazzler* toward the lifeboat and pulled up alongside it. ★

"Now!"

In response to Frisco Kid's command, Joe leaned over the side, grasped the towrope, and tied it to the railing. Then they turned around again and started on their way. Joe still felt bad about the trouble he had caused, but Frisco Kid quickly put him at ease.

"Oh, that's nothing," the Kid said. "Everybody does that when they're beginning. Now, some men forget all about the trouble they had in learning and get mad when a youngster makes a mistake. I never do. Why, I remember . . ."

Frisco Kid began to tell Joe about the problems he had when he first went on the water. He also told Joe about some of the punishments he had received.

As the two boys talked, they sat side by side and close against each other, next to the tiller.

"What place is that?" Joe asked as they sailed by a lighthouse perched on a rocky island.

"Goat Island. They've got a naval training station over on the other side. There's good fishing, too. We'll pass to the left of it. Then we'll go a bit farther and anchor in the shelter of Angel Island. When Pete wakes up, we'll know which direction he wants to go. You can turn in now and get some sleep. I can manage all right."

Joe shook his head. There had been too much excitement for him to feel like sleeping. He could not bear to think of it, with the *Dazzler* leaping and surging along and shattering the sea into clouds of spray. His clothes had half dried already, and he preferred to stay on deck.

The lights of Oakland made only a hazy flare against the sky, but to the south, the San Francisco lights stretched for miles. Starting from the great ferry building and passing on to Telegraph Hill, Joe saw all the principal places of the city. His home was somewhere over there in that maze of light and shadow. Perhaps even now his parents were thinking about him and worrying. Joe shivered. It was almost morning. Then, slowly, his head drooped over on Frisco Kid's shoulder. Soon he was fast asleep.

- How did Joe feel about Frisco Kid?
  (Ideas: *Joe admired him, even though he was a thief; Joe thought he was kind; Joe was drawn to him.*) (DCE)
- How much skill did Frisco Kid have as a sailor? Give an example. (Ideas: *He had lots of skill. For example, he lowered the mainsail in the wind; he guided the boat with the tiller; he turned the boat around; he knew the names of all the islands.*) (Sum)
- Explain how Joe tried to pull in the lifeboat. (Idea: *He held onto the railing with one hand while pulling in the boat with the other.*) (R)
- Why wasn't Frisco Kid upset when Joe lost the lifeboat? (Ideas: *He knew it was just a beginner's mistake; he knew Joe had done his best; he remembered when he was a beginner.*) (DCE)
- Why do you think Joe wanted to stay on deck instead of going to bed? (Ideas: *He wanted to be with Frisco Kid; he was too excited to sleep; he wanted to see everything.*) (H)

EXERCISE 9

Paired Practice (Optional)

1. Now you'll read in pairs.
- Whoever read second the last time will read first today.
- Remember to start at the diamond and switch at the star.
2. (Observe students and answer questions as needed.)

AFTER READING

EXERCISE 10

Independent Work

1. Do all the items in your workbook and textbook for this lesson.
2. (The independent work in this lesson includes the following activities.)
- Story details
- Vocabulary
- Cause and effect
- Story review
- Perspectives
- Deductions
- Main idea
- Vocabulary review
- Comprehension
- Writing

EXERCISE 11

Workcheck

1. (Using the Answer Key, read the questions and answers for the workbook.)
2. (Have students read their answers for the textbook activities.)
3. (Have two or three students read their writing assignments aloud. Comment on each assignment.)
4. (Have students correct and turn in their work.)

SPELLING

(Present Spelling lesson 64 after completing Reading lesson 64. See *Spelling Presentation Book.*)

BEFORE READING

(Have students find lesson 65, part A, in their textbooks.)

EXERCISE 1
Word Practice

1. Look at column 1.
- We're going to practice these words.

1. condensed	5. bungle
2. bicycle	6. bugle
3. bicyclists	7. smallpox
4. Alcatraz	

2. Word 1. Everybody, what word? (Signal.) *Condensed.*
- (Repeat this procedure for every word in the column.)
3. (Repeat the column until firm.)

EXERCISE 2
New Vocabulary

1. Look at column 2.
- First we'll read the words in this column. Then we'll read their definitions.

1. quarantine station	4. keg
2. stir	5. bait
3. mar	

2. Line 1. Everybody, what words? (Signal.) *Quarantine station.*
- (Repeat this procedure for every word in the column.)
3. (Repeat the column until firm.)

EXERCISE 3
Vocabulary Definitions

1. Everybody, find part B. ✔
- These are definitions for the words you just read.
2. (For each word, call on a student to read the definition and the item. Then ask the student to complete the item.)

1. **quarantine station**—A *quarantine station* is a place where people who may have diseases are kept. To prevent the diseases from spreading, only certain people can enter or leave the quarantine station.
- What is a quarantine station?

- What's the answer? (Idea: *A place where people who may have diseases are kept.*)

2. **stir**—When something *stirs* you, it creates strong emotion in you.
- What's another way of saying *The music created strong emotion in her*?

- What's the answer? (Response: *The music stirred her.*)

3. **mar**—When you *mar* something, you spoil or ruin part of it. If you ruin part of a floor, you mar the floor.
- What's another way of saying *He ruined part of his shirt?*

- What's the answer? (Response: *He marred his shirt.*)

4. **keg**—A *keg* is a small barrel.
- What do we call a small barrel?

- What's the answer? (Response: *A keg.*)

5. **bait**—*Bait* is anything that lures a person or an animal into a trap.
- What kinds of bait do fishermen put on hooks?

- What's the answer? (Ideas: *Worms, meat, flies.*)

EXERCISE 4
Conversations

1. Everybody, turn to part D at the end of today's story. ✔
- (Call on a student to read the instructions.)

The following conversation includes seven statements. Write which person makes each statement.

- Read up to the number in parentheses. Then tell me who made the statement.

  Amy said, "Linda, aren't you ever going to get up?" (1)

- Who made that statement? (Response: *Amy.*)

  "Go away!" (2)

- Who made that statement? (Response: *Linda.*)

  "Come on, Linda, it's almost noon." (3)

- Who made that statement? (Response: *Amy.*)

  "I'm sick," said the drowsy sister as she turned her face to the wall. (4)

- Who made that statement? (Response: *Linda.*)

  "Mom will be angry if she finds you in bed," Amy observed. (5)

- Who made that statement? (Response: *Amy.*)

  "Wait," she continued, "I think I hear her now." (6)

- Who made that statement? (Response: *Amy.*)

  "Oh no, I better get moving!" (7)

- Who made that statement? (Response: *Linda.*)
- You'll write the answers later.

READING

Focus Question

1. Everybody, turn back to part C. ✔

2. What's the focus question for today's lesson? (Response: *Why did ships have to stop at Angel Island?*)

Reading Aloud (Optional)

1. We're going to read aloud to the diamond.

- (Call on individual students to read several sentences each.)

Chapter 4
Angel Island

Focus Question: Why did ships have to stop at Angel Island?

"Come on! Wake up! We're going to anchor."

Joe woke up with a start, bewildered at the unusual scene. Sleep had made him forget his troubles for the time being, and he did not know where he was. Then he remembered.

The wind had dropped. The sea was still rolling, but the *Dazzler* was creeping up into the shelter of Angel Island. The sky was clear, and the air had the snap and vigor of early morning. The rippling water was laughing in the rays of the sun, which was just above the eastern skyline. To the south lay Alcatraz Island. In the west, the Golden Gate stood between the Pacific Ocean and San Francisco Bay. A huge ship was coming slowly through the Gate.

It was a pretty sight. Joe rubbed the sleep from his eyes. He continued gazing until Frisco Kid told him to go forward and get ready to drop the anchor.

"Pull out about three hundred feet of chain," Frisco Kid ordered, "and then stand by." Frisco Kid eased the sloop gently into the wind.

"Now!" Frisco Kid commanded. "Over with the anchor!"

Joe threw the anchor overboard, and the chain followed with startling speed. The *Dazzler* soon came to rest. Frisco Kid went forward to help, and together the two boys lowered the mainsail.

"Here's a bucket," Frisco Kid said. "Wash down the decks and don't be afraid of the water, nor of the dirt. Here's a broom. Sweep the deck when you're finished, and have everything shining.

When you get that done, bail out the lifeboat. She took in a little water last night. I'm going below to cook breakfast."

The water from Joe's bucket was soon splashing over the deck, while the smoke pouring from the cabin stove carried a promise of good things to come. Joe kept lifting his head from his work to take in the scene. Its beauty stirred him strangely. His happiness would have been complete if he could have forgotten who and what his companions were. But the thought of these companions marred the beauty of the day. Joe was not used to such people, and he was shocked at the harsh reality of their lives.

Instead of hurting him, the shock had the opposite effect. It strengthened his desire to be clean and strong and not to be ashamed of himself. He glanced around and sighed. Why couldn't men be honest and true? It seemed too bad that he had to go away and leave life on the bay. But then he remembered the events of last night, and he knew he must escape. ♦

EXERCISE 7

Silent Reading

1. Read the rest of the lesson to yourselves and be ready to answer some questions.

Just then, Joe was called to breakfast.

Frisco Kid was as good a cook as he was a sailor. There were mush and condensed milk, beefsteak and fried potatoes, and all topped off with good French bread, butter, and coffee. Pete did not join them, though Frisco Kid attempted to rouse him a couple of times. He mumbled and grunted, half opened his eyes, and started to snore again.

"Can't tell when Pete's going to sleep like that," Frisco Kid explained. "Sometimes he won't get that way for a month. Sometimes he's good-natured, and sometimes he's dangerous. So the best thing to do is to let him alone and keep out of his way. And don't cross him, for if you do, there's likely to be trouble."

"Come on, let's take a swim," Frisco Kid added, abruptly changing the subject. "Can you swim?"

Joe nodded, and the boys went on deck.

"What's that place?" Joe asked as they got ready to dive. He pointed to a sheltered beach on Angel Island, where there were several buildings and a large number of tents.

"Quarantine station. Lots of smallpox coming in now on the ships. The government makes the ships stay there till the doctors say they're safe to land. I tell you, they're strict about it, too."

Then Frisco Kid jumped into the water, and Joe dived in after him. A half hour later, the two boys were climbing back onto the deck.

"I'll tell you what," Frisco Kid suggested. "Let's catch a mess of fish for lunch and then turn in and make up for the sleep we lost last night. What do you say?"

Joe quickly agreed. Frisco Kid went into the cabin and brought out a pair of heavy fish lines and a keg of sardines.

"Bait," he said. "Just shove a whole sardine on the hook. The fish aren't a bit particular. They swallow the bait, hook and all. Last one to catch a fish has to clean 'em."

Both hooks were thrown overboard together, and seventy feet of line whizzed out. Joe instantly felt the struggling jerks of a hooked fish. As he began to haul in, he glanced at Frisco Kid and saw that he, too, had a fish on his line. ★

The race between the two boys was exciting. Hand over hand, the wet lines flashed on board. But Frisco Kid was the greater expert, and his fish tumbled on deck first. Joe's followed an instant later— a three-pound rock-cod. Joe was wild with joy. It was magnificent, the largest fish he had ever caught. The lines went over again, and up they came with two more fish. It was royal sport. Joe could have continued until he had fished the bay empty, but Frisco Kid persuaded him to stop.

"We've got enough for three meals now," Frisco Kid said, "so there's no use in having them spoil. Besides, the more you catch, the more you clean, and you'd better start right away. I'm going to take a nap."

Joe did not mind cleaning the fish. In fact, he was glad he had not caught the first fish, for he preferred to be alone. He wanted to carry out a little plan he had thought of while swimming.

After Joe threw the last cleaned fish into a bucket of water, he glanced around. The quarantine station was less than a half-mile away, and he could make out a soldier pacing up and down on the beach. Joe went into the cabin and listened to the heavy breathing of the sleepers. He had to pass so close to Frisco Kid to get his bundle of clothes that he decided not to take them. He returned outside and carefully pulled the lifeboat alongside the *Dazzler.* Then he got aboard the lifeboat and cast off.

At first, he rowed gently in the direction of the station. He did not want to make any noise. But he gradually increased the strength of his oar strokes. When he had covered half the distance, he glanced around. He had escaped, for he knew it would be impossible for the *Dazzler* to get underway and head him off before he reached the station.

Suddenly, Joe heard a shout from the shore. He turned to see who had made the noise. The soldier on the beach was pointing his rifle straight at Joe.

- Why did ships have to stop at Angel Island? (Ideas: *Because it was a quarantine station; because there was smallpox coming in on the ships.*) ⓒⒺ
- When Joe is cleaning the deck, the story says, "the thought of these companions marred the beauty of the day." Explain that statement. (Idea: *The beauty of the day was partly ruined because Joe knew he was working for pirates.*) ⓤ︀ⒸⒸⓂ
- Why do you think being with the pirates strengthened Joe's desire to be clean and strong? (Ideas: *Because he knew what they were doing was wrong; because he wanted to be better than they were.*) Ⓗ
- Describe the plan Joe thought of while swimming. (Idea: *When Frisco Kid and Pete were asleep, he would take the lifeboat and row to Angel Island.*) Ⓡ
- Why do you think the soldier was pointing his rifle at Joe? Explain your answer. (Idea: *The soldier didn't want Joe to land because Angel Island was a quarantine station.*) ⒹⒸⒺ

Paired Practice (Optional)

1. Now you'll read in pairs.
- Whoever read second the last time will read first today.
- Remember to start at the diamond and switch at the star.
2. (Observe students and answer questions as needed.)

AFTER READING

Independent Work

1. Do all the items in your workbook and textbook for this lesson.
2. (The independent work in this lesson includes the following activities.)
- Story details
- Vocabulary
- Contradictions
- Perspectives
- Conversations
- Vocabulary review
- Comprehension
- Writing

Workcheck

1. (Using the Answer Key, read the questions and answers for the workbook.)
2. (Have students read their answers for the textbook activities.)
3. (Have two or three students read their writing assignments aloud. Comment on each assignment.)
4. (Have students correct and turn in their work.)

ACTIVITIES ACROSS THE CURRICULUM

(Students should complete the appropriate project in *Activities across the Curriculum* after completing lesson 65. See *Activities across the Curriculum* book for details.)

SPELLING

(Present Spelling lesson 65 after completing Reading lesson 65. See *Spelling Presentation Book.*)

	Lesson 66	Lesson 67	Lesson 68	Lesson 69	Lesson 70
BEFORE READING	Vocabulary definitions Vocabulary review Referents	Vocabulary definitions Vocabulary review	Vocabulary definitions Vocabulary review	Vocabulary definitions Vocabulary review Missing words	Vocabulary definitions Vocabulary review Missing words
NEW VOCABULARY	complicate spurt defy wince spunk taunt	reform school arouse hail skirt untidy	give somebody the slip sic	survey strained muffled	loom gale hurtle
READING	*The Cruise of the Dazzler* (Chapter 5)	*The Cruise of the Dazzler* (Chapter 6)	*The Cruise of the Dazzler* (Chapter 7)	*The Cruise of the Dazzler* (Chapter 8)	*The Cruise of the Dazzler* (Chapter 9)
INDEPENDENT WORK	Story details Vocabulary Maps Character traits Referents Inference Conversations Comprehension Writing	Story details Vocabulary Rhyme scheme Comparisons Conversations Referents Metaphors Comprehension Writing	Story details Vocabulary Comparisons Character traits Inference Referents Comprehension Writing	Story details Vocabulary Settings Exaggeration Missing words Comprehension Writing	Story details Vocabulary Maps Spoonerisms Missing words Similes Comprehension Writing
SUPPLEMENTS	*Spelling*	*Spelling*	*Spelling*	*Spelling*	Mastery Test *Spelling* *Activities across the Curriculum*

Comprehension Questions Abbreviations Guide

Access Prior Knowledge = (APK)   Author's Point of View = (APoV)   Author's Purpose = (AP)   Cause/Effect = (C/E)   Charts/Graphs/Diagrams/Visual Aids = (VA)

Classify and Categorize = (C+C)   Compare/Contrast = (C/C)   Determine Character Emotions, Motivation = (DCE)   Drawing Conclusions = (DC)   Drawing Inferences = (DI)

Fact and Opinion = (F/O)   Hypothesizing = (H)   Main Idea = (MI)   Making Connections = (MC)   Making Deductions = (MD)   Making Judgements = (MJ)

Narrative Elements = (NE)   Noting Details = (ND)   Predict = (P)   Reality/Fantasy = (R/F)   Recall Facts/Rules = (RF/R)   Retell = (R)   Sequence = (Seq)

Steps in a Process = (SP)   Story Structure = (SS)   Summarize = (Sum)   Understanding Dialogue = (UD)   Using Context to Confirm Meaning(s) = (UCCM)   Visualize = (V)

BEFORE READING

(Have students find lesson 66, part A, in their textbooks.)

EXERCISE 1

Vocabulary Definitions

1. We're going to read these definitions.
2. (For each word, call on a student to read the definition and the item. Then ask the student to complete the item.)

1. **complicate**—When you *complicate* something, you make it difficult. If you make a game difficult, you complicate the game.
   - What's another way of saying *She made the arrangements difficult*?

   - What's the answer? (Response: *She complicated the arrangements.*)

2. **spurt**—A *spurt* is a quick burst.
   - What's another way of saying *a quick burst of energy*?

   - What's the answer? (Response: *A spurt of energy.*)

3. **defy**—When you *defy* somebody, you challenge or oppose that person.
   - What's another way of saying *He challenged the captain*?

   - What's the answer? (Response: *He defied the captain.*)

4. **wince**—When you *wince,* you suddenly tense up, usually because of pain.
   - What's another way of saying *The doctor's shot made the boy suddenly tense up*?

   - What's the answer? (Response: *The doctor's shot made the boy wince.*)

5. **spunk**—When you have *spunk,* you have spirit and determination.
   - What's another way of saying *She showed determination when she scolded the bully*?

   - What's the answer? (Response: *She showed spunk when she scolded the bully.*)

6. **taunt**—When you *taunt* people, you mock them and try to make them angry.
   - What's another way of saying *She mocked the prince*?

   - What's the answer? (Response: *She taunted the prince.*)

EXERCISE 2

Vocabulary Review

1. Everybody, find part B. ✔
   - We're going to review these words.
2. (Call on a student to read the words in the box.)

outwit	**marred**
surges	**principal**
puny	**bungles**
stirs	**bough**

3. (For each item, have a student read the item and say the answer.)

1. When something creates strong emotion in you, it ▩▩▩ you.

   - What's the answer? (Response: *Stirs.*)

2. Something that is small and weak is ▩▩▩.

   - What's the answer? (Response: *Puny.*)

3. Things that are partly spoiled or ruined are ▩▩▩.

   - What's the answer? (Response: *Marred.*)

4. When something moves forward like a wave, that thing ▓▓▓▓▓.

- What's the answer? (Response: *Surges.*)

5. When a person works awkwardly, that person ▓▓▓▓▓.

- What's the answer? (Response: *Bungles.*)

EXERCISE 3

Referents

1. Everybody, turn to part D at the end of today's story. ✔
- (Call on individual students to read several sentences each.)
- (At the end of each section, present the questions for that section.)

In the following passage, the **bold words** refer to people or objects. Write the people or objects to which the bold words refer.
1. Martha was sick. **She** stayed in bed all day long.

- To what person does **she** refer? (Response: *Martha.*)

2. Martha was watching a TV show, but she thought **it** was stupid.

- To what object does **it** refer? (Response: *The TV show.*)

3. She wished she had gone to the library. She could have checked out several books **there.**

- To what object does **there** refer? (Response: *The library.*)

4. The books would be far better than the TV show, because **they** would contain more information.

- To what objects does **they** refer? (Response: *The books.*)
- You'll write the answers later.

READING

EXERCISE 4

Focus Question

1. Everybody, find part C. ✔
2. What's the focus question for today's lesson? (Response: *Why did Frisco Kid defend Joe's actions?*)

> **Note:** The "Reading Aloud" exercise is recommended for this lesson.

EXERCISE 5

Reading Aloud

1. We're going to read aloud to the diamond.
- (Call on individual students to read several sentences each.)

Chapter 5
The Quarantine Station
Focus Question: Why did Frisco Kid defend Joe's actions?

Joe was in deep trouble. A few minutes of hard rowing would bring him to the beach and safety. But on that beach, for some unknown reason, a United States soldier was pointing a gun at him.

Joe brought the lifeboat to a standstill. The soldier lowered his rifle and regarded Joe intently.

"I want to come ashore! Important!" Joe shouted out to him.

The man in uniform shook his head no.

"But it's important, I tell you! Won't you let me come ashore?"

Joe quickly looked in the direction of the *Dazzler.* The shouts had evidently awakened Pete, for the mainsail had been hoisted. And as Joe looked, he saw the anchor being lifted.

"Can't land here!" the soldier shouted back. "Smallpox!"

"But I must!" Joe cried, choking down a half-sob and preparing to row.

"Then I'll shoot," said the soldier. And he brought his rifle to his shoulder again.

Joe thought rapidly. The island was large. Perhaps there were no soldiers farther on. If he could get ashore, he did not care how quickly the soldiers captured him. He might catch smallpox, but even that was better than going back to the bay pirates.

Joe whirled the lifeboat to the right and threw all his strength against the oars. The cove was quite wide, and the nearest landing place was a good distance away. Joe rowed as hard as he could, but the *Dazzler* started off and soon began to overtake him.

It was close for a while. The breeze was light and not very steady, so sometimes Joe gained and sometimes the *Dazzler* did. The wind blew the sloop to within a hundred yards of Joe. Then the wind suddenly dropped, and the *Dazzler*'s big mainsail flapped idly from side to side.

"Ah! You steal ze lifeboat, eh?" Pete howled at Joe, running into the cabin for his rifle. "I fix you! You come back queeck or I get you!" But Pete knew the soldier was watching from the shore, so he did not dare to fire. ♦

EXERCISE 6

Silent Reading

1. Read the rest of the lesson to yourselves and be ready to answer some questions.

Joe did not think of this. He had never been shot at in all his life, and already he had been threatened with guns twice in the last twenty-four hours. One more threat couldn't amount to much. So he pulled steadily away while Pete raved like a wild man. He threatened Joe with all sorts of punishments once he laid hands on him again. To complicate matters, Frisco Kid was trying to defend Joe.

"You'd better let him go," Frisco Kid yelled. "He's a good boy and all right and not raised for the life you and I are leading."

"You too, eh!" Pete shrieked in a rage. "Den I fix you, you rat!"

He made a rush for Frisco Kid, but he couldn't catch him. A sharp wind arrived just then, and Pete stopped trying to catch the boy. Instead, he sprang to the tiller and headed the sloop toward Joe. Joe made one tremendous spurt, then gave up in despair. Pete came up alongside the motionless lifeboat and dragged Joe out.

"Keep your mouth shut," Frisco Kid whispered to Joe while the angry Pete was busy fastening the rope. "Don't talk back. Let him say all he wants to, but you keep quiet. It'll be better for you."

But Joe did not listen to Frisco Kid's advice.

"Look here, Mr. Pete, or whatever your name is," Joe said. "I tell you I want to quit, and I'm going to quit. So you'd better put me ashore at once. If you don't, I'll put you in prison."

Pete was shocked. He was being defied on board his own sloop—and by a boy. He had never heard of such a thing. He could not let Joe go, because the boy knew too much about the sloop and its occupation. Joe had spoken the truth when he said he could send Pete to prison. The only thing for Pete to do was to bully Joe.

"You put me in preezon, eh?" Pete said in a shrill voice. "Den you come, too. You row ze boat last-a night—answer me dat! You steal ze metal—answer me dat! You run away—answer me dat! And den you say you put me in jail? Bah!"

"But I didn't know," Joe protested.

"Ha, ha! Dat is funny. You tell dat to ze judge; mebbe him laugh, eh?"

Joe said bravely, "I didn't know I'd been hired by a lot of pirates and thieves."

Frisco Kid winced at this statement. If Joe had been looking at him, he would have seen the shame in Frisco Kid's face. ★

"And now that I do know about you," Joe continued, "I want to be put ashore. I don't know anything about the law, but I do know right and wrong, and I'm willing to take my chance with any judge for whatever wrong I have done—with all the judges in the United States, for that matter. And that's more than you can say, Mr. Pete."

"You say dat, eh? Vairy good. But you are one big thief . . ."

"I'm not! Don't you dare call me that again!" Joe's face was pale, and he was trembling—but not with fear.

"Thief!" the Frenchman taunted back.

"You lie!"

"Say dat one time more," Pete screamed. He raised his fist and prepared to strike.

Tears of anger stood in Joe's eyes, but he was calm and in dead earnest. "When you say I am a thief, Pete, you lie. You can hit me, but still I will say you lie."

"No, you don't!" Frisco Kid yelled.

He darted between them like a wildcat and shoved Pete back.

"You leave him alone," Frisco Kid continued. He picked up an oar and stood between them. "This thing has gone just about as far as it's going to go. Joe's right, and he knows it, and you could hit him and he wouldn't give in."

Frisco Kid turned and extended his hand to Joe, and the boys shook hands. Then Frisco Kid said, "You've got spunk, and you're not afraid to show it."

Pete's mouth twisted itself in a sickly smile, but there was an evil gleam in his eyes. He shrugged his shoulders and said, "Ah! So? He does not deesire dat I call him pet-names? Ha, ha. It is only in play. Let us—what you call—forgeeve and forget, eh? Vairy good—forgeeve and forget."

Pete reached out his hand, but Joe refused to take it. The man shrugged his shoulders and walked into the cabin.

A moment later, Pete called out, "Take the sloop down to Hunter's Point. For once, I will cook ze lunch, and den you will say dat it is ze vairy good lunch. Ah! Pete is ze great cook!"

"That's the way he always does—gets nice and cooks when he wants to make up," Frisco Kid said. "But even then you can't trust him."

Joe nodded his head but did not speak. He was in no mood for conversation. He was still trembling from the excitement of the last few moments. Deep down, he questioned himself on how he had behaved, and he found nothing to be ashamed of.

- Why did Frisco Kid defend Joe's actions? (Ideas: *Because he admired Joe; because he knew Joe was a good person.*) ⒹⒸⒺ
- Why wouldn't the soldier let Joe land? (Ideas: *Because there was smallpox on the island; because the island was a quarantine station.*) ⒹⒸⒺ
- Why was Joe able to move the lifeboat faster than the *Dazzler* for a while? (Ideas: *Because the wind died down; because he kept rowing while the* Dazzler *waited for the wind.*) ⒸⒺ
- Why did Pete try to make friends with Joe at the end of the chapter? (Ideas: *Because he knows Joe could put him in prison; because he doesn't want Joe to escape.*) ⒹⒸⒺ

- What do you think Joe should do next? (Ideas: *Work with Frisco Kid to escape; jump from the sloop when it nears land.*) ⓂⒿ

EXERCISE 7

Paired Practice (Optional)

1. Now you'll read in pairs.
- Whoever read second the last time will read first today.
- Remember to start at the diamond and switch at the star.
2. (Observe students and answer questions as needed.)

AFTER READING

EXERCISE 8

Independent Work

1. Do all the items in your workbook and textbook for this lesson.
2. (The independent work in this lesson includes the following activities.)
- Story details
- Vocabulary
- Maps
- Character traits
- Referents
- Inference
- Conversations
- Comprehension
- Writing

EXERCISE 9

Workcheck

1. (Using the Answer Key, read the questions and answers for the workbook.)
2. (Have students read their answers for the textbook activities.)
3. (Have two or three students read their writing assignments aloud. Comment on each assignment.)
4. (Have students correct and turn in their work.)

SPELLING

(Present Spelling lesson 66 after completing Reading lesson 66. See *Spelling Presentation Book.*)

BEFORE READING

(Have students find lesson 67, part A, in their textbooks.)

Vocabulary Definitions

1. We're going to read these definitions.
2. (For each word, call on a student to read the definition and the item. Then ask the student to complete the item.)

1. **reform school**—A *reform school* is a special type of school for young people who have broken the law.
*   What is a reform school?

*   What's the answer? (Idea: *A special type of school for young people who have broken the law.*)

2. **arouse**—When you *arouse* something, you wake up that thing or make it active. If your comments make an active discussion, your comments arouse discussion.
*   What's another way of saying *The sunset made his imagination active*?

*   What's the answer? (Response: *The sunset aroused his imagination.*)

3. **hail**—When you *hail* people or objects, you greet or summon them by calling out. When you summon a taxi by calling out, you hail a taxi.
*   What's another way of saying *They greeted the ship by calling out*?

*   What's the answer? (Response: *They hailed the ship.*)

4. **skirt**—When you *skirt* a place, you move around the edge of that place.
*   What's another way of saying *They moved around the edge of the city*?

*   What's the answer? (Response: *They skirted the city.*)

5. **untidy**—When something is *untidy*, it is messy and disordered.
*   What's another way of saying *His room was messy and disordered*?

*   What's the answer? (Response: *His room was untidy.*)

Vocabulary Review

1. Everybody, find part B. ✔
*   We're going to review these words.
2. (Call on a student to read the words in the box.)

defy	taunt
marred	rebel
spunk	puny
complicate	forlorn
stirs	wince

3. (For each item, have a student read the item and say the answer.)

1. Someone with spirit and determination has ▩▩.

*   What's the answer? (Response: *Spunk.*)

2. When you suddenly tense up, you ▩▩.

*   What's the answer? (Response: *Wince.*)

3. When you mock people and try to make them angry, you ▩▩ them.

*   What's the answer? (Response: *Taunt.*)

4. When you make something more difficult, you ▩▩ it.

*   What's the answer? (Response: *Complicate.*)

5. When you challenge or oppose somebody, you ▩▩ that person.

*   What's the answer? (Response: *Defy.*)

6. When something creates strong emotion in you, it ▇▇▇▇ you.

- What's the answer? (Response: *Stirs.*)

7. Things that are partly spoiled or ruined are ▇▇▇▇.

- What's the answer? (Response: *Marred.*)

READING

EXERCISE 3

Focus Question

1. Everybody, find part C. ✔
2. What's the focus question for today's lesson? (Response: *How was Frisco Kid's life story different from Joe's?*)

EXERCISE 4

Reading Aloud (Optional)

1. We're going to read aloud to the diamond.

- (Call on individual students to read several sentences each.)

Chapter 6
Frisco Kid's Story

Focus Question: How was Frisco Kid's life story different from Joe's?

The afternoon sea breeze had sprung up and was now blasting in from the Pacific. The *Dazzler* plowed along in front of the waterfront of San Francisco. Soon the sloop was in the middle of the shipping lanes, passing in and out among vessels that had come from the ends of the earth. Later, the sloop crossed the fairway, where ferryboats crowded with passengers passed back and forth between San Francisco and Oakland.

One ferryboat came so close that the passengers crowded to the side to see the gallant little sloop. Joe gazed enviously at the rows of downturned faces. Those passengers were all going to their homes, while he was going wherever Pete Le Maire ordered.

Joe was half-tempted to cry out for help. But that would have been foolish, so he held his tongue and turned his head. His eyes wandered along the heights of the city, and he began thinking about the strange ways of men and ships on the sea.

Frisco Kid watched Joe from the corner of his eye and seemed to follow his thoughts. "Got a home over there somewhere?" he asked suddenly, waving his hand in the direction of the city.

Joe started in surprise. "Yes," he said simply.

"Tell me about it."

Joe began to describe his home and his parents and his sister. Frisco Kid was interested in everything.

"Now tell me about your home," Joe said when he at last had finished.

Frisco Kid seemed suddenly to harden, and his face took on a stern look Joe had never seen before. Frisco Kid swung his foot idly to and fro.

"Go ahead," Joe said.

"I haven't got a home."

It seemed that Frisco Kid had to use great effort to force out those five words.

Joe saw that he had touched a tender spot, so he tried to get out of it. "Then tell me about the home you did have," he said. Joe did not dream that there were boys in the world who never had known homes.

"Never had none."

"Oh." Joe's interest was aroused. "Any brothers or sisters?"

"Nope."

"Mother?"

"I was so young when she died that I don't remember her."

"Father?"

"I never saw much of him. He went to sea—anyhow, he disappeared."

"Oh." Joe did not know what to say, and a silence fell upon them. ◆

EXERCISE 5

Silent Reading

1. Read the rest of the lesson to yourselves and be ready to answer some questions.

Just then, Pete came out to take over the tiller while Joe and Frisco Kid went in to eat. Both boys hailed Pete with feelings of relief, and their awkwardness vanished during lunch. The lunch was delicious—all that Pete had claimed it would be. Afterward, Frisco Kid relieved Pete. While Pete was eating, Joe washed up the dishes and put the cabin shipshape. Then they all sat around the back of the sloop. Pete tried to cheer things up by telling them stories of life in the South Seas.

They spent the rest of the afternoon in that way. They had long since left San Francisco behind and had rounded Hunter's Point. Now they were skirting the south shore. Joe caught a glimpse of a group of bicyclists rounding a cliff on San Bruno Road. He remembered the time when he had gone over the same ground on his own bike. That was only a month or two before, but it seemed like ten years to him now.

By the time Joe, Pete, and Frisco Kid had eaten dinner and cleared the things away, they were far south in the bay. But the wind went down with the sun, and the *Dazzler* was making little headway. They sighted a sloop coming toward them in the dying wind. Frisco Kid instantly said it was the *Reindeer.* After a while, Pete agreed. He seemed greatly pleased to meet the *Reindeer.*

"Epont Nelson runs her," Frisco Kid informed Joe. "They've got big plans down here, and they're always after Pete to come in with them. He knows more about it, whatever it is."

Joe nodded and looked at the approaching sloop curiously. It was somewhat larger than the *Dazzler,* but it was built for speed. The mainsail was as big as a racing ship's. Everything was in place on the deck. Nothing was untidy.

The *Reindeer* came up slowly in the gathering twilight and anchored about a stone's throw away. Pete anchored the *Dazzler* and then went in the lifeboat to pay the *Reindeer* a visit. The two boys stretched themselves out on top of the cabin and awaited his return.

"Do you like this life?" Joe asked.

The other boy turned on his elbow. "Well . . . I do, and then again I don't. The fresh air and salt water and all that. And the freedom—that's all right. But I don't like the . . . the . . ." He paused a moment and then blurted out, "The stealing." ★

"Then why don't you quit it?"

"I will, just as soon as I can take up something else."

"But why not now?" Joe thought that if Frisco Kid wanted to leave, he should do it at once.

"Where can I go?" Frisco Kid asked. "What can I do? There's nobody in all the world to lend me a hand, just as there never has been. I tried it once, and I learned my lesson too well to do it again in a hurry."

"Well, when I get out of this, I'm going home," Joe said. "Guess my father was right, after all. And I don't see . . . maybe . . . say, why don't you go with me?"

"You don't know what you're talking about," Frisco Kid answered. "Picture me going off with you! What would your father say? What would he think of me? And what would he do?"

Joe felt sick at heart. He realized he had given an invitation that would be difficult to carry out. He tried to imagine how his father would receive a stranger like Frisco Kid.

"He might turn me over to the police," Frisco Kid went on, "and send me to reform school. I'd die before I'd let that happen to me. And besides, Joe, I'm not a city boy, and you know it. Why, I'd be like a fish out of water, with all the things I don't know. Nope, I guess I'll have to wait a little before I run away. But there's only one thing for you to do, and that's to go straight home. First chance I get, I'll land you, and then I'll deal with Pete . . ."

"No, you don't," Joe interrupted hotly. "When I leave, I'm not going to leave you in trouble on my account. So, don't you try anything like that."

Frisco Kid shook his head. He gazed up at the starlit sky and wandered off into daydreams of the life he would like to lead. The seriousness of life was striking deeper than ever into Joe's heart, and he lay silent, thinking hard. A mumble of heavy voices came over to them from the *Reindeer.* From the land, the solemn notes of a church bell floated across the water while the summer night wrapped the boys slowly in its warm darkness.

- How was Frisco Kid's life story different from Joe's? (Ideas: *Joe had grown up in a family, but Frisco Kid never had a family; Joe had a home, but Frisco Kid didn't; Joe had grown up on land, but Frisco Kid had grown up on the sea.*) Ⓒ/ⓒ
- When Joe remembers bicycling on San Bruno Road, the story says, "That was only a month or two before, but it seemed like ten years to him now." Explain what that statement means. (Ideas: *Joe's life had changed so much in the past few days that his past life seemed far away; Joe had grown up so much that his childhood seemed distant.*) ⓊⒸⒸⓂ
- How was the *Reindeer* different from the *Dazzler*? (Ideas: *The* Reindeer *was larger; the* Reindeer *was built for speed.*) Ⓒ/ⓒ
- Why would Joe's idea of escaping with Frisco Kid be difficult to carry out? (Ideas: *Joe's father might not accept Frisco Kid; Frisco Kid might be sent to reform school; Frisco Kid didn't know how to live on land.*) ⒹⒾ
- Why didn't Joe want Frisco Kid to stay behind? (Idea: *Frisco Kid would get in trouble with Pete; Frisco Kid would have to suffer because of Joe's escape.*) ⒹⒸⒺ

EXERCISE 6
Paired Practice (Optional)

1. Now you'll read in pairs.
- Whoever read second the last time will read first today.
- Remember to start at the diamond and switch at the star.
2. (Observe students and answer questions as needed.)

AFTER READING

EXERCISE 7
Independent Work

1. Do all the items in your workbook and textbook for this lesson.
2. (The independent work in this lesson includes the following activities.)
- Story details
- Vocabulary
- Rhyme scheme
- Comparisons
- Conversations
- Referents
- Metaphors
- Comprehension
- Writing

EXERCISE 8
Workcheck

1. (Using the Answer Key, read the questions and answers for the workbook.)
2. (Have students read their answers for the textbook activities.)
3. (Have two or three students read their writing assignments aloud. Comment on each assignment.)
4. (Have students correct and turn in their work.)

SPELLING

(Present Spelling lesson 67 after completing Reading lesson 67. See *Spelling Presentation Book*.)

BEFORE READING

(Have students find lesson 68, part A, in their textbooks.)

Vocabulary Definitions

1. We're going to read these definitions.
2. (For each word, call on a student to read the definition and the item. Then ask the student to complete the item.)

1. **give somebody the slip**—When you *give somebody the slip,* you escape or hide from that person. If Bill hides from the sheriff, he gives the sheriff the slip.
   - What's another way of saying *Thelma tried to escape from her father*?

   - What's the answer? (Response: *Thelma tried to give her father the slip.*)

2. **sic**—When you *sic* an animal, you order the animal to attack somebody. If you order a dog to attack somebody, you *sic a dog* on that person.
   - What are you doing when you sic a dog?

   - What's the answer? (Idea: *Ordering the dog to attack somebody.*)

Vocabulary Review

1. Everybody, find part B. ✔
   - We're going to review these words.
2. (Call on a student to read the words in the box.)

taunt	untidy
drab	wince
arouse	endure
collide	spurt

3. (For each item, have a student read the item and say the answer.)

1. When you wake up something or make it active, you ▬▬▬ that thing.
   - What's the answer? (Response: *Arouse.*)

2. Something that is messy and disorderly is ▬▬▬.
   - What's the answer? (Response: *Untidy.*)

3. A quick burst is a ▬▬▬.
   - What's the answer? (Response: *Spurt.*)

4. When you mock people or try to make them angry, you ▬▬▬ them.
   - What's the answer? (Response: *Taunt.*)

5. When you suddenly tense up, you ▬▬▬.
   - What's the answer? (Response: *Wince.*)

READING

Focus Question

1. Everybody, find part C. ✔
2. What's the focus question for today's lesson? (Response: *Why did Frisco Kid keep a picture of a family?*)

Reading Aloud (Optional)

1. We're going to read aloud to the diamond.
   - (Call on individual students to read several sentences each.)

Chapter 7

The Picture

Focus Question: Why did Frisco Kid keep a picture of a family?

The two boys stayed on top of the cabin for perhaps an hour. Then, without saying a word, Frisco Kid went below and lit the cabin lamp. Joe could hear him fumbling around, and a little later, Joe heard his own name called softly. He went into the cabin and saw Frisco Kid sitting on the edge of the bunk. He was holding a carefully folded page from a magazine.

"Do they look like this?" Frisco Kid asked as he smoothed the magazine page and turned it so Joe could see.

The page had a picture of a family sitting around a dinner table.

"Who?" Joe asked, glancing at Frisco Kid's face.

"Your family—do they look like this?" Then Frisco Kid added more slowly, "I thought . . . I kind of thought they might, and . . . and . . ."

Frisco Kid's lips trembled and his eyes glistened. He turned hastily away.

The next instant, Joe was by his side on the bunk. He did not understand what was bothering Frisco Kid, but he knew that, whatever it was, it was something important.

"Go ahead and tell me," Joe said. "I'll understand."

"No, you won't; you can't."

"Yes, sure. Go ahead."

Frisco Kid choked and shook his head. "I don't think I could, anyway. It's more the things I feel, and I don't know how to put them into words."

"Try," Joe said.

"Well, it's this way," Frisco Kid said at last. "You see, I don't know much about the land and people and homes, and I never had no brothers or sisters or playmates. All the time I didn't know it, but I was lonely—sort of missed them down in here somewhere." And Frisco Kid placed a hand over his chest.

"Did you ever feel downright hungry?" he continued. "Well, that's just the way I used to feel, only a different kind of hunger. But one day, oh, a long time back, I got hold of a magazine and saw a picture—this picture—with the family sitting together. I thought it must be fine to be like them, and I got to thinking about the things they said and did till it came to me all of a sudden, and I knew I was just lonely. That's what was wrong with me.

"But more than anything else, I got to wondering about the family. I was thinking about them all the time, and after a while,

they became real to me. You see, it was making believe, and I knew it. Whenever I'd think of the pirates and the work and the hard life, I'd know the family was make-believe; but when I'd look at the picture, it wasn't. I don't know; I can't explain it."

Joe nodded as he remembered all the adventures he had imagined on land and sea. He understood that make-believe could be very real. ♦

EXERCISE 5

Silent Reading

1. Read the rest of the lesson to yourselves and be ready to answer some questions.

"Of course, it was all foolishness," Frisco Kid continued. "As I said, it was a long while back, and I was only a little kid. But the family in the picture, I was always getting that picture out to look at them. Afterwards, when I was older, I began to look at the picture in another way. I thought: Suppose, Kid, someday you were to belong to a family like that, what would they think of you? Would they like you? And then I'd make up my mind to be better, to try and do something with myself so that the family would not be ashamed to know me.

"That's why I learned to read. That's why I ran away from the pirates once. It wasn't till after I learned to read that I found out there was something wrong in bay-pirating. I'd been used to it ever since I could remember, and everybody I knew made their living that way. But when I did find out it was wrong, I ran away, thinking to quit it for good. I'll tell you about it sometime.

"Of course, they seemed like a real family when I was a youngster, and even now they sometimes seem that way. But while I'm talking to you, I know what they mean to me. They just stand for . . . well . . . for a better life than this and one I'd like to live. So I was wondering about your family, and that's why . . . I don't know . . . I guess I was just wondering."

Joe nodded his head.

"Then tell me about your family," Frisco Kid asked eagerly, "something—anything."

"Oh, that's easy," Joe began. He thought he understood Frisco Kid's hunger, and it seemed simple enough to satisfy him. "To begin with, they're like . . . hmmm . . . why, they're like a family—just a family." Joe broke off. ★

Frisco Kid waited patiently.

Joe struggled to pull his ideas together. "All families are alike," he said at last. "They're just the same as the ones you know, Kid. Sure they are."

"I don't know any, but I seem to know as much about them as you do," Frisco Kid said, smiling.

Both boys laughed. But a moment later, Joe fell into deep thought. He realized he was grateful for the good things he had in life. His home, his father, and his mother suddenly became important to him. He never had appreciated them, he thought, but from now on—well, it would be different.

Just then, they heard Pete hailing them from the *Reindeer.* Both boys ran onto the deck.

"Get up ze mainsail, and pull up ze anchor!" Pete shouted. "And then follow us! No lights!"

"Grab that rope!" Frisco Kid ordered. "Now hoist, but don't hoist ahead of me."

The mainsail went up, and the *Dazzler* strained and tugged at her anchor like an impatient horse. Suddenly, the anchor left the bottom with a rush, and the *Dazzler* was free.

Frisco Kid continued to give Joe commands. "Come forward again, and lend a hand on the chain," he yelled. The boy who kept a picture of a family in a magazine had vanished, and Frisco Kid the sailor was on deck. He ran back and forth across the deck, adjusting all the sails. Just then the *Reindeer,* like a monstrous bat, passed to the left of them in the gloom.

"Ah! Dose boys! Dey take all night!" they heard Pete exclaim.

And then the boys heard the gruff voice of Epont Nelson, who said, "Never you mind, Pete. I taught the Kid his sailing, and I ain't never been ashamed of him yet."

- Why did Frisco Kid keep a picture of a family? (Ideas: *He wanted to belong to a family; he was lonely.*) ⒹⒸⒺ
- How was Frisco Kid like Sara Crewe? (Ideas: *Both were lonely; both had lost their families; both had a strong imagination.*) Ⓒ/Ⓒ
- The story says Joe "understood that make-believe could be very real." Explain why he understood that idea. (Ideas: *He had imagined that life on the sea would be fun and exciting; he had imagined that life was easy.*) Ⓓ Ⓘ
- Frisco Kid didn't think anything was wrong with pirating until he learned to read. Why do you think reading would change his mind about pirating? (Ideas: *Stories show the difference between right and wrong; writers explain why crime is wrong.*) Ⓜ Ⓙ
- Why did Joe's family suddenly become important to him? (Ideas: *He realized how much Frisco Kid wanted a family; he realized how much he needed his own family.*) ⒹⒸⒺ

EXERCISE 6

Paired Practice (Optional)

1. Now you'll read in pairs.
- Whoever read second the last time will read first today.
- Remember to start at the diamond and switch at the star.
2. (Observe students and answer questions as needed.)

AFTER READING

EXERCISE 7

Independent Work

1. Do all the items in your workbook and textbook for this lesson.
2. (The independent work in this lesson includes the following activities.)
- Story details
- Vocabulary
- Comparisons
- Character traits
- Inference
- Referents
- Comprehension
- Writing

Workcheck

1. (Using the Answer Key, read the questions and answers for the workbook.)
2. (Have students read their answers for the textbook activities.)
3. (Have two or three students read their writing assignments aloud. Comment on each assignment.)
4. (Have students correct and turn in their work.)

(Present Spelling lesson 68 after completing Reading lesson 68. See *Spelling Presentation Book.*)

BEFORE READING

(Have students find lesson 69, part A, in their textbooks.)

EXERCISE 1
Vocabulary Definitions

1. We're going to read these definitions.
2. (For each word, call on a student to read the definition and the item. Then ask the student to complete the item.)

1. **survey**—When you *survey* something, you look all around that thing. If you look all around the sky, you survey the sky.
   • What's another way of saying *They looked all around the mountains*?

   • What's the answer? (Response: *They surveyed the mountains.*)

2. **strained**—*Strained* is another word for *tense*.
   • What's another way of saying *The situation was tense*?

   • What's the answer? (Response: *The situation was strained.*)

3. **muffled**—Sounds that are *muffled* are softened or deadened.
   • What's another way of saying *They spoke in softened voices*?

   • What's the answer? (Response: *They spoke in muffled voices.*)

EXERCISE 2
Vocabulary Review

1. Everybody, find part B. ✔
   • We're going to review these words.
2. (Call on a student to read the words in the box.)

principal	marred
hoist	defy
outwit	spunk
complicate	taunt

3. (For each item, have a student read the item and say the answer.)

1. When you challenge or oppose people, you �858 them.
   • What's the answer? (Response: *Defy.*)

2. When you mock people and try to make them angry, you �858 them.
   • What's the answer? (Response: *Taunt.*)

3. The most important things are the �858 things.
   • What's the answer? (Response: *Principal.*)

4. When you make something more difficult, you �858 it.
   • What's the answer? (Response: *Complicate.*)

5. Things that are partly spoiled or ruined are �858.
   • What's the answer? (Response: *Marred.*)

EXERCISE 3
Missing Words

1. Everybody, turn to part D at the end of today's story. ✔
   • (Call on individual students to read several sentences each.)
   • (At the end of each section, present the questions for that section.)

Write the answers for items 1 and 2.

Some sentences have words missing. We can see how these sentences work by starting with a sentence that has no words missing, for example: *Tom's clothes were clean, but Huck's clothes weren't clean.*

Here's a sentence with one word missing: *Tom's clothes were clean, but Huck's weren't clean.*

- What belongings of Huck's were not clean?

- What's the answer? (Response: *His clothes.*)

Here's sentence with a different word missing: *Tom's clothes were clean, but Huck's clothes weren't.*
- What weren't Huck's clothes?

- What's the answer? (Response: *Clean.*)

Here's a sentence with two words missing: *Tom's clothes were clean, but Huck's weren't.*
- What's the first word that's missing?

- What's the answer? (Response: *Clothes.*)

- What's the next word that's missing?

- What's the answer? (Response: *Clean.*)

Here are two more sentences with missing words. Rewrite each sentence so it has no missing words.
1. Her face was clean, but his wasn't clean.

- What part of him wasn't clean? (Response: *His face.*)

2. She could climb the hill, but he couldn't.

- What couldn't he do? (Response: *Climb the hill.*)
- You'll write the answers later.

READING

EXERCISE 4
Focus Question

1. Everybody, find part C. ✔

2. What's the focus question for today's lesson? (Response: *How did Frisco Kid feel about life on land?*)

EXERCISE 5
Reading Aloud (Optional)

1. We're going to read aloud to the diamond.
- (Call on individual students to read several sentences each.)

Chapter 8
Across the Bay
Focus Question: How did Frisco Kid feel about life on land?

The *Reindeer* led the way east across the bay. She was the faster boat, but the *Dazzler* had enough speed that the boys could keep her in sight. The breeze came steadily in from the west. The stars were blotted out by clouds. Frisco Kid surveyed the sky. "Going to have a good stiff wind before morning," he predicted, and Joe agreed.

A couple of hours later, both boats stood near the land, and they dropped anchor not far from shore. Joe could see a little wharf and a small sailboat a short distance away.

The two sloops got ready for a hasty departure. The anchors could be lifted and the sails hoisted in a moment. The lifeboat and another skiff came over noiselessly from the *Reindeer.* One of Epont Nelson's men was with Pete in the lifeboat, and Nelson was in the *Reindeer's* skiff with another man. The men's faces had a savage seriousness that almost made Joe shiver.

Pete buckled on his pistol-belt and placed a rifle in the lifeboat. Nelson was also armed, and his men had knives. They were careful to avoid making any noise. Pete paused long enough to warn the boys to remain quietly aboard and not to try any tricks.

Then the lifeboat and the skiff vanished into the gloom of the land. "Now would be your chance, Joe, if they hadn't taken the lifeboat," Frisco Kid whispered.

"What's the matter with the *Dazzler*?" Joe answered. "We could sail away before you could say 'Jack Flash.'"

The boys crawled forward and began to hoist the mainsail. But at the first rattle, a warning "Hist!" came to them through the darkness, followed by a loudly whispered "Stop that!"

The boys glanced in the direction of the sound. They saw a pale face peering at them from over the railing of the other sloop.

"Aw, it's only the *Reindeer*'s boy," Frisco Kid said. "Come on."

Again they were interrupted at the first rattling of the sails.

"I say, you fellers, you'd better let go of them sails pretty quick, I'm a-tellin' you, or I'll shoot!"

This threat was accompanied by the click of a pistol. Frisco Kid obeyed and went back to the cabin. "Oh, there's plenty more chances to come," he whispered to Joe. "Pete thought you'd be trying to make a break, and he fixed it so you couldn't." ♦

EXERCISE 6

Silent Reading

1. Read the rest of the lesson to yourselves and be ready to answer some questions.

The boys could hear nothing from the shore. Not a dog barked, not a light flared, yet an alarm seemed about to burst forth. The night had taken on a strained feeling, as though it held all kinds of terrible things.

"You were going to tell me about your running away from the pirates," Joe whispered finally, "and why you came back again."

Frisco Kid spoke in a muffled tone close to Joe's ear.

"You see, when I made up my mind to quit the pirate life, there wasn't anybody who could help me. But I knew that the only thing for me to do was to get ashore and find some kind of work. I figured there would be more chance in the country than in the city. I was working for Nelson on the *Reindeer* then, and one night I gave him the slip and headed into the country. But they were all farmers around there, and none of them had work for me. Besides, it was in the wrong time of year—winter. That shows how much I knew about the land.

"I'd saved up a couple of dollars, and I kept traveling back, deeper and deeper into the country, looking for work and buying bread and cheese and such things from the storekeepers. I tell you it was cold at night, sleeping out without blankets, and I was always glad when morning came. But worse than that was the way everybody looked at me. They were all suspicious, and sometimes they'd sic their dogs on me and tell me to move along. Seemed as though there wasn't no place for me on the land. Then I ran out of money, and just about the time I was good and hungry, I got captured."

"Captured! What for?"

"Nothing. I crawled into a haystack to sleep one night because it was warmer, and along comes a police officer and arrests me for being a tramp. At first, they thought I was a runaway. I told them I didn't have no family, but they wouldn't believe me for a long while. And then, when nobody claimed me, the judge sent me to a reform school in San Francisco." ★

Frisco Kid stopped and peered toward the shore into the darkness. Nothing was stirring except the rising wind.

"I thought I'd die in that reform school. Just like being in jail. I was locked up and guarded like a prisoner. And the boys were mostly street boys, without one idea of square dealing and fair play. There was only one thing I did like, and that was the books. Oh, I did lots of reading, I tell you. But that couldn't make up for the rest. I wanted the freedom and the sunlight and the salt water. And what had I done to be kept in prison? Instead of doing wrong, I had tried to do good, to make myself better, and that's what I got for it.

"Sometimes I'd imagine the sunshine dancing on the water and the *Reindeer* cutting through it. I'd get so homesick that I wouldn't know what I was doing. And then the boys would gang up on me. I'd take on all of them. Then the men in charge would lock me up and punish me. After I couldn't stand it any longer, I escaped. It seemed as though there wasn't any place for me on the land, so I picked up with Pete and went back on the bay. That's about all there is to it."

"You're going to go back on the land with me," Joe said, laying a hand on Frisco Kid's shoulder. "That's what you're going to do. As for . . ."

Bang! A revolver shot rang out from the shore. Bang! Bang! More guns were speaking sharply. A man's voice rose wildly. Somebody began to cry for help. Both boys were on their feet in an instant, hoisting the mainsail and getting everything ready to run. The *Reindeer* boy was doing the same thing. The noise woke up a man on the nearby sailboat. He stuck his head out but withdrew it when he saw the two sloops ready to speed off into the bay.

- How did Frisco Kid feel about life on land? (Ideas: *He didn't like it; he was afraid of it.*) (DCE)
- Why did Frisco Kid feel that way? (Ideas: *He'd had bad experiences on land; he couldn't find work on land; he was put in a reform school on land.*) (C/E)
- How did Pete guard against a possible escape by Joe and Frisco Kid? (Idea: *He asked the* Reindeer's *boy to guard the* Dazzler.) (Sum)
- Explain how Frisco Kid ended up in reform school. (Idea: *He was arrested for being a tramp and put in reform school because he had no family.*) (R)
- Frisco Kid's experiences on land turned out badly. What could he have done to have better experiences? (Ideas: *He could have tried to find a job in town; he could have gone to a public school.*) (MJ)

EXERCISE 7

Paired Practice (Optional)

1. Now you'll read in pairs.
- Whoever read second the last time will read first today.
- Remember to start at the diamond and switch at the star.
2. (Observe students and answer questions as needed.)

AFTER READING

EXERCISE 8

Independent Work

1. Do all the items in your workbook and textbook for this lesson.
2. (The independent work in this lesson includes the following activities.)
- Story details
- Vocabulary
- Settings
- Exaggeration
- Missing words
- Comprehension
- Writing

EXERCISE 9

Workcheck

1. (Using the Answer Key, read the questions and answers for the workbook.)
2. (Have students read their answers for the textbook activities.)
3. (Have two or three students read their writing assignments aloud. Comment on each assignment.)
4. (Have students correct and turn in their work.)

SPELLING

(Present Spelling lesson 69 after completing Reading lesson 69. See *Spelling Presentation Book*.)

BEFORE READING

(Have students find lesson 70, part A, in their textbooks.)

EXERCISE 1

Vocabulary Definitions

1. We're going to read these definitions.
2. (For each word, call on a student to read the definition and the item. Then ask the student to complete the item.)

1. **loom**—When something *looms,* it appears suddenly and looks big.
   - What's another way of saying *The wave suddenly appeared in front of them*?

   - What's the answer? (Response: *The wave loomed in front of them.*)

2. **gale**—A *gale* is a strong wind.
   - What's another way of saying *The strong wind blew the boat off course*?

   - What's the answer? (Response: *The gale blew the boat off course.*)

3. **hurtle**—When something *hurtles,* it moves quickly and forcefully.
   - What's another way of saying *The train moved quickly and forcefully down the mountain*?

   - What's the answer? (Response: *The train hurtled down the mountain.*)

EXERCISE 2

Vocabulary Review

1. Everybody, find part B. ✔
   - We're going to review these words.
2. (Call on a student to read the words in the box.)

strained	**untidy**
defy	**survey**
bungle	**spunk**
muffled	**surge**

3. (For each item, have a student read the item and say the answer.)

1. When you look all around a scene, you ▮▮▮▮▮ that scene.

   - What's the answer? (Response: *Survey.*)

2. Another word for *tense* is ▮▮▮▮▮.

   - What's the answer? (Response: *Strained.*)

3. Sounds that are softened or deadened are ▮▮▮▮▮.

   - What's the answer? (Response: *Muffled.*)

4. When you challenge or oppose people, you ▮▮▮▮▮ them.

   - What's the answer? (Response: *Defy.*)

5. Someone with spirit and determination has ▮▮▮▮▮.

   - What's the answer? (Response: *Spunk.*)

EXERCISE 3

Missing Words

1. Everybody, turn to part D at the end of today's story. ✔
   - (Call on individual students to read several sentences each.)
   - (At the end of each section, present the questions for that section.)

Write the answers for items 1 and 2.
   Some sentences have words missing. We can see how these sentences work by starting with a sentence that has no words missing.
   Here's a sentence with no words missing: *Camila's necklace had twelve beads, and Fernanda's necklace had fifteen beads.*

Here's a sentence with one word missing: *Camila's necklace had twelve beads, and Fernanda's had fifteen beads.*
- What belonging of Fernanda's had fifteen beads?

- What's the answer? (Response: *Her necklace.*)

Here's a sentence with a different word missing: *Camila's necklace had twelve beads, and Fernanda's necklace had fifteen.*
- What did Fernanda's necklace have fifteen of?

- What's the answer? (Response: *Beads.*)

Here's a sentence with two words missing: *Camila's necklace had twelve beads, and Fernanda's had fifteen.*
- What's the first word that's missing?

- What's the answer? (Response: *Necklace.*)

- What's the next word that's missing?

- What's the answer? (Response: *Beads.*)

Here are two more sentences with missing words. Rewrite each sentence so it has no missing words.
1. Russell wanted to go to the play, but his friends didn't.

- His friends didn't what? (Response: *Want to go to the play.*)
- Say the whole sentence with no words missing. (Response: *Russell wanted to go to the play, but his friends didn't want to go to the play.*)

2. Velma's car was loud, yet it was quieter than Sophie's.

- What was quieter than Sophie's? (Response: *Velma's car.*)
- Say the whole sentence with no words missing. (Response: *Velma's car was loud, yet it was quieter than Sophie's car.*)
- You'll write the answers later.

READING

Focus Question
1. Everybody, find part C. ✔
2. What's the focus question for today's lesson? (Response: *Why was the safe particularly important to Joe?*)

Reading Aloud (Optional)
1. We're going to read aloud to the diamond.
- (Call on individual students to read several sentences each.)

Chapter 9
The Office Safe
Focus Question: Why was the safe particularly important to Joe?

Frisco Kid and Joe heaved up the anchor chain. Everything was ready. They strained their eyes in the direction of the shore. The commotion had died away, but here and there, lights were beginning to flash. Then they heard Epont Nelson's voice crying out, "Cast off!"

"They're takin' their time about it, ain't they?" the boy on the *Reindeer* called over to them.

"Guess they're all right," Frisco Kid answered.

The man on the nearby sailboat cried out without showing his head, "Say, you!" he called. "You'd better go away!"

"And you'd better stay below and keep quiet," Frisco Kid answered.

"We'll take care of ourselves. You do the same," said the boy on the *Reindeer.*

"Here they come!" Frisco Kid said.

The two skiffs shot out of the darkness and came alongside. Some kind of an argument was going on.

"No, no!" Pete cried. "Put it on ze *Dazzler.* Ze *Reindeer,* she sail too fast and run away, oh, so queeck, and never more I see it. Put it on ze *Dazzler,* eh? What you say?"

"All right," Nelson agreed. "We'll divide it up afterwards. But hurry up. Heave it up, boys. My arm's broken."

The men tumbled out of the skiffs and jumped onto the *Dazzler*. From the shore, Joe could hear the shouting of men, the sound of oars, and the slapping of sails. He figured the men on shore were going to chase the pirates.

The pirates began to lift something heavy out of the skiff. "Now!" Nelson commanded. "All together! Be careful, or you'll smash the skiff. There! A long pull and a strong pull! Once again!"

Joe glanced into the skiff to see what the heavy object was. He saw the vague outlines of a small office safe.

Straining and gasping, with tense muscles and heaving chests, the men brought the safe over the side, rolled it onto the top of the railing, and lowered it onto the deck of the *Dazzler*. The cabin doors were thrown open, and the safe was moved along until it lay on the cabin floor. Nelson had followed it aboard. His left arm hung helpless at his side. He did not seem to mind, however, nor did he mind the sounds of people coming toward the sloops.

"Set your course for the Golden Gate," he said to Pete as he turned to go. "I'll try to stand by you, but if you get lost in the dark, I'll meet you near the Farallon Islands tomorrow." Then he sprang into the skiff after his men and cried heartily, "And then we'll head to Mexico, my jolly rovers—Mexico and summer weather!" ◆

EXERCISE 6

Silent Reading

1. Read the rest of the lesson to yourselves and be ready to answer some questions.

Just as the *Dazzler* began to sail away, the sails of a police boat loomed up behind her. The police boat was crowded with men, and they raised their voices angrily when they saw the pirates. Joe had half a mind to run forward and cut down the sails so the *Dazzler* could be captured. But the thought of Frisco Kid held him back. He wanted to take the Kid ashore with him, but he did not want to take him to jail. So he decided to help the *Dazzler* escape, after all.

The police boat started to come after them, but in the darkness, it collided with the nearby sailboat. The man on board the sailboat let out a wild yell and ran onto the deck, screaming for help. In the confusion, the *Dazzler* slipped away into the night.

The *Reindeer* had already disappeared. The wind was picking up, and the *Dazzler* surged quickly through the water. Before an hour had passed, they could see the lights of Hunter's Point. Frisco Kid went below to make coffee, but Joe remained on deck.

As Joe watched the lights of South San Francisco grow, he thought about his destination. Mexico! They were going to sea in a frail sloop! Impossible! At least, it seemed so to Joe. He thought ocean travel was limited to steamers and big ships, and he was beginning to feel sorry he had not cut the sails.

Joe longed to ask Pete a thousand questions, but just as the first question was on his lips, Pete ordered him to the cabin. Pete remained at the lonely task of steering the *Dazzler*. ★

Shortly after dawn, the boys were called and came sleepily on deck. The day was cold, the sky was gray, and the wind had almost the force of a gale. Joe saw they were near the quarantine station on Angel Island. San Francisco was a blur on the southern horizon. The night still lingered in the west, but it slowly withdrew before their eyes. Pete was carefully regarding a police boat half a mile away.

"Dey tink to catch ze *Dazzler*, eh? Bah!" And he turned the *Dazzler* straight for the Golden Gate.

The police boat did the same thing. Joe watched her a few moments. She seemed to be moving much faster than the *Dazzler*.

"Why, at this rate, they'll have us in no time!" Joe cried.

Pete laughed. "You tink so? Bah! Dey are scared of ze wind. We weel use ze wind. Ah! You wait—you see!"

"They're traveling ahead faster," Frisco Kid explained, "but we're better sailors. In the end, we'll beat them, even if they have the nerve to go through the Gate, which I don't think they have. Look!"

Joe could see the great ocean waves ahead. They were flinging themselves skyward and bursting into roaring caps of foam. In the middle of the Gate, a coasting steam ship was struggling slowly into the bay. It was magnificent, this battle between people and nature. Joe's eyes began to flash at the nearness of the upcoming struggle.

Joe and the others put on raincoats. Then Pete sent the two boys into the cabin to tie down the safe. In the middle of this task, Joe glanced at the name on the safe and read "Díaz and Tate, Inc." Why, those were the names of Joe's father and his father's partner! That was their safe! That was their money inside the safe!

- Why was the safe particularly important to Joe? (Ideas: *Because it belonged to his father's company; because it contained his father's money.*) (DCE)
- The story calls sailing through the Golden Gate "a battle between people and nature." Explain why it's a battle. (Idea: *The wind and water in the Golden Gate are rough, and ships have to struggle to go through the Gate safely.*) (DI)
- Why did Pete think the *Dazzler* would win the race against the police boat? (Ideas: *Pete thought the police were scared of the wind; he thought they didn't have the nerve to sail through the Golden Gate.*) (DCE)
- Why did Joe decide against cutting the sails so the police could catch the *Dazzler*? (Idea: *He didn't want Frisco Kid to go to prison.*) (DCE)
- Why do you think the Pacific Ocean is more dangerous for the *Dazzler* than San Francisco Bay? (Ideas: *The waves in the ocean are bigger; the wind is stronger on the ocean; there's less protection from storms.*) (MJ)

EXERCISE 7
Paired Practice (Optional)

1. Now you'll read in pairs.
- Whoever read second the last time will read first today.
- Remember to start at the diamond and switch at the star.
2. (Observe students and answer questions as needed.)

AFTER READING

EXERCISE 8
Independent Work

1. Do all the items in your workbook and textbook for this lesson.
2. (The independent work in this lesson includes the following activities.)
- Story details
- Vocabulary
- Maps
- Spoonerisms
- Missing words
- Similes
- Comprehension
- Writing

EXERCISE 9
Workcheck

1. (Using the Answer Key, read the questions and answers for the workbook.)
2. (Have students read their answers for the textbook activities.)
3. (Have two or three students read their writing assignments aloud. Comment on each assignment.)
4. (Have students correct and turn in their work.)

MASTERY TEST

(The Lesson 70 Mastery Test should be administered after students complete lesson 70. See *Curriculum-Based Assessment and Fluency Handbook* for details.)

ACTIVITIES ACROSS THE CURRICULUM

(Students should complete the appropriate project in *Activities across the Curriculum* after completing lesson 70. See *Activities across the Curriculum* book for details.)

SPELLING

(Present Spelling lesson 70 after completing Reading lesson 70. See *Spelling Presentation Book.*)

Lessons 71–75 • Planning Page

	Lesson 71	Lesson 72	Lesson 73	Lesson 74	Lesson 75
BEFORE READING	Vocabulary definitions Vocabulary review Referents	Vocabulary definitions Vocabulary review Referents	Vocabulary definitions Vocabulary review	Hard words Word practice Vocabulary definitions Combined sentences	Hard words Word practice Vocabulary definitions Vocabulary review Combined sentences
NEW VOCABULARY	summit poised	forge ahead vengeance	show promise reception	despise unheeded	scornful writhe
READING	*The Cruise of the Dazzler* (Chapter 10)	*The Cruise of the Dazzler* (Chapter 11)	*The Cruise of the Dazzler* (Chapter 12)	"Casey at the Bat" (Part 1)	"Casey at the Bat" (Part 2)
INDEPENDENT WORK	Story details Vocabulary Missing words Sarcasm Sequencing Referents Comprehension Writing	Story details Vocabulary Contradictions Missing words Poem review Referents Similes Comprehension Writing	Story details Vocabulary Maps Missing words Referents Comprehension Writing	Character traits Vocabulary Referents Maps Relevant information Combined sentences Comprehension Writing	Vocabulary Referents Sequencing Poem review Spoonerisms Combined sentences Comprehension Writing
SUPPLEMENTS	*Spelling*	*Spelling*	*Spelling*	*Spelling*	*Spelling* *Activities across the Curriculum*

Comprehension Questions Abbreviations Guide

Access Prior Knowledge = (APK)   Author's Point of View = (APoV)   Author's Purpose = (AP)   Cause/Effect = (C/E)   Charts/Graphs/Diagrams/Visual Aids = (VA)

Classify and Categorize = (C+C)   Compare/Contrast = (C/C)   Determine Character Emotions, Motivation = (DCE)   Drawing Conclusions = (DC)   Drawing Inferences = (DI)

Fact and Opinion = (F/O)   Hypothesizing = (H)   Main Idea = (MI)   Making Connections = (MC)   Making Deductions = (MD)   Making Judgements = (MJ)

Narrative Elements = (NE)   Noting Details = (ND)   Predict = (P)   Reality/Fantasy = (R/F)   Recall Facts/Rules = (RF/R)   Retell = (R)   Sequence = (Seq)

Steps in a Process = (SP)   Story Structure = (SS)   Summarize = (Sum)   Understanding Dialogue = (UD)   Using Context to Confirm Meaning(s) = (UCCM)   Visualize = (V)

BEFORE READING

(Have students find lesson 71, part A, in their textbooks.)

EXERCISE 1

Vocabulary Definitions

1. We're going to read these definitions.
2. (For each word, call on a student to read the definition and the item. Then ask the student to complete the item.)

1. **summit**—The *summit* of something is the top or the peak of that thing.
   • What's another way of saying *the peak of a mountain*?

   • What's the answer? (Response: *The summit of a mountain.*)

2. **poised**—When something is *poised,* it is balanced.
   • What's another way of saying *The ship was balanced on top of the wave*?

   • What's the answer? (Response: *The ship was poised on top of the wave.*)

EXERCISE 2

Vocabulary Review

1. Everybody, find part B. ✔
   • We're going to review these words.
2. (Call on a student to read the words in the box.)

arouse	survey
defy	muffled
hurtles	looms
gale	surges
strained	

3. (For each item, have a student read the item and say the answer.)

1. When something suddenly appears and looks big, it ▮▮▮▮.
   • What's the answer? (Response: *Looms.*)

.2. A strong wind is a ▮▮▮▮.
   • What's the answer? (Response: *Gale.*)

3. When something moves forward like a wave, that thing ▮▮▮▮.
   • What's the answer? (Response: *Surges.*)

4. When something moves quickly and forcefully, it ▮▮▮▮.
   • What's the answer? (Response: *Hurtles.*)

5. Sounds that are softened or deadened are ▮▮▮▮.
   • What's the answer? (Response: *Muffled.*)

6. When you wake up something or make it active, you ▮▮▮▮ that thing.
   • What's the answer? (Response: *Arouse.*)

7. Another word for *tense* is ▮▮▮▮.
   • What's the answer? (Response: *Strained.*)

EXERCISE 3

Referents

1. Everybody, turn to part D at the end of today's story. ✔
   • (Call on individual students to read several sentences each.)
   • (At the end of each section, present the questions for that section.)

Write the answers for items 1 and 2.
  Sometimes words refer to an entire sentence or a group of sentences. Here is an example:
  Wanda walked along the crest of the hill. Suddenly, she slipped and fell. She

tumbled down the side of the hill, bouncing against several large boulders. **Her misfortune** made her more careful when she returned to the crest of the hill.

The words *her misfortune* refer to all the bad things that happened to Wanda.

- Which sentence or sentences tell what *her misfortune* was?

- What's the answer? (Response: *Suddenly, she slipped and fell. She tumbled down the side of the hill, bouncing against several large boulders.*)

1. Write a main idea that tells what *her misfortune* was.

- What's the answer? (Idea: *Wanda fell down the hill.*)

Here is another example:

The *Dazzler* was now headed south. Joe caught a glimpse of a group of bicyclists rounding a cliff on the San Bruno Road. He remembered the time when he had gone over the same ground on his own bike. He remembered how tired his legs had become. **That** was only a month or two before, but it seemed like ten years to him now.

- Which sentence or sentences tell what *That* was?

- What's the answer? (Response: *He remembered the time when he had gone over the same ground on his own bike. He remembered how tired his legs had become.*)

2. Write a main idea that tells what *That* was.

- What's the answer? (Idea: *Joe bicycled and got tired.*)
- You'll write the answers later.

READING

EXERCISE 4

Focus Question

1. Everybody, turn back to part C. ✔
2. What's the focus question for today's lesson? (Response: *What did the boys plan to do if they reached the shore?*)

> ***Note:*** The "Reading Aloud" exercise is recommended for this lesson.

EXERCISE 5

Reading Aloud

1. We're going to read aloud to the diamond.
- (Call on individual students to read several sentences each.)

Chapter 10

The Golden Gate

Focus Question: What did the boys plan to do if they reached the shore?

Frisco Kid looked up and followed Joe's gaze. "Is that your father's safe?" he whispered.

Joe nodded yes. He could see it all now. Joe's father, Mr. Díaz, and his partner, Mr. Tate, owned a large factory south of Oakland. That was the place the pirates had robbed. The safe probably contained the wages of the people who worked in the factory.

"Don't say anything," Joe cautioned.

Frisco Kid agreed. "Pete can't read, anyway," he added, "and the chances are that Nelson won't know what your name is. Just the same, the situation is pretty rough. They'll break the safe open and divide up the money as soon as they can, so I don't see what you're going to do about it."

"Wait and see." Joe had made up his mind that he would protect his father's property. He had a fighting chance to recover the safe.

Responsibilities were showering upon Joe thick and fast. Three days before, he had only himself to consider. Then he had felt a responsibility for Frisco Kid's future. And now, he had to recover his father's safe. He responded bravely. While the future might be doubtful, he had no doubt in himself. This self-confidence gave him added strength.

"Now she takes it!" Pete cried from the deck.

Both boys ran onto the deck. The sloop was in the middle of the Gate. A huge forty-foot wave reared a foam-crested head far above them. The wave was so tall that it blocked the wind for a moment and threatened to crush the tiny sloop like an eggshell. Joe held his breath. Pete went straight into the wave, and the *Dazzler* mounted the steep slope with a rush, poised a moment on the summit, and fell into the yawning valley beyond.

The *Dazzler* worked its way across the dangerous stretch of water. Once, the sloop was almost buried by a wave, but otherwise it bobbed and ducked like a cork.

To Joe, it seemed as though he had been lifted into a new world. This was life! This was action! The sailors on the deck of the steamer waved their hats at the brave sloop.

"Ah! You see! You see!" Pete yelled as he pointed behind them.

The police boat had been afraid to sail through the Gate. The chase had ended. ♦

EXERCISE 6

Silent Reading

1. Read the rest of the lesson to yourselves and be ready to answer some questions.

Half an hour later, the *Dazzler* was sliding up and down on the long Pacific Ocean waves. The wind had increased in strength, and the *Dazzler* took off for the Farallon Islands, which were thirty miles away. By the time breakfast was cooked and eaten, Pete saw the *Reindeer* anchored near the shore of one of the islands. There was not a soul on deck.

Pete said, "Dat Nelson is something. He no care. He is afraid of nothing. Some day he will drown, oh so very queeck! You see! You see!"

The *Dazzler* circled the *Reindeer* three times. Then the crew appeared on the *Reindeer*'s deck and lifted her sails at once. Together the two sloops plunged south toward Mexico. Pete explained they would keep just out of sight of the California coast. That way, no one on land could see them during the day, and they could get food and water by landing at night.

"I'll tell you what we'll do," Frisco Kid whispered to Joe while cooking dinner. "Tonight we'll drag Pete down . . ."

"Drag Pete down?"

"Yes, and tie him up good and snug—as soon as it gets dark. Then we'll put out the lights and make a run for it. Get to shore anyway, anywhere, just so long as we shake loose from Nelson. You'll save your father's money, and I'll go away somewhere, over on the other side of the world, and begin all over again."

"I won't go for that plan," Joe said. "I'll not have a thing to do with it. I'll go on to Mexico if you don't make me one promise."

"And what's the promise?"

"Just this: You place yourself in my hands from the moment we get ashore, and trust me. You don't know anything about the land. And I'll fix it up with my father—I know I can—so you can get to study and get an education and be something other than a bay pirate. That's what you'd like, isn't it?" ★

Though he said nothing, Frisco Kid showed how well he liked it by the expression on his face.

"And you'll have earned it," Joe continued. "If you help me recover my father's money, he'll owe it to you."

"But I don't do things that way," Frisco Kid said.

"Now you keep quiet. Just remember, it would cost my father thousands of dollars to recover that safe. He'll be grateful, and if you don't like it on the land, you can back out. Come on. That's fair."

They shook hands and proceeded to map out their plans for the night.

But the storm from the northwest had something entirely different in store for the *Dazzler* and her crew. By the time lunch was over, the wind was so strong that they were forced to lower their sails. But the gale had still not reached its height. The sea had been blown into a series of mountainous waves. It was frightful to look at them. The only time the boys could see the *Reindeer* was when the two sloops were tossed up on the crests of the waves at the same time. Occasionally, waves poured onto the deck or dashed clear over the cabin. Before long, Joe was using a small pump to keep the sloop dry.

At three o'clock in the afternoon, Pete motioned to the *Reindeer* that he was going to stop and get out a sea anchor.

Nelson waved his hand in response that he understood.

Joe asked Frisco Kid, "What's a sea anchor?"

Frisco Kid replied, "A large bucket that we drag. It slows the sloop down but keeps it heading with the wind."

Pete went forward to launch the sea anchor himself. He stood on the slippery deck, waiting for an opportunity. But at that moment the *Dazzler* was lifted by an unusually large wave. As she came to the summit of the wave, she was blasted by a heavy snort of the gale.

Snap! Crash! The mast, the mainsail, the sea anchor, and Pete went over the side. Almost by a miracle, he clutched the side of the *Dazzler.* The boys ran forward to drag him into safety. Nelson observed the disaster and instantly ran the *Reindeer* down to the rescue.

- What did the boys plan to do if they reached the shore? (Ideas: *Get the safe back to Mr. Díaz; get Frisco Kid an education.*) (Sum)
- When Joe sailed through the Golden Gate, he felt "as though he had been lifted into a new world." Explain why he felt that way. (Ideas: *Joe had never experienced that kind of sailing before; Joe had never felt so alive; sailing through the Gate was completely different from the rest of Joe's life.*) (DI)
- Why did Pete want to stay just out of sight of the coast? (Idea: *No one could see them during the day, but they could still land at night for food and water.*) (DCE)
- Why would Joe take charge if the boys reached the shore? (Ideas: *Because Joe knew about the land; because Frisco Kid didn't know about the land.*) (MD)
- Why do you think Nelson wants to rescue Pete? (Ideas: *They're friends; Nelson doesn't want Pete to die; Nelson doesn't want to lose the safe.*) (DCE)

Paired Practice (Optional)

1. Now you'll read in pairs.
- Whoever read second the last time will read first today.
- Remember to start at the diamond and switch at the star.
2. (Observe students and answer questions as needed.)

AFTER READING

Independent Work

1. Do all the items in your workbook and textbook for this lesson.
2. (The independent work in this lesson includes the following activities.)
- Story details
- Vocabulary
- Missing words
- Sarcasm
- Sequencing
- Referents
- Comprehension
- Writing

Workcheck

1. (Using the Answer Key, read the questions and answers for the workbook.)
2. (Have students read their answers for the textbook activities.)
3. (Have two or three students read their writing assignments aloud. Comment on each assignment.)
4. (Have students correct and turn in their work.)

(Present Spelling lesson 71 after completing Reading lesson 71. See *Spelling Presentation Book.*)

BEFORE READING

(Have students find lesson 72, part A, in their textbooks.)

EXERCISE 1
Vocabulary Definitions

1. We're going to read these definitions.
2. (For each word, call on a student to read the definition and the item. Then ask the student to complete the item.)

1. **forge ahead**—When you *forge ahead,* you move forward powerfully.
- What's another way of saying *The ship moved forward powerfully through the stormy sea?*

- What's the answer? (Response: *The ship forged ahead through the stormy sea.*)

2. **vengeance**—*Vengeance* is another word for *revenge.*
- What's another word for *revenge?*

- What's the answer? (Response: *Vengeance.*)

EXERCISE 2
Vocabulary Review

1. Everybody, find part B. ✔
- We're going to review these words.
2. (Call on a student to read the words in the box.)

poised	gale
taunt	untidy
strained	muffled
spunky	summit
arouse	

3. (For each item, have a student read the item and say the answer.)

1. Sounds that are softened or deadened are ▮▮▮▮▮.
- What's the answer? (Response: *Muffled.*)

2. The top or peak of something is the ▮▮▮▮▮ of that thing.
- What's the answer? (Response: *Summit.*)

3. When something is balanced, it is ▮▮▮▮▮.
- What's the answer? (Response: *Poised.*)

4. Another word for tense is ▮▮▮▮▮.
- What's the answer? (Response: *Strained.*)

5. When you mock people and try to make them angry, you ▮▮▮▮▮ them.
- What's the answer? (Response: *Taunt.*)

6. When you wake up something or make it active, you ▮▮▮▮▮ it.
- What's the answer? (Response: *Arouse.*)

EXERCISE 3
Referents

1. Everybody, turn to part D at the end of today's story. ✔
- (Call on individual students to read several sentences each.)
- (At the end of each section, present the questions for that section.)

Write the answers for items 1 and 2.
Sometimes words refer to an entire sentence or a group of sentences. Here is an example:
Both hooks were thrown overboard together, and seventy feet of line whizzed out. Joe instantly felt the struggling jerks of a hooked fish. As he began to haul the fish in, he glanced at Frisco Kid and saw that he, too, had captured a fish on his line.

The race between them was exciting. Hand over hand, the wet lines flashed on board. **It** was royal sport.

The word *it* refers to what Joe and Frisco Kid were doing.
- Which sentence or sentences tell what Joe and Frisco Kid were doing?

- What's the answer? (Idea: *As he began to haul the fish in, he glanced at Frisco Kid and saw that he, too, had captured a fish on his line. The race between them was exciting. Hand over hand, the wet lines flashed on board.*)

1. Write a main idea that tells what Joe and Frisco Kid were doing.

- What's the answer? (Idea: *Joe and Frisco Kid had a fishing race.*)

Here is another example:
In Greenwich Village, there is a squat three-story building. Sue and Joan have their painting studio there. Sue is from Maine, Joan from California. They met at a restaurant and found their tastes in art similar. While they were at the restaurant, they decided to share a studio. **That** was in May.
- Which sentence or sentences tell what *that* was?

- What's the answer? (Idea: *While they were at the restaurant, they decided to share a studio.*)

2. Write a main idea that tells what *that* was.

- What's the answer? (Idea: *Sue and Joan decided to share a studio.*)
- You'll write the answers later.

READING

EXERCISE 4

Focus Question
1. Everybody, find part C. ✔
2. What's the focus question for today's lesson? (Response: *What was the fate of the* Reindeer?)

EXERCISE 5

Reading Aloud (Optional)
1. We're going to read aloud to the diamond.
- (Call on individual students to read several sentences each.)

Chapter 11
The Fate of the *Reindeer*
Focus Question: What was the fate of the *Reindeer*?

Pete was not injured from the fall overboard, but the sloop had not escaped so easily. It was leaning dangerously toward the sea. It could flip over at any moment.

"Goodbye, old *Dazzler*," Pete said. "Never no more you sail into ze wind."

Pete stood near the tiller with the boys and surveyed the sloop with wet eyes. Even Joe felt sorry for him at this moment. Another heavy blast of wind caught the crest of a wave and hurled it upon the helpless craft.

"Can't we save her?" Joe spluttered.

Frisco Kid shook his head no.

"Or the safe?"

"Impossible," Frisco Kid answered. "With these waves, it's impossible to get the *Reindeer* alongside. We'll be lucky to save ourselves."

Another wave swept over them, and the lifeboat dashed itself to pieces against the side of the *Dazzler*. Then the *Reindeer* towered above them on a mountain of water. Joe shrank back, for it seemed she would fall on top of them. But the next instant, she dropped and they rose. Now they were looking down on the *Reindeer*. It was a striking picture. The *Reindeer* was wallowing in the foam. The water whipped across her decks. The air was filled with flying spray, making the scene appear misty and unreal.

One of Nelson's men was clinging to the lower deck and pulling in the *Reindeer*'s skiff. The cabin boy was leaning far over the railing and trying to help. Another man stood at the tiller and attempted to steer the sloop through the waves.

Nelson was standing by this man. His arm was in a sling, and his hat had blown away. His wet hair was plastered around his face. But his whole appearance breathed courage and strength. Joe looked at Nelson in admiration, and he felt sorrow for the way in which the man used his courage. He was a pirate! A robber!

These thoughts came to Joe in the flash of a second. Then the *Reindeer* swept up to the top of the wave and hurtled by the *Dazzler*.

"Ze wild man! Ze wild man!" Pete shrieked, watching the *Reindeer* in amazement. "He wants us to jump on his sloop. He thinks he can turn around in this gale! He will die! We will all die! Oh, ze fool! Ze fool!"

But Nelson tried the impossible. At the right moment, he turned the *Reindeer* around and hauled back toward the *Dazzler*.

"Here she comes! Get ready to jump!" Pete cried. Frisco Kid and Joe only looked at each other. They said nothing, but they both sensed that they should stay with the *Dazzler* and rescue the safe.

The *Reindeer* dashed by them again. She was so close that it appeared she would run them down. Pete was the only one to jump. He sprang for the *Reindeer* like a cat and caught onto the railing with both hands. Then the *Reindeer* forged ahead. Pete clung to the railing and worked his way up until he dropped onto the deck.

And then, to Joe's amazement, the *Reindeer* turned around again. She plowed back toward the *Dazzler* at breakneck speed. She was tilted at such an angle that it seemed she would sink.

Just then, the storm burst in fury, and the shouting wind made the sea churn. The *Reindeer* dipped from view behind an immense wave. The wave rolled on, but the boys could see only the angry waters where the *Reindeer* had been. They looked a second time. There was no *Reindeer*. They were alone on the ocean. ◆

EXERCISE 6

Silent Reading

1. Read the rest of the lesson to yourselves and be ready to answer some questions.

Joe was too horrified to utter a sound. "She went straight to the bottom," Frisco Kid gasped. "Pete always said Nelson would drown himself someday! And now

they're all gone. It's dreadful—dreadful. But now we've got to look out for ourselves, I tell you! The sea will kick up worse yet. Lend a hand, and hang on with the other. We've got to bail her out."

The two boys raced to the cabin. Using a couple of buckets, they proceeded to fling the water overboard. It was heartbreaking work, for the sea flung most of the water back. But they kept on, and the storm soon began to die down. When night fell, the *Dazzler* was still afloat. The storm had passed, and the wind had shifted to the west.

"We have no sail," Frisco Kid observed, "so we'll just have to drift along with the current. If the wind keeps blowing in this direction, we'll get to the coast sometime tomorrow. There's nothing to do now but wait."

They said little. They were overcome with exhaustion and huddled against each other for warmth and companionship. It was a miserable night, and they shivered constantly from the cold. There was nothing dry on board. Everything was soaked with saltwater. Sometimes the boys dozed, but their sleep was anxious. They kept waking up with sudden starts. ★

At last, day broke. The boys looked around. Wind and sea had calmed down considerably, and the *Dazzler* was definitely out of danger. The coast was nearer than they had expected. They could see dark and forbidding cliffs in the gray dawn. But they could also see yellow beaches, and beyond—it seemed too good to be true—the houses and smoking chimneys of a town!

"It's Santa Cruz!" Frisco Kid cried. "And the beach is soft, so we'll run no risk of being wrecked in the surf!"

"Then you think we'll be able to rescue the safe?" Joe asked.

"Yes, indeed we will! There isn't much of a harbor, but with this breeze, we'll run right up the mouth of the San Lorenzo River. Then there's a little lake where the water is smooth as glass. Come on. We'll be just in time for breakfast."

And then Frisco Kid went into the cabin and grabbed a couple of spare oars and some blankets. In just a little while, he had made a temporary sail. The *Dazzler* headed straight for the mouth of the river.

- What was the fate of the *Reindeer*? (Ideas: *It sank to the bottom of the ocean; it sank in the storm.*) (Sum)
- The story says that Joe "felt sorrow for the way in which Nelson used his courage." Explain what that statement means. (Idea: *Joe was sorry Nelson used his courage to be a robber.*) (UCCM)
- How else could Nelson have used his courage? (Ideas: *He could have worked for the police; he could have served in the navy; he could have worked for a shipping line.*) (MJ)
- Explain how Nelson tried to save Pete and the boys. (Idea: *He turned the* Reindeer *around and sailed next to the* Dazzler, *hoping that Pete and the boys would jump onto the* Reindeer.) (R)
- Why were Joe and Frisco Kid able to bring the *Dazzler* to Santa Cruz? (Ideas: *The storm died down; they went with the current; they made a temporary sail from oars and blankets.*) (C/E)

EXERCISE 7
Paired Practice (Optional)

1. Now you'll read in pairs.
- Whoever read second the last time will read first today.
- Remember to start at the diamond and switch at the star.
2. (Observe students and answer questions as needed.)

AFTER READING

EXERCISE 8
Independent Work

1. Do all the items in your workbook and textbook for this lesson.
2. (The independent work in this lesson includes the following activities.)
- Story details
- Vocabulary
- Contradictions
- Missing words
- Poem review
- Referents
- Similes
- Comprehension
- Writing

EXERCISE 9
Workcheck

1. (Using the Answer Key, read the questions and answers for the workbook.)
2. (Have students read their answers for the textbook activities.)
3. (Have two or three students read their writing assignments aloud. Comment on each assignment.)
4. (Have students correct and turn in their work.)

SPELLING

(Present Spelling lesson 72 after completing Reading lesson 72. See *Spelling Presentation Book*.)

BEFORE READING

(Have students find lesson 73, part A, in their textbooks.)

EXERCISE 1
Vocabulary Definitions

1. We're going to read these definitions.
2. (For each word, call on a student to read the definition and the item. Then ask the student to complete the item.)

1. **show promise**—When people *show promise,* they show they have the talent to learn something.
   - What's another way of saying *She was a musician who showed talent to learn?*

   - What's the answer? (Response: *She was a musician who showed promise.*)

2. **reception**—One meaning of *reception* is "greeting."
   - What's another way of saying *He didn't know what kind of greeting he would receive?*

   - What's the answer? (Response: *He didn't know what kind of reception he would receive.*)

EXERCISE 2
Vocabulary Review

1. Everybody, find part B. ✔
   - We're going to review these words.
2. (Call on a student to read the words in the box.)

hurtles	poised
suppress	forge
vengeance	loot
gale	hoist

3. (For each item, have a student read the item and say the answer.)

1. A strong wind is a ▮▮▮▮.
   - What's the answer? (Response: *Gale.*)
2. When something moves quickly and forcefully, it ▮▮▮▮.
   - What's the answer? (Response: *Hurtles.*)
3. When you move forward powerfully, you ▮▮▮▮ ahead.
   - What's the answer? (Response: *Forge.*)
4. Another word for revenge is ▮▮▮▮.
   - What's the answer? (Response: *Vengeance.*)
5. When something is balanced, it is ▮▮▮▮.
   - What's the answer? (Response: *Poised.*)

READING

EXERCISE 3
Focus Question

1. Everybody, find part C. ✔
2. What's the focus question for today's lesson? (Response: *What did Joe learn from his adventures?*)

EXERCISE 4
Reading Aloud (Optional)

1. We're going to read aloud to the diamond.
   - (Call on individual students to read several sentences each.)

Chapter 12
Home at Last
Focus Question: What did Joe learn from his adventures?

"How's that?" said Frisco Kid as he finished tying up the *Dazzler* to a tiny wharf in the lake near Santa Cruz.

Frisco Kid's face suddenly broke into a broad smile. "You're in charge now," he said. "So, what'll we do next, captain?"

Joe looked at him in surprise. "Why . . . I . . . what's the matter?"

"Well, aren't you the captain now? Haven't we reached land? I'm the crew from now on, you know. What are your orders?"

Joe caught the spirit. "All hands for breakfast—in a restaurant."

Joe went into the cabin, got some money out of his bundle, and locked the cabin door. Then the two boys went in search of restaurants. They soon found one, and they planned their next move over bacon and eggs.

After eating, Joe and Frisco Kid went to the train station. Joe found out when the next train left for San Francisco and glanced at the clock.

"I just have time to catch it," he said to Frisco Kid. "Here's the key to the cabin door. Keep it locked, and don't let anybody come aboard. Here's some money. Eat at the restaurants. Dry your blankets and sleep on board. I'll be back tomorrow. And don't let anybody into that cabin. Goodbye."

Then Joe ran down the steps to the train. The conductor looked at Joe with surprise. It was not usual for passengers to wear seaboots. But Joe did not mind. He did not even notice the conductor's amazed look. Joe had bought a newspaper and was reading it carefully. Before long, his eyes caught an interesting story.

**Pirate Ships Vanish
Without a Trace**

Two pirate sloops, one of which carried a stolen safe, have vanished off the coast of California. A tugboat hired by Díaz and Tate, owners of the safe, has failed to turn up any clues.

On Wednesday morning, the lighthouse keeper at the Farallon Islands saw the two sloops heading south into a treacherous gale. Authorities believe the ships sank in the storm.

The safe is rumored to contain gold and several important papers. The Díaz and Tate Company is still offering a $5,000 reward for its return.

Joe felt great relief when he read that story. No one suspected that the *Dazzler* was docked near Santa Cruz. ♦

Silent Reading

1. Read the rest of the lesson to yourselves and be ready to answer some questions.

When Joe reached the train station in San Francisco, he hailed a cab and dashed away. He was in a hurry.

The secretary, Mr. Willis, scowled at Joe when he pushed open the office door and asked to see Mr. Díaz.

"Don't you know me, Mr. Willis?" Joe asked.

Mr. Willis looked a second time. "Why, it's Joe Díaz! Of all things under the sun, where did you come from? Go right in. Your father's in there."

Mr. Díaz looked up and said, "Hello! Where have you been?"

"To sea," Joe answered. He wasn't sure what kind of a reception he would get, and he fingered his coat nervously.

"Short trip, eh? How did you do?"

"Not bad." Joe had caught the twinkle in his father's eye and knew that it was all right. "Not so bad . . . er . . . that is, considering."

"Considering what?"

"Well, it might have been worse, and, well . . . I don't know that it could have been better."

Joe could hardly keep from crying. His father had received him so kindly and naturally, as if nothing had occurred. It was as if Joe had just returned from a vacation or a business trip.

"Now go ahead, Joe. Tell me all about it," Mr. Díaz said.

Then Joe sat down and told what had happened—all that had happened—from the previous Monday night to that moment. He related each little incident and every detail. He emphasized his conversations with Frisco Kid and his plans for him. His face flushed as he was carried away with the excitement of the story. Mr. Díaz remained silent.

"So you see," Joe said at last, "it couldn't possibly have turned out any better." ★

But the next instant, Joe was sobbing as though his heart would break. He had never understood his father before, and he knew now the pain he must have caused him, to say nothing of his mother and his sister. The four days he had spent at sea had given him a clearer view of the world. He had always been able to put his thoughts into speech, so he spoke of the lessons he had learned. And Mr. Díaz listened and seemed to understand.

"But what about Frisco Kid, Father?" Joe asked as he wiped his eyes.

"There's a great deal of promise in the boy from what you say of him," Mr. Díaz said. "I think he'll be happy with his money."

"What money?" Joe asked.

"Frisco Kid is entitled to half of five thousand dollars. The other half belongs to you. It was you two who rescued the safe, and if you had only waited a little longer, Mr. Tate and I might have increased the reward."

"But that isn't exactly what Frisco Kid wants," Joe said. "He wants friends and a chance for an education—not just twenty-five hundred dollars."

"Don't you think it would be better that he choose for himself?"

"No. We've already arranged it."

"Arranged it?"

"Yes, sir. He's captain on sea, and I'm captain on land. So he's under my charge now."

"Good. Then I'll make an offer. I'll hold his twenty-five hundred dollars for him and give him money as he needs it. Then he can move in with us and have the same opportunities for an education that you have. It all depends on him. What do you say to that?"

Father and son shook hands.

"What are you going to do now, Joe?"

"I'm going to send a telegram to Frisco Kid and hurry home."

"Then wait a minute while I call up Mr. Tate with the good news, and I'll go with you."

- What did Joe learn from his adventures? (Ideas: *Just because somebody is a pirate doesn't mean he or she is a bad person; living on the sea is dangerous; doing the right thing can be dangerous but is worth it; his family is the most important thing.*) Ⓓ︎ⒸⒺ

- How did Joe's feelings about his family change during the story? Why? (Ideas: *He realized how important they were to him because he missed them; he realized how important they were because Frisco Kid didn't have a family.*) Ⓒ/Ⓒ
- Why do you think Mr. Díaz wasn't mad at Joe? (Ideas: *He was happy to see Joe safe; he realized that Joe needed to find out about the world.*) Ⓜ︎Ⓙ
- Explain what will happen to Frisco Kid. (Ideas: *He'll move in with Joe and go to school; Mr. Díaz will hold on to Frisco Kid's reward money and give it to him as needed.*) Ⓡ
- Do you think Joe will run away again? Explain your answer. (Ideas: *No, because he's learned that family is more important than adventure; no, because he's had enough adventure to last him a lifetime; yes, because he'll get tired of going to school.*) Ⓜ︎Ⓙ

EXERCISE 6

Paired Practice (Optional)

1. Now you'll read in pairs.
- Whoever read second the last time will read first today.
- Remember to start at the diamond and switch at the star.
2. (Observe students and answer questions as needed.)

AFTER READING

EXERCISE 7

Independent Work

1. Do all the items in your workbook and textbook for this lesson.
2. (The independent work in this lesson includes the following activities.)
- Story details
- Vocabulary
- Maps
- Missing words
- Referents
- Comprehension
- Writing

EXERCISE 8

Workcheck

1. (Using the Answer Key, read the questions and answers for the workbook.)
2. (Have students read their answers for the textbook activities.)
3. (Have two or three students read their writing assignments aloud. Comment on each assignment.)
4. (Have students correct and turn in their work.)

SPELLING

(Present Spelling lesson 73 after completing Reading lesson 73. See *Spelling Presentation Book.*)

BEFORE READING

(Have students find lesson 74, part A, in their textbooks.)

Hard Words

1. Look at column 1.
- These are hard words from your textbook stories.

1. despise	**4. defiance**
2. pallor	**5. writhe**
3. spheroid	**6. melancholy**

2. Word 1 is **despise.** Everybody, what word? (Signal.) *Despise.*
- (Repeat this procedure for every word in the column.)
3. Let's read the words again.
4. Word 1. Everybody, what word? (Signal.) *Despise.*
- (Repeat this procedure for every word in the column.)
5. (Repeat the column until firm.)

Word Practice

1. Look at column 2.
- We're going to practice these words.

1. multitude	**3. patron**
2. recoil	

2. Word 1. Everybody, what word? (Signal.) *Multitude.*
- (Repeat this procedure for every word in the column.)
3. (Repeat the column until firm.)

Vocabulary Definitions

1. Everybody, find part B. ✔
- We're going to read these definitions.
2. (For each word, call on a student to read the definition and the item. Then ask the student to complete the item.)

1. **despise**—When you *despise* something, you really hate it.
- What's another way of saying *She really hated snakes*?
- What's the answer? (Response: *She despised snakes.*)

2. **unheeded**—When something is *unheeded,* nobody pays attention to it. A warning that nobody pays attention to is an unheeded warning.
- What's another way of saying *advice that nobody pays attention to*?
- What's the answer? (Response: *Unheeded advice.*)

Combined Sentences

1. Everybody, turn to part E at the end of today's story. ✔
- (Call on individual students to read several sentences each.)
- (At the end of each section, present the questions for that section.)

Write the answers for items 1 and 2.

Some sentences give information about the meaning of a new word. Here's a sentence that contains a new word in **bold type:** *The **ibex** lives in the mountains.*

Here's a sentence that tells the meaning of the new word: *The ibex is a wild goat.*

To combine the sentences, we start with the first sentence and leave a space after the new word: *The ibex ▬▬▬▬ lives in the mountains.*

Then we put in the meaning of the new word. We put a comma at the beginning of the meaning and another comma at the end of the meaning. We also take out the word *is.* Here's the combined sentence: *The ibex, a wild goat, lives in the mountains.*

- Which new word is presented in the sentence?

- What's the answer? (Response: *Ibex.*)

- What is an ibex?

- What's the answer? (Response: *A wild goat.*)

- What else does the sentence say about the ibex?

- What's the answer? (Idea: *It lives in the mountains.*)

1. Write the combined sentence.

- What's the combined sentence? (Response: *The ibex, a wild goat, lives in the mountains.*)

  Here are two more sentences. The first presents a new word, and the second tells what that word means. *The **torque** was worn many years ago. The torque is a metal necklace.*
- Which new word is presented in the first sentence?

- What's the answer? (Response: *Torque.*)

- What does that word mean?

- What's the answer? (Response: *A metal necklace.*)

- What else does the first sentence tell about the new word?

- What's the answer? (Idea: *It was worn many years ago.*)

2. Write the combined sentence. Remember to put commas at the beginning and end of the meaning.

- What's the combined sentence? (Response: *The torque, a metal necklace, was worn many years ago.*)
- You'll write the answers later.

READING

EXERCISE 5

Story Background

1. Everybody, turn back to part C. ✔
- We're going to read this passage aloud.

2. (Call on individual students to read several sentences each.)

A Game in Mudville

In today's lesson, you will begin reading a long poem about a baseball game. The poem is called "Casey at the Bat," and it was written by Ernest Lawrence Thayer.

At the beginning of the poem, the home team, Mudville, is losing the game by a score of four to two, with only one inning left to play. The first two batters for the home team, Cooney and Barrows, are thrown out at first base. But the next two batters, Flynn and Blake, both get on base.

The last batter, Casey, has a chance to win the game if he can hit a home run. If he does, the final score will be five to four in favor of the Mudville team.

- What is the title of the poem? (Response: *"Casey at the Bat."*) (NE)
- What is the score of the game when the poem starts? (Response: *Four to two.*) (ND)
- Which team is winning, the Mudville team or the visiting team? (Response: *The visiting team.*) (ND)
- What happens to the first two Mudville batters? (Idea: *They get thrown out at first base.*) (Seq)
- What happens to the next two Mudville batters? (Idea: *They get on base.*) (Seq)
- How can Casey win the game? (Idea: *By hitting a home run.*) (C/E)

EXERCISE 6

Poem Interpretation

1. Everybody, find part D. ✔
- We're going to read the poem aloud.
2. (Call on a student to read the first stanza.)

Casey at the Bat
by Ernest Lawrence Thayer
Part 1

The outlook wasn't brilliant for the Mudville
   nine that day;
The score was four to two, with just an
   inning left to play.
And then when Cooney died at first, and
   Barrows did the same,
A sickly silence fell upon the patrons of the
   game.

- What is the "Mudville nine"? (Idea: *The Mudville baseball team.*) ⓓⓘ
- Why wasn't the outlook brilliant for the Mudville nine? (Ideas: *They were losing; there was just an inning left to play.*) ⓓⓘ
- What does "Cooney died at first" mean? (Idea: *Cooney made an out at first base.*) ⓓⓘ
- Who else made an out? (Response: *Barrows.*) ⓝⒹ
- Who are the "patrons of the game"? (Ideas: *The spectators; the fans.*) ⓓⓘ
- Why did a "sickly silence" fall upon the spectators? (Idea: *They thought the Mudville team would lose.*) ⓓⓘ

3. (Call on a student to read the second stanza.)

A straggling few got up to go in deep
  despair. The rest
Clung to that hope which springs eternal in
  the human breast.
They thought, "If only Casey could but get
  a whack at that,
We'd give even chances now, with Casey
  at the bat."

- What does "A straggling few go up to go in deep despair" mean? (Idea: *A few of the spectators left because they had lost hope.*) ⓤⒸⒸⓂ
- What did the rest of the spectators cling to? (Idea: *The hope that Casey could win the game.*) ⓓⓘ
- What did the spectators hope Casey could whack? (Idea: *The ball.*) ⓓⓘ
- What does "We'd give even chances" mean? (Idea: *Our chance of winning is the same as our chance of losing.*) ⓤⒸⒸⓂ

4. (Call on a student to read the third stanza.)

But Flynn preceded Casey, as did also
  Jimmy Blake,
And the former was a lulu, and the latter
  was a fake.
So on that stricken multitude grim
  melancholy sat;
For there seemed but little chance of
  Casey's getting to the bat.

- Which player was a lulu? (Response: *Flynn.*) ⒹⒸ
- Which player was a fake? (Response: *Jimmy Blake.*) ⒹⒸ
- Who is the "stricken multitude"? (Ideas: *The spectators; the fans.*) ⓓⓘ

- Why did the spectators think Casey had little chance of batting? (Idea: *Because Flynn and Blake preceded him.*) ⓜⒿ

5. In the next stanza, the word *despised* has an accent mark on the last syllable. That means you should say the word like this: **dee SPY zed.**

- (Call on a student to read the fourth stanza.)

But Flynn let drive a single, to the
  wonderment of all.
And Blake, the much despisèd, tore the
  cover off the ball.
And when the dust had lifted, and they
  saw what had occurred,
There was Jimmy safe at second and
  Flynn a-hugging third.

- Why do you think the poet added a syllable by accenting the word *despised*? (Ideas: *It keeps the rhythm steady; it sounds better.*) ⒶⓅ
- What does "Blake tore the cover off the ball" mean? (Idea: *Blake hit the ball hard.*) ⓤⒸⒸⓂ
- Where did the runners end up after Blake's hit? (Idea: *On second and third base.*) ⓝⒹ
- Who's batting next? (Response: *Casey.*) ⓓⓘ
- How could Casey win the game? (Idea: *By hitting a home run.*) ⒶⓅⓀ

6. (Call on a student to read the fifth stanza.)

Then from five thousand throats and more
  there rose a lusty yell;
It rumbled through the valley, it rattled in
  the dell;
It knocked upon the mountain and recoiled
  upon the flat;
For Casey, mighty Casey, was advancing
  to the bat.

- Why did the crowd let out a yell? (Idea: *Because Casey was coming to bat.*) ⒹⒸⒺ
- In what places could the yell be heard? (Idea: *In the valley, the dell, the mountain, and the flat.*) ⓝⒹ
- What kind of place could "the flat" be? (Ideas: *A plain; a field; a meadow.*) ⓓⓘ

7. (Call on a student to read the sixth stanza.)

There was ease in Casey's manner as he
   stepped into his place;
There was pride in Casey's bearing and a
   smile on Casey's face;
And when, responding to the cheers, he
   lightly doffed his hat,
No stranger in the crowd could doubt 'twas
   Casey at the bat.

- What does "he lightly doffed his hat"
  mean? (Idea: *He lifted his hat off his
  head.*) Ⓓ
- How confident does Casey seem to be?
  Explain your answer. (Idea: *Very
  confident, because he's relaxed and
  smiling.*) Ⓜ

EXERCISE 7
Poem Reading

1. Now we'll read the poem again without
   stopping.
- When you read, try to keep a steady
  rhythm. Also pause briefly at the end of
  each line.
- (Call on individual students to read one
  stanza each.)

Casey at the Bat
by Ernest Lawrence Thayer
Part 1

The outlook wasn't brilliant for the Mudville
   nine that day;
The score was four to two, with just an
   inning left to play.
And then when Cooney died at first, and
   Barrows did the same,
A sickly silence fell upon the patrons of the
   game.

A straggling few got up to go in deep
   despair. The rest
Clung to that hope which springs eternal in
   the human breast.
They thought, "If only Casey could but get
   a whack at that,
We'd give even chances now, with Casey
   at the bat."

But Flynn preceded Casey, as did also
   Jimmy Blake,
And the former was a lulu, and the latter
   was a fake.
So on that stricken multitude grim
   melancholy sat;
For there seemed but little chance of
   Casey's getting to the bat.

But Flynn let drive a single, to the
   wonderment of all.
And Blake, the much despisèd, tore the
   cover off the ball.
And when the dust had lifted, and they
   saw what had occurred,
There was Jimmy safe at second and
   Flynn a-hugging third.

Then from five thousand throats and more
   there rose a lusty yell;
It rumbled through the valley, it rattled in
   the dell;
It knocked upon the mountain and recoiled
   upon the flat;
For Casey, mighty Casey, was advancing
   to the bat.

There was ease in Casey's manner as he
   stepped into his place;
There was pride in Casey's bearing and a
   smile on Casey's face;
And when, responding to the cheers, he
   lightly doffed his hat,
No stranger in the crowd could doubt 'twas
   Casey at the bat.

EXERCISE 8
Paired Practice (Optional)

1. Now you'll read in pairs.
- Whoever read second the last time will
  read first today.
- The first person should read the first
  three stanzas, and the second person
  should read the rest.
2. (Observe students and answer questions
   as needed.)

AFTER READING

Independent Work

1. Do all the items in your workbook and textbook for this lesson.
2. (The independent work in this lesson includes the following activities.)
- Character traits
- Vocabulary
- Referents
- Maps
- Relevant information
- Combined sentences
- Comprehension
- Writing

EXERCISE 10

Workcheck

1. (Using the Answer Key, read the questions and answers for the workbook.)
2. (Have students read their answers for the textbook activities.)
3. (Have two or three students read their writing assignments aloud. Comment on each assignment.)
4. (Have students correct and turn in their work.)

SPELLING

(Present Spelling lesson 74 after completing Reading lesson 74. See *Spelling Presentation Book.*)

BEFORE READING

(Have students find lesson 75, part A, in their textbooks.)

EXERCISE 1

Hard Words

1. Look at column 1.
- These are hard words from your textbook stories.

1. haughty	**4. grandeur**
2. Christian	**5. tumult**
3. visage	

2. Word 1 is **haughty.** Everybody, what word? (Signal.) *Haughty.*
- (Repeat this procedure for every word in the column.)
3. Let's read the words again.
4. Word 1. Everybody, what word? (Signal.) *Haughty.*
- (Repeat this procedure for every word in the column.)
5. (Repeat the column until firm.)

EXERCISE 2

Word Practice

1. Look at column 2.
- We're going to practice these words.

1. defy	**4. fraud**
2. defiance	**5. spheroid**
3. pallor	

2. Word 1. Everybody, what word? (Signal.) *Defy.*
- (Repeat this procedure for every word in the column.)
3. (Repeat the column until firm.)

EXERCISE 3

Vocabulary Definitions

1. Everybody, find part B. ✔
- We're going to read these definitions.

2. (For each word, call on a student to read the definition and the item. Then ask the student to complete the item.)

1. **scornful**—When something is *scornful,* it is full of disrespect and dislike. An expression full of disrespect is a scornful expression.
- What's another way of saying *comments full of dislike?*

- What's the answer? (Response: *Scornful comments.*)

2. **writhe**—When something *writhes,* it twists and turns.
- What's another way of saying *She twisted and turned around the dance floor?*

- What's the answer? (Response: *She writhed around the dance floor.*)

EXERCISE 4

Vocabulary Review

1. Everybody, find part C. ✔
- We're going to review these words.
2. (Call on a student to read the words in the box.)

despise	poised
reception	summit
vengeance	unheeded
muffled	

3. (For each item, have a student read the item and say the answer.)

1. When you really hate something, you ▮▮▮▮ that thing.

- What's the answer? (Response: *Despise.*)

2. Another word for *revenge* is ▮▮▮▮.

- What's the answer? (Response: *Vengeance.*)

3. A party that takes place after an important event is a ▮▮▮▮.

- What's the answer? (Response: *Reception.*)

4. When nobody pays attention to something, that thing is ▮▮▮▮.

- What's the answer? (Response: *Unheeded.*)

EXERCISE 5

Combined Sentences

1. Everybody, turn to part E at the end of today's story. ✔
- (Call on individual students to read several sentences each.)
- (At the end of each section, present the questions for that section.)

Write the answers for items 1–8.
   Below are two sentences. One introduces a new word; the other tells what the word means.
- *The toucan has bright feathers.*
- *The toucan is a tropical bird.*
1. Combine the sentences so the meaning comes right after the new word. Remember to put commas before and after the meaning. Also remember to take out the word *is*.

- What's the combined sentence? (Response: *The toucan, a tropical bird, has bright feathers.*)

2. What is the new word in the combined sentence?

- What's the answer? (Response: *Toucan.*)

3. What does the new word mean?

- What's the answer? (Response: *A tropical bird.*)

4. What else does the combined sentence say about the new word?

- What's the answer? (Idea: *It has bright feathers.*)
- You'll write the answers later.

READING

EXERCISE 6

Poem Rereading

1. Everybody, turn to part D of lesson 74. ✔
2. Let's reread part 1 of "Casey at the Bat" aloud.

- (Call on individual students to read one stanza each.)

Casey at the Bat
by Ernest Lawrence Thayer
Part 1

The outlook wasn't brilliant for the Mudville
    nine that day;
The score was four to two, with just an
    inning left to play.
And then when Cooney died at first, and
    Barrows did the same,
A sickly silence fell upon the patrons of the
    game.

A straggling few got up to go in deep
    despair. The rest
Clung to that hope which springs eternal in
    the human breast.
They thought, "If only Casey could but get
    a whack at that,
We'd give even chances now, with Casey
    at the bat."

But Flynn preceded Casey, as did also
    Jimmy Blake,
And the former was a lulu, and the latter
    was a fake.
So on that stricken multitude grim
    melancholy sat;
For there seemed but little chance of
    Casey's getting to the bat.

But Flynn let drive a single, to the
    wonderment of all.
And Blake, the much despisèd, tore the
    cover off the ball.
And when the dust had lifted, and they
    saw what had occurred,
There was Jimmy safe at second and
    Flynn a-hugging third.

Then from five thousand throats and more
 there rose a lusty yell;
It rumbled through the valley, it rattled in
 the dell;
It knocked upon the mountain and recoiled
 upon the flat;
For Casey, mighty Casey, was advancing
 to the bat.

There was ease in Casey's manner as he
 stepped into his place;
There was pride in Casey's bearing and a
 smile on Casey's face;
And when, responding to the cheers, he
 lightly doffed his hat,
No stranger in the crowd could doubt 'twas
 Casey at the bat.

- What will happen if Casey hits a home
  run? (Idea: *The Mudville team will win
  the game.*) (APK)
- Does Casey think he's going to hit a
  home run? Explain your answer. (Ideas:
  *Yes, because he's acting so confident;
  no, because he doesn't know for sure.*) (MJ)

EXERCISE 7
Poem Interpretation

1. Everybody, turn to part D of lesson 75. ✔
- We're going to read the rest of the poem
  aloud.
2. (Call on a student to read the first
   stanza.)

Casey at the Bat
Part 2

Ten thousand eyes were on him as he
 rubbed his hands with dirt;
Five thousand tongues applauded when
 he wiped them on his shirt;
Then while the writhing pitcher ground the
 ball into his hip,
Defiance gleamed in Casey's eye, a sneer
 curled Casey's lip.

- What does "Five thousand tongues
  applauded" mean? (Idea: *Five thousand
  voices shouted.*) (DI)
- Is "Five thousand tongues applauded" a
  metaphor or a simile? (Response: *A
  metaphor.*) (MJ)
- Explain the metaphor. (Idea: *The
  tongues were like something that
  applauds.*) (R)

- What kind of expression did Casey have
  in the last line? (Idea: *Mean and
  determined.*) (Sum)
3. (Call on a student to read the second
   stanza.)

And now the leather-covered sphere came
 hurtling through the air,
And Casey stood a-watching it in haughty
 grandeur there.
Close by the sturdy batsman the ball
 unheeded sped—
"That ain't my style," said Casey. "Strike
 one!" the umpire said.

- What is the "leather-covered sphere"?
  (Idea: *The baseball.*) (DI)
- What do you think "in haughty grandeur"
  means? (Idea: *In a proud way.*) (UCCM)
- Who is the "sturdy batsman"?
  (Response: *Casey.*) (DI)
- Why didn't Casey swing at the ball?
  (Idea: *It wasn't his style.*) (C/E)
4. (Call on a student to read the third
   stanza.)

From the benches, black with people,
 there went up a muffled roar,
Like the beating of the storm waves on a
 stern and distant shore.
"Kill him! Kill the umpire!" shouted
 someone in the stand;
And it's likely they'd have killed him had
 not Casey raised his hand.

- What's the simile in this stanza? (Idea:
  *There went up a muffled roar, / Like the
  beating of the storm waves on a stern
  and distant shore.*) (C+C)
- Why did Casey raise his hand? (Ideas:
  *To quiet the crowd; to protect the
  umpire.*) (DI)
5. (Call on a student to read the fourth
   stanza.)

With a smile of Christian charity great
 Casey's visage shone;
He stilled the rising tumult; he bade the
 game go on;
He signaled to the pitcher, and once more
 the spheroid flew;
But Casey still ignored it, and the umpire
 said, "Strike two!"

- What is "Christian charity"? (Ideas:
  Kindness; sympathy for others.) (APK)

- What is "Casey's visage"? (Idea: *His face.*) ⓓⓘ
- What is the "rising tumult"? (Idea: *The increasing noise of the crowd.*) ⓓⓘ
- What does "he bade the game go on" mean? (Idea: *He asked the umpire to keep the game going.*) ⓓⓘ
- Why do you think Casey ignored the second pitch? (Ideas: *He didn't like it; he knew he had another pitch left.*) ⓓⒸⒺ

6. (Call on a student to read the fifth stanza.)

> "Fraud!" cried the maddened thousands, and echo answered "Fraud!"
> But one scornful look from Casey and the audience was awed.
> They saw his face grow stern and cold, they saw his muscles strain,
> And they knew that Casey wouldn't let that ball go by again.

- What did the crowd think of the umpire's call? (Ideas: *They thought it was a fraud; they disliked it.*) ⓓⒸⒺ
- How could the crowd tell Casey was going to swing at the next pitch? (Ideas: *His face grew stern and cold; his muscles strained; it was his last chance.*) ⒸⒺ

7. (Call on a student to read the sixth stanza.)

> The sneer is gone from Casey's lip, his teeth are clenched in hate;
> He pounds with cruel violence his bat upon the plate.
> And now the pitcher holds the ball, and now he lets it go,
> And now the air is shattered by the force of Casey's blow.

- Is "the air is shattered" a simile or a metaphor? (Response: *A metaphor.*) ⓂⒿ
- What does the metaphor compare the air to? (Idea: *Something that shatters; glass.*) ⒸⒸ
- Do you think Casey hit the ball? Explain your answer. (Idea: *Probably not, because only the air was shattered, not the ball.*) ⓂⒿ

8. (Call on a student to read the last stanza.)

> Oh, somewhere in this favored land the sun is shining bright;
> The band is playing somewhere, and somewhere hearts are light,
> And somewhere men are laughing, and somewhere children shout;
> But there is no joy in Mudville—mighty Casey has struck out.

- Why is there no joy in Mudville? (Ideas: *Casey has struck out; the Mudville team has lost the baseball game.*) ⓓⒸⒺ
- How is this stanza different from the other stanzas? (Ideas: *It tells about places other than Mudville; it changes the setting.*) ⒸⒸ
- Why is Mudville a good name for Casey's town? (Ideas: *It's an unhappy place; it's stuck in the mud.*) ⓂⒿ

EXERCISE 8
Poem Memorization

1. Everybody, close your textbook.
- Let's see if we can memorize the last stanza of "Casey at the Bat."
- I'll read a line. Then we'll say it together.
2. First line: **Oh, somewhere in this favored land the sun is shining bright.**
- Say the line with me. (The students say the line with you.)
- All by yourselves. (The students say the line by themselves.)
3. Next line. **The band is playing somewhere, and somewhere hearts are light.**
- Say the line with me. (The students say the line with you.)
- Say both lines from the beginning. (The students say both lines by themselves.)
4. Next line. **And somewhere men are laughing, and somewhere children shout.**
- Say the line with me. (The students say the line with you.)
- All by yourselves. (The students say the line by themselves.)
- Say all three lines from the beginning. (The students say the first three lines by themselves.)

5. Last line. **But there is no joy in Mudville—mighty Casey has struck out.**
   - Say the line with me. (The students say the line with you.)
   - All by yourselves. (The students say the line by themselves.)
   - Say the whole stanza from the beginning. (The students say the whole stanza by themselves.)
6. Who wants to say the stanza?
   - (Call on individual students to say the stanza.)

EXERCISE 9
Paired Practice (Optional)

1. Now you'll read in pairs.
   - One person will read the first three stanzas.
   - Then the other person will read the rest.
2. (Observe students and answer questions as needed.)

AFTER READING

EXERCISE 10
Independent Work

1. Do all the items in your workbook and textbook for this lesson.
2. (The independent work in this lesson includes the following activities.)
   - Vocabulary
   - Referents
   - Sequencing
   - Poem review
   - Spoonerisms
   - Combined sentences
   - Comprehension
   - Writing

EXERCISE 11
Workcheck

1. (Using the Answer Key, read the questions and answers for the workbook.)
2. (Have students read their answers for the textbook activities.)
3. (Have two or three students read their writing assignments aloud. Comment on each assignment.)
4. (Have students correct and turn in their work.)

ACTIVITIES ACROSS THE CURRICULUM

(Students should complete the appropriate project in *Activities across the Curriculum* after completing lesson 75. See *Activities across the Curriculum* book for details.)

SPELLING

(Present Spelling lesson 75 after completing Reading lesson 75. See *Spelling Presentation Book*.)

Lessons 76–80 • Planning Page   *Looking Ahead*

	Lesson 76	**Lesson 77**	**Lesson 78**	**Lesson 79**	**Lesson 80**
BEFORE READING	Hard words Word practice Vocabulary definitions Combined sentences	Hard words Word practice Vocabulary definitions Vocabulary review		Combined sentences	Outlining
NEW VOCABULARY	plantation ruts	fit licking snicker	(none)	(none)	(none)
READING	"Harriet Tubman" (Part 1)	"Harriet Tubman" (Part 2)	"Harriet Tubman" (Part 3)	"Harriet Tubman" (Part 4)	"Harriet Tubman" (Part 5)
INDEPENDENT WORK	Story details Vocabulary Maps Combined sentences Inference Comprehension Writing	Story details Metaphors Related facts Combined sentences Comprehension Writing	Story details Combined sentences Similes Maps Comprehension Writing	Story details Vocabulary Maps Settings Combined sentences Conversations Comprehension Writing	Story details Vocabulary Maps Combined sentences Outlining Comprehension Writing
SUPPLEMENTS	*Spelling*	*Spelling*	*Spelling*	*Spelling*	Mastery Test *Spelling* *Activities across the Curriculum*

Comprehension Questions Abbreviations Guide

Access Prior Knowledge = (APK)   **Author's Point of View =** (APoV)   **Author's Purpose =** (AP)   **Cause/Effect =** (C/E)   **Charts/Graphs/Diagrams/Visual Aids =** (VA)

Classify and Categorize = (C+C)   **Compare/Contrast =** (C/C)   **Determine Character Emotions, Motivation =** (DCE)   **Drawing Conclusions =** (DC)   **Drawing Inferences =** (DI)

Fact and Opinion = (F/O)   **Hypothesizing =** (H)   **Main Idea =** (MI)   **Making Connections =** (MC)   **Making Deductions =** (MD)   **Making Judgements =** (MJ)

Narrative Elements = (NE)   **Noting Details =** (ND)   **Predict =** (P)   **Reality/Fantasy =** (R/F)   **Recall Facts/Rules =** (RF/R)   **Retell =** (R)   **Sequence =** (Seq)

Steps in a Process = (SP)   **Story Structure =** (SS)   **Summarize =** (Sum)   **Understanding Dialogue =** (UD)   **Using Context to Confirm Meaning(s) =** (UCCM)   **Visualize =** (V)

BEFORE READING

(Have students find lesson 76, part A, in their textbooks.)

Hard Words

1. Look at column 1.
- These are hard words from your textbook stories.

1. quatrain	4. biography
2. noria	5. Confederacy
3. omnivore	6. territory

2. Word 1 is **quatrain.** Everybody, what word? (Signal.) *Quatrain.*
- (Repeat this procedure for every word in the column.)
3. Let's read the words again.
4. Word 1. Everybody, what word? (Signal.) *Quatrain.*
- (Repeat this procedure for every word in the column.)
5. (Repeat the column until firm.)

Word Practice

1. Look at column 2.
- We're going to practice these words.

1. Maryland	4. tobacco
2. Pennsylvania	5. runaway
3. Kentucky	

2. Word 1. Everybody, what word? (Signal.) *Maryland.*
- (Repeat this procedure for every word in the column.)
3. (Repeat the column until firm.)

Vocabulary Definitions

1. Everybody, find part B. ✔
- We're going to read these definitions.

2. (For each word, call on a student to read the definition and the item. Then ask the student to complete the item.)

1. **plantation**—A *plantation* is a large farm. Plantations in some parts of the United States once had slaves.
- What's another way of saying *The large farm grew cotton and tobacco?*

- What's the answer? (Response: *The plantation grew cotton and tobacco.*)

2. **ruts**—*Ruts* are grooves or tracks in a road, particularly a dirt road. When vehicles drive over a road many times, their wheels make *ruts* in the road.
- What are ruts?

- What's the answer? (Idea: *Grooves or tracks in a road.*)

Combined Sentences

1. Everybody, turn to part E at the end of today's story. ✔
- (Call on individual students to read several sentences each.)
- (At the end of each section, present the questions for that section.)

Write the answers for items 1–6.
The following combined sentence presents a new word and tells what the word means: *This carved box was made in a hong, a Chinese factory.*
1. What is the new word?

- What's the answer? (Response: *Hong.*)

2. What does the new word mean?

- What's the answer? (Response: *A Chinese factory.*)

3. What else does the sentence say about the new word?

- What's the answer? (Idea: *That a carved box was made there.*)
- You'll write the answers later.

READING

Poem Memorization

1. Everybody, close your textbook.
- Who wants to recite the last stanza of "Casey at the Bat" from memory?
2. (Call on individual students to recite the last stanza. If students don't remember the stanza, repeat the "Poem Memorization" exercise in lesson 75.)

> Oh, somewhere in this favored land the
>   sun is shining bright;
> The band is playing somewhere, and
>   somewhere hearts are light,
> And somewhere men are laughing, and
>   somewhere children shout;
> But there is no joy in Mudville—mighty
>   Casey has struck out.

Story Background

1. Everybody, find lesson 76, part C, in your textbook. ✔
- We're going to read this passage aloud.
2. (Call on individual students to read several sentences each.)
- (After each section, present the questions for that section.)

The Civil War

In this lesson, you will begin reading a biography of Harriet Tubman, a famous American woman who helped more than three hundred slaves escape to freedom before the Civil War. She was born around 1820 and lived until 1913—almost a hundred years.

The map below shows the United States during the Civil War, which began in 1861. One of the main causes of the war was slavery. The blue states belonged to the Union, which was opposed to slavery. The gray states belonged to the Confederacy, which was in favor of slavery. (The other areas were not yet states and were called *territories*.) In 1865, the Union won the war and ended slavery.

- What is slavery? (Idea: *Ownership of one person by another person.*) (APK)
- Why do you think the people in the Confederacy were in favor of slavery? (Ideas: *People in the Confederacy owned slaves; they made money by owning slaves.*) (H)
- Why do you think the people in the Union were opposed to slavery? (Idea: *They thought slavery was wrong.*) (H)
- Everybody, look at the map. (VA)

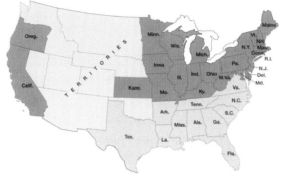

The United States in 1863

- In which part of the United States were the Confederate states located? (Ideas: *In the south; in the southeast.*) (VA)
- In which part were most of the Union states located? (Ideas: *In the north; in the northeast.*) (VA)
- If it's on this map, was our state Union, Confederate, or one of the territories? (Accept correct response.) (MC)
- Alaska and Hawaii aren't on this map because they didn't belong to the United States until long after the Civil War.

Most of the Union states banned slavery long before the Civil War. These "free" states were all in the north. A few slave states in between the north and the south, such as Maryland and Kentucky, joined the Union and banned slavery during the war. Before then, thousands of slaves—including Harriet Tubman—escaped from these "border" states to the free states of the north.

The following biography of Harriet Tubman begins in Maryland in 1855. At that time, Maryland was still a slave state. The biography is narrated by a character named Jim Johnson. Jim is fictional, but the facts he tells about Harriet Tubman are true.

- Why do you think Maryland and Kentucky joined the Union even though they were slave states? (Ideas: *The people in these states thought the Union would win; they were on the Union's southern border; many people in those states were opposed to slavery.*) (MJ)
- Why would it be easier for slaves to escape to freedom from Maryland than from Florida? (Idea: *Maryland is closer to the free states than Florida is.*) (MJ)
- How many years before the Civil War does this biography begin? (Response: *Six years.*) (Seq)
- Which parts of the biography are fictional? (Idea: *The parts about Jim Johnson.*) (SS)
- Which parts of the biography are true? (Idea: *The facts about Harriet Tubman.*) (SS)

EXERCISE 7

Focus Question

1. Everybody, find part D. ✔
2. What's the focus question for today's lesson? (Response: *Why did Jim want to run away?*)

Note: The "Reading Aloud" exercise is recommended for this lesson.

EXERCISE 8

Reading Aloud

1. We're going to read aloud to the diamond.
2. (Call on individual students to read several sentences each.)

Harriet Tubman
by Talbot Bielefeldt
Part 1
Focus Question: Why did Jim want to run away?

My name is Jim Johnson. In the winter of 1855, I was sixteen years old, and I was running for my life. I had been a slave in Maryland, but now I was trying to escape from my master and the plantation. I was leaving the only life I had ever known.

Ever since I was old enough to hold a shovel, I had worked with other slaves in the tobacco fields of my master's plantation. The master owned us and used us to farm his fields. He could sell us or trade us, as if we were horses or cows. When I was very young, my mother and father were sold to plantations far away in Georgia. I cried when the slave traders came to take my parents away. My three older brothers took care of me until they were sold to different plantations.

By the time my brothers were sold, I was old enough to work in the fields. The older I got, the harder my master made me work. When I was sixteen, I was hauling pine logs out of the woods with a horse and wagon. I worked from dawn to darkness. At night, I would go to sleep in the one-room cabin I shared with five other slaves. I was so tired each evening that I would fall asleep before the cook brought around our dinner of cornmeal and bacon. I was so hungry and weak each morning that it took me a long time to harness the horses. When I was slow getting to work, the master hit me with his whip.

It was a hard life, so some slaves ran away. We knew that the states north of Maryland—such as Pennsylvania and New York—did not allow slavery. Slaves who could escape to one of those states would be free. But the trip to freedom was dangerous. A runaway slave had to travel at night and hide during the day.

The masters hired slave catchers to hunt for runaway slaves, and they offered rewards to anyone who helped a slave catcher bring back a runaway. Any runaway who was caught would be whipped. Slaves who ran away more than once would often be sold to plantations far to the south, where they would be farther away from the free northern states. Yet some slaves did escape, and there were stories about runaways who came back to the south to free other slaves. ♦

EXERCISE 9

SILENT READING

1. Read the rest of the lesson to yourselves and be ready to answer some questions.

One cold night, I heard some slaves talking about a woman named Moses.

Old George said, "Moses has led so many runaways out of the South that the masters will pay to have her captured—dead or alive."

"She's eight feet tall," Old George continued in a whisper. "She can carry a grown man under each arm and still run faster than any slave catcher."

"That can't be," I said. "I don't believe there is a Moses."

"Yes, there is," Henry said. He was a new slave on the plantation.

"How do you know?" I asked.

"Moses is an old friend of mine," he said. "Her real name is Harriet Tubman. She will come for me one of these days, and she will take any of you who are brave enough to go."

Moses was real! For the first time in my life, I believed I had a chance to be free. I had been a slave all my life, and I wanted freedom. I had heard stories about how free blacks lived in the north. A free man could own property. He could work for anyone he wanted to, and no one could treat him like an animal.

I wanted to be free, but fear kept me from running away. On the plantation, I had food every day, even if it was never enough. The master gave us clothes to wear and a cabin to sleep in.

How did a free man get food, clothing, and shelter? I did not know, and I was afraid of the unknown world outside the plantation. One thing I did know was that if I ran away and got caught, the master would beat me so hard I might die.

• • •

A few weeks later, I hauled a load of wood out of the forest. The horse I was driving slipped on some ice, stumbled, and broke its leg. The master blamed me for the accident, even though it wasn't my fault. He beat me with a whip until I bled. When he had finished, I could barely crawl through the door of my cabin.

I lay on the floor, hurting all over. I knew I could be beaten for running away. But as long as I was a slave, I could be beaten anyway, for no reason. I might as well try to escape. ★

That night, Henry came into my cabin and whispered, "I got a message from Moses. She's on her way. When you hear a child singing about a chariot coming, you'll know she's here. I'm going with Moses. If you want to come along, meet us in the woods behind the cabins."

I went out to work the next day, even though I could hardly walk. The master would have beaten me again if I had stayed in bed. The day was cold, and a brisk wind cut through the ragged jacket I wore. The ground was frozen and covered with snow. My fingers became numb, and I had trouble tying ropes to the fallen logs. But I continued to work as well as I could.

At noon, a young slave girl brought some food to us. As she walked toward us, she sang the following words:
Good news, chariot's coming!
Good news, chariot's coming!
Good news, chariot's coming,
And I don't want it to leave me behind!
A white man was guarding us while we worked. The man did not pay any attention to the song, but all the slaves knew that the girl was bringing us a secret message. If anyone wanted to run away, now was the time. Moses was here.

A guard counted the slaves every night to make sure all of us were in our cabins. That night, as soon as the guard had finished and gone away, I wrapped my blanket around me for a coat, walked out of the little cabin, and slipped into the woods.

I soon approached three figures in the dark. One was Henry. The second was a pretty woman named Catherine. She was holding Henry's arm. Next to them was a third figure, a small black woman, no more than five feet tall. She looked about thirty years old.

Henry gestured toward the small woman and announced, "Jim, this is Harriet Tubman, the one they call Moses."

I had thought that Moses would be a big, powerful person, but she was so small that I stared at her in amazement.

"You're the last one in the party," Moses said to me. "Now all of you walk where I walk and don't make a sound. Step in the wagon ruts so you don't leave fresh tracks in the snow. Follow me."

- Why did Jim want to run away? (Ideas: *He wanted to be free; he wanted to escape slavery.*) (DCE)
- Jim said, "I wanted to be free, but fear kept me from running away." Explain what he meant. (Ideas: *Even though he wanted to run away, he didn't know how*

*he would survive on his own; even
though he wanted to run away, he was
afraid of being caught and beaten.)* (UCCM)

- Why was running away so dangerous for
  slaves? (Ideas: *They could be whipped;
  they could be sold to plantations farther
  south; they had to travel by night.*) (C/E)
- What incident made Jim change his mind
  about running away? Why? (Idea: *When
  the master beat him, Jim realized he
  would rather be beaten for running away
  than for no reason.*) (DCE)
- How was Harriet Tubman like the words
  of the song? (Ideas: *She was like a
  chariot coming to rescue people; if
  slaves didn't escape with her, they might
  get left behind.*) (C/C)

Paired Practice (Optional)

1. Now you'll read in pairs.
- Whoever read second the last time will
  read first today.
- Remember to start at the diamond and
  switch at the star.
2. (Observe students and answer questions
   as needed.)

AFTER READING

Independent Work

1. Do all the items in your workbook and
   textbook for this lesson.
2. (The independent work in this lesson
   includes the following activities.)
- Story details
- Vocabulary
- Maps
- Combined sentences
- Inference
- Comprehension
- Writing

Workcheck

1. (Using the Answer Key, read the
   questions and answers for the
   workbook.)
2. (Have students read their answers for
   the textbook activities.)
3. (Have two or three students read their
   writing assignments aloud. Comment on
   each assignment.)
4. (Have students correct and turn in their
   work.)

(Present Spelling lesson 76 after completing
Reading lesson 76. See *Spelling
Presentation Book.*)

BEFORE READING

(Have students find lesson 77, part A, in their textbooks.)

EXERCISE 1
Hard Words

1. Look at column 1.
- These are hard words from your textbook stories.

1. ocelot	**3. limpkin**
2. ocarina	

2. Word 1 is **ocelot.** Everybody, what word? (Signal.) *Ocelot.*
- (Repeat this procedure for every word in the column.)
3. Let's read the words again.
4. Word 1. Everybody, what word? (Signal.) *Ocelot.*
- (Repeat this procedure for every word in the column.)
5. (Repeat the column until firm.)

EXERCISE 2
Word Practice

1. Look at column 2.
- We're going to practice these words.

1. rickets	**3. dull**
2. rickety	**4. dully**

2. Word 1. Everybody, what word? (Signal.) *Rickets.*
- (Repeat this procedure for every word in the column.)
3. (Repeat the column until firm.)

EXERCISE 3
Vocabulary Definitions

1. Everybody, find part B. ✔
- We're going to read these definitions.
2. (For each word, call on a student to read the definition and the item. Then ask the student to complete the item.)

1. **fit**—A *fit* is an attack brought on by a disease. Some people who have fits may writhe around or even faint.
- What's a fit?

- What's the answer? (Idea: *An attack brought on by a disease.*)

2. **licking**—A *licking* is a beating. When a person gets a licking, that person is beaten up.
- What's another way of saying *They gave the bully a beating?*

- What's the answer? (Response: *They gave the bully a licking.*)

3. **snicker**—When you *snicker,* you hide your laughter.
- What's another way of saying *The woman hid her laughter at the badly dressed man?*

- What's the answer? (Response: *The woman snickered at the badly dressed man.*)

EXERCISE 4
Vocabulary Review

1. Everybody, find part C. ✔
- We're going to review these words.
2. (Call on a student to read the words in the box.)

rut	**scornful**
writhe	**plantation**

3. (For each item, have a student read the item and say the answer.)

1. A groove in a road is a ▮▮▮▮.

- What's the answer? (Response: *Rut.*)

2. A large farm is a ▮▮▮▮.

- What's the answer? (Response: *Plantation.*)

3. When you twist and turn, you ▆▆▆▆.

- What's the answer? (Response: *Writhe.*)

READING

EXERCISE 5

Focus Question

1. Everybody, find part D. ✔
2. What's the focus question for today's lesson? (Response: *How did Harriet Tubman become a conductor on the Underground Railroad?*)

EXERCISE 6

Reading Aloud (Optional)

1. We're going to read aloud to the diamond.
- (Call on individual students to read several sentences each.)

Harriet Tubman

Part 2

Focus Question: How did Harriet Tubman become a conductor on the Underground Railroad?

Moses led us down a small road and into a thick woods. We walked carefully through the trees. Every stick that cracked sounded like the slave catchers hot on our trail. We were terrified when Moses stepped onto another road and marched straight across it to a farmhouse.

Moses knocked at the farmhouse door. A white woman instantly opened the door and stepped aside to let us in. I wanted to look more closely at her, but I was embarrassed. So I just glanced and quickly followed Henry up a rickety ladder to the attic. Nobody said a word. The last person up the ladder was Harriet. She was carrying a basket of food and a lantern the white woman had given her. When we were all upstairs, Moses smiled and passed out the food. "Welcome to the Underground Railroad," she said.

While we ate, Moses explained the Underground Railroad. There were people in the South who did not approve of slavery. Those people helped runaway slaves reach freedom in the North. They would hide the slaves in their homes during the day. The slaves would go from one building to another at night, only at night. Night after night, they would travel until they reached the free state of Pennsylvania.

It was against the law to help runaway slaves, so the location of each hiding place was a secret. A runaway needed a guide to find the next hiding place each night. These guides were former slaves. The guides were called conductors, and the trail of hiding places was called the Underground Railroad.

Harriet Tubman, the woman called Moses, was our conductor. She looked around at our frightened faces and said, "All of you get some sleep now. And don't worry. We'll be in Pennsylvania next week. I'm a good conductor. I never run my train off the track, and I've never lost a passenger yet." ♦

EXERCISE 7

Silent Reading

1. Read the rest of the lesson to yourselves and be ready to answer some questions.

During the next day, I tried to sleep in the attic, but I couldn't. I kept asking myself a thousand questions. "What are you doing here, hiding in this attic? What's going to happen to you if you get caught? Who are these people who are hiding you? Why are they doing it?" I had no answers to these questions, but that didn't stop me from asking them.

That night, as we traveled to a new hiding place, we suddenly heard sounds that weren't cracking twigs or owls in the woods. They were the sounds of fast horses and lots of them. Harriet quickly darted into the woods next to the road. Nobody had to tell me to follow, even though my heart was pounding so much that I could hardly move.

White men were riding the horses. One of the men shouted, "The runaways may be in that field ahead. Spread out and move fast!"

The masters must have found out that Moses had come and taken some of their slaves. When we could no longer hear the sound of hooves, I stood up and began to plead, "Let me go home, let me see my old cabin again, let me walk back to my master and take my licking, but don't let me be caught by those slave catchers."

Suddenly I was looking down the barrel of Harriet Tubman's pistol. "No one goes back on the Underground Railroad," Moses said as she pointed the pistol straight at my head. "I can't let your master or the slave catchers have someone who knows where the hiding places are. You go with us, Jim, or you die right here!"

I thought I would die of fright, but I managed to nod my head up and down to indicate I would go with her. We walked through the cold December night until we came to a small town. I shivered as I followed Moses down a back street. In a whisper, she explained that a black man in town had been freed by his master. This freedman would hide us for the day. Moses knocked at the door of a house as we huddled close behind her.

When the door opened, I could see Harriet's expression grow cold. On the other side of the door was a white man, not a black man. He was wearing a nightshirt, and he looked as if he had just crawled out of bed. In a thick, unfriendly voice, he said, "What do you want?"

Harriet stared at him for a long moment. Then she asked quietly, "Is Mr. Booker here?"

"Him?" the man asked dully as he rubbed his eyes. "He got chased out of town for helping runaways."

The man muttered something I could not understand and slammed the door. In an instant, Harriet was running. "Quick!" she said. "Follow me!"

After we had reached the edge of town, she stopped and explained between gulps of air, "As soon as that man wakes up fully, he'll realize he was talking to a band of runaways, and he'll sound the alarm. So we must keep moving."

Moses led us off the road, through a pine woods, and into a field of high grass. The grass was as tall as a man, and it was covered with frost from the cold. I started to follow Moses into the grass, but I stepped back when my foot sank into cold water. I couldn't see where we were going, and I was afraid to walk in that cold water.

Moses turned around and grabbed my arm. I followed. I had nowhere else to go. ★

We waded through the swampy grass until it hid us on all sides. I heard hoofbeats on the road and shouts in the trees. A cold fear around my heart chilled me more than the water around my legs. I began to shake. Moses looked at me and whispered, "The Lord has been with us before. He will not desert us now."

Suddenly Moses' eyes closed and her head tipped forward. In a second, she was asleep. It was as if someone had struck her over the head, but she just stood there like a statue.

"Wake up!" I pleaded. "Don't leave us here!"

"Quiet, Jim," whispered Henry. "It's just one of her fits. It'll pass." He crouched next to me, and in a voice no louder than the rustling of the tall grass, he told me Harriet's story.

When Harriet was thirteen years old, she was still a slave. One morning, she was in a country store when a runaway slave suddenly darted into the room. A white man was chasing the slave. He ordered Harriet to help him catch the slave, but Harriet shook her head. The slave ran out of the store, and Harriet stepped into the doorway to detain the white man. Just as Harriet stepped into the doorway, the man threw a heavy weight he had picked up from the counter. He was trying to hit the runaway, but the weight struck Harriet on the forehead instead, leaving a large scar.

Henry continued, "The injury nearly killed Harriet. She was taken to her parents' cabin, where she lay unconscious for many days. After a while, she was well enough to work in the fields again, but she never recovered from her injury. Our master tried to sell her to other plantation owners, but nobody wanted to buy an injured slave, especially one that was disobedient. So Harriet worked on the plantation, but she was never the same as she used to be. Without any warning, she would drop off to sleep, just the way you see her sleeping right now. I've seen her fall asleep right in the middle of a conversation. She'll sleep for some time. Then she'll wake up and pick up the conversation where she left off, just as if nothing had happened."

Henry shook his head and smiled as I stared at Harriet's sleeping form. He said, "Our master used to think Harriet was stupid because of her sleeping fits. But when she wasn't sleeping, she was the best worker for a hundred miles around. She was as strong as a man at field work. The other planters paid our master to let her work on their plantations. She would do such a good job that our master sometimes let her keep some of the money she made at the other plantations."

"Why did she run away?" I asked.

"Everything changed," said Henry. "Our master died. His sister wanted to sell Harriet and her brothers to different plantations. Other slaves found out about this plan and told Harriet. She said they had to run away or the whole family would be broken up. Her brothers said they'd go with her. One night, they finally did run away. Before long, her brothers got scared and went back to the plantation, but Harriet decided to keep on going. The Underground Railroad took her all the way to Philadelphia, up in Pennsylvania."

"Why'd she come back?" I asked.

"Once she got to Pennsylvania, she realized her real home was still down here in Maryland," Henry said. "She didn't want to be a slave anymore, so she figured she had to bring her home and family up North. After a year passed, she came back and helped her sister and many other slaves escape. The next year, she came for one of her brothers. This time, she's taking me."

Henry stopped talking. He looked nervously in the direction of the road. Suddenly, we heard a low voice. Henry put out his hand and touched Harriet's shoulder.

- How did Harriet Tubman become a conductor on the Underground Railroad? (Idea: *After she escaped slavery, she decided to help other slaves escape as well.*) ⓡ
- Why do you think the escape system for slaves was called the Underground Railroad? (Ideas: *Because it was a secret way of getting people from one place to another; because it operated only at night; because it was like a subway that nobody could see above ground.*) ⓓⓘ

- What did conductors on the Underground Railroad do? (Idea: *Guided escaped slaves from one hiding place to the next.*) Ⓢⓤⓜ
- Harriet told Jim, "No one goes back on the Underground Railroad." Explain what would happen if somebody did go back. (Idea: *The masters and slave catchers would discover the hiding places.*) ⓡ
- Why did Harriet have sleeping fits? (Idea: *When she was young, she was hit on the head with a heavy weight.*) Ⓒ/ⓔ

SPELLING

(Present Spelling lesson 77 after completing Reading lesson 77. See *Spelling Presentation Book.*)

READING

(Have students find lesson 78, part A, in their textbooks.)

> **Note:** There are no "Before Reading" exercises for this lesson. Instead, the "Reading Aloud" exercise is recommended for this lesson.

EXERCISE 1

Reading Aloud

1. What's the focus question for today's lesson? (Response: *Why did Harriet and the others have to go to Canada?*)
2. We're going to read aloud to the diamond.
- (Call on individual students to read several sentences each.)

Harriet Tubman

Part 3

Focus Question: Why did Harriet and the others have to go to Canada?

I could hear somebody on the road, talking in a low voice. I wanted to run, but I stood there as Henry put his hand on Harriet's shoulder. She was motionless.

"Harriet," Henry said softly.

And suddenly, without warning, Harriet opened her eyes and looked wide awake. Henry pointed toward the road.

The man on the road was saying, "My wagon stands in the barnyard of the farm across the road. The horse is in the stable. The harness hangs on a nail." He repeated those words over and over again as he walked past the swamp where we hid.

"Crazy man!" I whispered. "Who's he talking to?"

"Quiet!" said Moses. "He's talking to us. We are in a special hiding place. He knows that if we are not in Mr. Booker's place, we are here."

After the man had passed the swamp, Moses led us across the road to the farm.

The horse, the wagon, and the harness were where the man had said they would be. We hid in the back of the wagon while Moses climbed up on the seat, grabbed the reins, and set off.

The next morning, we were in Delaware, a slave state next to Maryland. As the first light of dawn tinted the sky, Harriet guided the tired horse to a large farmhouse. A white family greeted us warmly and gave us a hot meal. We were far out in the country, so we did not have to hide. I slept well that day and felt sad when we set out again the next night.

We walked from the farmhouse to the outskirts of Wilmington, the biggest city in Delaware. There, a wagon met us. We hid in the back of the wagon under a pile of laundry. It was nice and warm under those clothes. Before dawn, we were inside the city on an empty street in front of a shoe store. We quickly slipped out of the wagon, into the shoe store, and upstairs to a secret room.

The store was owned by a man named Thomas Garret. He belonged to the Society of Friends. This group believed that slavery was evil, and they helped runaways whenever they could. Moses told us that Garret had been punished by the government for helping runaway slaves, but he refused to stop helping them. ♦

EXERCISE 2

Silent Reading

1. Read the rest of the lesson to yourselves and be ready to answer some questions.

We spent the next day sitting very quietly above Garret's shoe store. We could hear the customers coming and going in the room below. Whenever the store was empty, one of us would smile and whisper to the others, "Tomorrow we'll be in Pennsylvania. Tomorrow we'll be free."

After the last customer had left the store, Garret opened the door of the secret room and called for Moses. The two of them talked for a long time.

When Moses came back, Catherine asked, "Are we leaving now? How long until we're safe in Pennsylvania?"

"We'll be there tonight," said Moses. "But Mr. Garret tells me that we won't be safe in Pennsylvania. We'll have to keep on going farther north."

"How much farther will we go?" I asked.

Without looking at me, Harriet replied, "To Canada." She explained that the United States government had recently passed a law that helped slave owners and made it hard for runaways to escape. According to that law, runaway slaves could be arrested in the free states of the North, such as New York or Pennsylvania. The only place that was safe for runaways was Canada.

As we sneaked out of Garret's store that night, I felt as if I were in a nightmare that would never end. Our journey to freedom was not over—it was just beginning.

When we got to Philadelphia that night, Moses took us to meet William Still, a free black man who ran the office of the Anti-Slavery Society.

"Harriet Tubman!" he called and grinned broadly after we were inside the office. He counted us and then shook his head. "That's amazing," he said, looking at Harriet. Then he looked right at me and smiled. He said, "You may not know it, but you are with the best conductor on the Underground Railroad. So far, she has delivered forty people from the South—counting the three people in your group."

I didn't know what to say. Mr. Still was telling me Harriet was a very good conductor, but I was terrified half the time. The other half I was cold and hungry. Even when I wasn't hungry, I kept wondering what had made me leave the plantation in the first place. Harriet was certainly the strongest and bravest person I had ever known. But in some ways she was unlike anybody I had ever seen before. Whoever heard of somebody falling asleep standing up?

After a few moments, I said, "I know we're not safe here, but could you tell me how far we are from Canada?"

Mr. Still took a map from his desk and carefully unfolded it. It was old and tattered and covered with lines. I didn't know how to read a map, so he explained it to me.

He began by pointing to a place near the bottom. "Here's where you started out, in Maryland," he said. Then he moved up to the middle of the map. "Here you are now, in Philadelphia." Then his finger began to follow a pencil line up to the top of the map. "Here's where you're going," he said. "All the way up here to Canada. You've already traveled about two hundred miles. But you've got another four hundred miles to go." ★

"Four hundred miles," I said as I stared at that map. "Four hundred miles."

"I'm afraid so," Mr. Still said, shaking his head. "And it won't be easy, because Canada is north, and you know what happens to the weather when you go that far north."

"I've heard it's really cold," I said.

"That's right," he replied.

I could picture myself hiding in old wagons with the wind howling and my bones chattering from the cold. I turned away from the map.

Moses said, "Well, now, maybe the trip won't be all that bad. We'll be going on the railroad."

"I know," I said. "We've been on the railroad from Maryland."

"No," Moses said, "the real railroad. We're going to take a real train. In fact, we'll take two of them. The first one will take us to New York City. The next one will take us from New York all the way to Canada. Mr. Still has given me money for our tickets."

• • •

When we entered the crowded Philadelphia train station, my heart was pounding so loudly that I was sure everybody in the place could hear it. I tried to look natural, but I felt my eyes darting this way and that every time something made the slightest sound.

I stood with Henry and the others as Harriet bought tickets for all of us. I nervously watched the man behind the counter. When Harriet first talked to him, he didn't look up. He counted out four tickets. Then he glanced over at us and back at her. I wondered what he would do next, when suddenly he gave Harriet a faint smile. At that moment, I realized he was a member of the Underground Railroad. I can't tell you how good it felt to know he was on our side.

Harriet had told us to be very quiet and not to talk to anybody, and that's just what we did. I kept wishing I could get so small that nobody would know I was there.

At last, a train conductor walked into the station and announced that the train was ready to leave. People stood up and started to move toward the platform. Some of them hugged friends and relatives. Some of them cried. Some of them got onto the train and waved back to little groups of people.

I followed Harriet and the others in our party as quietly as I could. I didn't look up, and I didn't look down. I just followed and tried not to breathe so loudly that people would hear me. We found seats inside the car and sat down. I was next to Harriet, while Henry and Catherine sat across from us.

We had just sat down when I saw Catherine's mouth fall open. She was looking at something in back of Harriet and me. In little more than a whisper, she said, "Look." I glanced up and saw a big sign with some writing on it, but I couldn't read.

Harriet said to Catherine, "Child, don't keep us in suspense. You know I can't read. My master never allowed us to get that kind of learning. So if you want me to know what that sign says, you'd better read it."

Catherine said in a whisper, "The sign tells about you, Harriet. It says they're offering a reward of five thousand dollars for your capture. Five thousand dollars."

- Why did Harriet and the others have to go to Canada? (Ideas: *Because they could be arrested in New York or Pennsylvania; because Canada was the only safe place for runaways.*) (DCE)
- Why did the Society of Friends help runaway slaves? (Ideas: *Because they believed slavery was evil; because they believed helping slaves was the right thing to do.*) (DCE)
- Why do you think the government had passed a law that helped slave owners? (Ideas: *Because slave owners were powerful; because some people in the government supported slavery.*) (MJ)
- Mr. Still said that Harriet was the best conductor on the Underground Railroad. Why was that statement surprising to Jim? (Ideas: *Because he was cold, hungry, and terrified; because Harriet had sleeping fits.*) (DCE)

- Do you think it was wise of Harriet and the others to take a real train? Explain your answer. (Ideas: *Yes, because the train would get them to Canada quickly; no, because they would be traveling in public; no, because there were reward posters for Harriet.*) (MJ)

EXERCISE 3

Paired Practice (Optional)

1. Now you'll read in pairs.
- Whoever read second the last time will read first today.
- Remember to start at the diamond and switch at the star.
2. (Observe students and answer questions as needed.)

AFTER READING

EXERCISE 4

Independent Work

1. Do all the items in your workbook and textbook for this lesson.
2. (The independent work in this lesson includes the following activities.)
- Story details
- Combined sentences
- Similes
- Maps
- Comprehension
- Writing

EXERCISE 5

Workcheck

1. (Using the Answer Key, read the questions and answers for the workbook.)
2. (Have students read their answers for the textbook activities.)
3. (Have two or three students read their writing assignments aloud. Comment on each assignment.)
4. (Have students correct and turn in their work.)

SPELLING

(Present Spelling lesson 78 after completing Reading lesson 78. See *Spelling Presentation Book*.)

BEFORE READING

(Have students find lesson 79 in their
textbooks.)

Combined Sentences

1. Everybody, turn to part B at the end of
today's story. ✔
• (Call on individual students to read
several sentences each.)
• (At the end of each section, present the
questions for that section.)

Write the answers for items 1–5.
   Some sentences combine a main
sentence and a part. The main sentence
tells what is important. The part tells more
about something in the main sentence.
Here's an example: *The sun, red and pale,
sank slowly in the west.*
• Here's the main sentence: *The sun sank
slowly in the west.*
• Here's the part: *red and pale*
1. The part tells more about a word in the
main sentence. What is that word?

• What's the answer? (Response: *Sun.*)

2. What does the part tell about the sun?

• What's the answer? (Idea: *It was red
and pale.*)

   Here's how to combine a main sentence
and a part that tells more about something
in the main sentence. Start with the main
sentence and leave a space for the part:
The sun ▰▰▰ *sank slowly in the west.*
Then add the part that tells more about the
sun: *The sun, red and pale, sank slowly in
the west.*
   Here's a main sentence and a part:
• *The sail was raised to the top of the
mast.*
• *snarling in the wind*
3. The part tells more about a word in the
main sentence. What is that word?

• What's the answer? (Response: *Sail.*)

4. What does the part tell about the sail?

• What's the answer? (Idea: *It was
snarling in the wind.*)

5. Write the combined sentence.

• What's the combined sentence?
(Response: *The sail, snarling in the wind,
was raised to the top of the mast.*)
• You'll write the answers later.

READING

Focus Question

1. Everybody, turn back to part A. ✔
2. What's the focus question for today's
lesson? (Response: *When did Jim
become a free man?*)

Reading Aloud (Optional)

1. We're going to read aloud to the
diamond.
• (Call on individual students to read
several sentences each.)

Harriet Tubman

Part 4

Focus Question: When did Jim
become a free man?

   Moses stared at the sign for a moment;
then she shook her head. "My, my," she
laughed. "Last year the reward was only
one thousand dollars. Now I'm worth five
thousand dollars. My value has gone up a
lot. When I was a slave, after I got hit on
the head, the traders thought I was so
worthless they wouldn't buy me for any
price."
   Just then two white men walked through
the car. One of them said to the other,
"There are a lot of Negroes heading north
on this train."

"Yeah," the other said and pointed to the poster over my head. "Who knows? Maybe Harriet Tubman is on this train right now."

"Five thousand dollars," the other man said and began to read the sign aloud. "Harriet Tubman, sometimes called Moses, is a runaway slave from Maryland." He stood there, right above me, as he read how she had helped other slaves escape. He read that she was a small woman, about thirty, with a large scar on her forehead.

The man stopped reading and looked at us for a long moment. I could feel his eyes, even though I didn't look back. I glanced at Harriet. She was sitting there very calmly, holding a book and pretending to read.

The man continued, "It says here that she has sleeping fits and that she can't read or write." Both men stared at Harriet. For a moment, I thought they would recognize her from the description. Suddenly, one of them said, "No, I don't think we'll get a reward today. She's got a scar, but she can read."

They both laughed and walked slowly down the aisle. The train rocked gently from side to side. I could feel sweat forming on my forehead.

After they left, Harriet pointed to the book and said, "This book is the best disguise I ever used. If you just hold a book, people think you can read." ♦

EXERCISE 4

Silent Reading

1. Read the rest of the lesson to yourselves and be ready to answer some questions.

The train station in New York City was the most amazing sight I had ever seen in my life. There were tracks and tracks in all directions and smoke and people — thousands and thousands of them, moving along like armies of ants. The inside of the station was so big that I couldn't even see from one side to the other. The ceiling was so high that when I bent back and looked straight up, I got dizzy.

Conductors shouted announcements about trains that were departing and trains that were arriving. People rushed this way and that, stumbling along with heavy bags. I felt as if I had just stepped into a different world.

I tried to stay close to Harriet and the others. We walked toward three people who were standing near a pillar.

Catherine said, "You could put a whole plantation inside this place."

I nodded above the clattering and the shouting and the sounds of train whistles.

The people who met us were members of the Society of Friends. They took us in a large horsedrawn carriage to the Friends' meeting hall, where we spent the night. I didn't sleep well. I kept remembering all those amazing sights I had seen in the train station.

Early the next morning, the Friends drove us back to the train station. We moved from one long line to another — first the ticket line, then the line to go to the train platform, then the line outside the train. Finally we were on the train. Less than a half hour later, we had left New York City, but its sights were burned into my memory.

Most of the passengers in our train car were black people, but there were a few whites at the far end of the car. They ignored us, and I was glad to see there were no posters about Harriet Tubman on this train.

We traveled for half a day after leaving New York City, and everything was peaceful. I was beginning to think we would travel all the way to Canada without any trouble. I changed my mind when we stopped in Buffalo, New York, which is right across the river from Canada.

At the Buffalo station, we waited in the train as some passengers got off and others got on. Just before the train was ready to leave, a white man walked into our train car, carrying a poster. He looked at the black people in the car, one at a time. Behind this man was a white police officer.

I could feel my hands start to tremble as the man and the officer moved slowly down the aisle. When they were only a few rows from us, the officer put his hand on the other man's shoulder and said, "Mister, I'm not going to delay this train any longer just because you think there might be a runaway on it."

The man turned quickly toward the police officer and snapped, "Yes, you will delay it!" Then he pointed toward us. In fact, it seemed he was pointing right at me. He said, "It's the law. The law says that if I find any slaves who are listed on this poster, you have to arrest them and send them back to their owners."

I glanced over at Moses and couldn't believe what I saw. She was sound asleep. I could see by the way she was breathing that she wasn't just pretending. She was having one of her sleeping fits. The slave catcher and the police officer stopped in front of our seats. The slave catcher paused and looked at his poster. I saw a smile form on his face as he glanced at me. ★

Just then one of the white men at the far end of the train said, "You're wasting our time, Mister. I saw those people on my trip down to the United States. They're from Canada."

"You're lying," the slave catcher said. He thrust his finger in my face. "This one is listed on the poster."

I looked at the slave catcher's face and then back at his finger, which was only a couple of inches from my nose. The slave catcher shook his poster and said, "This young man is a slave who ran away from Maryland last week. And he's going right back where he came from."

The slave catcher grabbed me by the collar of my jacket and jerked me to my feet. I could hear the jacket tear.

One of the white women at the end of the car stood up and shouted, "Take your hands off that young man! He's a Canadian. I was on the train he took from Canada."

The slave catcher gave her a grim smile as he held me firmly by the collar. Then he turned to me and said, "So you're a Canadian. Well, tell me, Canadian, what were you doing in New York City?"

The man gave my collar a sudden tug. My throat was so dry that I could hardly talk. I don't know where the words came from, but I found myself saying, "I . . . I visited some friends."

The woman in the back of the car shouted, "You heard what the young man said, Officer. Now get this slave catcher off the train. I have important business back in Canada, and I don't want to be late!"

"Let's go," the officer said, slapping his hand on the slave catcher's shoulder.

"No!" the slave catcher shouted. "This man is a runaway slave. I'm sending him back to Maryland in chains, and you're going to help me!"

"Mister," the police officer said, "if you're not off this train in ten seconds, I'm going to send *you* back to Maryland in chains."

The slave catcher looked angrily at everyone in the car. Some of the white people were quietly snickering at him. Suddenly he let go of my collar, stomped down the aisle, and disappeared through the door.

I sat there trembling and sweating as the train slowly chugged out of the Buffalo station. I wanted to run, but there was no place to go. I wanted to hide, but I was trapped inside the railroad car. I wanted to cry, but I felt that everybody was looking at me.

From time to time, I looked out the window. About an hour after we left Buffalo, the train started across a long bridge over a river. The river was a beautiful sight, but I didn't feel excited about it. The people in the seat behind us were exclaiming about the view.

Moses woke up. She looked at me and said, "Why aren't you enjoying the view?"

I said, "The slave catchers know I'm on this train. They'll get me the next time the train stops."

"No, they won't be able to get you anymore," Moses said with a twinkle in her eye. "We just passed the middle of the bridge that goes between the United States and Canada, so we are no longer in the United States. You are a free man, Jim."

Without thinking, I stood up and began to cheer. Then I noticed that everyone else in the car was standing and cheering. A moment later, they started to sing.

Goodbye, old master,
Don't think hard of me.
I'm going off to Canada
Where all the slaves are free.

- When did Jim become a free man? (Ideas: *When he left the United States; when the train crossed the bridge to Canada.*) (Seq)
- Why was Harriet amused that the reward for her was five thousand dollars? (Idea: *When she was a slave, nobody wanted to buy her.*) (DCE)
- What trick did Harriet use to fool the two men who read the poster? Why did that trick work? (Idea: *For her trick, she pretended to read. The trick worked because the poster said she couldn't read.*) (Sum)
- How did the people in the train help Jim when the slave catcher appeared? (Ideas: *They said he had come from Canada; they told the officer to take the slave catcher away.*) (R)
- Do you think Harriet will stay in Canada? Explain your answer. (Ideas: *Yes, because the Underground Railroad is getting too dangerous; no, because she wants to keep helping slaves escape.*) (MJ)

EXERCISE 5

Paired Practice (Optional)

1. Now you'll read in pairs.
- Whoever read second the last time will read first today.
- Remember to start at the diamond and switch at the star.
2. (Observe students and answer questions as needed.)

AFTER READING

EXERCISE 6

Independent Work

1. Do all the items in your workbook and textbook for this lesson.
2. (The independent work in this lesson includes the following activities.)
- Story details
- Vocabulary
- Maps
- Settings
- Combined sentences
- Conversations
- Comprehension
- Writing

EXERCISE 7

Workcheck

1. (Using the Answer Key, read the questions and answers for the workbook.)
2. (Have students read their answers for the textbook activities.)
3. (Have two or three students read their writing assignments aloud. Comment on each assignment.)
4. (Have students correct and turn in their work.)

SPELLING

(Present Spelling lesson 79 after completing Reading lesson 79. See *Spelling Presentation Book.*)

BEFORE READING

(Have students find lesson 80 in their textbooks.)

Outlining

1. Everybody, turn to part B at the end of today's story. ✔
- (Call on individual students to read several sentences each.)
- (At the end of each section, present the questions for that section.)

Write the answers for items 1 and 2.

The passage below tells about two main things that happened. One main thing happens in each paragraph.

- How many paragraphs are in the passage? (Response: *Two.*)
- Each paragraph has its own main idea.

Just then, Frisco Kid called Joe in for breakfast. The Kid was as good a cook as he was a sailor. They ate beefsteak and fried potatoes, topped off with good French bread, butter, and coffee.

Pete did not join the boys. He kept sleeping, even though Frisco Kid attempted to rouse him. Pete just mumbled and half opened his eyes, but then he started snoring again.
1. Write the main idea and three supporting details for the first paragraph.

- What's the main idea of the first paragraph? (Idea: *The boys ate breakfast.*)
- What are the supporting details for that main idea? (Ideas: *Frisco Kid called Joe to breakfast; Frisco Kid was a good cook; the boys had beefsteak, fried potatoes, bread, butter, and coffee.*)
- You'll write the answers later. Remember to write a number in front of each main idea and a letter in front of each supporting detail.

READING

Focus Question

1. Everybody, turn back to part A. ✔
2. What's the focus question for today's lesson? (Response: *How did Harriet help Joe Nalle?*)

Reading Aloud (Optional)

1. We're going to read aloud to the diamond.
- (Call on individual students to read several sentences each.)

Harriet Tubman
Part 5
Focus Question: How did Harriet help Joe Nalle?

By the spring of 1859, I had lived in Hamilton, Canada, for more than four years. I was a different person than when I arrived on that train from the United States. I had learned to read because I knew that reading would be important in my new life. I had a house of my own, and I had a good job as a cabinet maker.

Just as a lot had happened to me since 1855, a lot had happened to Harriet. She had gone back to the South to free her brothers. Slave catchers were everywhere. The reward for Harriet had gone up to ten thousand dollars, and the reward posters now showed her picture. Still, she managed to bring her brothers and others to safety.

Harriet later returned on a dangerous mission to free her parents, who were over eighty years old. She made other trips as well, and the number of slaves she freed kept going up. By 1859, Harriet had freed more than two hundred slaves.

Things looked good for me that year—until I had to take a trip to Troy, New York. I didn't want to go, but the cabinet maker I worked for insisted on it. We had just finished making a special desk of solid oak for a lawyer in Troy. It was the most elegant and costly desk we had ever made, and it had taken us over a month.

"You've got to deliver that desk," the cabinet maker said. "We can't just put it on the train and hope it gets there in one piece."

I objected and explained that I might be arrested in the United States.

"Don't worry," the cabinet maker said. "I'll give you papers that show you're a Canadian. All you have to do is ride in the baggage car with the desk to Troy, drop it off at the lawyer's office, and come right back. You'll be in no danger at all."

The cabinet maker's prediction was wrong. ♦

EXERCISE 4

Silent Reading

1. Read the rest of the lesson to yourselves and be ready to answer some questions.

At first, everything went well. I rode with the desk to Troy, where a wagon met the train. Some workers and I loaded the desk onto the wagon and drove through crowded streets to the lawyer's office. But the lawyer wasn't in. His assistant told us he had gone to the sheriff's office to help a black man named Joseph Nalle, who used to be a slave.

The assistant said. "This morning, Nalle's master came up from Virginia to take Nalle back with him. Nalle's now locked up in the sheriff's office. I think there's going to be trouble. The people around here are tired of slave catchers."

As the lawyer's assistant talked, I felt a terrible panic. I didn't want to be in this place any longer. I tried not to show my fear as we unloaded the desk, but my mind was fixed on one thought: Get out of here fast.

As soon as the desk was unloaded, I started walking back toward the train station, which was less than a mile away. I figured I could make better time than the wagon because the streets were so crowded. Before I reached the train station, I came upon a huge mob of angry people. They shouted insults and shook their fists. A young boy added to the confusion by screaming, "Fire! Fire!"

People were swarming out of buildings and joining the angry mob in the street. I pushed through the crowd toward the boy.

"There's no fire," I shouted when I reached the boy at last.

He looked at me and smiled. "A woman told me to shout 'Fire!' She gave me some money to do it."

The boy pointed toward the steps of a building. A small woman wearing a large bonnet was curled up on the steps, right in front of the door. Above the door was a sign: Sheriff's Office. Although I couldn't see the woman's face, I knew instantly who she was.

I couldn't decide what to do. The mob was going to make trouble, and there would be violence. But I couldn't leave Harriet Tubman, not after all she'd done for me.

Suddenly, the crowd let out a roar. All eyes turned toward the second floor of the sheriff's office. A black man was halfway out the open window, struggling with other men.

"That's Nalle!" somebody shouted.

"Jump!" the people below shouted and held their arms high. "We'll catch you!"

A moment later, strong white arms wrapped around Nalle and pulled him back inside the office.

"Let him go!" people below called. "We'll buy his freedom from his master. How much does the master want?"

A white man stuck his head out of the window and said, "I'm his master! I'll sell him for twelve hundred dollars!"

"Come on," somebody yelled. "We can raise that money right now."

"I have fifty!" the man next to me yelled.

"I can give a hundred!" a well-dressed woman announced.

In five minutes, the crowd had collected twelve hundred dollars.

"We've got the money!" somebody shouted. "Let Joe Nalle go!"

The master appeared at the window again. "The price is now fifteen hundred dollars," he shouted.

People in the mob hollered and shook their fists. Just then, the sheriff opened the front door. He was holding Nalle by the arm. "Clear these steps," he shouted. "We're taking this man to the train station."

Without standing up, Harriet slowly moved to one side of the door. "Out of the way, old woman," the sheriff shouted. "Clear the steps!" ★

But Harriet stopped moving. Instead, she just sat there, blocking the sheriff's path. To get past Harriet, the sheriff had to let go of Nalle for an instant. In that instant, Harriet jumped to her feet and shoved Nalle into the crowd at the bottom of the steps.

"Grab him!" she shouted.

She quickly shoved the sheriff back into the doorway. Before he could grab her, she darted down the stairs and into the crowd. I could still see her large bonnet bobbing up and down.

Fights were breaking out in the crowd. Some of the people were on the sheriff's side, and others were on Nalle's. I figured Harriet was in danger. Although I desperately wanted to run away, I followed Harriet's bonnet. I couldn't stand the thought of her being injured by this mob.

I caught up to Harriet in a tangle of shouting people who were waving their arms and fists. I grabbed her shoulder and spun her around. But it was not Harriet. It was Joe Nalle. Harriet must have slipped the bonnet on Nalle's head during all the confusion.

Nalle was in terrible condition. His clothes were torn, and his body was covered with bruises. His wrists had large cuts from the handcuffs he had been wearing.

Suddenly, I heard a familiar voice behind me. "Don't just stand there, Jim," Harriet shouted. "Help us get Nalle out of here."

Before I knew what I was doing, I was rushing down the street with the mob. I didn't know where we were going, but I was in the middle of it. We rushed down to the river, where a rowboat was docked. Harriet and I helped Nalle into the rowboat. Then two other men jumped into the boat and began rowing Nalle to the other side of the river.

"He's not safe yet," Harriet warned. "The police can still arrest him."

Harriet and I ran with the rest of the mob to a large ferryboat that was about to cross the river. Everybody crowded on board—

hundreds of people. The ferry was so crowded that some people fell into the water.

As the ferry began to move, people swarmed to the rails and watched the tiny rowboat crossing the river. The rowboat reached the other side before we did. Then we witnessed a dismal sight. As soon as the men got out of the rowboat, police officers grabbed Nalle.

The officers put Nalle into a wagon and drove toward a police station on their side of the river. Meanwhile, people on the ferry shouted, "We'll free him! We'll free him!"

By the time the ferry reached the shore, the people had become like wild animals. They poured off the ferry and ran toward the police station. The police shot into the crowd. Two men were wounded, but the mob continued with more determination than ever.

The police locked themselves inside the station, but some people from the mob smashed through the front door. Moments later, they emerged with Joe Nalle. Wild shouts rose from the crowd.

Meanwhile, Harriet had found a carriage. The people holding Nalle rushed him over to the vehicle. Harriet whispered something to the driver, who drove away as soon as Nalle was safely aboard.

"Nalle will be safe now," Harriet said to me as the carriage headed off. "I told the driver about a hiding place where the police can't find him."

Then Harriet turned and lost herself in the crowd. I turned the other way and headed back to Canada. The United States was still not a safe country for runaway slaves.

- How did Harriet help Joe Nalle? (Ideas: *She helped him escape from the sheriff's office; she put him into the rowboat; she found a carriage for him to escape in.*) (SUM)
- Why did Jim have to travel to Troy, New York? (Idea: *He had to deliver a fancy desk to a lawyer.*) (ND)
- Why do you think Harriet asked the boy to shout "Fire"? (Ideas: *She wanted to create confusion; she wanted people to gather on the street.*) (DCE)

- Explain how Harriet freed Nalle from the sheriff in the doorway. (Idea: *She blocked the door. To get by her, the sheriff had to let go of Nalle. Then she shoved Nalle into the crowd.*) Ⓡ
- The people who freed Joe Nalle from the police station were breaking the law. Do you think they were right to break the law? Explain your answer. (Ideas: *Yes, because freeing Joe Nalle was more important than the law about runaway slaves; no, because people should always obey the law.*) ⓂⒿ

EXERCISE 5
Paired Practice (Optional)

1. Now you'll read in pairs.
- Whoever read second the last time will read first today.
- Remember to start at the diamond and switch at the star.
2. (Observe students and answer questions as needed.)

AFTER READING

EXERCISE 6
Independent Work

1. Do all the items in your workbook and textbook for this lesson.
2. (The independent work in this lesson includes the following activities.)
- Story details
- Vocabulary
- Maps
- Combined sentences
- Outlining
- Comprehension
- Writing

EXERCISE 7
Workcheck

1. (Using the Answer Key, read the questions and answers for the workbook.)
2. (Have students read their answers for the textbook activities.)
3. (Have two or three students read their writing assignments aloud. Comment on each assignment.)
4. (Have students correct and turn in their work.)

MASTERY TEST

(The Lesson 80 Mastery Test should be administered after students complete lesson 80. See *Curriculum-Based Assessment and Fluency Teacher Handbook* for details.)

SPELLING

(Present Spelling lesson 80 after completing Reading lesson 80. See *Spelling Presentation Book.*)

ACTIVITIES ACROSS THE CURRICULUM

(Students should complete the appropriate project in *Activities across the Curriculum* after completing lesson 80. See *Activities across the Curriculum* book for details.)

Lessons 81–85 • Planning Page

	Lesson 81	Lesson 82	Lesson 83	Lesson 84	Lesson 85

BEFORE READING	Hard words
	Word practice
	New vocabulary
	Vocabulary
	  definitions
	Following directions
		Hard words
		New vocabulary
		Vocabulary
		  definitions
		Following directions
			Hard words
			New vocabulary
			Vocabulary
			  definitions
				Hard words
				Word practice
				New vocabulary
				Vocabulary
				  definitions
					Word practice
					Vocabulary review
					Reference books

NEW VOCABULARY	regiment groggy agony reap sensation raid surrender	in debt staggering artificial deception hobble testify	rising inflection at rise beforehand majority unanimous dumbfounded initials	shy exception sulk dryly astound gavel	(none)
READING	"Harriet Tubman" (Part 6)	"Harriet Tubman" (Part 7)	*All in Favor* (Part 1)	*All in Favor* (Part 2)	*All in Favor* (Part 3)
INDEPENDENT WORK	Story details Combined sentences Sequencing Outlining Following directions Comprehension Writing	Story details Combined sentences Character traits Outlining Following directions Vocabulary review Comprehension Writing	Story details Vocabulary Character traits Combined sentences Following directions Vocabulary review Outlining Comprehension Writing	Story details Vocabulary Following directions Similes Vocabulary review Outlining Comprehension Writing	Story details Vocabulary Contradictions Character traits Story review Reference books Comprehension Writing
SUPPLEMENTS	*Spelling*	*Spelling*	*Spelling*	*Spelling*	*Spelling* *Activities across the* *Curriculum*

Comprehension Questions Abbreviations Guide

Access Prior Knowledge = (APK)   Author's Point of View = (APoV)   Author's Purpose = (AP)   Cause/Effect = (C/E)   Charts/Graphs/Diagrams/Visual Aids = (VA)

Classify and Categorize = (C+C)   Compare/Contrast = (C/C)   Determine Character Emotions, Motivation = (DCE)   Drawing Conclusions = (DC)   Drawing Inferences = (DI)

Fact and Opinion = (F/O)   Hypothesizing = (H)   Main Idea = (MI)   Making Connections = (MC)   Making Deductions = (MD)   Making Judgements = (MJ)

Narrative Elements = (NE)   Noting Details = (ND)   Predict = (P)   Reality/Fantasy = (R/F)   Recall Facts/Rules = (RF/R)   Retell = (R)   Sequence = (Seq)

Steps in a Process = (SP)   Story Structure = (SS)   Summarize = (Sum)   Understanding Dialogue = (UD)   Using Context to Confirm Meaning(s) = (UCCM)   Visualize = (V)

BEFORE READING

(Have students find lesson 81, part A, in their textbooks.)

EXERCISE 1

Hard Words

1. Look at column 1.
- These are hard words from your textbook stories.

1. Abraham Lincoln	4. regiment
2. Syracuse	5. agony
3. Beaufort	6. conscious

2. Line 1 is **Abraham Lincoln.** Everybody, what words? (Signal.) *Abraham Lincoln.*
- (Repeat this procedure for every word in the column.)
3. Let's read the words again.
4. Line 1. Everybody, what words? (Signal.) *Abraham Lincoln.*
- (Repeat this procedure for every word in the column.)
5. (Repeat the column until firm.)

EXERCISE 2

Word Practice

1. Look at column 2.
- We're going to practice these words.

1. crutches	3. realization
2. realize	

2. Word 1. Everybody, what word? (Signal.) *Crutches.*
- (Repeat this procedure for every word in the column.)
3. (Repeat the column until firm.)

EXERCISE 3

New Vocabulary

1. Look at column 3.
- First we'll read the words in this column. Then we'll read their definitions.

1. regiment	5. sensation
2. groggy	6. raid
3. agony	7. surrender
4. reap	

2. Word 1. Everybody, what word? (Signal.) *Regiment.*
- (Repeat this procedure for every word in the column.)
3. (Repeat the column until firm.)

EXERCISE 4

Vocabulary Definitions

1. Everybody, find part B. ✔
- These are definitions for the words you just read.
2. (For each word, call on a student to read the definition and the item. Then ask the student to complete the item.)

1. **regiment**—An army is often divided into units called *regiments.* Each regiment has a certain number of soldiers.
- What is a regiment?

- What's the answer? (Idea: *A unit in an army.*)

2. **groggy**—When you are *groggy,* you are unsteady and half asleep.
- What's another way of saying *He felt unsteady and half asleep after the long trip*?

- What's the answer? (Response: *He felt groggy after the long trip.*)

3. **agony**—*Agony* is great pain.
- What's another way of saying *The wounded soldiers were in great pain*?

- What's the answer? (Response: *The wounded soldiers were in agony.*)

4. **reap**—When you *reap* a crop from a field, you cut down the crop and gather it.
- What's another way of saying *The farmer is cutting down and gathering the wheat?*

- What's the answer? (Response: *The farmer is reaping the wheat.*)

5. **sensation**—*Sensation* is another word for feeling. A feeling of fear is a sensation of fear.
- What's another way of saying *He had no feeling in his toes?*

- What's the answer? (Response: *He had no sensation in his toes.*)

6. **raid**—A *raid* is a surprise attack by a small group.
- What is a raid?

- What's the answer? (Idea: *A surprise attack by a small group.*)

7. **surrender**—When an army *surrenders,* it gives up and stops fighting.
- What's another way of saying *The army gave up?*

- What's the answer? (Response: *The army surrendered.*)

EXERCISE 5
Following Directions

1. Everybody, turn to part D at the end of today's story. ✔
- (Call on individual students to read several sentences each.)
- (At the end of each section, present the questions for that section.)

Use the facts below to answers items 1–4.
Facts: Your name is Homer Price. You are sixteen years old. You are applying for a job at a factory that makes doughnut machines. You know how the machines work, and you have fixed them before. You live at 417 Central Street in Centerburg, Ohio.
1. Write your full name, last name first.

- What's the answer? (Response: *Price, Homer.*)

2. What is your age?

- What's the answer? (Response: *Sixteen.*)

3. Write your address, including street, city, and state.

- What's the answer? (Response: *417 Central Street, Centerburg, Ohio.*)

4. List at least two qualifications you have for this job.

- What's the answer? (Ideas: *I know how the machines work; I have fixed them before.*)
- You'll write the answers later.

READING

EXERCISE 6
Focus Question

1. Everybody, find part C. ✔
2. What's the focus question for today's lesson? (Response: *How did Harriet help the Union during the Civil War?*)

> *Note:* The "Reading Aloud" exercise is recommended for this lesson.

EXERCISE 7
Reading Aloud

1. We're going to read aloud to the diamond.
2. (Call on individual students to read several sentences each.)

Harriet Tubman
Part 6
Focus Question: How did Harriet help the Union during the Civil War?

The next time I saw Harriet was in 1860, when I married a wonderful young woman named Elizabeth. Harriet attended the wedding and led us in songs at the reception. After that, she disappeared for a long time, but hardly a week passed that we didn't hear about her adventures. She was busy in the southern states, telling slaves they would soon be free from their masters' rule.

In November 1860, Abraham Lincoln was elected president of the United States. Within the next few months, several southern states broke away from the United States and formed the Confederacy. The states that remained in the United States were called the Union. In April 1861, Confederate soldiers attacked a Union fort in South Carolina, and the Civil War began.

During the war, slave catchers could no longer go to northern states and hunt for runaways. Elizabeth and I moved back to New York, where I opened my own cabinet shop in the town of Syracuse.

I was proud of my accomplishment, and I planned to work in that shop until I was an old man. But shortly after the shop opened, some of my best friends from Canada visited me. They wanted me to join the Union army and fight the Confederates. They reminded me of my life as a slave and of the beatings I had taken.

I resisted their arguments all day, but I was beginning to weaken by that evening. I looked over at Elizabeth, who was sitting near the window of my shop. She gave me a faint smile and nodded her head. That was her way of telling me I should join the army and fight against slavery.

A few months later, I was beginning to wonder about the wisdom of my decision. I was part of an all-black regiment in a place called Beaufort, South Carolina.

Our regiment had just marched off a large boat that had sailed all the way down the east coast of the United States. I was groggy, seasick, and hungry. Hundreds of black soldiers met us. They cheered and we cheered, but I don't think anybody felt very happy. We were close to battlegrounds where thousands of soldiers had lost their lives. ♦

EXERCISE 8

Silent Reading

1. Read the rest of the lesson to yourselves and be ready to answer some questions.

During my first day in South Carolina, I must have heard fifty stories about Harriet Tubman. One soldier told me how she had sneaked around to all the plantations and told the slaves that President Lincoln had set them free. She said they no longer had to work on the plantations because they were no longer slaves.

Another soldier told me how Harriet had helped free hundreds of slaves. Working with the Union army, she set fire to plantations all along a large river. The slaves ran down to the river, where rowboats took them to ships and freedom.

The soldier who told me about this adventure shook his head and smiled. "Harriet is a sly one," he said.

He then explained what Harriet had done. The slaves had panicked at the bank of the river because there weren't enough rowboats to carry all the people to the ships at one time. The people on shore held onto the crowded boats so the boats couldn't move.

Suddenly, Harriet stood up in one of the boats and began to sing and clap her hands. The slaves near the boats began to clap as well. They let go of the rowboats, which finally began to move toward the ships. The rowboats returned to shore again and again until all the people were safe on board.

When the soldier finished his story, I smiled and said, "That's like Harriet."

The soldier looked at me. "Do you know her?" he asked.

I replied, "I've met her a time or two."

The next day was horrible. Our regiment attacked Fort Wagner, which was next to the ocean. At dawn, with the sky behind us turning pink, our boats approached the broad, sandy beach. I crouched down near the back of the boat. My teeth were chattering, and my mind was racing. I wondered what I would do in the face of enemy guns.

I soon found out. We jumped from the boats about ten yards from shore and started to slosh through the knee-deep water. A moment after I got out of the boat, I heard something hit the water near me. It sounded like a stone, but it was a bullet. The Confederate soldiers were shooting at us. ★

We started to run. The soldier directly in front of me fell face first into the water. I kept going until I reached the shore. As I charged toward the fort, I suddenly fell forward and landed in the sand. I felt a terrible pain in my right leg. I rolled over in agony and realized I had been shot. The beach whirled around and around and . . .

I have only dim memories of the events that occurred after I fell. I remember a huge man lifting me up and carrying me. I remember moaning voices, but I don't know whether I was moaning or somebody else was. I remember someone bending over me and telling me I was lucky to be alive.

My first clear memory occurred several days later. When I opened my eyes, I found myself in a large hospital filled with wounded soldiers. The floors were so crowded that doctors and nurses had to step over the wounded to get from one place to another.

I looked around the room anxiously. Suddenly, my eyes met the familiar twinkling gaze of Harriet Tubman.

She said, "When are you going to learn to stay out of trouble, Jim? Seems like I've been taking care of you ever since you ran away on the Underground Railroad."

"What happened?" I asked.

So she told me about the battle at Fort Wagner. Over half my regiment was killed before they reached the fort. The boats finally returned and picked up the soldiers who were still alive.

"The battle was like a storm over a field of corn," she said. "We saw the lightning and that was the guns. Then we heard the thunder, and that was the big guns. And then we came to get in the crops. It was dead men that we reaped."

Harriet put her hand on my shoulder and said, "You're one of the lucky ones, Jim. You're still alive, and the war is over for you. But . . ."

She paused and pointed toward my legs. As I looked down, a deadly sick feeling came over me. I could see the outline of my left leg clearly under the sheet. But the sheet lay flat where my right leg should have been.

- How did Harriet help the Union during the Civil War? (Ideas: *She went to plantations and freed slaves; she freed hundreds of slaves along a river; she helped care for wounded men.*) ⓢ̄ᵘᵐ
- At first, why was Jim reluctant to join the Union army? (Ideas: *He had his own cabinet shop; he wanted to work in the shop.*) ⓓᶜᵉ
- What reasons did Jim have for changing his mind? (Ideas: *He remembered his life as a slave; he remembered the beatings he had received; his wife gave him her permission.*) ⓓᶜᵉ
- Explain how Harriet got the slaves to let go of the rowboats. (Idea: *She began singing and clapping her hands. When the slaves began clapping, they let go of the rowboats.*) Ⓡ
- Harriet said, "The battle was like a storm over a field of corn." Explain what she meant. (Idea: *The lightning and thunder were the guns, and the dead men were the crops.*) ⓤᶜᶜᵐ

EXERCISE 9

Paired Practice (Optional)

1. Now you'll read in pairs.
- Whoever read second the last time will read first today.
- Remember to start at the diamond and switch at the star.
2. (Observe students and answer questions as needed.)

AFTER READING

EXERCISE 10

Independent Work

1. Do all the items in your workbook and textbook for this lesson.
2. (The independent work in this lesson includes the following activities.)
- Story details
- Combined sentences
- Sequencing
- Outlining
- Following directions
- Comprehension
- Writing

EXERCISE 11

Workcheck

1. (Using the Answer Key, read the questions and answers for the workbook.)
2. (Have students read their answers for the textbook activities.)
3. (Have two or three students read their writing assignments aloud. Comment on each assignment.)
4. (Have students correct and turn in their work.)

SPELLING

(Present Spelling lesson 81 after completing Reading lesson 81. *See Spelling Presentation Book.*)

BEFORE READING

(Have students find lesson 82, part A, in their textbooks.)

Hard Words

1. Look at column 1.
• These are hard words from your textbook stories.

1. deception	**4. artificial**
2. Auburn	**5. testify**
3. debt	**6. sweetener**

2. Word 1 is **deception.** Everybody, what word? (Signal.) *Deception.*
• (Repeat this procedure for every word in the column.)
3. Let's read the words again.
4. Word 1. Everybody, what word? (Signal.) *Deception.*
• (Repeat this procedure for every word in the column.)
5. (Repeat the column until firm.)

New Vocabulary

1. Look at column 2.
• First we'll read the words in this column. Then we'll read their definitions.

1. in debt	**4. deception**
2. staggering	**5. hobble**
3. artificial	**6. testify**

2. Line 1. Everybody, what words? (Signal.) *In debt.*
• (Repeat this procedure for every word in the column.)
3. (Repeat the column until firm.)

Vocabulary Definitions

1. Everybody, find part B. ✔
• These are definitions for the words you just read.

2. (For each word, call on a student to read the definition and the item. Then ask the student to complete the item.)

1. **in debt**—When somebody is *in debt,* that person owes money. If John owes money, John is *in debt.*
• What's another way of saying *Mary owes money*?
• What's the answer? (Response: *Mary is in debt.*)

2. **staggering**—When something is *staggering,* it is astonishing. An astonishing number of people is a *staggering* number of people.
• What's another way of saying *an astonishing home run*?
• What's the answer? (Response: *A staggering home run.*)

3. **artificial**—When something is *artificial,* it is made by people, not nature. A flower made by people is an *artificial* flower.
• What is a leg made by people?
• What's the answer? (Response: *An artificial leg.*)

4. **deception**—*Deception* is another word for trickery.
• What's another way of saying *The magician used trickery to fool the children*?
• What's the answer? (Response: *The magician used deception to fool the children.*)

5. **hobble**—When you *hobble,* you walk with a limp.
• What's another way of saying *She walked with a limp across the room*?
• What's the answer? (Response: *She hobbled across the room.*)

6. **testify**—When you *testify,* you make a statement about something you have observed, such as an accident. People often testify in court.
   • What's another way of saying *The witness made a statement about the robbery to the judge?*
   • What's the answer? (Response: *The witness testified about the robbery to the judge.*)

EXERCISE 4
Following Directions

1. Everybody, turn to part D at the end of today's story. ✔
   • (Call on individual students to read several sentences each.)
   • (At the end of each section, present the questions for that section.)

Use the facts to complete the items.
   Facts: Your name is Kathy Tanaka, and you would like to be a camp counselor. You live in Houston, Texas. You have worked as a lifeguard, and you know how to ride horses. You have just graduated from Bowie High School. You can speak both Spanish and English.
1. Name (last name first).

   • What's the answer? (Response: *Tanaka, Kathy.*)

2. State highest grade completed:

   • What's the answer? (Idea: *Twelfth grade.*)

3. What job would you like to have?

   • What's the answer? (Idea: *Camp counselor.*)

4. What languages do you speak?

   • What's the answer? (Idea: *English and Spanish.*)

5. What special qualifications, if any, do you have for the job you want?

   • What's the answer? (Ideas: *Worked as a lifeguard; can ride horses.*)
   • You'll write the answers later.

READING

EXERCISE 5
Focus Question

1. Everybody, turn back to part C. ✔
2. What's the focus question for today's lesson? (Response: *What were Harriet Tubman's main accomplishments?*)

EXERCISE 6
Reading Aloud (Optional)

1. We're going to read aloud to the diamond.
   • (Call on individual students to read several sentences each.)

Harriet Tubman
Part 7
Focus Question: What were Harriet Tubman's main accomplishments?

   The war raged on, and soldiers on both sides continued to die in staggering numbers. But for me, the war was over. In fact, most of my life seemed to be over. I was an old man at the age of twenty-five. I had a wooden leg and a pair of crutches. My dreams and my future were dark.

   After returning to Syracuse, I didn't work for several months. I sat around the house staring and thinking. Elizabeth earned money by sewing and washing clothes.

   Things changed that spring. Harriet's parents lived in a nearby town, and once a week, Elizabeth visited them. Everybody tried to help them while Harriet continued her work with the United States Army. Every time Elizabeth visited Harriet's parents, she invited me to go with her, and every time I mumbled the same answer. I didn't feel like going out.

One evening after Elizabeth had visited Harriet's parents, the front door swung open. There was Harriet, carrying an armful of fresh pine boards. With that familiar twinkle in her eyes, she told me she needed shelves for her parents' house. She said, "I need you to make the shelves. I've even brought you the wood."

I told her I couldn't work anymore because I had only one leg.

She replied, "A cabinetmaker works with his hands, not with his legs."

Without saying another word, she walked outside and left me with a pile of boards in the middle of the floor.

I stared at those boards for a long time. Harriet's words kept running through my head—"A cabinetmaker works with his hands, not with his legs."

After a while, I felt a little foolish. She was right, of course. My life wasn't over, and I could be as good at cabinetmaking as I had ever been before my injury.

Once I decided to make the shelves, my life changed greatly. I took out my old tools. Then I went outside for the first time since I'd been back home. I purchased nails and glue. I had to build a stool because I couldn't stand for long periods of time on my wooden leg.

Before I had completed the shelves, three people came to the shop and ordered cabinetwork. Within two days, I was back in business, and I felt happy and useful. I realized how stupid I had been for pitying myself. I was still a good cabinetmaker, and there was no reason I couldn't become even better.

When I completed the shelves, I took them to Harriet's parents. I looked around the inside of the house to see where they would fit best. Suddenly, I realized that Harriet had deceived me. There were plenty of shelves inside the house. Harriet hadn't ordered the shelves because her parents needed them. She had ordered them because *I* needed them. ♦

EXERCISE 7
Silent Reading

1. Read the rest of the lesson to yourselves and be ready to answer some questions.

The next time I visited Harriet's parents, I witnessed a terrible sight. Harriet was having a long sleeping fit. Her mother told me that Harriet had been sleeping for three days without waking. She looked thin and frail, and I feared she would die.

A while later, Harriet finally woke up, but she was quite weak. She stayed with her parents for several months as the Civil War continued to rage.

The war was nearly over when Harriet was well enough to rejoin the army. Before she left, she stopped at my cabinet shop to see how I was doing. I thanked her for tricking me into becoming a useful person again.

Harriet smiled and reminded me that she was quite good at deception. She said, "A lot of white men lost their slaves because they thought a little black woman who had sleeping fits couldn't be smart enough to work on the Underground Railroad."

Harriet's last mission during the war was in Virginia, where she worked as a nurse until the Confederacy surrendered in 1865. The war was finally over, and the slaves were free at last. That was worth celebrating.

Harriet had worked as a soldier during the war. She had spied; she had led raiding parties; she had fought in furious battles; she had convinced slaves to leave their plantations; and she had worked as an army nurse. Her great job was completed, but her troubles were not over.

When Harriet returned to Auburn, New York, in 1865, she was treated as a hero. But she had no money. She had never been paid one cent for her efforts during the war, and she was now deep in debt.

A woman named Sarah Bradford helped Harriet earn money. Sarah helped Harriet write a book about her adventures. The book made a fair amount of money, and Sarah gave every cent to Harriet. But the government still refused to pay Harriet for her services.

A lot of people testified that Harriet deserved the money. A general from the North wrote, "She made many a raid inside the enemy lines, displaying remarkable courage." A doctor who worked in a hospital in South Carolina praised her for her "kindness and attention to the sick and suffering." Others told about the unselfish deeds Harriet had done. But the government still refused to pay her. ★

Harriet married Nelson Davis in 1867. He had been a soldier in South Carolina, and Harriet had met him when she was conducting raiding parties during the war. The wedding was a joyous event, and they were happily married for eighteen years until his death.

Harriet finally received money from the government because Nelson had been a soldier. However, she was never paid for her own services.

Harriet's parents also died, but Harriet continued to work as only she could. She tried to raise money for a hospital that would care for old people. She made speeches around the country about why women should be able to vote. (Back then, only men could vote.) She worked year after year, until 1913.

I remember that year very well. At the time, I was seventy-seven years old, but I had not retired. I continued to work as a cabinetmaker. My business was prospering, and I had two men working for me.

Harriet was more than ninety years old in 1913. She was confined to a wheelchair, but she still had that twinkle in her eyes. The twinkle came out brightest when she retold her adventures. People from all over the world came to visit her and to hear those incredible tales of long ago.

One sunny afternoon, Elizabeth walked into the cabinet shop and told me that Harriet was dying. I tossed my tools aside and hobbled out to the wagon. It was almost dark when we arrived at Harriet's house. By then, she was dead.

Elizabeth ran into the house, but I didn't move—not for a long time. In the gathering darkness, I saw flashes of myself as a frightened sixteen-year-old boy looking down the barrel of the pistol that Moses held. I saw Moses sitting on the train as she pretended to read. I saw Moses in Troy, New York, saving Joe Nalle. I saw Moses in the hospital in South Carolina. I saw Moses holding a pile of boards and tricking me into making shelves for her parents' house.

Many months later, I was able to express what I thought about Harriet's life. Harriet Tubman always did what she knew

was right, no matter how difficult, no matter what the danger, and no matter what anyone else told her to do. She was born a slave, but she lived like a free person all her life.

- What were Harriet Tubman's main accomplishments? (Ideas: *Working as a conductor on the Underground Railroad; freeing hundreds of slaves; helping the Union army during the Civil War; working as a nurse; writing a book about her life.*) (Sum)
- Harriet told Jim, "A cabinetmaker works with his hands, not with his legs." Explain what she meant. (Idea: *Jim could still make cabinets even though he'd lost his leg.*) (UCCM)
- Why did Harriet deceive Jim about the shelves? (Idea: *She wanted him to start working again.*) (DCE)
- Why do you think the government refused to pay Harriet for her help during the Civil War? (Ideas: *She was black; she was a woman; they wanted to save money.*) (MJ)
- Jim said, "Harriet Tubman always did what she knew was right." Give an example of a belief Harriet knew was right. Then explain how she acted on that belief. (Ideas: *Harriet believed that people should be free, so she worked to free the slaves; Harriet believed the Union should win the war, so she worked for the Union army; Harriet believed people should be cared for, so she worked as a nurse.*) (R)

EXERCISE 8

Discussion

1. (Lead students in a general discussion of the problems involved in "doing the right thing." Use the following questions as a guide.)
- Harriet Tubman believed that slavery was wrong. How did she act on her belief? (Ideas: *She helped slaves escape; she made raids on plantations; she helped the Union army.*)
- When she helped slaves escape, Harriet was breaking the law. Do you think it was right for her to break the law? Explain your answer. (Ideas: *Yes, because the law was wrong; yes, because people shouldn't be slaves; no, because people should always follow the law.*)

- Do you think the law is always right? Use an example to explain your answer. (Ideas: *No, because people often make bad laws, such as permitting slavery and denying women the right to vote; yes, because the law says that murder and robbery are crimes.*)
- What would happen if people disobeyed certain laws? (Ideas: *The laws might get changed; there would be a lot of crime; society wouldn't have order.*)
- Do you think it's right to disobey laws you don't agree with? Explain your answer. (Ideas: *Yes, because some laws are wrong; no, because we should always obey the law.*)

EXERCISE 9
Paired Practice (Optional)

1. Now you'll read in pairs.
- Whoever read second the last time will read first today.
- Remember to start at the diamond and switch at the star.
2. (Observe students and answer questions as needed.)

AFTER READING

EXERCISE 10
Independent Work

1. Do all the items in your workbook and textbook for this lesson.
2. (The independent work in this lesson includes the following activities.)
- Story details
- Combined sentences
- Character traits
- Outlining
- Following directions
- Vocabulary review
- Comprehension
- Writing

EXERCISE 11
Workcheck

1. (Using the Answer Key, read the questions and answers for the workbook.)
2. (Have students read their answers for the textbook activities.)
3. (Have two or three students read their writing assignments aloud. Comment on each assignment.)
4. (Have students correct and turn in their work.)

SPELLING

(Present Spelling lesson 82 after completing Reading lesson 82. *See Spelling Presentation Book.*)

LESSON 83

BEFORE READING

(Have students find lesson 83, part A, in their textbooks.)

Hard Words

1. Look at column 1.
- These are hard words from your textbook stories.

> 1. inflection   4. unanimously
> 2. dumbfounded   5. initials
> 3. majority

2. Word 1 is **inflection.** Everybody, what word? (Signal.) *Inflection.*
- (Repeat this procedure for every word in the column.)
3. Let's read the words again.
4. Word 1. Everybody, what word? (Signal.) *Inflection.*
- (Repeat this procedure for every word in the column.)
5. (Repeat the column until firm.)

EXERCISE 2

New Vocabulary

1. Look at column 2.
- First we'll read the words in this column. Then we'll read their definitions.

> 1. rising inflection   5. unanimous
> 2. at rise   6. dumbfounded
> 3. beforehand   7. initials
> 4. majority

2. Line 1. Everybody, what words? (Signal.) *Rising inflection.*
- (Repeat this procedure for every word in the column.)
3. (Repeat the column until firm.)

EXERCISE 3

Vocabulary Definitions

1. Everybody, find part B. ✔
- These are definitions for the words you just read.
2. (For each word, call on a student to read the definition and the item. Then ask the student to complete the item.)

1. **rising inflection**—When people use a *rising inflection,* they say certain words louder or higher in pitch than normal. People almost always use a rising inflection for questions.
- Say this question with a rising inflection: *Can you believe that?*

- What's the answer? (Response: *Student should read Can you believe that? with a rising inflection.*)

2. **at rise**—*At rise* is an instruction in a play. *At rise* means "This is what's happening on stage as the curtain rises."
- What does *at rise* mean?

- What's the answer? (Idea: *This is what's happening on stage as the curtain rises.*)

3. **beforehand**—When something happens *beforehand,* it happens before another event.
- If a woman took out her wallet and then paid a bill, which of those two things did she do beforehand?

- What's the answer? (Response: *Took out her wallet.*)

4. **majority**—The *majority* of a group is more than half the group.
- If there are five people in a group, what's the smallest number needed to form a majority?

- What's the answer? (Response: *Three.*)

5. **unanimous**—When a vote is *unanimous,* all the votes are the same.
- If there are seven people in a group, how many votes are needed for a unanimous vote?

- What's the answer? (Response: *Seven.*)

6. **dumbfounded**—When you are *dumbfounded,* you are briefly astonished by something.
- What's another way of saying *She was briefly astonished by his rude remark*?

- What's the answer? (Response: *She was dumbfounded by his rude remark.*)

7. **initials**—Your *initials* are the first letter of your first name and the first letter of your last name.
- If your name is Joan Armstrong, what are your initials?

- What's the answer? (Response: *J.A.*)

READING

EXERCISE 4

Focus Question

1. Everybody, find part C. ✔
2. What's the focus question for today's lesson? (Response: *What did Nancy have to get before she could join the club?*)

EXERCISE 5

Reading Drama

1. Today's selection is a play. We're going to read the play out loud over the next three lessons.
- After we complete the reading, we may decide to put on the play as a class project.
2. What's the title of the play? (Response: *All in Favor.*) (NE)
- Who's the author? (Response: *Morton K. Schwartz.*) (NE)
3. Now we'll read the instructions for the play.
- (Call on individual students to read one instruction each.)

All in Favor
by Morton K. Schwartz
Part 1
Focus Question: What did Nancy have to get before she could join the club?

Characters
EDDIE
NANCY
SIDNEY
HARRIET
TOM
DOROTHY
ALVIN

TIME: *A summer afternoon.*

SETTING: *A backyard, just outside a shack—the Aces' clubhouse.*

AT RISE: NANCY, *a neatly-dressed girl of about 13, is patiently leaning against the wall of the shack, next to the door. Presently* EDDIE, *a little boy of about 10, comes walking on.*

- Who are the characters in the play? (Response: *Eddie, Nancy, Sidney, Harriet, Tom, Dorothy, and Alvin.*) (SS)
- When does the play take place? (Idea: *During a summer afternoon.*) (SS)
- Where does the play take place? (Idea: *In a backyard, just outside a shack.*) (SS)
- What is the purpose of the shack? (Idea: *It's the Aces' clubhouse.*) (MI)
- What is Nancy doing when the curtain rises? (Idea: *Leaning against the wall of the shack.*) (Seq)
- What does Eddie do? (Idea: *Walks on stage.*) (Seq)
4. The rest of this selection is the play.
- At the beginning of each speech is the name of the character who makes that speech.
- Who's the first character to speak in the play? (Response: *Eddie.*) (SS)
- What does Eddie say? (Response: *Hello, Nancy.*) (SS)
5. Now we'll read the play.
- (Assign one student to be Eddie, another to be Nancy, and so on. Periodically reassign roles during the reading.)
- When you are reading aloud, don't say the name at the beginning of the speech. Just say your character's lines.

- Also, don't say any words in parentheses. Those words are instructions that tell what the character does. We'll use the instructions when we perform the play.
- Let's begin.

EDDIE: Hello, Nancy.

NANCY: Hello.

EDDIE: What are you doing?

NANCY: Can't you see? I'm standing here waiting. *(She is annoyed.)*

EDDIE: Oh. *(He moves next to NANCY, and leans on the wall the way she is doing.)* What are you waiting for?

NANCY: We're having a meeting.

EDDIE: Who's having a meeting?

NANCY: We . . . our club.

EDDIE: What club?

NANCY: The Aces.

EDDIE: How soon does it begin?

NANCY *(Annoyed)*: Why don't you stop bothering me, Eddie? You have your own friends to play with.

EDDIE: I can't find any of them.

NANCY: Then play ball or something. I'm busy.

EDDIE: You won't be busy till the meeting begins, will you?

NANCY: It's going on right now.

EDDIE: Where?

NANCY: In the clubhouse, of course. *(She motions back to it.)*

EDDIE: Well, if the meeting is going on in the clubhouse, how come you're out here?

NANCY: Because this is my first meeting, and I have to be elected to the club. Now stop asking questions.

EDDIE: Then you're not in the club yet?

NANCY: I told you to stop asking questions!

EDDIE: That wasn't a question. I just said "then you're not in the club yet."

NANCY: Well, you said it with a rising inflection, and that makes it a question.

EDDIE: What's a rising inflection?

NANCY: It's a rising tone in your voice when you ask a question—and anyway I said I won't answer any more questions, so I won't tell you.

EDDIE: All right then, I'll just say it plain— you're not in the club yet.

NANCY: That's right. But I will be in it in about five minutes, because they're electing me right now.

EDDIE: Maybe they won't let you in.

NANCY: Don't be silly. Of course they will.

EDDIE: I don't see how you can tell beforehand.

NANCY: I only need a majority to vote for me. There are only five kids in the club, so all I need is three votes.

EDDIE: Maybe you won't get three.

NANCY: Of course I will. Why, three of the kids are my best friends. There's Harriet, Sidney, and Tom. They'll all vote for me, I'm certain. That makes a majority without even counting the other two.

EDDIE: Then I guess you'll get in. Can I join the club?

NANCY *(Impatiently)*: Of course not!

EDDIE: Why not?

NANCY: You're too young. And you have different friends.

EDDIE: I know Harriet, and Sidney and Tom. . . and you. You'll vote for me, won't you?

NANCY: Well . . . yes, I would vote for you. But you wouldn't be elected anyway, because the others wouldn't.

EDDIE: I think I would. When you get inside, tell them that I want to join. *(There is the sound of movement inside the clubroom. NANCY stands and straightens her shirt. In a few moments, SIDNEY opens the door, steps out, and closes the door behind him. SIDNEY is about the same age as NANCY.)*

NANCY: Hello, Sidney. Is the voting done yet?

SIDNEY *(Hesitantly)*: Er . . . yes, Nancy . . . yes, it's done.

NANCY: Let's go inside then. *(She starts in.)*

EDDIE: Don't forget I want to join, Nancy.

SIDNEY *(Keeping NANCY back)*: Er . . . wait a second, Nancy. There's er . . . something I want to talk to you about.

NANCY *(Wonderingly)*: Why . . . what is it, Sidney?

SIDNEY: Well, er . . . it's about, er . . .

NANCY *(Noticing that EDDIE is listening)*: Go away, Eddie! (EDDIE *doesn't move.*) Eddie! I said go away! Sidney has something to tell me. It might be some secret rules of the club or something, and you're not supposed to hear. (EDDIE *moves a step or two away, but remains in earshot.*)

SIDNEY: Er . . . no, Nancy . . . it isn't about the rules.

NANCY: What is it then?

SIDNEY: It's about the vote. I have to explain . . .

NANCY: Isn't the vote done? Do you have to vote again?

SIDNEY: Yes, yes . . . it's done. I want to explain the way it came out. You see . . . er . . .

NANCY *(Joyfully)*: Was I elected unanimously?

SIDNEY: Er, no . . . no, Nancy . . . not exactly. That is . . . you weren't elected.

NANCY: Unanimously?

SIDNEY: No, no . . . you weren't elected . . . er . . . at all. (NANCY *is dumbfounded.*) What I mean to say is that . . . you, er . . . didn't get in.

EXERCISE 6

Comprehension

1. Now let's discuss the play.
- What did Nancy have to get before she could join the club? (Idea: *A majority of the votes.*) (C/E)

- Why do you think Nancy was annoyed when Eddie started talking to her? (Ideas: *She thinks he's a pest; she thinks he's too young.*) (MJ)
- Why was Nancy certain she'd get into the club? (Idea: *She was friends with three of the members, and she only needed three votes.*) (DCE)
- Nancy thought Eddie wouldn't be elected to the club. Explain why not. (Ideas: *He was too young; he had different friends.*) (DCE)
- Why do you think Nancy didn't get into the club? (Ideas: *One of her friends didn't vote for her; the other kids convinced Nancy's friends to vote against her; there was a mistake in the counting.*) (MJ)

EXERCISE 7

Small-Group Practice (Optional)

1. Now you'll read in groups of three.
- There are three characters in part 1 of the play, so each one of you will play a character.
- Decide who will play each character; then read all of part 1.
2. (Observe students and answer questions as needed.)

AFTER READING

EXERCISE 8

Independent Work

1. Do all the items in your workbook and textbook for this lesson.
2. (The independent work in this lesson includes the following activities.)
- Story details
- Vocabulary
- Character traits
- Combined sentences
- Following directions
- Vocabulary review
- Outlining
- Comprehension
- Writing

Workcheck

1. (Using the Answer Key, read the questions and answers for the workbook.)
2. (Have students read their answers for the textbook activities.)
3. (Have two or three students read their writing assignments aloud. Comment on each assignment.)
4. (Have students correct and turn in their work.)

(Present Spelling lesson 83 after completing Reading lesson 83. *See Spelling Presentation Book.*)

BEFORE READING

(Have students find lesson 84, part A, in their textbooks.)

Hard Words

1. Look at column 1.
- These are hard words from your textbook stories.

1. astound	4. gavel
2. sulkily	5. succinct
3. treasurer	

2. Word 1 is **astound.** Everybody, what word? (Signal.) *Astound.*
- (Repeat this procedure for every word in the column.)
3. Let's read the words again.
4. Word 1. Everybody, what word? (Signal.) *Astound.*
- (Repeat this procedure for every word in the column.)
5. (Repeat the column until firm.)

Word Practice

1. Look at column 2.
- We're going to practice these words.

1. pronounce	3. hasty
2. pronouncing	4. hastily

2. Word 1. Everybody, what word? (Signal.) *Pronounce.*
- (Repeat this procedure for every word in the column.)
3. (Repeat the column until firm.)

New Vocabulary

1. Look at column 3.
- First we'll read the words in this column. Then we'll read their definitions.

1. shy	4. dryly
2. exception	5. astound
3. sulk	6. gavel

2. Word 1. Everybody, what word? (Signal.) *Shy.*
- (Repeat this procedure for every word in the column.)
3. (Repeat the column until firm.)

Vocabulary Definitions

1. Everybody, find part B. ✔
- These are definitions for the words you just read.
2. (For each word, call on a student to read the definition and the item. Then ask the student to complete the item.)

1. **shy**—One meaning of *shy* is "short." If a person is an inch short of five feet tall, the person is an inch shy of five feet tall.
- What's another way of saying *one vote short of a majority*?

- What's the answer? (Response: *One vote shy of a majority.*)

2. **exception**—When you make an *exception,* you break the rules for a special case. If you break the rules for Henry's case, you make an exception for Henry.
- What's another way of saying *The teacher broke the rules for the student who was sick*?

- What's the answer? (Response: *The teacher made an exception for the student who was sick.*)

3. **sulk**—When people *sulk*, they are moody and quiet. They behave *sulkily.*
- What do people do when they sulk?

- What's the answer? (Ideas: *They are moody and quiet; they behave sulkily.*)

4. **dryly**—When you speak *dryly*, you speak without enthusiasm.
   - What's another way of saying *She congratulated the winner without enthusiasm*?

   - What's the answer? (Response: *She congratulated the winner dryly.*)

5. **astound**—*Astound* is another word for amaze.
   - What's another way of saying *Her performance amazed me*?

   - What's the answer? (Response: *Her performance astounded me.*)

6. **gavel**—A *gavel* is a wooden hammer used by people who lead meetings. The person pounds the gavel on a table to control the meeting.
   - What is a gavel?

   - What's the answer? (Idea: *A wooden hammer used by people who lead meetings.*)

READING

EXERCISE 5

Reading Drama

1. Everybody, find part C. ✔
   - What's the focus question for today's lesson? (Response: *How did Nancy's friends seem to feel about the vote?*)
2. We're going to read this lesson aloud.
   - (Assign roles to students. Periodically reassign roles during the reading.)

All in Favor
Part 2

Focus Question: How did Nancy's friends seem to feel about the vote?

NANCY *(Astounded)*: Didn't get in!

SIDNEY: No, no . . . you, er . . . you see, you didn't receive a majority of the votes.

NANCY: B-but . . . th-that's impossible! You . . . y-you must have counted them incorrectly . . . or gotten them mixed up or something! It's . . . it's impossible!

SIDNEY: We counted them a few times. That's the way it came out.

NANCY: B-but . . . I only needed three votes to get in, isn't that right?

SIDNEY: Yes, that's right. I guess you . . . er . . . you didn't get the three, that's all. *(Hastily)* Of course I voted for you; you know that. I tried to get you in. I spoke for you and everything . . . but, well . . . the others, I guess.

NANCY: B-but . . . how many votes did I get?

SIDNEY *(Quickly)*: Oh, you almost made it. You were barely one vote shy, that's all. Only one vote. You needed three and you got . . . er . . . two . . . just one short, that's all.

NANCY *(A catch in her voice)*: C-couldn't you do something . . . make an exception or . . .?

SIDNEY: We'd like to, Nancy, honestly. But you know how those things are. It would be all right with me, of course . . . but the others . . . you know how it is.

NANCY *(Near tears)*: Well . . . well . . .

SIDNEY: I'm really sorry, Nancy, honestly. Well . . . have to, er, get back inside . . . meeting going on. See you later, Nancy. *(He starts for the clubhouse door.)*

NANCY *(Barely keeping back her tears)*: Sidney . . .

SIDNEY: Yes, Nancy? Glad to do anything for you.

NANCY: C-could you ask Harriet to come out?

SIDNEY: I'll try, Nancy . . . but the meeting is going on . . . I'll tell her, and she'll probably be able to come out in a few minutes, if you want to wait.

NANCY: All right. Tell her to try to make it as soon as she can. And . . . thanks for voting for me and everything.

SIDNEY: Oh, er . . . sure, Nancy. I certainly wanted you in the club. *(He exits into the clubhouse. A moment or two later, NANCY bursts into tears, and covers her mouth and nose with a handkerchief as she cries.)*

EDDIE (After a while): I told you.

NANCY (Sobbing): Go away.

EDDIE: Now you're not going to the meeting.

NANCY: Go away.

EDDIE: Do you want to play ball with me?

NANCY (Still sobbing): No.

EDDIE: Do you think I'll be elected to the club now?

NANCY (Sobbing and angry): No!

EDDIE: I guess they won't even vote for me. (Pauses) Are you going to try to get in again next week?

NANCY: No.

EDDIE: The week after?

NANCY: No. (Wipes tears from her eyes with handkerchief. After a few moments' silence, the door to the clubhouse opens, and HARRIET slips out—and shuts the door again.) Harriet!

HARRIET: I'm . . . I'm awfully sorry, Nancy. Sidney told you what happened, didn't he?

NANCY: Y-yes . . . b-b-but . . .

HARRIET: You just missed by one vote. Of course I voted for you. You know that.

NANCY: Yes, Harriet . . . b-b-but . . .

HARRIET: It was the others, I guess . . .

NANCY: It couldn't have been a mistake . . .?

HARRIET: I, er . . . I thought it was at first . . . and we recounted the votes. But it was correct the first time . . . you only had two votes. I really thought you were going to get many more than that, but . . . well, I don't know what happened. Of course . . . you know we only have a small clubhouse and everything . . . and maybe some of the members figured . . . well, you know. (NANCY sobs and cries) You . . . er, you don't feel bad, do you?

NANCY (Through tears): N-no. I d-don't mind.

HARRIET: We're having a party at my house this Saturday, and . . .

NANCY: Y-your house?

HARRIET (Hastily): Well . . . I'm not giving it myself . . . it's the club. And only the members can come . . .

NANCY: Oh. (More tears)

HARRIET: Er . . . how about . . . er . . . how about going to the movies with me later today?

NANCY: N-no thanks. I'm going home.

HARRIET: All right. Well, I better get back to the meeting. See you later, Nancy. (She exits into the clubhouse.)

EDDIE (After a pause): Nancy . . . (She doesn't answer.) Nancy . . .

NANCY (After a little while): What? (She wipes tears from her eyes.)

EDDIE: Why don't we start a club?

NANCY: I don't want to be in any club. I never want to be in one.

EDDIE: You felt just the opposite five minutes ago.

NANCY: I changed my mind.

EDDIE (After a silence): How do you start a club?

NANCY: Oh . . . I don't know exactly. You get a few people together and start one.

EDDIE: How many people?

NANCY: I don't know. (Sobbing) Can't you stop asking me silly questions?

EDDIE: Is three enough?

NANCY: I suppose. There's no exact amount.

EDDIE: Is two enough?

NANCY (Impatiently): Any amount is enough!

EDDIE: How about one?

NANCY: Let me alone.

EDDIE: I guess one is enough too, then. I guess I could start a club myself.

NANCY: Do anything you please.

EDDIE (After thinking for a few moments): I'm starting a club. Do you want to be in it, Nancy?

NANCY: No.

EDDIE: Well, I'm in it. That makes one. Let's see . . . I guess I'm president.

NANCY: Go away.

EDDIE: Does the president decide when there are going to be meetings? (*No answer*) Nancy . . . does the president . . .

NANCY (*Angrily*): Yes, yes! Can't you be still? (*Sobs a bit.*)

EDDIE: Well, let's see . . . (*Ponders*) I think I'll have a meeting. (*Thinks another moment.*) Nancy, you'll have to go away. Only members can attend meetings.

NANCY: Go away yourself. (EDDIE *thinks again, and then moves a few steps away and sits down, to start his "meeting." After a short silence, the clubroom door opens again, and* TOM *emerges, shutting the door after him.*)

TOM: Hello, Nancy.

NANCY: Hello.

TOM: Did they tell you what happened?

NANCY (*Sulkily*): Yes.

TOM: It's really a shame. Of course, *I* voted for you. I thought you would surely be elected.

NANCY: Thanks, Tom.

TOM: You only missed by one vote, you know. I thought maybe we could make an exception, but you know how clubs are . . .

NANCY (*Sobs*): Yes.

TOM: We're having a picnic Sunday . . . would you like to . . . er . . .

NANCY: No.

TOM: Well, all right. They probably wouldn't want anyone who wasn't a member to come along anyway. Well . . . (*Awkwardly*) I'll . . . I'll see you later. Have to get back to the meeting . . . (*He goes back into the clubhouse.*)

EDDIE (*Getting up and coming over to* NANCY *after a pause*): Nancy . . . I have good news for you. (*No answer*) You were just elected to my club.

NANCY: I don't want to be in your club.

EDDIE: You have to be. You were elected. (*No answer*) You were barely elected by one vote. But it was a majority, and you're a member.

NANCY (*Dryly*): That's good.

Comprehension

1. Now let's discuss the play.
- How did Nancy's friends seem to feel about the vote? (Ideas: *They were sorry she lost the vote; they all said they voted for her.*) (DCE)
- Sidney, Harriet, and Tom said they voted for Nancy. Why couldn't that be true? (Idea: *If all three had voted for her, she would have received three votes, not two.*) (MD)
- Which character do you think is lying to Nancy? Explain your answer. (Ideas: *Sidney, because he spoke hastily; Harriet, because she didn't want Nancy to come to the party; Tom, because he didn't want Nancy to come to the picnic; all three, because each acted suspiciously.*) (MJ)
- Do you think Nancy should join Eddie's club? Explain your answer. (Ideas: *Yes, because she can't get into the Aces; no, because Eddie's too young.*) (MJ)
- How do you think Nancy could find out what really happened during the vote? (Ideas: *Talk to the other two members of the club; talk to Sidney, Tom, and Harriet in private; peek inside the clubhouse.*) (MJ)

Small-Group Practice (Optional)

1. Now you'll read in groups of five.
- There are five characters in part 2, so each one of you will play a character.
- Decide who will play each character, then read all of part 2.

2. (Observe students and answer questions as needed.)

AFTER READING

Independent Work

1. Do all the items in your workbook and textbook for this lesson.
2. (The independent work in this lesson includes the following activities.)

- Story details
- Vocabulary
- Following directions
- Similes
- Vocabulary review
- Outlining
- Comprehension
- Writing

Workcheck

1. (Using the Answer Key, read the questions and answers for the workbook.)
2. (Have students read their answers for the textbook activities.)
3. (Have two or three students read their writing assignments aloud. Comment on each assignment.)
4. (Have students correct and turn in their work.)

(Present Spelling lesson 84 after completing Reading lesson 84. *See Spelling Presentation Book.*)

LESSON 85

BEFORE READING

(Have students find lesson 85, part A, in their textbooks.)

EXERCISE 1

Word Practice

1. Look at column 1.
- We're going to practice these words.

1. Syracuse	4. pronouncing
2. treasurer	5. scrapping
3. succinct	6. scraping

2. Word 1. Everybody, what word? (Signal.) *Syracuse.*
- (Repeat this procedure for every word in the column.)
3. (Repeat the column until firm.)

EXERCISE 2

Vocabulary Review

1. Everybody, find part B. ✔
- We're going to review these words.
2. (Call on a student to read the words in the box.)

astound	reap
dumbfounded	gavel
unanimous	dryly
majority	

3. (For each item, have a student read the item and say the answer.)

1. When you speak without enthusiasm, you speak ▮▮▮▮▮.

- What's the answer? (Response: *Dryly.*)

2. Another word for *amaze* is ▮▮▮▮▮.

- What's the answer? (Response: *Astound.*)

3. A wooden hammer is a ▮▮▮▮▮.

- What's the answer? (Response: *Gavel.*)

4. More than half of a group is the ▮▮▮▮▮ of the group.

- What's the answer? (Response: *Majority.*)

EXERCISE 3

Reference Books

1. Everybody, turn to part D at the end of today's story. ✔
- (Call on individual students to read several sentences each.)
- (At the end of each section, present the questions for that section.)

Write the answers for items 1–6.
There are several kinds of reference books you can use to find information:
- A **dictionary** gives facts about words. It shows how to spell a word and how to pronounce it. It tells what part of speech a word is and what the word means. A dictionary also tells the history of words.
- An **atlas** gives facts about places. It contains maps of states, countries, and continents. It shows the distance from one place to another. It tells how many people live in each place.
- An **encyclopedia** gives facts about nearly everything. It tells about plants, planets, animals, agriculture, history, and famous people, among many other topics.

Which would be the best reference book for the following questions? Choose **dictionary, atlas,** or **encyclopedia.**
1. How do you spell the word *doughnut*?

- What's the answer? (Response: *Dictionary.*)

2. How far is it from Denver to Kansas City?

- What's the answer? (Response: *Atlas.*)

3. What were the main events in Duke Ellington's life?

- What's the answer? (Response: *Encyclopedia.*)

4. When did the Civil War take place?

- What's the answer? (Response: *Encyclopedia.*)

5. How many people live in Mexico City?

- What's the answer? (Response: *Atlas.*)

6. How do you pronounce the word *succinct*?

- What's the answer? (Response: *Dictionary.*)
- You'll write the answers later.

READING

Reading Drama

1. Everybody, turn back to part C. ✔
- What's the focus question for today's lesson? (Response: *Why did some of the characters lie to Nancy?*)
2. We're going to read this lesson aloud.
- (Assign roles to students. Periodically reassign roles during the reading.)

All in Favor

Part 3

Focus Question: Why did some of the characters lie to Nancy?

EDDIE: And you got in unan . . . unanimous . . . ly . . . (*He has trouble pronouncing it*) . . . by one vote. (NANCY *says nothing*) Now there are two members in my club. (A pause) Nancy . . .

NANCY: What?

EDDIE: Am I still the president?

NANCY: If you want to be.

EDDIE: All right. You're the vice president. Should we have any treasurer?

NANCY: You don't need a treasurer.

EDDIE: But my father is in a club, and they have a treasurer. My father is the treasurer.

NANCY: You don't need a treasurer unless there's some money.

EDDIE: What's the treasurer's job? To spend the money?

NANCY: He keeps the money. That's what a treasurer is for.

EDDIE: Well, whose money is it?

NANCY: The club's money.

EDDIE: Where are we going to get any money?

NANCY: We're not going to get any.

EDDIE: Do you think we'll need a treasurer then? (*Their conversation is interrupted by noises coming from inside the clubhouse. There is a sound of moving benches, and then a pounding of a gavel. Then* TOM's *voice is heard saying, "Meeting adjourned." There is more scraping of benches, and the door opens and* SIDNEY *emerges. A moment later* HARRIET *and* TOM *step out.*)

SIDNEY (*Seeing* NANCY): Oh hello, Nancy. Are you still here?

NANCY: Yes.

SIDNEY: We . . . er . . . just finished our meeting.

HARRIET: Nancy . . . we decided you can come to the party Saturday night. Er . . . a couple of the other kids won't be able to be there.

NANCY: I . . . I'm not coming.

TOM: But it's all right, Nancy, even if you aren't a member.

NANCY: Thanks, but I can't.

SIDNEY (*To* HARRIET): Never mind, Harriet—we'll have enough.

HARRIET: Well . . .

TOM (*To* HARRIET *and* SIDNEY): Let's go to the drugstore and have a soda.

SIDNEY: All right. Come on.

HARRIET (*To* NANCY): You can come with us if you want to, Nancy.

NANCY: No . . . I have to go home. *(She barely keeps from crying.)*

HARRIET: Well . . . 'bye, Nancy.

NANCY: Goodbye.

TOM and SIDNEY: Goodbye, Nancy. (HARRIET, TOM *and* SIDNEY *exit to one side.*)

EDDIE *(After the three are off)*: If they don't want you in the club, why do they want you to have a soda with them?

NANCY: But they do want me. They're my friends. Harriet, Tom, and Sidney voted for me.

EDDIE: Didn't you only get two votes?

NANCY: Yes . . .

EDDIE: Then how could they all have voted for you? Harriet, Tom and Sidney make three.

NANCY *(Counting on her fingers)*: Harriet . . . Tom . . . Sidney.

EDDIE: See? Three.

NANCY: But . . . but you heard what they said, didn't you? They all wanted me in the club. *(At this point, DOROTHY and ALVIN, the other two club members, are coming out of the door of the clubhouse.)*

DOROTHY: Oh . . . there she is, Alvin.

ALVIN: Hello . . . er . . . what was your name again?

NANCY *(Turning)*: Nancy.

DOROTHY: Oh, that's right. Where do you live?

NANCY: On Jay Street. Near the school.

DOROTHY: Oh.

ALVIN: Are you going to be at the party Saturday night?

NANCY: No. Only club members can attend.

DOROTHY: Well, Alvin and I aren't going.

NANCY: You're not?

ALVIN: No. We had a big argument just before, in the meeting. We didn't like that rule.

NANCY: Oh.

DOROTHY *(To NANCY)*: I'm sorry you didn't get in the club. You seem like a nice girl.

NANCY: I . . . only got two votes.

ALVIN: Don't you have any friends in the club that you know? Don't you know Harriet, or Sidney, or Tom?

NANCY: I know all three of them. They're all my friends.

DOROTHY: All? I don't see how that could be. You only need three votes to get in.

NANCY: Well . . . Harriet said she voted for me. And so did Tom, and so did Sidney. That's three right there. *(She sobs a bit again)* But I only got two.

DOROTHY *(Surprised)*: But I voted for you!

ALVIN: And so did I!

DOROTHY: Even though we never met you before, Alvin and I both thought you seemed like a nice girl, and would be a good member for the club; and we voted for you.

NANCY: B-but . . .

ALVIN: Why, I counted the votes myself. Here . . .! *(He reaches into a pocket)* I crushed them up and put them into my pocket. *(He pulls out the votes and smoothes them open one by one.)* Here's mine . . . see? We put our initials on them. A. H. It says "yes." (NANCY *looks over* ALVIN's *shoulder and nods*.) And here's another "yes."

DOROTHY: That's mine! Those are my initials—D. M.

ALVIN: And these other three are "No's." Tom, Harriet and Sidney wrote those.

NANCY: Then *none* of them voted for me! And they all said they did!

ALVIN: Gosh!

DOROTHY: That was certainly mean of them!

ALVIN *(To DOROTHY)*: You know, Dorothy, I think I'm going to quit the Aces. I'm sorry we started the club with them. We ought to have a club with some other kids, like Nancy.

DOROTHY: That's a good idea. Do you want to start a club with us, Nancy?

NANCY: Why, I guess I . . .

EDDIE (*To* ALVIN *and* DOROTHY): Wait a minute! She can't be in your club!

DOROTHY: Why not?

EDDIE: She's already in one. She's in my club. She was elected at the last meeting!

DOROTHY: Oh.

ALVIN (*Not giving* NANCY *a chance to speak*): Well, why don't we join their club, Dorothy?

DOROTHY: All right. Let's do that.

EDDIE: Wait a minute . . . you can't just "join." We have to elect you at a meeting.

ALVIN: When is your next meeting?

EDDIE: Whenever I decide. I'm the president, you see. Now . . . let me see . . . I think we'll have one right away. Come on, Nancy. (*He pulls* NANCY *into the clubhouse.*)

NANCY: But Eddie!

EDDIE (*Pulling her along*): Hurry up . . . we have to vote. (*He gets her inside and shuts the door.* ALVIN *and* DOROTHY *stand by and look on curiously. In a moment,* NANCY *opens the clubhouse door and pokes her head out.*)

NANCY: You only got two votes.

EDDIE (*Poking his head out beside* NANCY's): You were elected an . . . unan . . . unanimous . . . ly. (*He has the same trouble pronouncing the word.* ALVIN *and* DOROTHY *look at each other, and then happily start into the clubhouse as the curtain falls.*)

THE END

EXERCISE 5

Comprehension

1. Now let's discuss the play.

- Why did some of the characters lie to Nancy? (Ideas: *They weren't really her friends; they didn't want to admit what they'd done.*) (DCE)

- Why did Dorothy and Alvin decide to leave the Aces? (Ideas: *They didn't like Sidney, Harriet, and Tom; they were unhappy with the vote.*) (DCE)

- How did Nancy react when she didn't get into the Aces? (Ideas: *She was unhappy; she cried.*) (DCE)

- How did Eddie react when Nancy told him he wouldn't get into the Aces? (Idea: *He started his own club.*) (DCE)

- What do you think this play says about joining and starting clubs or other groups? (Ideas: *If you can't get into a club, start your own; people act differently when they're in a club than when they're by themselves; clubs look different from the outside than from the inside.*) (MJ)

EXERCISE 6

Performance of Play

1. This play was about voting, so let's vote on performing the play. If a majority votes for doing the play, we'll do it.

- First we have to figure out how many students are in the class. How many? (Accept correct response.)

- We need more than half the students to vote "yes" to have a majority. How many "yes" votes would we need? (Accept correct response.)

- Raise your hand if you vote "yes" for putting on the play. (The students raise their hands.)

- Did we receive a majority? (Accept correct response.)

- (If a majority of the students voted "yes," assign roles and arrange for the production.)

AFTER READING

Independent Work

1. Do all the items in your workbook and textbook for this lesson.
2. (The independent work in this lesson includes the following activities.)
   - Story details
   - Vocabulary
   - Contradictions
   - Character traits
   - Story review
   - Reference books
   - Comprehension
   - Writing

EXERCISE 8

Workcheck

1. (Using the Answer Key, read the questions and answers for the workbook.)
2. (Have students read their answers for the textbook activities.)
3. (Have two or three students read their writing assignments aloud. Comment on each assignment.)
4. (Have students correct and turn in their work.)

SPELLING

(Present Spelling lesson 85 after completing Reading lesson 85. See *Spelling Presentation Book.*)

ACTIVITIES ACROSS THE CURRICULUM

(Students should complete the appropriate project in *Activities across the Curriculum* after completing lesson 85. See *Activities across the Curriculum* book for details.)

Lessons 86–90 • Planning Page

Looking Ahead

	Lesson 86	**Lesson 87**	**Lesson 88**	**Lesson 89**	**Lesson 90**
BEFORE READING	Hard words New vocabulary Vocabulary definitions Vocabulary review Reference books	Hard words New vocabulary Vocabulary definitions Vocabulary review Maps	Hard words New vocabulary Vocabulary definitions Vocabulary review Irony	Hard words New vocabulary Vocabulary definitions Vocabulary review Irony	Hard words New vocabulary Vocabulary definitions Vocabulary review Irony
NEW VOCABULARY	cubic inch forenoon	corridor landing tradition	rigid ambush legend	dwindle bulky plush settler	supernatural systematically endure junction
READING	"Miracles"	"Life in the 1840s" Part 1	"Life in the 1840s" Part 2	"Life in the 1840s" Part 3	"Life in the 1840s" Part 4
INDEPENDENT WORK	Vocabulary Story review Combined sentences Poem review Reference books Inference Writing	Story details Vocabulary Reference books Following directions Settings Maps Comprehension Writing	Story details Reference books Exaggeration Maps Sarcasm Story review Irony Comprehension Writing	Story details Vocabulary Character traits Maps Descriptions Irony Reference books Comprehension Writing	Story details Vocabulary Maps Irony Reference books Comprehension Writing
SUPPLEMENTS	*Spelling*	*Spelling*	*Spelling*	*Spelling*	Mastery Test *Spelling* *Activities across the Curriculum*

Comprehension Questions Abbreviations Guide

Access Prior Knowledge = (APK)   Author's Point of View = (APoV)   Author's Purpose = (AP)   Cause/Effect = (C/E)   Charts/Graphs/Diagrams/Visual Aids = (VA)

Classify and Categorize = (C+C)   Compare/Contrast = (C/C)   Determine Character Emotions, Motivation = (DCE)   Drawing Conclusions = (DC)   Drawing Inferences = (DI)

Fact and Opinion = (F/O)   Hypothesizing = (H)   Main Idea = (MI)   Making Connections = (MC)   Making Deductions = (MD)   Making Judgements = (MJ)

Narrative Elements = (NE)   Noting Details = (ND)   Predict = (P)   Reality/Fantasy = (R/F)   Recall Facts/Rules = (RF/R)   Retell = (R)   Sequence = (Seq)

Steps in a Process = (SP)   Story Structure = (SS)   Summarize = (Sum)   Understanding Dialogue = (UD)   Using Context to Confirm Meaning(s) = (UCCM)   Visualize = (V)

BEFORE READING

(Have students find lesson 86, part A, in their textbooks.)

EXERCISE 1

Hard Words

1. Look at column 1.
- These are hard words from your textbook stories.

1. Manhattan	4. continual
2. district	5. organism
3. interior	6. digest

2. Word 1 is **Manhattan.** Everybody, what word? (Signal.) *Manhattan.*
- (Repeat this procedure for every word in the column.)
3. Let's read the words again.
4. Word 1. Everybody, what word? (Signal.) *Manhattan.*
- (Repeat this procedure for every word in the column.)
5. (Repeat the column until firm.)

EXERCISE 2

New Vocabulary

1. Look at column 2.
- First we'll read the words in this column. Then we'll read their definitions.

1. cubic inch	2. forenoon

2. Line 1. Everybody, what words? (Signal.) *Cubic inch.*
- (Repeat this procedure for *forenoon.*)
3. (Repeat the column until firm.)

EXERCISE 3

Vocabulary Definitions

1. Everybody, find part B. ✔
- These are definitions for the words you just read.

2. (For each word, call on a student to read the definition and the item. Then ask the student to complete the item.)

1. **cubic inch**—A *cubic inch* is a cube that is one inch long and one inch wide on each side.
- What's a cubic inch?

- What's the answer? (Idea: *A cube that is one inch long and one inch wide on each side.*)

2. **forenoon**—*Forenoon* is another word for *morning.* It's the time before noon.
- What's another way of saying *We're leaving in the morning*?

- What's the answer? (Response: *We're leaving in the forenoon.*)

EXERCISE 4

Vocabulary Review

1. Everybody, find part C. ✔
- We're going to review these words.
2. (Call on a student to read the words in the box.)

reap	gavel
testify	artificial
dryly	agony
dumbfounded	

3. (For each item, have a student read the item and say the answer.)

1. Great pain is �   .

- What's the answer? (Response: *Agony.*)

2. When you make a statement about an event you observed, you ▆▆▆.

- What's the answer? (Response: *Testify.*)

3. When you cut down and gather grain, you ▆▆▆ the grain.

- What's the answer? (Response: *Reap.*)

4. When you are briefly astonished, you are ▓▓▓▓.
- What's the answer? (Response: *Dumbfounded*.)

Reference Books

1. Everybody, turn to part E at the end of today's poem. ✔
- (Call on individual students to read several sentences each.)
- (At the end of each section, present the questions for that section.)

Write the answers for items 1–6.
There are several kinds of reference books you can use to find information:
- A **dictionary** gives facts about words. It shows how to spell a word and how to pronounce it. It tells what part of speech a word is and what the word means. A dictionary also tells the history of words.
- An **atlas** gives facts about places. It contains maps of states, countries, and continents. It shows the distance from one place to another. It tells how many people live in different places.
- An **encyclopedia** gives facts about nearly everything. It tells about plants, planets, animals, agriculture, history, and famous people, among many other topics.

Which would be the best reference book for the following questions? Choose **dictionary, atlas,** or **encyclopedia.**

1. How many states border Missouri?
- What's the answer? (Response: *Atlas.*)

2. What does *dispute* mean?
- What's the answer? (Response: *Dictionary.*)

3. How is *dominion* spelled?
- What's the answer? (Response: *Dictionary.*)

4. How do engines work?
- What's the answer? (Response: *Encyclopedia.*)

5. What are William Wordsworth's most famous poems?
- What's the answer? (Response: *Encyclopedia.*)

6. How large is Kentucky?
- What's the answer? (Response: *Atlas.*)
- You'll write the answers later.

READING

Poem Reading

1. Everybody, find part D. ✔
- We're going to read this poem aloud.
2. What's the title of this poem? (Response: *"Miracles".*)
- Who is the author? (Response: *Walt Whitman.*)
3. This is a poem that doesn't rhyme, but it has the sound and rhythm of a poem.
- The poem tells about the miracles we see every day.
4. The stanzas are different lengths. I'll read the first stanza. (Read the first stanza.)

Miracles
by Walt Whitman

Why, who makes much of a miracle?
As to me I know of nothing else but
miracles,
Whether I walk the streets of Manhattan,
Or dart my sight over the roofs of houses
toward the sky,
Or wade with naked feet along the beach
just in the edge of the water,
Or stand under trees in the woods,
Or watch honey-bees busy around the
hive of a summer forenoon,
Or animals feeding in the fields,
Or birds, or the wonderfulness of insects
in the air,
Or the wonderfulness of the sundown, or
of the stars shining so quiet and bright,
Or the exquisite delicate thin curve of the
new moon in spring;
These with the rest, one and all, are to me
miracles,
The whole referring, yet each distinct and
in its place.

- The poem begins with the question "Why, who makes much of a miracle?" What do you think that question means? (Ideas: *Who thinks miracles are so special; what's so unusual about a miracle?*) (DI)
- The next line says, "I know of nothing else but miracles." What does that mean? (Ideas: *Everything is a miracle; everything I know is a miracle.*) (DI)
- What are some of the miracles the poem describes? (Ideas: *Walking the streets of Manhattan; looking at the sky; wading in the water; standing under trees; watching bees and other animals; observing the sundown, the stars, and the moon.*) (Sum)
- The second-to-last line says, "These with the rest, one and all, are to me miracles." What does that mean? (Idea: *All these things are miracles.*) (DI)
- The first part of the last line says, "The whole referring." What do you think that means? (Ideas: *All these miracles are part of the whole; all these miracles refer to the whole.*) (DI)
- The second part says, "yet each distinct and in its place." What does that mean? (Ideas: *Each miracle is special; each miracle is unique.*) (DI)

5. I'll read the next two stanzas. (Read the second and third stanzas.)

> To me every hour of the light and dark is a miracle,
> Every cubic inch of space is a miracle,
> Every square yard of the surface of the earth is spread with the same,
> Every foot of the interior swarms with the same.
>
> To me the sea is a continual miracle,
> The fishes that swim—the rocks—the motion of the waves—the ships with men in them,
> What stranger miracles are there?

- What miracles does the poem mention in the second stanza? (Ideas: *Light and dark; space; the surface of the earth; the interior of the earth.*) (Sum)
- What units of measurement does the poem use to describe miracles? (Ideas: *Cubic inches; square yards; feet.*) (Sum)
- What is the main miracle in the last stanza? (Idea: *The sea.*) (MI)

- What are some parts of that miracle? (Ideas: *Fishes; rocks; waves; ships.*) (Sum)
- Do you think there are any stranger miracles than the ones described in the poem? Explain your answer. (Ideas: *No, because everything is a miracle and is equally strange; yes, because some things are more like miracles than others.*) (MJ)
- Why do you think the poem ends with a question? (Ideas: *The poet doesn't have all the answers; the poet wants readers to think of their own answers.*) (MJ)

6. Now you'll read the poem aloud.
- (Call on different students to read several lines each.)

Paired Practice (Optional)

1. Now you'll read in pairs.
- One person will read the first stanza.
- Then the other person will read the last two stanzas.
2. (Observe students and answer questions as needed.)

AFTER READING

Independent Work

1. Do all the items in your workbook and textbook for this lesson.
2. (The independent work in this lesson includes the following activities.)
- Vocabulary
- Story review
- Combined sentences
- Poem review
- Reference books
- Inference
- Writing

Workcheck

1. (Using the Answer Key, read the questions and answers for the workbook.)
2. (Have students read their answers for the textbook activities.)
3. (Have two or three students read their writing assignments aloud. Comment on each assignment.)
4. (Have students correct and turn in their work.)

(Present Spelling lesson 86 after completing Reading lesson 86. *See Spelling Presentation Book.*)

BEFORE READING

(Have students find lesson 87, part A, in their textbooks.)

EXERCISE 1

Hard Words

1. Look at column 1.
- These are hard words from your textbook stories.

1. Tom Sawyer	4. Saint Louis
2. Saint Petersburg	5. Hannibal
3. Huckleberry Finn	6. Mississippi

2. Line 1 is **Tom Sawyer.** Everybody, what words? (Signal.) *Tom Sawyer.*
- (Repeat this procedure for every word in the column.)
3. Let's read the words again.
4. Line 1. Everybody, what words? (Signal.) *Tom Sawyer.*
- (Repeat this procedure for every word in the column.)
5. (Repeat the column until firm.)

EXERCISE 2

Hard Words

1. Look at column 2.
- Here are some more hard words.

1. Palermo	4. Naples
2. Albania	5. syrup
3. Sarajevo	

2. Word 1 is **Palermo.** Everybody, what word? (Signal.) *Palermo.*
- (Repeat this procedure for every word in the column.)
3. Let's read the words again.
4. Word 1. Everybody, what word? (Signal.) *Palermo.*
- (Repeat this procedure for every word in the column.)
5. (Repeat the column until firm.)

EXERCISE 3

New Vocabulary

1. Look at column 3.
- First we'll read the words in this column. Then we'll read their definitions.

1. corridor	3. tradition
2. landing	

2. Word 1. Everybody, what word? (Signal.) *Corridor.*
- (Repeat this procedure for every word in the column.)
3. (Repeat the column until firm.)

EXERCISE 4

Vocabulary Definitions

1. Everybody, find part B. ✔
- These are definitions for the words you just read.
2. (For each word, call on a student to read the definition and the item. Then ask the student to complete the item.)

1. **corridor**—*Corridor* is another word for *hallway.*
- What's another way of saying *She stood in the hallway*?

- What's the answer? (Response: *She stood in the corridor.*)

2. **landing**—A *landing* is a platform between two flights of stairs.
- What is a landing?

- What's the answer? (Idea: *A platform between two flights of stairs.*)

3. **tradition**—When you follow a *tradition,* you do things in the same way that other people have done them for many years. Going to school is a tradition.
- What are you doing when you follow a tradition?

- What's the answer? (Idea: *Doing things in the same way that other people have done them for many years.*)

Vocabulary Review

1. Everybody, find part C. ✔
• We're going to review these words.
2. (Call on a student to read the words in the box.)

majority	dryly
astound	exception
unanimous	sulk

3. (For each item, have a student read the item and say the answer.)

1. Another word for *amaze* is ▇▇▇.

• What's the answer? (Response: *Astound.*)

2. When you break the rules for a special case, you make an ▇▇▇.

• What's the answer? (Response: *Exception.*)

3. When you are moody and quiet, you ▇▇▇.

• What's the answer? (Response: *Sulk.*)

Maps

1. Everybody, turn to part E at the end of today's story. ✔
• (Call on individual students to read several sentences each.)
• (At the end of each section, present the questions for that section.)

Write the answers for items 1–7.
The map shows countries and some cities. Stars (★) show cities that are capitals of countries. Dots (•) show cities that are not capitals.
1. What is the capital of Italy?

• What's the answer? (Response: *Rome.*)

2. Which capital on the map is farthest north?

• What's the answer? (Response: *Zagreb.*)

3. Which country is bigger, Greece or Albania?

• What's the answer? (Response: *Greece.*)

4. Does Sarajevo border on the sea?

• What's the answer? (Response: *No.*)

5. Which direction do you go to get from Athens to Palermo?

• What's the answer? (Response: *West.*)

6. Which is the shorter route from Tirane to Thessaloniki, going by water or going by land?

• What's the answer? (Response: *Going by land.*)

7. The map shows the location of a story you read. Which story?

• What's the answer? (Response: *The Odyssey.*)
• You'll write the answers later.

READING

Reading Aloud

1. Everybody, turn back to part D. ✔
• What's the focus question for today's lesson? (Response: *How were houses in the 1840s different from modern houses?*)
2. We're going to read part of this lesson aloud.

- (Call on individual students to read several sentences each.)
- (At the end of each section, ask the questions for that section.)

Life in the 1840s
Part 1

Focus Question: How were houses in the 1840s different from modern houses?

In lesson 91, you will begin reading a novel titled *Tom Sawyer.* The novel takes place in a small town on the Mississippi River in the 1840s. The main character is a boy named Tom Sawyer, and the novel tells about his adventures with his friends Huckleberry Finn and Becky Thatcher.

The novel was written by Mark Twain. In many ways, the book is really about Mark Twain's own childhood in a small Mississippi River town. In the novel, the town is called Saint Petersburg, but in real life it is Hannibal, Missouri, which still exists today. Hannibal is located about one hundred and twenty miles northwest of Saint Louis.

- What's the title of the next novel you will read? (Response: *Tom Sawyer.*) (NE)
- Who is the author of the novel? (Response: *Mark Twain.*) (NE)
- Why do you think the author changed the name of the town in the novel? (Ideas: *Because the novel is just a story, not real life; because he wanted to change some parts of the town.*) (AP)
- What other things do you think an author might change when he or she is writing about real life? (Ideas: *People's names; events; endings.*) (AP)
- Everybody, look at the map. (VA)

- Which river does the map show? (Response: *The Mississippi River.*) (VA)
- Which town is northwest of Saint Louis? (Response: *Hannibal.*) (VA)
- What is that town called in the novel? (Response: *Saint Petersburg.*) (ND)

What was it like to live in Hannibal in the 1840s? The best way to answer that question is to imagine you're one of Mark Twain's friends growing up with him in Hannibal.

• • •

A rooster crowing outside your window wakes you up early on a Monday morning in March. You don't have an electric alarm clock because electric clocks haven't been invented yet. Even if you had one, you wouldn't be able to plug it in because your house doesn't have any electricity, nor do any of the other houses in town. Scientists already know what electricity is, but many years will pass before they discover how to bring electricity to houses. ♦

- Why didn't houses have electricity in the 1840s? (Idea: *Scientists hadn't yet discovered how to bring electricity to houses.*) (C/E)
- Name some electrical appliances people didn't have in the 1840s. (Ideas: *Refrigerators; computers; toasters; television sets.*) (Sum)

- What other things do you think people didn't have in the 1840s? (Ideas: *Indoor plumbing; cars; furnaces; telephones.*) Ⓗ

EXERCISE 8

Silent Reading

1. Read the rest of the lesson to yourselves and be ready to answer some questions.

Early in the morning, your room is cold because there's no electric or gas heater to warm it up. There's a fireplace downstairs in the living room and a wood stove in the kitchen. Those rooms stay warm. But your room is not heated, and in the winter, it sometimes gets very cold.

You get dressed as quickly as possible and try to ignore the cold. If you're a boy, you put on a simple white shirt and a pair of pants that end about halfway between your knees and ankles. If you're a girl, you put on a long dress that covers almost every part of your body except your head, hands, and feet.

The first thing you do after getting dressed is to make your bed. Your mother is a strict housekeeper, and she is always telling you to keep the house clean and neat. On Saturdays, you spend most of the day helping her clean the house; but on weekdays, you just have to make your bed.

As soon as your bed is made, you go into the corridor and then downstairs to the kitchen. Like most of the other houses in town, your house has two stories and is made of wood. The bedrooms are all upstairs, and the kitchen, dining room, and living room are downstairs. There's also a small landing halfway up the stairs. There's no bathroom because the house doesn't have running water. If you need to use the bathroom, you go outside to a little shack in the backyard called an outhouse.

When you come into the kitchen, your mother is cooking breakfast on the wood stove. The kitchen is warm and cheerful, and it feels good to stand next to the stove and smell the food cooking. Before long, however, your mother asks you to go outside to get more wood from the woodpile. When you come back, she asks you to set the table.

The dining room is really the main room of the house. It's where the whole family gathers to eat breakfast, lunch, and dinner. It has a long wooden table with simple chairs. Along one wall is a large cabinet called a sideboard. The sideboard holds all the plates and silverware, as well as the cotton napkins and the fancy tablecloth your mother uses when guests come to dinner. ★

As soon as the table is set, you go upstairs to call your father. He has just finished dressing for his job at one of the stores in town. He earns a dollar a day, just as most of the other workers in the area do. Even though he works in the store all day, you see your father almost as much as you see your mother. He comes home every day for lunch, and he's usually home from the store by late afternoon.

Your father walks downstairs with you, and the two of you go into the kitchen and help your mother carry breakfast into the dining room.

Breakfast is huge. You eat oatmeal, soft-boiled eggs, sausage, potatoes, cheese, and bread. On some days, you also have pancakes and maple syrup. You wash all this down with hot coffee or tea. In keeping with tradition, nobody says much during breakfast or during any other meal; the dining room is for eating, not for talking. In some families, children are not even permitted to talk at the dining room table, but your parents are not that strict. Still, you eat quickly and silently. Your body will be working hard all day long, and you need all the food you can get.

After breakfast, you help your mother clear the table. Then you take a bucket outside to the water pump. After cranking the pump several times, you finally get enough water to fill the bucket. Your mother will use the water to wash the dishes. Someday soon, your father is going to put a water storage tank on top of the house. The tank will catch rainwater and send it down to the kitchen through a pipe. But for now, you still have to bring all water into the house by hand.

You help your mother do a few more chores around the kitchen before setting off to school, which is on the other side of town. There's no bus, car, or even a bicycle to take you there. These vehicles haven't been invented yet. Some of the richer people in town own horse-drawn wagons, but your family doesn't have a horse or a wagon. The only way for you to get to school is to walk.

- Why didn't houses in the 1840s have indoor bathrooms? (Idea: *They didn't have running water.*) Ⓒ/Ⓔ
- In the 1840s, the whole family ate three meals together every day. How have family eating habits changed since then? (Ideas: *Many families just eat dinner together now; some families skip breakfast or lunch.*) Ⓒ/Ⓒ
- In the 1840s, store clerks earned a dollar a day. About how much do you think store clerks earn now? (Ideas: *At least fifty dollars a day; a lot more.*) Ⓜ Ⓒ
- Why do you think people didn't talk much during meals? (Ideas: *They didn't want their food to get cold; they had plenty of time to talk later; they were hungry.*) Ⓜ Ⓙ
- Explain how the water storage tank will work. (Idea: *A tank on top of the house will catch rainwater and send it to the kitchen through a pipe.*) Ⓡ

EXERCISE 9

Paired Practice (Optional)

1. Now you'll read in pairs.
- Whoever read second the last time will read first today.
- Remember to start at the diamond and switch at the star.
2. (Observe students and answer questions as needed.)

AFTER READING

EXERCISE 10

Independent Work

1. Do all the items in your workbook and textbook for this lesson.
2. (The independent work in this lesson includes the following activities.)
- Story details
- Vocabulary
- Reference books
- Following directions
- Settings
- Maps
- Comprehension
- Writing

EXERCISE 11

Workcheck

1. (Using the Answer Key, read the questions and answers for the workbook.)
2. (Have students read their answers for the textbook activities.)
3. (Have two or three students read their writing assignments aloud. Comment on each assignment.)
4. (Have students correct and turn in their work.)

SPELLING

(Present Spelling lesson 87 after completing Reading lesson 87. *See Spelling Presentation Book.*)

BEFORE READING

(Have students find lesson 88, part A, in their textbooks.)

Hard Words

1. Look at column 1.
- These are hard words from your textbook stories.

1. irony	**5. New Orleans**
2. geography	**6. Memphis**
3. unmistakable	**7. Mississippi**
4. Minneapolis	

2. Word 1 is **irony.** Everybody, what word? (Signal.) *Irony.*
- (Repeat this procedure for every word in the column.)
3. Let's read the words again.
4. Word 1. Everybody, what word? (Signal.) *Irony.*
- (Repeat this procedure for every word in the column.)
5. (Repeat the column until firm.)

New Vocabulary

1. Look at column 2.
- First we'll read the words in this column. Then we'll read their definitions.

1. rigid	**3. legend**
2. ambush	

2. Word 1. Everybody, what word? (Signal.) *Rigid.*
- (Repeat this procedure for every word in the column.)
3. (Repeat the column until firm.)

Vocabulary Definitions

1. Everybody, find part B. ✔
- These are definitions for the words you just read.
2. (For each word, call on a student to read the definition and the item. Then ask the student to complete the item.)

1. **rigid**—When something is *rigid,* it is stiff.
- What's another way of saying *His arm was stiff?*

- What's the answer? (Response: *His arm was rigid.*)

2. **ambush**—When you *ambush* people, you attack them from a hiding place. If rebels attack an army from a hiding place, the rebels ambush the army.
- What's another way of saying *The cat attacked the rat from a hiding place?*

- What's the answer? (Response: *The cat ambushed the rat.*)

3. **legend**—A *legend* is an old story about characters who may really have lived.
- What is a legend?

- What's the answer? (Idea: *An old story about characters who may really have lived.*)

Vocabulary Review

1. Everybody, find part C. ✔
- We're going to review these words.
2. (Call on a student to read the words in the box.)

corridor	reap
agony	testify
tradition	landing

3. (For each item, have a student read the item and say the answer.)

1. Another word for *hallway* is ▭.

- What's the answer? (Response: *Corridor.*)

2. A platform between two flights of stairs is a ▭.

- What's the answer? (Response: *Landing.*)

3. When you do things the same way that other people have done them for many years, you are following a ▭.

- What's the answer? (Response: *Tradition.*)

EXERCISE 5

Irony

1. Everybody, turn to part E at the end of today's story. ✔

- (Call on individual students to read several sentences each.)
- (At the end of each section, present the questions for that section.)

Write the answers for items 1–3.
Here's how irony works:
- A character believes something.
- The character acts in a certain way because of his or her belief.
- Later, the character finds out the belief was mistaken.

Here's an example of irony from "The Necklace."

1. Matilda had a mistaken belief about the necklace. What was that belief?

- What's the answer? (Idea: *That the necklace was valuable.*)

2. Matilda did something because of her belief. What did she do?

- What's the answer? (Idea: *Bought an expensive necklace to replace the lost necklace.*)

3. What would Matilda have done if she had known the truth about the necklace?

- What's the answer? (Ideas: *Bought a necklace made of fake diamonds; told Mrs. Forester the truth.*)
- You'll write the answers later.

READING

EXERCISE 6

Focus Question

1. Everybody, turn back to part D. ✔
2. What's the focus question for today's lesson? (Response: *How were schools in the 1840s different from modern schools?*)

EXERCISE 7

Reading Aloud (Optional)

1. We're going to read aloud to the diamond.

- (Call on individual students to read several sentences each.)

Life in the 1840s
Part 2
Focus Question: How were schools in the 1840s different from modern schools?

Walking to school takes about twenty minutes. You walk along a dirt street that's filled with ruts and garbage. Many people are walking on the street, along with a few horses and an occasional wagon. Several pigs are roaming around as well. Hannibal has no garbage collection, so people just dump their garbage into the streets for the pigs to eat.

Within a few minutes, you reach the center of Hannibal. There are two hotels, two churches, and dozens of stores and small factories. But these buildings are not nearly as important to Hannibal as the mighty Mississippi River rolling by the wharf at the end of Market Street. Without the Mississippi, there would be no Hannibal. The river carries just about everything and everybody that comes or goes from the little town.

There are no boats at the wharf this morning, but you know that a steamboat will arrive after school today, and you plan to be there when it does. For now, you only glance at the wharf and hurry on to school.

The school has only one classroom and one teacher. Most of the children in town start school when they're six years old and finish when they're fourteen. After that, they start working in town or on the farms. A few of the richer students might go on to a private high school in Saint Louis and maybe even to college. For most, however, this little one-room school is the only one they'll ever attend.

The classroom holds about sixty students, all of whom sit on long, rigid benches. The boys sit on one side of the room and the girls on the other. The teacher, who is a man, has a big desk at the front of the room.

His job is difficult because he must somehow teach reading, writing, and arithmetic to a class filled with students of all ages and abilities. At the same time, he must maintain strict order. He keeps a pile of birch rods in a corner, and he's not afraid to whack a misbehaving student with one of these rods. If the rod breaks, he picks out another. Most of the students are smart enough to behave themselves, but a few get whacked every day. ♦

EXERCISE 8

Silent Reading

1. Read the rest of the lesson to yourselves and be ready to answer some questions.

The teacher begins the class by working with the younger students. During this time, you and the other older students study your reading books. Your school uses McGuffey's Readers, and so do most other American schools of the 1840s. These small books contain pages and pages of stories, legends, poems, articles, and speeches. There are no pictures.

Today's selection is a poem that praises the United States. It says:

My country, 'tis of thee,
Sweet land of liberty,
Of thee I sing;
Land where my fathers died,
Land of the pilgrims' pride;
From every mountain side,
Let freedom ring.

When the teacher finishes with the younger students, he asks you to read the poem aloud. He pays close attention to how well you pronounce each word and to how dramatic your reading is. In the 1840s, people loved to listen to poetry, so the teacher spends a lot of time teaching you how to read poetry well. After you finish reading the poem, the teacher asks you to memorize it so you can recite it to the entire class later in the week. This doesn't surprise you, because you usually have to memorize at least one poem a week.

The class continues until noon, when it breaks up for lunch. You run back home and eat a lunch that's almost as big as your breakfast was. You have soup, meat, potatoes, and maybe some pudding. You also drink root beer that your father has brought home from the store. ★

An hour later, you're back at school. The afternoon class begins with a geography lesson on the Mississippi River. You learn that the river starts in northern Minnesota and flows south all the way to New Orleans. Thousands of boats go up and down the river, carrying goods and passengers from one city to another. The boats pick up lumber in Minneapolis, corn in Saint Louis, tobacco in Memphis, and cotton in New Orleans. New Orleans is a busy port where ships from all over the world pick up these goods and leave others behind. Everything moves by water. For now, it's the best way to send goods from one place to another.

You also learn about the trains that people ride in the eastern states. You have never seen a train, but your teacher describes them and predicts that trains will reach the Mississippi within a few years. The trains will be much faster than the riverboats, and your teacher wonders if people may start using the trains instead of the boats.

The class continues until four in the afternoon. You have been sitting on the same rigid wooden bench for most of the day, so it feels good to get out of school and run around. You play a few games with your friends, mostly races, tag, and make-believe war. Sports such as baseball, football, and basketball haven't been invented yet, so you can't play those.

As you are waiting to ambush one of your friends in a game of war, you hear the unmistakable sound of a steam whistle coming from the river. You and your friends instantly stop playing and race down to the wharf.

- How were schools in the 1840s different from modern schools? (Ideas: *In the 1840s, all students were in one classroom with one teacher; most students finished when they were fourteen; students sat on benches; the teacher hit students with birch rods; books had no pictures; students went home for lunch; school lasted until four in the afternoon.*) Ⓒ/Ⓒ
- Why did people in Hannibal dump their garbage in the street? (Ideas: *Because there was no garbage collection; because the pigs ate the garbage.*) ⒹⒸⒺ
- Why was the Mississippi River particularly important to Hannibal? (Idea: *The Mississippi brought everything and everybody to and from town.*) Ⓒ/Ⓔ
- Why do you think poetry was more popular in the 1840s than it is today? (Ideas: *In the 1840s, people didn't have television or movies, so they read more; in the 1840s, people listened to poetry instead of to the radio.*) ⓂⒿ
- What advantages did trains have over riverboats? (Ideas: *Trains could go anywhere; trains were faster.*) Ⓒ/Ⓒ

EXERCISE 9
Paired Practice (Optional)

1. Now you'll read in pairs.
- Whoever read second the last time will read first today.
- Remember to start at the diamond and switch at the star.
2. (Observe students and answer questions as needed.)

AFTER READING

EXERCISE 10
Independent Work

1. Do all the items in your workbook and textbook for this lesson.
2. (The independent work in this lesson includes the following activities.)
- Story details
- Reference books
- Exaggeration
- Maps
- Sarcasm
- Story review
- Irony
- Comprehension
- Writing

EXERCISE 11
Workcheck

1. (Using the Answer Key, read the questions and answers for the workbook.)
2. (Have students read their answers for the textbook activities.)
3. (Have two or three students read their writing assignments aloud. Comment on each assignment.)
4. (Have students correct and turn in their work.)

SPELLING

(Present Spelling lesson 88 after completing Reading lesson 88. *See Spelling Presentation Book.*)

BEFORE READING

(Have students find lesson 89, part A, in their textbooks.)

Hard Words

1. Look at column 1.
• These are hard words from your textbook stories.

1. paddlewheel	**3. bushel**
2. biscuit	

2. Word 1 is **paddlewheel.** Everybody, what word? (Signal.) *Paddlewheel.*
• (Repeat this procedure for every word in the column.)
3. Let's read the words again.
4. Word 1. Everybody, what word? (Signal.) *Paddlewheel.*
• (Repeat this procedure for every word in the column.)
5. (Repeat the column until firm.)

New Vocabulary

1. Look at column 2.
• First we'll read the words in this column. Then we'll read their definitions.

1. dwindle	**3. plush**
2. bulky	**4. settler**

2. Word 1. Everybody, what word? (Signal.) *Dwindle.*
• (Repeat this procedure for every word in the column.)
3. (Repeat the column until firm.)

Vocabulary Definitions

1. Everybody, find part B. ✔
• These are definitions for the words you just read.

2. (For each word, call on a student to read the definition and the item. Then ask the student to complete the item.)

1. **dwindle**—When something *dwindles,* it becomes less and less.
• What's another way of saying *Their supplies became less and less*?

• What's the answer? (Response: *Their supplies dwindled.*)

2. **bulky**—When something is *bulky,* it is large and heavy.
• What's another way of saying *large and heavy furniture*?

• What's the answer? (Response: *Bulky furniture.*)

3. **plush**—When something is *plush,* it is fancy and expensive.
• What's another way of saying *They had a fancy and expensive lifestyle*?

• What's the answer? (Response: *They had a plush lifestyle.*)

4. **settler**—A *settler* is somebody who moves into a conquered area. After the Native Americans were conquered in the 1800s, the white people who moved into the western United States were called *settlers.*
• What is a settler?

• What's the answer? (Idea: *Somebody who moves into a conquered area.*)

Vocabulary Review

1. Everybody, find part C. ✔
• We're going to review these words.
2. (Call on a student to read the words in the box.)

corridor	legend
rigid	ambush
tradition	landing

3. (For each item, have a student read the item and say the answer.)

1. Something that is stiff is ▬▬▬.

- What's the answer? (Response: *Rigid.*)

2. When you attack someone from a hiding place, you ▬▬▬ that person.

- What's the answer? (Response: *Ambush.*)

3. An old story about characters who may really have lived is a ▬▬▬.

- What's the answer? (Response: *Legend.*)

EXERCISE 5
Irony

1. Everybody, turn to part E at the end of today's story. ✔
- (Call on individual students to read several sentences each.)
- (At the end of each section, present the questions for that section.)

Write the answers for items 1–3.
　Here's how irony works:
- A character believes something.
- The character acts in a certain way because of his or her belief.
- Later, the character finds out the belief was mistaken.

Here's an example of irony from "Persephone."

1. When Persephone examined the pomegranate, she had a mistaken belief about how long Hades was going to keep her. What was her belief?

- What's the answer? (Idea: *That Hades was going to keep her forever.*)

2. Persephone did something because of her belief. What did she do?

- What's the answer? (Idea: *Tasted the pomegranate.*)

3. What would Persephone have done if she had known the truth about how much longer Hades would keep her?

- What's the answer? (Idea: *Not tasted the pomegranate.*)
- You'll write the answers later.

READING

EXERCISE 6
Reading Aloud

1. Everybody, turn back to part D. ✔
- What's the focus question for today's lesson? (Response: *Why were steamboats important to Hannibal?*)
2. We're going to read part of this lesson aloud.
- (Call on individual students to read several sentences each.)

Life in the 1840s
Part 3
Focus Question: Why were steamboats important to Hannibal?

　The steamboat is just pulling in as you and your friends reach the wharf. The boat has large steam engines that drive paddlewheels on both sides of the boat. When the paddlewheels turn, the boat moves forward.

- Everybody, look at the picture.

- The arrow shows the direction the paddlewheel is turning. Is it turning clockwise or counterclockwise? (Response: *Clockwise.*) ⓋⒶ
- The paddlewheel is moving the boat. Is the boat moving toward the right side of the picture or toward the left side? (Response: *Toward the right side.*) ⓂⒹ

- Which direction would the boat move if the paddlewheel turned counterclockwise? (Ideas: *Backward; toward the left side of the picture.*) Ⓜ🄳

You know a lot about steamboats, and you love to talk about them with your friends. You know that steamboats are much better for river travel than the old sailboats. For one thing, steamboats have shallow hulls, so there's little danger of their scraping the bottom of the river. Also, the paddlewheels are strong enough to fight against the current when the steamboats go upstream from New Orleans to Minneapolis.

In contrast, sailboats have deep hulls that often scrape the bottom of the river. Their sails don't sometimes give them even enough power to go upstream. It's no wonder that steamboats have taken over.

- If a boat were going from Minneapolis to New Orleans, would it have to fight the current? (Response: *No.*) Ⓜ🄳
- Why not? (Ideas: *New Orleans is downstream from Minneapolis; the boat is going in the same direction as the current.*) Ⓡ
- What advantages did steamboats have over sailboats? (Ideas: *Steamboats had shallow hulls, so they didn't scrape the bottom of the river; steamboats had enough power to go upstream.*) 🅒🄬🅒

The steamboat coming into the wharf seems ten times bigger than your house. It has enough room to carry tons of bulky freight and several hundred passengers.

The outside of the steamboat is covered with spectacular designs. It has beautifully carved wooden railings, windows for all the passenger cabins, smokestacks for the engines, and, of course, the giant steam whistle that blows from time to time. You can see the captain in his cabin at the top of the boat, slowly steering the boat into the wharf. After several minutes, the steam whistle gives one last blast, and the boat begins to unload. ◆

- Why do you think the captain's cabin is at the top of the steamboat? (Ideas: *So he can see all around; because that's the most powerful spot.*) Ⓜ🄹

- How do modern boats differ from steamboats? (Ideas: *Modern boats are made of metal; modern boats use gas engines; modern boats move faster.*) 🅒🄬🅒

EXERCISE 7

Silent Reading

1. Read the rest of the lesson to yourselves and be ready to answer some questions.

The passengers get off first. Most of them are settlers who are moving into Hannibal or onto farms in the surrounding area. It's easy to spot the settlers because they always have lots of baggage and look a little lost and bewildered. It's also easy to spot the gamblers and con men. They're well dressed and have confident looks.

You can tell about other passengers by what they carry. Peddlers are carrying merchandise in tin boxes. They'll be stopping by your house sometime soon, trying to sell your mother pins, silverware, fabrics, and perfume. Lawyers and business people are carrying their important papers in briefcases and looking serious.

You're excited about seeing the visitors, but you're a little disappointed, too. You keep hoping that a circus will come to town. One of your friends saw a circus in Saint Louis, and she says it had a man who was one hundred sixty-one years old, a mermaid from the South Seas, and a woman with a beard.

After the passengers leave the ship, workers begin to unload the freight. There are fabrics for the dressmaker, tools for the hardware store, plush furniture for the new hotel, and all kinds of merchandise for the general store. There are boxes of books and biscuits and barrels full of nails. There are even some cows and a crate of chickens. ★

As merchants pick up these goods and take them to their stores, the amount of freight on the wharf dwindles. When the wharf is finally clear, the workers begin to load the boat with goods from Hannibal. Most of these goods come from the surrounding farms. There are wagons full of corn, bags of tobacco, and bushels of wheat. There are also plenty of pigs and plenty of hides. The pigs grunt noisily as they trot by.

The workers load the boat quickly. Soon, the captain sounds the whistle, and a few passengers get on. The steam engines fire up; the paddlewheels begin to move. The boat slowly leaves the wharf, moves out into the river, and turns downstream for Saint Louis. An entire day will pass before another steamboat comes. Someday you might even be riding on one as it heads out into the big muddy river.

It's almost time to go home for dinner. You walk down the main street of the town. You pass the hotels, the restaurant, the shoemaker's shop, and the drugstore.

By the time you reach home, dinner is almost ready. Once again, you help your mother with the cooking and then set the table. Meanwhile, your father reads the local newspaper in the living room. When everything is ready, you sit down to a huge meal of soup, meat, vegetables, and pie.

- Why were steamboats important to Hannibal? (Ideas: *They brought people and freight to the town; they picked up products from the town; they connected the town to the rest of the world.*) (Sum)
- Why were settlers easy to spot? (Ideas: *Because they always had lots of baggage; because they looked lost and bewildered.*) (C/E)
- The article says you can figure out what passengers do based on what they carry. Do you think that's still true? Give an example. (Ideas: *Yes, at the airport, students carry backpacks, tourists carry big suitcases, and business people carry briefcases; no, modern luggage looks so much alike that it's hard to tell what the owners do.*) (MJ)
- How was the freight the steamboat unloaded different from the freight it picked up? (Idea: *It unloaded mostly manufactured goods, but it picked up farm products.*) (C/C)
- How would Hannibal be different if no steamboats stopped there? (Ideas: *The residents would have to make everything themselves; the residents would have too many farm products and not enough manufactured products; the town would be cut off from the world.*) (C/C)

Paired Practice (Optional)

1. Now you'll read in pairs.
- Whoever read second the last time will read first today.
- Remember to start at the diamond and switch at the star.
2. (Observe students and answer questions as needed.)

AFTER READING

EXERCISE 9

Independent Work

1. Do all the items in your workbook and textbook for this lesson.
2. (The independent work in this lesson includes the following activities.)
- Story details
- Vocabulary
- Character traits
- Maps
- Descriptions
- Irony
- Reference books
- Comprehension
- Writing

EXERCISE 10

Workcheck

1. (Using the Answer Key, read the questions and answers for the workbook.)
2. (Have students read their answers for the textbook activities.)
3. (Have two or three students read their writing assignments aloud. Comment on each assignment.)
4. (Have students correct and turn in their work.)

SPELLING

(Present Spelling lesson 89 after completing Reading lesson 89. *See Spelling Presentation Book.*)

BEFORE READING

(Have students find lesson 90, part A, in their textbooks.)

EXERCISE 1
Hard Words

1. Look at column 1.
- These are hard words from your textbook stories.

1. sensational	4. cholera
2. bilious	5. malaria
3. dropsy	

2. Word 1 is **sensational.** Everybody, what word? (Signal.) *Sensational.*
- (Repeat this procedure for every word in the column.)
3. Let's read the words again.
4. Word 1. Everybody, what word? (Signal.) *Sensational.*
- (Repeat this procedure for every word in the column.)
5. (Repeat the column until firm.)

EXERCISE 2
New Vocabulary

1. Look at column 2.
- First we'll read the words in this column. Then we'll read their definitions.

1. supernatural	3. endure
2. systematically	4. junction

2. Word 1. Everybody, what word? (Signal.) *Supernatural.*
- (Repeat this procedure for every word in the column.)
3. (Repeat the column until firm.)

EXERCISE 3
Vocabulary Definitions

1. Everybody, find part B. ✔
- These are definitions for the words you just read.

2. (For each word, call on a student to read the definition and the item. Then ask the student to complete the item.)

1. **supernatural**—When something is *supernatural,* it seems magical and cannot be explained by science.
- What's another way of saying *a magical event*?
- What's the answer? (Response: *A supernatural event.*)

2. **systematically**—When something is done *systematically,* it is done in an organized way. If you clean a room in an organized way, you clean the room *systematically.*
- What's another way of saying *They examined the house in an organized way*?
- What's the answer? (Response: *They examined the house systematically.*)

3. **endure**—One meaning of *endure* is "continue." If a memory lives on or continues, that memory endures.
- What's another way of saying *The legend continued*?
- What's the answer? (Response: *The legend endured.*)

4. **junction**—A *junction* is a place where two or more things join.
- What is a junction?
- What's the answer? (Idea: *A place where two or more things join.*)

EXERCISE 4
Vocabulary Review

1. Everybody, find part C. ✔
- We're going to review these words.
2. (Call on a student to read the words in the box.)

dwindles	bulky
rigid	plush

3. (For each item, have a student read the item and say the answer.)

1. Something fancy and expensive is ▮▮▮▮.

• What's the answer? (Response: *Plush.*)

2. Something that gets smaller and smaller ▮▮▮▮.

• What's the answer? (Response: *Dwindles.*)

3. Something large and heavy is ▮▮▮▮.

• What's the answer? (Response: *Bulky.*)

EXERCISE 5

Irony

1. Everybody, turn to part E at the end of today's story. ✔
• (Call on individual students to read several sentences each.)
• (At the end of each section, present the questions for that section.)

Write the answers for items 1–3.
Here's how irony works:
• A character believes something.
• The character acts in a certain way because of his or her belief.
• Later, the character finds out the belief was mistaken.
Here's an example of irony from "The Last Leaf."

1. Joan had a mistaken belief about the painted leaf that she saw through her window. What was that?

• What's the answer? (Idea: *That it was real.*)

2. Joan did something because of her belief. What did she do?

• What's the answer? (Idea: *She decided to live.*)

3. What would Joan have done if she had known the truth about the leaf?

• What's the answer? (Idea: *She would have decided to die.*)
• You'll write the answers later.

READING

EXERCISE 6

Focus Question

1. Everybody, turn back to part D. ✔
2. What's the focus question for today's lesson? (Response: *How was medical care in the 1840s different from modern care?*)

EXERCISE 7

Reading Aloud (Optional)

1. We're going to read aloud to the diamond.
• (Call on individual students to read several sentences each.)

Life in the 1840s

Part 4

Focus Question: How was medical care in the 1840s different from modern care?

After dinner is over and the dishes are washed, you sit with your family by the warm fire in the living room. Your father has lit the oil lamps and is sitting in the corner reading a book. Your mother is sitting on the sofa reading a magazine called *Godey's Lady's Book.* The magazine comes all the way from Philadelphia and has short stories and pictures of the latest fashions.

You decide to read the Hannibal newspaper, which is printed in a building near the wharf. The newspaper crams lots of news and ads into just a few pages. Some of the news stories tell about new states called Texas and Florida. Others describe new inventions, such as the McCormick reaper, an amazing machine that cuts wheat five times as fast as a person can.

The news stories you like best are the sensational ones that tell about strange creatures and supernatural events. These stories are printed right next to the more boring ones, and it seems to you they must be just as true. Of course, your parents often tell you not to believe everything you read in the newspaper. ♦

EXERCISE 8

Silent Reading

1. Read the rest of the lesson to yourselves and be ready to answer some questions.

The newspaper has many ads for medicines and cures. One of these ads is for Lee's Bilious Pills, which are supposed to be "useful against yellow fever, dropsy, and worms." Another ad promotes Old Sachem Bitters Wigwam Tonic. The ad says if you drink this tonic systematically, you will become just as strong as an Indian chief. From time to time, your mother buys some of these pills and tonics, but you've noticed that they've never had any effect other than to give you a stomachache.

As you turn the pages of the newspaper, an article about diseases catches your eye. The article says that yellow fever may spread again in the southern states. But that's not all: the article also says that cholera may break out again in the East. Cholera is far worse than yellow fever and spreads much more quickly.

You feel lucky that the only really bad disease around Hannibal is malaria. Many of your friends have had this disease. They got a very high fever and had to stay in bed for weeks, but most of them survived. Your brother was not so fortunate: he died from malaria last year.

The article goes on to say that doctors are trying to conquer these diseases against great odds. Medical schools are being established all over the country. Many of the doctors at these schools complain that the laws won't let them cut up dead people for students to examine. The article reports that some doctors have been accused of robbing graves to find

bodies, although nothing has been proved. ★

You think of your own family doctor, who travels many miles each day to deliver babies and set broken legs. There are many diseases he cannot cure, but he does his best. Of course, your mother only calls for the doctor when something really serious happens, such as when you broke your arm. Most of the time, she tries to cure you herself. When you had a sore throat last month, for example, she put you in bed, wrapped a thick piece of meat around your neck, and put a plaster of goose fat, onion, and mustard on your chest. Three days of that were enough to cure anything.

Many of your friends think diseases can be cured by magic spells. Some of them wear a spider on a necklace to prevent malaria. Others say you can cure a toothache by touching the tooth with wood from a tree that's been struck by lightning. And everybody knows you can heal a wound by using the right eye of a wolf.

You look up from the newspaper and see that it's getting late. Your father has just finished winding the clock, and your mother is turning the last pages of her magazine. All evening long, the house has been quiet. There's no refrigerator humming, no computer beeping, no television set jabbering away, and no telephone ringing. These things don't exist yet, and they won't for many years.

You take a candle in your hand and go up to your room. It's cold and dark, just as it was this morning. You get into bed quickly and snuff out the candle. As you fall asleep, you think back on your experiences of the day: doing chores for your mother; reading the poem in your McGuffey's Reader; learning about trains; finding out about diseases. Most of all, you think about the beautiful steamboat and all the things it brings to and from Hannibal. The steamboats may pass, but your memory of them will endure forever.

• • •

The version of *Tom Sawyer* you will be reading is shorter than the original version by Mark Twain. Some parts have been taken out, and some words have been changed, but the basic story remains the same.

- How was medical care in the 1840s different from modern medical care? (Ideas: *In the 1840s, doctors couldn't cure many diseases; in the 1840s, it was against the law to cut up dead people for research; in the 1840s, people cured themselves with home remedies and magic spells.*) (C/C)

- How is modern medical care still the same as medical care in the 1840s? (Ideas: *People use doctors for serious illnesses; medical science still doesn't have cures for many diseases.*) (C/C)

- Do you think the Hannibal newspaper was a reliable source of news? Explain your answer. (Idea: *Probably not, because it carried sensational stories about strange creatures and supernatural events.*) (MJ)

- Do you think television is a reliable source of news? Explain your answer. (Ideas: *Yes, because television news can show you events as they happen; no, because some television news is one-sided.*) (MJ)

- How was spending an evening at home in the 1840s different from spending an evening at home now? (Idea: *In the 1840s, reading and conversation were the main entertainments, but now many people watch TV or play on computers.*) (C/C)

EXERCISE 9

Paired Practice (Optional)

1. Now you'll read in pairs.
- Whoever read second the last time will read first today.
- Remember to start at the diamond and switch at the star.
2. (Observe students and answer questions as needed.)

AFTER READING

EXERCISE 10

Independent Work

1. Do all the items in your workbook and textbook for this lesson.
2. (The independent work in this lesson includes the following activities.)
- Story details
- Vocabulary
- Maps
- Irony
- Reference books
- Comprehension
- Writing

EXERCISE 11

Workcheck

1. (Using the Answer Key, read the questions and answers for the workbook.)
2. (Have students read their answers for the textbook activities.)
3. (Have two or three students read their writing assignments aloud. Comment on each assignment.)
4. (Have students correct and turn in their work.)

MASTERY TEST

(The Lesson 90 Mastery Test should be administered after students complete lesson 90. See *Curriculum-Based Assessment and Fluency Handbook* for details.)

SPELLING

(Present Spelling lesson 90 after completing Reading lesson 90. *See Spelling Presentation Book.*)

ACTIVITIES ACROSS THE CURRICULUM

(Students should complete the appropriate project in *Activities across the Curriculum* after completing lesson 90. See *Activities across the Curriculum* book for details.)

Lessons 91–95 • Planning Page

	Lesson 91	Lesson 92	Lesson 93	Lesson 94	Lesson 95
BEFORE READING	Hard words Word practice New vocabulary Vocabulary definitions Maps	Hard words Word practice New vocabulary Vocabulary definitions Vocabulary review Graphs	Hard words Word practice New vocabulary Vocabulary definitions Graphs	Hard words Word practice New vocabulary Vocabulary definitions Logic	Hard words Word practice New vocabulary Vocabulary definitions Logic
NEW VOCABULARY	perplexed conscience smug smother traitor vicious sidle	brim waver tranquil resume suits absorbed fragment philosopher	casual worship contemplate drone	justice of the peace lapse minister sermon congregation pew gingerly logic	ailment considerable aggravate genuine mortified
READING	*Tom Sawyer* (Chapter 1)	*Tom Sawyer* (Chapter 2)	*Tom Sawyer* (Chapter 3)	*Tom Sawyer* (Chapter 4)	*Tom Sawyer* (Chapter 5)
INDEPENDENT WORK	Story details Character traits Combined sentences Crossword puzzle Poem review Maps Vocabulary review Comprehension Writing	Story details Vocabulary Maps Graphs Comprehension Writing	Story details Vocabulary Maps Irony Graphs Vocabulary review Comprehension Writing	Story details Vocabulary Graphs Character traits Logic Vocabulary review Reference books Comprehension Writing	Story details Vocabulary Graphs Perspectives Logic Maps Vocabulary review Comprehension Writing
SUPPLEMENTS	*Spelling*	*Spelling*	*Spelling*	*Spelling*	*Spelling* *Activities across the Curriculum*

Comprehension Questions Abbreviations Guide

Access Prior Knowledge = (APK)   Author's Point of View = (APoV)   Author's Purpose = (AP)   Cause/Effect = (C/E)   Charts/Graphs/Diagrams/Visual Aids = (VA)

Classify and Categorize = (C+C)   Compare/Contrast = (C/C)   Determine Character Emotions, Motivation = (DCE)   Drawing Conclusions = (DC)   Drawing Inferences = (DI)

Fact and Opinion = (F/O)   Hypothesizing = (H)   Main Idea = (MI)   Making Connections = (MC)   Making Deductions = (MD)   Making Judgements = (MJ)

Narrative Elements = (NE)   Noting Details = (ND)   Predict = (P)   Reality/Fantasy = (R/F)   Recall Facts/Rules = (RF/R)   Retell = (R)   Sequence = (Seq)

Steps in a Process = (SP)   Story Structure = (SS)   Summarize = (Sum)   Understanding Dialogue = (UD)   Using Context to Confirm Meaning(s) = (UCCM)   Visualize = (V)

BEFORE READING

(Have students find lesson 91, part A, in their textbooks.)

EXERCISE 1

Hard Words

1. Look at column 1.
- These are hard words from your textbook stories.

> 1. conscience   3. vicious
> 2. sidling

2. Word 1 is **conscience.** Everybody, what word? (Signal.) *Conscience.*
- (Repeat this procedure for every word in the column.)
3. Let's read the words again.
4. Word 1. Everybody, what word? (Signal.) *Conscience.*
- (Repeat this procedure for every word in the column.)
5. (Repeat the column until firm.)

EXERCISE 2

Word Practice

1. Look at column 2.
- We're going to practice these words.

> 1. newcomer   6. Palermo
> 2. holiday   7. antelope
> 3. Albania   8. smug
> 4. shabby   9. smudge
> 5. shabbier

2. Word 1. Everybody, what word? (Signal.) *Newcomer.*
- (Repeat this procedure for every word in the column.)
3. (Repeat the column until firm.)

EXERCISE 3

New Vocabulary

1. Look at column 3.
- First we'll read the words in this column. Then we'll read their definitions.

> 1. perplexed   5. traitor
> 2. conscience   6. vicious
> 3. smug   7. sidle
> 4. smother

2. Word 1. Everybody, what word? (Signal.) *Perplexed.*
- (Repeat this procedure for every word in the column.)
3. (Repeat the column until firm.)

EXERCISE 4

Vocabulary Definitions

1. Everybody, find part B. ✔
- These are definitions for the words you just read.
2. (For each word, call on a student to read the definition and the item. Then ask the student to complete the item.)

1. **perplexed**—When you are *perplexed,* you are puzzled.
- What's another way of saying *She had a puzzled expression*?

- What's the answer? (Response: *She had a perplexed expression.*)

2. **conscience**—Your *conscience* is your sense of right and wrong.
- What is your conscience?

- What's the answer? (Idea: *Your sense of right and wrong.*)

3. **smug**—When you feel *smug,* you feel satisfied with yourself.
- What's another way of saying *She had a self-satisfied smile*?

- What's the answer? (Response: *She had a smug smile.*)

4. **smother**—When you *smother* something, you cut off its air.
- What's another way of saying *The foam cut off the air from the fire*?

- What's the answer? (Response: *The foam smothered the fire.*)

5. **traitor**—A *traitor* is someone who seems to be your friend but then betrays you.
- What do we call somebody who betrays you?

- What's the answer? (Response: *A traitor.*)

6. **vicious**—When something is *vicious,* it is cruel or violent.
- What's another way of saying *The captain had a violent dog*?

- What's the answer? (Response: *The captain had a vicious dog.*)

7. **sidle**—When you *sidle,* you move sideways.
- What's another way of saying *He moved sideways toward the door*?

- What's the answer? (Response: *He sidled toward the door.*)

EXERCISE 5

Maps

1. Everybody, turn to part E at the end of today's story. ✔
- (Call on individual students to read several sentences each.)
- (At the end of each section, present the questions for that section.)

Write the answers for items 1–6.

On the map, the dots show large cities, and the stars show capitals of countries.

Assume the map is accurate. Examine the map carefully and then read the statements below the map. Some of the statements contradict what is shown on the map.

Tirane is the capital of Albania.
1. Does that statement contradict what the map shows?

- What's the answer? (Response: *No.*)

2. If the statement is a contradiction, write what the map really shows about Tirane.

- Is the statement a contradiction? (Response: *No.*)
- So what do you have to write? (Idea: *Nothing.*)

Athens is farther west than Rome.
3. Does that statement contradict what the map shows?

- What's the answer? (Response: *Yes.*)

4. If the statement is a contradiction, write what the map really shows about Athens.

- Is the statement a contradiction? (Response: *Yes.*)
- So what do you have to write? (Idea: *What the map really shows about Athens.*)
- What does the map really show about Athens? (Idea: *Athens is farther east than Rome.*)
- You'll write the answers later.

READING

Title Page

1. Everybody, turn back to part C. ✔
• This is the title page for the novel *Tom Sawyer*.

Tom Sawyer
by Mark Twain

2. The picture shows Tom Sawyer.
• What can you tell about Tom Sawyer from the picture? (Ideas: *He's a boy who has adventures; he's a boy who gets into trouble; he dresses casually*.) (MJ)

EXERCISE 7

Focus Question

1. Everybody, find part D. ✔
2. What's the focus question for today's lesson? (Response: *What kind of boy was Tom Sawyer?*)

Note: The "Reading Aloud" exercise is recommended for this lesson.

EXERCISE 8

Reading Aloud

1. We're going to read aloud to the diamond.
• (Call on individual students to read several sentences each.)

Chapter 1
Tom Runs, Fights, and Hides
Focus Question: What kind of boy was Tom Sawyer?

"Tom!"
No answer.
"Tom!"
No answer.
"Where is that boy, I wonder? TOM!"
No answer.

Aunt Polly pulled her spectacles down and looked over them as she peered around the room. Then she pushed the spectacles up and looked out under them. She seldom looked through them for so small a thing as a boy. The spectacles were her best pair, the pride of her heart, and they were built for "style," not service. She could have seen through a pair of bottle caps just as well. She looked perplexed for a moment and then said:

"Well, if I get a hold of him, I'll . . ."

She did not finish, for by this time, she was bending down and sweeping under the bed with the broom.

"I never did see a boy like that!" she exclaimed at last.

She went to the open door and stood in it and looked out at her garden. No Tom. So she lifted up her voice and shouted:

"Y-o-u-u, Tom!"

There was a slight noise from the closet behind her, and she turned just in time to see a small boy start to sneak out of the open door. She quickly seized him by the back of his pants.

"There! I might have thought of that closet. What have you been doing in there?"

"Nothing."

"Nothing! Look at your hands. And look at your mouth. What is that stuff?"

"I don't know, Aunt Polly."

"Well, I know. It's jam—that's what it is. Forty times I've said if you didn't let that jam alone, I'd punish you. So . . ."

"My! Look behind you, Aunt Polly!"

The old lady whirled around and saw nothing. Meanwhile, the lad fled through the open door, scrambled up the high board fence, and disappeared.

Aunt Polly stood surprised for a moment and then broke into a gentle laugh.

"Can't I ever learn anything? Hasn't Tom played enough tricks like that for me to know what he's up to? But old fools are the biggest fools. Can't teach an old dog new tricks, as the saying goes. But my goodness, he never plays two tricks alike, and how am I supposed to know what's coming? He appears to know just how long he can torment me before I get angry, and he knows if he can put me off for a minute that I can't stay mad at him. I'm not doing my duty by that boy, and that's the truth."

Tom was the son of Polly's dead sister, and Polly didn't have the heart to punish him. Every time she let him off, her conscience hurt her; and every time she punished him, her old heart almost broke.

At last, Polly decided to make Tom work tomorrow. It would be mighty hard to make him work on Saturday, when all the boys were having a holiday. But Tom hated work more than he hated anything else, and Polly had to "do her duty" by making sure Tom did his chores. Otherwise, he might never change. ♦

EXERCISE 9
Silent Reading

1. Read the rest of the lesson to yourselves and be ready to answer some questions.

While Polly was deciding on the punishment, Tom was running down the road. He was not the Model Boy of the village. He knew the Model Boy very well, though—and hated him.

It was a beautiful summer evening, and it was not dark, yet. Suddenly, Tom stopped. A stranger was in front of him—a boy a shade larger than himself. A newcomer of any age was a curiosity in the poor little shabby village of Saint Petersburg. This newcomer was well dressed, too; this was simply astounding.

The newcomer's cap was dainty; his blue cloth coat was new and handsome, and so were his pants. Tom observed with wonder that the newcomer had shoes on, and that he even wore a necktie. He had a smug expression that drove Tom mad. The more Tom stared at the newcomer, the higher Tom turned up his nose at the newcomer's clothes, and the shabbier

Tom's own clothes seemed to grow.

Neither boy spoke. If one moved, the other moved—but only sideways, in a circle. They kept face to face and eye to eye all the time. Finally Tom said:

"I can lick you!"

"I'd like to see you try it."

"Well, I can do it."

"No, you can't, either."

"Yes, I can."

"No, you can't."

"I can."

"You can't."

"Can!"

"Can't!"

A brief pause. Then Tom said:

"What's your name?"

"None of your business."

"Well, I'll make it my business."

"Well, why don't you?"

"If you say much, I will."

"Much—much—much. There now."

"Oh, you think you're mighty smart, don't you?" Tom said. "I could lick you with one hand tied behind me, if I wanted to."

"Well, why don't you do it? You say you can do it."

"Well, I will, if you fool with me."

"Oh, sure you will."

Another pause, and more eyeing and sidling around each other. Presently they were shoulder to shoulder. Tom said:

"Get away from here!"

"Go away yourself!"

"I won't."

"I won't either."

So they stood, shoving each other back and forth and glaring at each other with hate. But neither could get an advantage. They struggled until they were both hot and flushed; then each relaxed and Tom said, lying:

"I'll tell my big brother on you, and he can thrash you with his little finger, and I'll make him do it, too."

"What do I care for your big brother? I've got a brother that's bigger than he is—and what's more, he can throw your big brother over that fence, too." (Both big brothers were imaginary.) ★

"That's a lie," Tom said.

"Your saying so doesn't make it so."

Tom drew a line in the dust with his big toe and said:

"I dare you to step over that, and I'll lick you till you can't stand up."

The new boy stepped over the line promptly and said:

"Now you said you'd do it, now let's see you do it."

"Don't you crowd me now; you better look out."

Well, you said you'd do it—why don't you do it?"

"For two cents I will do it."

The new boy took two copper pennies out of his pocket and held them out. Tom struck them to the ground. In an instant both boys were rolling and tumbling in the dirt, gripped together like cats. For almost a minute, they tugged and tore at each other's hair and clothes, punched and scratched each other's noses, and covered themselves with dust. Tom finally appeared, seated on top of the new boy and pounding him with his fists.

"Holler if you've had enough," Tom said.

The boy only struggled to free himself. He was crying—mainly from rage.

"Holler enough!" Tom said again.

At last the stranger got out a smothered "Enough!" Tom let him up and said, "Now that'll teach you. Better look out who you're fooling with next time."

The new boy went off brushing the dust from his clothes, sobbing, sniffling, and occasionally looking back and shaking his head and threatening what he would do to Tom the next time he saw him. Tom responded with a sneer and started off. But as soon as Tom's back was turned, the new boy picked up a chunk of dirt from the ground, threw it, and hit Tom between the shoulders. Then he turned tail and ran like an antelope.

Tom chased the traitor home, and thus found out where he lived. He then stood at the gate for some time, daring the enemy to come outside; but the enemy only made faces at him through the window. At last, the enemy's mother appeared and called Tom a bad, vicious, rude child and ordered him away. So he went away, but he said he'd "get" that boy.

He got home pretty late that night. When he climbed through the window, he discovered an ambush—his aunt. Seeing the state his clothes were in, she resolved more firmly than ever to turn his Saturday holiday into a day of hard labor.

- What kind of boy was Tom Sawyer? (Ideas: *Disobedient; full of tricks; talkative; prone to exaggeration; the kind who gets into fights; free-spirited; the kind who hates work.*) (MJ)
- How did Aunt Polly feel about Tom? (Ideas: *She disliked his tricks, but she still loved him; she didn't have the heart to punish him; he was special to her because he was her dead sister's son.*) (DCE)
- What did Aunt Polly mean when she said, "I'm not doing my duty by that boy"? (Ideas: *She wasn't bringing him up properly; she wasn't punishing him enough.*) (UCCM)
- Why do you think Tom hated the Model Boy? (Ideas: *Because Tom was not a Model Boy; because Tom disliked boys who behaved properly.*) (MJ)
- What boasts and lies did Tom make to the new boy? (Ideas: *He said he could lick the new boy with one hand tied behind his back; he said he had a big brother who could thrash the new boy.*) (R)

EXERCISE 10

Paired Practice (Optional)

1. Now you'll read in pairs.
- Whoever read second the last time will read first today.
- Remember to start at the diamond and switch at the star.
2. (Observe students and answer questions as needed.)

AFTER READING

EXERCISE 11

Independent Work

1. Do all the items in your workbook and textbook for this lesson.
2. (The independent work in this lesson includes the following activities.)
- Story details
- Character traits
- Combined sentences
- Crossword puzzle
- Poem review
- Maps
- Vocabulary review
- Comprehension
- Writing

Workcheck

1. (Using the Answer Key, read the questions and answers for the workbook.)
2. (Have students read their answers for the textbook activities.)
3. (Have two or three students read their writing assignments aloud. Comment on each assignment.)
4. (Have students correct and turn in their work.)

(Present Spelling lesson 91 after completing Reading lesson 91. See *Spelling Presentation Book.*)

LESSON 92

BEFORE READING

(Have students find lesson 92, part A, in their textbooks.)

EXERCISE 1

Hard Words

1. Look at column 1.
- These are hard words from your textbook stories.

1. philosopher	**3. contemplate**
2. resume	**4. casual**

2. Word 1 is **philosopher.** Everybody, what word? (Signal.) *Philosopher.*
- (Repeat this procedure for every word in the column.)
3. Let's read the words again.
4. Word 1. Everybody, what word? (Signal.) *Philosopher.*
- (Repeat this procedure for every word in the column.)
5. (Repeat the column until firm.)

EXERCISE 2

Word Practice

1. Look at column 2.
- We're going to practice these words.

1. whitewash	**4. locust**
2. inspiration	**5. alongside**
3. melancholy	

2. Word 1. Everybody, what word? (Signal.) *Whitewash.*
- (Repeat this procedure for every word in the column.)
3. (Repeat the column until firm.)

EXERCISE 3

New Vocabulary

1. Look at column 3.
- First we'll read the words in this column. Then we'll read their definitions.

1. brim	**5. suits**
2. waver	**6. absorbed**
3. tranquil	**7. fragment**
4. resume	**8. philosopher**

2. Word 1. Everybody, what word? (Signal.) *Brim.*
- (Repeat this procedure for every word in the column.)
3. (Repeat the column until firm.)

EXERCISE 4

Vocabulary Definitions

1. Everybody, find part B. ✔
- These are definitions for the words you just read.
2. (For each word, call on a student to read the definition and the item. Then ask the student to complete the item.)

1. **brim**—When something *brims,* it is filled or overflowing. If a pond is filled with fish, the pond brims with fish.
- What's another way of saying *The cup overflowed with water?*
- What's the answer? (Response: *The cup brimmed with water.*)

2. **waver**—When you *waver,* you can't make up your mind.
- What's another way of saying *He couldn't make up his mind?*
- What's the answer? (Response: *He wavered.*)

3. **tranquil**—*Tranquil* is another word for calm.
- What's another way of saying *Her mood was calm?*
- What's the answer? (Response: *Her mood was tranquil.*)

---

144   *Lesson 92*

4. **resume**—When you *resume* doing something, you start doing it again.
- What's another way of saying *He started working on his homework again*?
- What's the answer? (Response: *He resumed working on his homework.*)

5. **suits**—If something *suits* you, you like it. If you like melons, melons suit you.
- What's another way of saying *I like singing*?
- What's the answer? (Response: *Singing suits me.*)

6. **absorbed**—When you are *absorbed* in an activity, you are deeply involved in it.
- What's another way of saying *She was deeply involved in her thoughts*?
- What's the answer? (Response: *She was absorbed in her thoughts.*)

7. **fragment**—A *fragment* is a small piece of something.
- What's another way of saying *a small piece of chalk*?
- What's the answer? (Response: *A fragment of chalk.*)

8. **philosopher**—A *philosopher* is someone who seeks truth and wisdom.
- What is a philosopher?
- What's the answer? (Idea: *Someone who seeks truth and wisdom.*)

EXERCISE 5
Vocabulary Review
1. Everybody, find part C. ✔
- We're going to review these words.
2. (Call on a student to read the words in the box.)

traitor	smother
perplexed	bulky
conscience	legends
smug	vicious

3. (For each item, have a student read the item and say the answer.)

1. When you are puzzled, you are ▮▮▮▮.
- What's the answer? (Response: *Perplexed.*)

2. Someone who betrays you is a ▮▮▮▮.
- What's the answer? (Response: *Traitor.*)

3. When you cut off something's air, you ▮▮▮▮ it.
- What's the answer? (Response: *Smother.*)

4. When you feel satisfied with yourself, you feel ▮▮▮▮.
- What's the answer? (Response: *Smug.*)

5. Something that is cruel or violent is ▮▮▮▮.
- What's the answer? (Response: *Vicious.*)

6. Your sense of right and wrong is your ▮▮▮▮.
- What's the answer? (Response: *Conscience.*)

EXERCISE 6
Graphs
1. Everybody, turn to part F at the end of today's story. ✔
- (Call on individual students to read several sentences each.)
- (At the end of each section, present the questions for that section.)

APPLE PRODUCTION AT THE EDEN APPLE ORCHARDS

Write the answers for items 1–6.

On the graph above, the numbers along the left side of the graph tell how many bushels of apples were picked during a year.

- What's the label on the left side of the graph? (Response: *Bushels of apples.*)
- What do the numbers on the left side of the graph show? (Idea: *How many bushels of apples were picked during a year.*)

The numbers along the bottom of the graph name the years from 1991 to 2001.

- What's the label at the bottom of the graph? (Response: *Years.*)
- What do the numbers at the bottom of the graph show? (Idea: *The names of years.*)

- Look at dot R. Find out what year R shows by going straight down from R.
1. What year is on the same line as R?

- What's the answer? (Response: *1994.*)
- So what year does R tell about? (Response: *1994.*)

- Find out how many apples were picked during that year by going across from R to the apple numbers.
2. What number is on the same line as R?

- What's the answer? (Response: *Four thousand.*)

- So how many apples were picked in 1994? (Response: *Four thousand bushels.*)

- Now look at dot M.
3. Which year does M tell about?

- What's the answer? (Response: *1998.*)

4. How many apples were picked in that year?

- What's the answer? (Response: *Six thousand bushels.*)

- Now look at dot J.
5. Which year does J tell about?

- What's the answer? (Response: *1991.*)

6. How many apples were picked in that year?

- What's the answer? (Response: *Five thousand bushels.*)
- You'll write the answers later.

READING

EXERCISE 7

Story Background

1. Everybody, turn back to part D. ✔
- (Call on individual students to read.)
- (After each section, present the questions for that section.)

Tom's Rule

In Chapter 2, Tom learns this rule about human nature: All you need to do to make a person want something is to make the thing difficult to get.
- How do you make somebody want something?

- What's the answer? (Idea: *Make the thing difficult to get.*) ®

- If you used the rule, how would you make somebody want a piece of wood?

- What's the answer? (Idea: *Make the piece of wood difficult to get*.) (MD)

- If you used the rule, how would you make somebody want to do a hard job, such as shoveling snow?

- What's the answer? (Idea: *Make the job difficult to get*.) (MD)

Chapter 2 also tells about whitewash. In the 1840s, people used whitewash to paint wood. Whitewash was mostly water mixed with different kinds of white powder. To use whitewash, people filled a bucket with the white, runny substance. Then they used a paint brush to spread the whitewash onto the wood.

Unlike modern paint, whitewash did not last long. When it faded away, people had to apply another coating of whitewash to keep the wood looking clean and white. Children were often given the job of whitewashing fences and other wooden objects.

- How are whitewash and paint the same? (Idea: *Both are used to paint wood*.) (C/C)
- How are whitewash and paint different? (Idea: *Whitewash doesn't last as long as paint*.) (C/C)

EXERCISE 8

Focus Question

1. Everybody, find part E. ✔
2. What's the focus question for today's lesson? (Response: *Why did the other boys want to whitewash the fence?*)

EXERCISE 9

Reading Aloud (Optional)

1. We're going to read aloud to the diamond.
- (Call on individual students to read several sentences each.)

Chapter 2
The Glorious Whitewasher

Focus Question: Why did the other boys want to whitewash the fence?

Saturday morning came, and all the summer world was bright and fresh and brimming with life. There was a song in every heart; there was cheer in every face and a spring in every step. The locust trees were in bloom, and the fragrance of the blossoms filled the air.

Tom appeared on the sidewalk with a bucket of whitewash and a long-handled brush. He viewed the fence. All gladness left him, and a deep melancholy settled down on his spirit. He had to whitewash thirty yards of board fence nine feet high. Life to him seemed hollow, and living just a burden.

He sighed, then dipped his brush and passed it along the topmost plank of the fence. He repeated the operation; then he did it again. He compared the tiny whitewashed streak with the vast unwhitewashed fence—and sat down discouraged.

Tom's younger brother, Sid, came skipping out at the gate with a tin pail, singing "Buffalo Gals." Bringing water from the town pump had always seemed like hateful work to Tom, but now it did not strike him so. He remembered that there was company at the pump. Boys and girls were always there waiting their turns, resting, trading playthings, and quarreling. Although the pump was only a hundred and fifty yards off, Sid never got back with a bucket of water in less than an hour.

Tom said, "Say, Sid, I'll fetch the water if you'll whitewash some."

Sid shook his head and said, "Can't, Tom. Old Polly, she told me I have to go and get this water and not fool around with anybody. She said she expected you were going to ask me to whitewash, and she told me to go along and tend to my own business."

"Oh, never mind what she said, Sid. That's the way she always talks. Gimme the bucket—I'll only be gone a minute. She won't ever know."

"Oh, I shouldn't, Tom. Old Polly, she'd tear my head off. Indeed she would."

"Oh, come on. The worst punishment she ever gives is when she whacks you over the head with her thimble—and who's afraid of that, I'd like to know? She talks awful, but talk doesn't hurt—at least if she doesn't cry. Sid, I'll give you a marble—my best white one."

Sid began to waver.

"My white marble, Sid! And it's big."

"My! That's a mighty fine marble, I tell you! But, Tom, I'm afraid old Polly . . ."

"And besides, if you will, I'll show you my sore toe."

Sid was only human—this attraction was too much for him. He put down his pail, took the white marble, and bent over the toe with great interest as Tom unwound the bandage.

A moment later, everything changed when a third person appeared on the scene. Suddenly Sid was flying down the street with his pail, Tom was whitewashing with vigor, and Aunt Polly was marching triumphantly back into the house. ♦

EXERCISE 10

Silent Reading

1. Read the rest of the lesson to yourselves and be ready to answer some questions.

Tom's energy with the whitewash brush did not last. He began to think of the fun he had planned for this day, and his sorrows increased. Soon the free boys would come skipping along. They would make a world of fun of him for having to work. The very thought of it burned Tom like fire.

He got out his worldly wealth and examined it. He had bits of toys, marbles, and trash—it wasn't enough to buy even half an hour of freedom. So he returned his wealth to his pocket and gave up the idea. At that dark and hopeless moment, he had a terrific idea—an inspiration. It was a great, magnificent inspiration.

Tom took up his brush and went tranquilly to work. Ben Rogers came in sight presently. Tom dreaded Ben's ridicule most of all. Ben hopped, jumped, and skipped along. In between hops, he bit into an apple.

Tom went on whitewashing and paid no attention to him. Ben stared a moment and then said, "You've got a lot of chores, don't you?"

No answer. Tom surveyed his last touch with the eye of an artist. Then he gave his brush another gentle sweep and looked at the result with admiration. Ben came up alongside him. Tom's mouth watered for the apple, but he stuck to his work. Ben said, "You got to work, hey?"

Tom wheeled suddenly and said, "Why, it's you, Ben. I didn't notice you."

Then Ben said in a mocking tone, "Say—I'm going in swimming. Don't you wish you could? But of course you'd rather work—wouldn't you? Course you would!"

Tom gazed thoughtfully at the boy and said, "What do you call work?"

"Why, ain't that work?"

Tom resumed his whitewashing and answered carelessly, "Well, maybe it is, and maybe it isn't. All I know is, it suits Tom Sawyer."

"Oh, come now, you don't mean to let on that you like it?"

The brush continued to move.

"Like it? Well, I don't see why I oughtn't to like it. Does a boy get a chance to whitewash a fence every day?"

That put the whitewashing in a new light. Ben stopped nibbling his apple. Tom swept his brush daintily back and forth—stepped back to note the effect—added a touch here and there—and noted the effect again. Ben watched every move and got more and more interested, more and more absorbed. Presently he said, "Say, Tom, let me whitewash a little."

Tom considered and was about to agree, but he changed his mind. ★

"No . . . no . . . I reckon it wouldn't hardly do, Ben. You see, Aunt Polly's awful particular about this fence. It's got to be done very carefully. I reckon there ain't one boy in a thousand, maybe two thousand, that can do it the way it's got to be done."

"No—is that so? Oh, come on—lemme just try. Only just a little. I'd let you whitewash if you were me, Tom."

"Ben, I'd like to, honest; but Aunt Polly . . . Sid wanted to do it, but she wouldn't let him. Now don't you see my problem? If you were to tackle this fence and anything happened to it . . ."

"Oh, shucks, I'll be careful. Now let me try. Say—I'll give you the core of my apple."

"No, Ben. I'm afraid."

"I'll give you all the rest of my apple."

Tom gave up the brush with sorrow in his face but lightness in his heart. And while Ben worked and sweated in the sun, the retired artist sat on a barrel in the shade close by, dangled his legs, munched his apple, and planned how to deceive more innocent boys.

Boys came along every little while. They came to make fun, but they remained to whitewash. By the time Ben was tired out, Billy Fisher had given Tom a kite for a chance to whitewash. And when Billy tired out, Johnny Miller took over. He gave Tom a key that wouldn't unlock anything. And so on, and so on, hour after hour.

When the middle of the afternoon came, Tom was rolling in wealth. He had twelve marbles, a piece of blue bottle glass to look through, a spool of thread, a fragment of chalk, a tin soldier, a couple of tadpoles, six firecrackers, a brass doorknob, a dog collar—but no dog—the handle of a knife, and part of an orange.

He had a nice, good, idle time all the while—plenty of company—and the fence had three coats of whitewash on it! If he hadn't run out of whitewash, he would have had the prize possessions of every boy in the village.

Tom said to himself that it was not such a hollow life after all. He had discovered a great law of human nature without knowing it—all you need to do to make a person want something is to make the thing difficult to get. If he had been a great and wise philosopher, he would now have understood that work consists of whatever someone is required to do and that play consists of whatever someone is not required to do.

Tom thought about the sudden increase in his wealth and then headed back to the house.

- Why did the other boys want to whitewash the fence? (Ideas: *Because Tom told them they couldn't; because Tom made it seem hard to get.*) (DCE)

- Explain how Tom tried to tempt Sid to whitewash the fence. (Ideas: *Tom offered to give Sid a marble; Tom offered to show Sid his sore toe.*) (R)

- What made Tom realize he'd have to come up with a better plan for getting other boys to whitewash the fence? (Ideas: *He didn't have enough wealth to bribe the boys; Aunt Polly might catch him paying the boys.*) (DCE)

- Why did Tom pretend not to notice Ben Rogers at first? (Ideas: *Tom wanted to appear absorbed in his work; Tom wanted to make whitewashing seem fun.*) (DCE)

- According to the story, what's the difference between work and play? (Idea: *Work is what you're required to do, and play is what you're not required to do.*) (C/C)

EXERCISE 11
Paired Practice (Optional)

1. Now you'll read in pairs.
- Whoever read second the last time will read first today.
- Remember to start at the diamond and switch at the star.
2. (Observe students and answer questions as needed.)

AFTER READING

EXERCISE 12
Independent Work

1. Do all the items in your workbook and textbook for this lesson.
2. (The independent work in this lesson includes the following activities.)
- Story details
- Vocabulary
- Maps
- Graphs
- Comprehension
- Writing

EXERCISE 13

Workcheck

1. (Using the Answer Key, read the questions and answers for the workbook.)

2. (Have students read their answers for the textbook activities.)

3. (Have two or three students read their writing assignments aloud. Comment on each assignment.)

4. (Have students correct and turn in their work.)

SPELLING

(Present Spelling lesson 92 after completing Reading lesson 92. See *Spelling Presentation Book.*)

BEFORE READING

(Have students find lesson 93, part A, in their textbooks.)

EXERCISE 1
Hard Words

1. Look at column 1.
- These are hard words from your textbook stories.

1. Staten Island	3. Harlem
2. congregation	

2. Line 1 is **Staten Island.** Everybody, what words? (Signal.) *Staten Island.*
- (Repeat this procedure for every word in the column.)
3. Let's read the words again.
4. Line 1. Everybody, what words? (Signal.) *Staten Island.*
- (Repeat this procedure for every word in the column.)
5. (Repeat the column until firm.)

EXERCISE 2
Word Practice

1. Look at column 2.
- We're going to practice these words.

1. crumpled	3. drowsing
2. maidservant	4. absurd

2. Word 1. Everybody, what word? (Signal.) *Crumpled.*
- (Repeat this procedure for every word in the column.)
3. (Repeat the column until firm.)

EXERCISE 3
New Vocabulary

1. Look at column 3.
- First we'll read the words in this column. Then we'll read their definitions.

1. casual	3. contemplate
2. worship	4. drone

2. Word 1. Everybody, what word? (Signal.) *Casual.*
- (Repeat this procedure for every word in the column.)
3. (Repeat the column until firm.)

EXERCISE 4
Vocabulary Definitions

1. Everybody, find part B. ✔
- These are definitions for the words you just read.
2. (For each word, call on a student to read the definition and the item. Then ask the student to complete the item.)

1. **casual**—When something is *casual,* it happens by chance or at random. A meeting that happens by chance is a casual meeting.
- What's another way of saying *a visit that happens by chance*?

- What's the answer? (Response: *A casual visit.*)

2. **worship**—When you *worship* something, you treat it with great respect.
- What's another way of saying *He treated his older brother with great respect*?

- What's the answer? (Response: *He worshipped his older brother.*)

3. **contemplate**—When you *contemplate* something, you look at it closely.
- What's another way of saying *She looked closely at the painting*?

- What's the answer? (Response: *She contemplated the painting.*)

4. **drone**—When you *drone*, you speak at length in a dull voice.
- What's another way of saying *The judge spoke at length in a dull voice*?

- What's the answer? (Response: *The judge droned.*)

EXERCISE 5

Graphs

1. Everybody, turn to part D at the end of today's story. ✔
- (Call on individual students to read several sentences each.)
- (At the end of each section, present the questions for that section.)

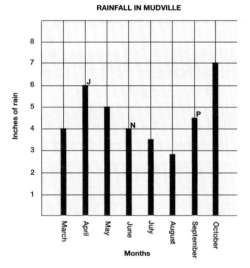

RAINFALL IN MUDVILLE

Write the answers for items 1–6.

On the graph above, the numbers along the left side of the graph tell how many inches of rain fell during a month.

- What's the label on the left side of the graph? (Response: *Inches of rain.*)
- What do the numbers on the left side of the graph show? (Idea: *How many inches of rain fell during a month.*)

The words along the bottom of the graph name the months from March to October.

- What's the label on the bottom of the graph? (Response: *Months.*)
- What do the words on the bottom of the graph show? (Idea: *The names of months.*)

- Find bar J.
1. What month does bar J tell about?

- What's the answer? (Response: *April.*)
- So what month does J tell about? (Response: *April.*)

- Find out how much rain fell during that month by going across from J to the rainfall numbers.
2. What number is on the same line as J?

- What's the answer? (Response: *Six.*)
- So how much rain fell in April? (Response: *Six inches.*)

- Now look at bar N.
3. Which month does bar N tell about?

- What's the answer? (Response: *June.*)

4. How much rain fell during that month?

- What's the answer? (Response: *Four inches.*)

- Now look at bar P.
5. Which month does bar P tell about?

- What's the answer? (Response: *September.*)

6. How much rain fell during that month?

- What's the answer? (Idea: *About four and a half inches.*)
- You'll write the answers later.

READING

EXERCISE 6

Focus Question

1. Everybody, turn back to part C. ✔
2. What's the focus question for today's lesson? (Response: *Why did Tom try to impress the Adored Unknown Girl?*)

EXERCISE 7

Reading Aloud (Optional)

1. We're going to read aloud to the diamond.
- (Call on individual students to read several sentences each.)

Chapter 3
Busy at War and Love

Focus Question: Why did Tom try to impress the Adored Unknown Girl?

Tom walked into the house. Aunt Polly was sitting by an open window in a pleasant room that was bedroom, breakfast room, dining room, and library combined. The warm summer air, the restful quiet, the odor of the flowers, and the drowsing murmur of the bees had had their effect on her, and she was nodding over her knitting. She had no company but the cat, and it was asleep in her lap. Her spectacles were propped up on her gray head for safety. She had thought that Tom had deserted long ago, and she was amazed to see him.

He said, "May I go and play now, Aunt Polly?"

"What, already? How much have you done?"

"It's all done, Aunt Polly."

"Tom, don't lie to me—I can't bear it."

"I ain't, Aunt Polly; it is all done."

Aunt Polly did not trust Tom's statement. She went out to see for herself. She would have been content to find a small part of the fence finished. When she found the entire fence whitewashed, and not only whitewashed but skillfully coated and recoated, her astonishment was great.

She said, "Well, I never! There's no getting round it, you can work when you want to, Tom." And then she weakened the compliment by adding, "But it's seldom you want to, I'm bound to say. Well, go along and play, but get back sometime in a week."

She was so overcome by the splendor of Tom's achievement that she called him in and selected a choice apple and handed it to him. As she did so, she told him about the added value and flavor of a treat that was earned by hard work. And as she spoke, Tom stole a doughnut.

Then he skipped out and was over the fence and gone. There was a gate, but as a general rule he was in too much of a hurry to make use of it. ♦

Silent Reading

1. Read the rest of the lesson to yourselves and be ready to answer some questions.

Tom ran down the block and came to a muddy alley behind his aunt's cow stable. He hurried toward the public square of the village, where two groups of boys were playing soldiers. Tom became general of one army, Joe Harper general of the other. These two great commanders did not fight in person—that was for the smaller boys. Instead, the two commanders sat together on a hill and sent orders to the troops. Tom's army won a great victory, after a long and hard-fought battle. Then the prisoners were exchanged, and the day for the next battle was agreed upon. At last, the armies fell into line and marched away, and Tom turned homeward alone.

As he was passing by the house where Jeff Thatcher lived, he saw a new girl in the garden—a lovely little blue-eyed creature with yellow hair in two long pigtails. Tom fell in love at once. His last love, Amy Lawrence, vanished out of his heart. He had taken months to win Amy, and she had confessed her love for him hardly a week ago. He had been the happiest and proudest boy in the world for seven short days, and here in one instant Amy had gone out of his heart like a casual stranger whose visit is done.

He secretly worshipped this new angel till he saw that she had discovered him. Then he pretended he did not know she was present. He began to "show off" in all sorts of absurd boyish ways in order to win her admiration. He kept up his foolishness for some time. But by and by, while he was in the middle of some dangerous feat in a tree, he glanced aside and saw that the little girl was walking back toward the house.

Tom came up to the fence and leaned on it. He hoped she would stay a while longer. She halted on the steps and then moved toward the door. Tom heaved a great sigh of disappointment as she put her foot on the threshold. But suddenly his face lit up, for she tossed a flower over the fence a moment before she disappeared.

Tom was fascinated with the flower, but he didn't want anybody to see him pick it up. So he ran around and stopped within a foot or two of the flower. Then he shaded his eyes with his hand and began to look down the street. Presently he picked up a straw and began trying to balance it on his nose, with his head tilted far back. As he moved from side to side, he edged nearer and nearer to the flower. Finally, his bare foot rested upon it, and he hopped away with the treasure between his toes. He disappeared around the corner. It took him only a minute to button the flower inside his jacket, next to his heart. ★

He returned, now, and stayed near the girl's fence till nightfall, "showing off" as before; but the girl never appeared again. Tom comforted himself a little with the hope that she had been near some window and had seen his incredible performance. Finally, he went away, with his poor head full of visions.

He wandered away aimlessly. Soon, a log raft in the river caught his attention. He seated himself on the log raft and contemplated the vastness of the river. He wondered how people would feel if he drowned. Then he thought of his flower. He took it out. It was crumpled and wilted. He wondered if she would pity him if he drowned. Would she cry, and wish that she could put her arms around his neck and comfort him? Or would she turn coldly away? He worked this thought over and over again in his mind and set it up in new and varied ways till he wore it out. At last, he rose up sighing and departed in the darkness.

About half past nine or ten o'clock, Tom returned to the deserted street to where the Adored Unknown Girl lived. He paused a moment. No sound fell upon his listening ear. A candle was casting a dull glow upon the curtain of a second-story window. Was the Adored Unknown Girl there? He climbed the fence and tiptoed through the plants until he stood under that window. He looked up at it long, and with emotion.

Tom lay down on his back under the window. His hands were folded on his chest, holding his poor wilted flower. As he lay there, Tom imagined that he would look this way if he were dying, with no shelter over his head, no loving face to bend over him. And thus she would see him when she looked out in the morning. Would she drop one little tear upon his poor, lifeless form? Would she heave one little sigh to see a bright young life so rudely cut down?

The window went up, a maidservant's voice broke the calm, and a torrent of water drenched poor Tom and brought him back to life. Tom sprang up with a snort, went over the fence, and shot away in the gloom.

Later that night, Polly mentioned that Jeff Thatcher's cousin Becky had moved to Saint Petersburg. Tom said nothing.

- What was the Adored Unknown Girl's real name? (Response: *Becky.*) (ND)
- Why did Tom try to impress Becky? (Ideas: *He wanted her to fall in love with him; he wanted her to admire him; he was in love with her.*) (DCE)
- Tom had spent months winning Amy Lawrence's love. Why do you think he forgot Amy so quickly? (Ideas: *He was more in love with Becky; he was no longer interested in Amy after winning her love.*) (MJ)
- Why do you think Becky tossed a flower over the fence? (Ideas: *She wanted to give Tom a gift; she was signaling to Tom that she'd seen him; she was just throwing the flower away.*) (DCE)
- Why do you think Tom imagined he was dying? (Ideas: *He wanted Becky to feel sorry for him; he wondered if anybody loved him.*) (MJ)
- Do you think Becky was impressed with Tom? Explain your answer. (Ideas: *Yes, because she tossed the flower to him; no, because she left in the middle of his performance.*) (MJ)

Paired Practice (Optional)

1. Now you'll read in pairs.
- Whoever read second the last time will read first today.
- Remember to start at the diamond and switch at the star.
2. (Observe students and answer questions as needed.)

AFTER READING

Independent Work

1. Do all the items in your workbook and textbook for this lesson.
2. (The independent work in this lesson includes the following activities.)
- Story details
- Vocabulary
- Maps
- Irony
- Graphs
- Vocabulary review
- Comprehension
- Writing

Workcheck

1. (Using the Answer Key, read the questions and answers for the workbook.)
2. (Have students read their answers for the textbook activities.)
3. (Have two or three students read their writing assignments aloud. Comment on each assignment.)
4. (Have students correct and turn in their work.)

(Present Spelling lesson 93 after completing Reading lesson 93. See *Spelling Presentation Book.*)

LESSON 94

BEFORE READING

(Have students find lesson 94, part A, in their textbooks.)

EXERCISE 1
Hard Words

1. Look at column 1.
   - These are hard words from your textbook stories.

1. gingerly	3. vulgar
2. hymn	4. logic

2. Word 1 is **gingerly**. Everybody, what word? (Signal.) *Gingerly.*
   - (Repeat this procedure for every word in the column.)
3. Let's read the words again.
4. Word 1. Everybody, what word? (Signal.) *Gingerly.*
   - (Repeat this procedure for every word in the column.)
5. (Repeat the column until firm.)

EXERCISE 2
Word Practice

1. Look at column 2.
   - We're going to practice these words.

1. aisle	4. fertile
2. postmaster	5. furry
3. mansion	6. fury

2. Word 1. Everybody, what word? (Signal.) *Aisle.*
   - (Repeat this procedure for every word in the column.)
3. (Repeat the column until firm.)

EXERCISE 3
New Vocabulary

1. Look at column 3.
   - First we'll read the words in this column. Then we'll read their definitions.

1. justice of	5. congregation
the peace	6. pew
2. lapse	7. gingerly
3. minister	8. logic
4. sermon	

2. Line 1. Everybody, what words? (Signal.) *Justice of the peace.*
   - (Repeat this procedure for every word in the column.)
3. (Repeat the column until firm.)

EXERCISE 4
Vocabulary Definitions

1. Everybody, find part B. ✔
   - These are definitions for the words you just read.
2. (For each word, call on a student to read the definition and the item. Then ask the student to complete the item.)

1. **justice of the peace**—A *justice of the peace* is a type of judge with limited powers.
   - What is a justice of the peace?
   - What's the answer? (Idea: *A type of judge with limited powers.*)

2. **lapse**—When you *lapse,* you slowly sink or slip. If you slowly sink into sleep, you lapse into sleep.
   - What's another way of saying *She slowly slipped into a dream*?
   - What's the answer? (Response: *She lapsed into a dream.*)

3. **minister**—A *minister* is the person who directs the services in some churches.
   - What is a minister?
   - What's the answer? (Idea: *A person who directs the services in some churches.*)

4. **sermon**—A *sermon* is a speech that a minister delivers in church.
   - What do we call a speech that a minister delivers in church?

- What's the answer? (Response: *A sermon.*)

5. **congregation**—A *congregation* is a group of people who attend a church service.
- What is a congregation?

- What's the answer? (Response: *A group of people who attend a church service.*)

6. **pew**—A *pew* is a long bench that people sit on in church.
- What's another way of saying *The congregation sat on long benches*?

- What's the answer? (Response: *The congregation sat on pews.*)

7. **gingerly**—When you do something *gingerly,* you do it cautiously.
- What's another way of saying *They entered the cave cautiously*?

- What's the answer? (Response: *They entered the cave gingerly.*)

8. **logic**—*Logic* is the science of reasoning. People use logic to figure out how things work.
- What is the science of reasoning called?

- What's the answer? (Response: *Logic.*)

EXERCISE 5

Logic

1. Everybody, turn to part D at the end of today's story. ✔
- (Call on individual students to read several sentences each.)
- (At the end of each section, present the questions for that section.)

Write the answers for items 1 and 2.
Here's one rule of logic: *Just because two events happen around the same time doesn't mean one event causes the other event.*
The following statement by a writer breaks that rule: "The last five times Sally tapped home plate, she hit a home run. She should always remember to tap home plate when she goes up to bat."

1. What two events happen around the same time?

- What's the answer? (Idea: *Sally tapping home plate and hitting a home run.*)

2. What event does the writer think causes the home run?

- What's the answer? (Idea: *Sally tapping home plate.*)
- You'll write the answers later.

READING

EXERCISE 6

Focus Question

1. Everybody, turn back to part C. ✔
2. What's the focus question for today's lesson? (Response: *How did Tom feel about going to church?*)

EXERCISE 7

Reading Aloud (Optional)

1. We're going to read aloud to the diamond.
- (Call on individual students to read several sentences each.)

Chapter 4
The Pinch Bug and Its Prey
Focus Question: How did Tom feel about going to church?

The next morning was Sunday. About half past ten, the cracked bell of the small church began to ring, and people began to gather for the morning sermon. Aunt Polly came, and Tom and Sid sat with her. Tom was placed next to the aisle—as far away as possible from the open window and the appealing summer weather.

Tom watched the crowd file up the aisles. He saw the aged postmaster, the mayor and his wife, the justice of the peace, and the Widow Douglas. The Widow Douglas was beautiful, smart, and forty years old. She was a generous, good-hearted person and very rich. Her mansion on the hill was the only palace in town.

Next, Tom saw Major and Mrs. Ward; then the beauty of the village, followed by a troop of young suitors; and last of all came the Model Boy, Willie Mufferson. Willie was the pride of all the mothers. The boys all hated him because he was so good. His white handkerchief was hanging out of his pocket. Tom had no handkerchief, and he looked upon boys who had handkerchiefs as snobs.

The congregation was all there now. The bell rang once more, and then a hush fell upon the church. The hush was broken only by the whispering of the choir. The choir always whispered all through service.

The minister announced to the congregation the hymn to be sung. Then he read the hymn. He was regarded as a wonderful reader. At church "socials," he was always called upon to read poetry. At those times, the ladies would blink their eyes and shake their heads, as if to say, "Words cannot express it; it is too beautiful, too beautiful for this earth."

After the hymn had been sung, the minister turned himself into a bulletin board and read off "notices" of meetings till it seemed to Tom the list would never end.

Now the minister prayed. His prayer pleaded for the church and the little children of the church, for the other churches of the village, for the village itself, for the county, for the state, for the state officers, for the United States, for the churches of the United States, for the president, and for poor sailors tossed by stormy seas. He closed with a hope that the words he was about to speak might be like seed sown in fertile ground, producing in time a grateful harvest of good. Amen. ◆

EXERCISE 8

Silent Reading

1. Read the rest of the lesson to yourselves and be ready to answer some questions.

There was a rustling of dresses, and the congregation sat down. Tom did not enjoy the prayer; he only endured it. In the middle of the prayer, a fly had landed on the back of the pew in front of Tom. It had tortured his spirit by calmly rubbing its hands together, embracing its head with its arms, and polishing its head so vigorously that the head almost seemed to separate from the body. The fly then scraped its wings with its hind legs and smoothed them to its body. It went through all these motions as if it knew it was perfectly safe. And indeed it was; for as much as Tom's hands itched to grab for the fly, they did not dare. But with the closing sentence of the prayer, his hand began to curve and move forward. At the instant the "Amen" was out, the fly was a prisoner in Tom's hand. But Tom's aunt detected the act and made Tom let the fly go.

Now the minister began his sermon. He droned along in such a boring way that many heads began to nod. Tom counted the pages of the sermon. After church he always knew how many pages there had been, but he seldom knew anything else about the sermon.

Tom lapsed into suffering as the sermon continued. Presently he remembered a treasure he had and took it out. It was a large black beetle with huge jaws—a "pinch bug," he called it. It was in a small box. The first thing the beetle did was to grab Tom by the finger. A fight followed, and the beetle went floundering into the aisle and ended up on its back. Meanwhile, the hurt finger went into the boy's mouth.

The beetle lay there working its helpless legs, unable to turn over. Tom eyed it and longed for it, but it was out of his reach. Other people uninterested in the sermon found relief in the beetle, and they eyed it, too. Presently, a vagrant poodle dog came along. The dog spied the beetle, and his drooping tail lifted and wagged. He surveyed the prize, walked around it, smelled it from a safe distance, walked around it again, grew bolder, and took a closer smell. Then he lifted his lip and made a gingerly snatch at the bug, just missing it. He made another snatch and another. He began to enjoy himself. He lay down on his stomach with the beetle between his paws and continued his experiments. ★

At last, the dog grew weary. His head nodded, and little by little his chin descended and touched the beetle. The beetle instantly seized it. There was a sharp yelp, and the beetle fell a couple of yards away, on its back once more. The neighboring spectators laughed quietly, hiding their faces behind their fans and handkerchiefs. Tom was entirely happy.

The dog looked foolish, and probably felt so, but he had a craving for revenge. So he went to the beetle and began a cautious attack. He jumped at it from every direction. He brought his paws within an inch of the bug. He made even closer snatches at it with his teeth, and he jerked his head till his ears flapped again. But he grew tired once more. He tried to amuse himself with a fly but found no relief. He followed an ant around, with his nose close to the floor, and quickly wearied of that. Then he yawned, sighed, forgot the beetle entirely—and sat down on it.

There was a wild yelp of agony, and the poodle went sailing up the aisle. The yelps continued, and so did the dog. He flew up one aisle; he flew down the other aisle; he crossed before the doors. As his anguish grew, he ran faster, until he was like a furry comet moving with the gleam and speed of light. At last, the frantic dog sprang into his master's lap. But the master carried the dog outside, and the howls of distress quickly thinned away and faded in the distance.

By this time, the whole church was red-faced and choking with silent laughter, and the sermon had come to a dead standstill. The sermon was resumed presently, and the minister stammered through it. But the congregation no longer felt serious.

Everybody was relieved when the sermon finally ended. Tom Sawyer went home quite cheerful. He had only one disturbing thought: He didn't mind the dog playing with his pinch bug, but he did not think it was fair of him to carry it off.

- How did Tom feel about going to church? (Ideas: *He didn't like it; he thought church was boring.*) ⒹⒸⒺ
- Why did Tom dislike the Model Boy? (Ideas: *The Model Boy was good; the Model Boy was well behaved.*) ⒸⒺ
- Why do you think Tom is so interested in flies and bugs? (Ideas: *They're fun to watch; they're small; he can keep them in his pocket.*) ⒹⒸⒺ
- Explain how the pinch bug ended up in the aisle. (Idea: *When Tom took the bug out of its box, it bit him on the finger. A fight followed, and the bug ended up in the aisle on its back.*) Ⓡ

- The story says the dog was "like a furry comet." Explain why the dog looked like that. (Idea: *The dog was furry, and he was running so fast that he looked like a comet.*) ⒸⒸ

EXERCISE 9

Paired Practice (Optional)

1. Now you'll read in pairs.
- Whoever read second the last time will read first today.
- Remember to start at the diamond and switch at the star.
2. (Observe students and answer questions as needed.)

AFTER READING

EXERCISE 10

Independent Work

1. Do all the items in your workbook and textbook for this lesson.
2. (The independent work in this lesson includes the following activities.)
- Story details
- Vocabulary
- Graphs
- Character traits
- Logic
- Vocabulary review
- Reference books
- Comprehension
- Writing

EXERCISE 11

Workcheck

1. (Using the Answer Key, read the questions and answers for the workbook.)
2. (Have students read their answers for the textbook activities.)
3. (Have two or three students read their writing assignments aloud. Comment on each assignment.)
4. (Have students correct and turn in their work.)

SPELLING

(Present Spelling lesson 94 after completing Reading lesson 94. See *Spelling Presentation Book*.)

BEFORE READING

(Have students find lesson 95, part A, in their textbooks.)

EXERCISE 1

Hard Words

1. Look at column 1.
   - These are hard words from your textbook stories.

1. aggravated	**3. mortified**
2. genuine	**4. juvenile**

2. Word 1 is **aggravated.** Everybody, what word? (Signal.) *Aggravated.*
   - (Repeat this procedure for every word in the column.)
3. Let's read the words again.
4. Word 1. Everybody, what word? (Signal.) *Aggravated.*
   - (Repeat this procedure for every word in the column.)
5. (Repeat the column until firm.)

EXERCISE 2

Word Practice

1. Look at column 2.
   - We're going to practice these words.

1. infect	**3. hymn**
2. bedpost	**4. admirable**

2. Word 1. Everybody, what word? (Signal.) *Infect.*
   - (Repeat this procedure for every word in the column.)
3. (Repeat the column until firm.)

EXERCISE 3

New Vocabulary

1. Look at column 3.
   - First we'll read the words in this column. Then we'll read their definitions.

1. ailment	**4. genuine**
2. considerable	**5. mortified**
3. aggravate	

2. Word 1. Everybody, what word? (Signal.) *Ailment.*
   - (Repeat this procedure for every word in the column.)
3. (Repeat the column until firm.)

EXERCISE 4

Vocabulary Definitions

1. Everybody, find part B. ✔
   - These are definitions for the words you just read.
2. (For each word, call on a student to read the definition and the item. Then ask the student to complete the item.)

1. **ailment**—*Ailment* is another word for sickness.
   - What's another way of saying *He had a strange sickness*?

   - What's the answer? (Response: *He had a strange ailment.*)

2. **considerable**—*Considerable* is another word for *large* or *great.*
   - What's another way of saying *She had a large amount of money*?

   - What's the answer? (Response: *She had a considerable amount of money.*)

3. **aggravate**—When you *aggravate* something, you make it worse.
   - What's another way of saying *His scratching made the wound worse*?

   - What's the answer? (Response: *His scratching aggravated the wound.*)

4. **genuine**—When something is *genuine,* it is real.
   - What's another way of saying *The couch was made of real leather*?

- What's the answer? (Response: *The couch was made of genuine leather.*)

5. **mortified**—If a part of your body is dead, that part is *mortified*.
- What's another way of saying *His little finger seemed dead*?

- What's the answer? (Response: *His little finger seemed mortified.*)

EXERCISE 5

Logic

1. Everybody, turn to part D at the end of today's story. ✔
- (Call on individual students to read several sentences each.)
- (At the end of each section, present the questions for that section.)

Write the answers for items 1 and 2.

Here's a rule of logic: *Just because two events happen around the same time doesn't mean one event causes the other event.*

The following statement by a writer breaks that rule: "When I went to Nova Scotia last year, it was snowing. When I went to Chicago later that year, it snowed. When I went to Buffalo this year, it was also snowing. I think I'll go to Philadelphia next year and make it snow there."

1. What two events happen around the same time?

- What's the answer? (Idea: *The writer goes someplace, and it snows in that place.*)

2. What event does the writer think causes the snow?

- What's the answer? (Idea: *The writer goes someplace.*)
- You'll write the answers later.

READING

EXERCISE 6

Focus Question

1. Everybody, find part C. ✔

2. What's the focus question for today's lesson? (Response: *How did Aunt Polly cure Tom's ailments?*)

EXERCISE 7

Reading Aloud (Optional)

1. We're going to read aloud to the diamond.
- (Call on individual students to read several sentences each.)

Chapter 5
Monday Morning

Focus Question: How did Aunt Polly cure Tom's ailments?

The next day was Monday. That morning, Tom Sawyer was miserable. Monday morning always found him so, because it began another week's slow suffering in school. He generally began Mondays by wishing he had had no weekend, because it made going back to school so much more hateful.

As Tom thought about his situation, it occurred to him that he could be sick; then he could stay home from school. Here was a possibility. He felt his body. He found no ailment, so he investigated again. Suddenly he discovered something. One of his upper front teeth was loose. This was lucky—he was about to begin with a groan when it occurred to him that if he told his aunt about the tooth, she would pull it out, and that would hurt. So he thought he would not mention the tooth unless he could find no other ailment.

Tom found nothing, but then he remembered hearing the doctor tell about a disease that laid up a patient for two or three weeks and threatened to make him lose a finger. Tom eagerly drew his sore toe from under the sheet and held it up for inspection. He did not know what to look for, but it seemed worth a chance, so he began to groan with considerable spirit.

Tom hoped that Sid, who slept next to him, would hear his groans. But Sid slept on.

Tom groaned louder and thought that he began to feel pain in the toe.

No result from Sid.

Tom was panting by this time. He took a rest and then swelled himself up and made a series of admirable groans.

Sid snored on.

Tom was aggravated. He said, "Sid, Sid!" and shook him. This worked well, and Tom began to groan again. Sid yawned and stretched, then brought himself up on his elbow with a snort and began to stare at his brother. Tom went on groaning. ◆

EXERCISE 8
Silent Reading

1. Read the rest of the lesson to yourselves and be ready to answer some questions.

Sid said, "Tom!" (No response.) "Tom! What is the matter?" Sid shook Tom and looked into his face anxiously.

Tom moaned out, "Oh, don't, Sid. Don't shake me."

"Why, what's the matter, Tom? I must call Aunt Polly."

"No—never mind. It'll be over in a while, maybe. Don't call anybody."

"But I must! Don't groan so, Tom, it's awful. How long have you been this way?"

"Hours. Ouch! Oh, don't move around, Sid, you'll kill me."

"Tom, why didn't you wake me sooner? Oh, Tom, don't! It scares me to hear you. Tom, what is the matter?"

In a solemn voice Tom announced, "I forgive you for everything, Sid." (Groan.) "Everything you've ever done to me. When I'm dead and gone . . ."

"Oh, Tom, you ain't dying, are you? Don't, Tom—oh, don't!"

"I forgive everybody, Sid." (Groan.) "Tell 'em so, Sid. And, Sid, you give my kite to that new girl that's come to town, and tell her . . ."

But Sid had snatched his clothes and left. Tom was suffering in reality, now, because his imagination was working so well. His groans had an almost genuine tone.

Sid flew downstairs and called, "Oh, Aunt Polly, come! Tom's dying!"

"Dying!"

"Yes'm. Don't wait—come quick!"

"Rubbish! I don't believe it!"

But she fled upstairs, nevertheless, with Sid at her heels. And her face grew pale, too, and her lip trembled. When she reached the bedside, she gasped, "Tom, what's the matter with you?"

"Oh, Auntie, I'm . . ."

"What's the matter with you—what is the matter with you, child?"

"Oh, Auntie, my sore toe's mortified!"

The old lady sank into a chair and laughed a little, then cried a little, then did both together. This restored her, and she said, "Tom, what a fright you did give me. Now you shut up that nonsense and climb out of bed." ★

The groan ceased, and the pain vanished from the toe. The boy felt a little foolish, and he said, "Aunt Polly, it seemed mortified, and it hurt so I never noticed my tooth at all."

"Your tooth, indeed! What's the matter with your tooth?"

"One of them's loose, and it aches perfectly awful."

"There, there, now, don't begin that groaning again. Open your mouth. Well . . . your tooth is loose, but you're not going to die from that. Sid, get me a chunk of hot coal out of the kitchen stove, and a silk thread."

Tom said, "Oh, please, Auntie, don't pull it out. It don't hurt anymore. Please don't, Auntie. I don't want to stay home from school."

"Oh, you don't, don't you? So all this nonsense was because you thought you'd get to stay home from school and go fishing? Tom, Tom, I love you so, and you seem to try every way you can to break my old heart with your tricks."

By this time Sid had returned with the thread and the hot coal. He carried the coal in a potholder. Aunt Polly tied one end of the silk thread to Tom's tooth and the other end to the bedpost. Then she seized the hot coal and suddenly moved it toward Tom's face. The boy jerked back, and in an instant the tooth was dangling by the bedpost.

But Tom's suffering brought rewards.

As Tom walked to school after breakfast, he was the envy of every boy he met because the gap in his upper row of teeth helped him to spit in a new and admirable way. He gathered quite a following of younger boys who were fascinated by his performance.

- How did Aunt Polly cure Tom's ailments? (Ideas: *She laughed at his "mortified" toe; she pulled out his tooth.*) (Sum)

- Why did Tom seek another ailment after discovering his tooth was loose? (Idea: *He knew that pulling the tooth would hurt.*) (DCE)
- Why did Tom actually begin to feel pain in his toe? (Idea: *Because he had such a good imagination.*) (C/E)
- Why do you think Aunt Polly laughed when Tom said his toe was mortified? (Ideas: *Because his toe wasn't dead; because he didn't know what* mortified *meant.*) (MJ)
- Explain how Aunt Polly pulled out Tom's tooth. (Idea: *She tied one end of a silk thread to Tom's tooth and the other end to a bedpost. Then she moved a hot coal toward Tom's face. When Tom moved back from the hot coal, the thread pulled the tooth out.*) (R)

EXERCISE 9

Paired Practice (Optional)

1. Now you'll read in pairs.
- Whoever read second the last time will read first today.
- Remember to start at the diamond and switch at the star.
2. (Observe students and answer questions as needed.)

AFTER READING

EXERCISE 10

Independent Work

1. Do all the items in your workbook and textbook for this lesson.
2. (The independent work in this lesson includes the following activities.)
- Story details
- Vocabulary
- Graphs
- Perspectives
- Logic
- Maps
- Vocabulary review
- Comprehension
- Writing

EXERCISE 11

Workcheck

1. (Using the Answer Key, read the questions and answers for the workbook.)
2. (Have students read their answers for the textbook activities.)
3. (Have two or three students read their writing assignments aloud. Comment on each assignment.)
4. (Have students correct and turn in their work.)

SPELLING

(Present Spelling lesson 95 after completing Reading lesson 95. See *Spelling Presentation Book*.)

ACTIVITIES ACROSS THE CURRICULUM

(Students should complete the appropriate project in *Activities across the Curriculum* after completing lesson 95. See *Activities across the Curriculum* book for details.)

Lessons 96–100 • Planning Page *Looking Ahead*

	Lesson 96	**Lesson 97**	**Lesson 98**	**Lesson 99**	**Lesson 100**
BEFORE READING	Word practice New vocabulary Vocabulary definitions	Hard words Word practice New vocabulary Vocabulary definitions Vocabulary review	Word practice New vocabulary Vocabulary definitions Vocabulary review Logic	Hard words Word practice New vocabulary Vocabulary definitions Vocabulary review Logic	Word practice Vocabulary review Graphs
NEW VOCABULARY	juvenile vulgar tick wistful doze lull	critical foolhardy scrawl scuffle harass prod	engaged blunder coffin pathetic	oath swear tannery	(none)
READING	*Tom Sawyer* (Chapter 6)	*Tom Sawyer* (Chapter 7)	*Tom Sawyer* (Chapter 8)	*Tom Sawyer* (Chapter 9)	*Tom Sawyer* (Chapter 10)
INDEPENDENT WORK	Story details Vocabulary Graphs Similes Character traits Vocabulary review Logic Irony Comprehension Writing	Story details Vocabulary Graphs Drawing conclusions Character traits Logic Comprehension Writing	Story details Vocabulary Maps Logic Comprehension Writing	Story details Vocabulary Logic Sequencing Poem review Comprehension Writing	Story details Vocabulary Logic Character traits Graphs Comprehension Writing
SUPPLEMENTS	*Spelling*	*Spelling*	*Spelling*	*Spelling*	Mastery Test *Spelling* *Activities across the Curriculum*

Comprehension Questions Abbreviations Guide

Access Prior Knowledge = (APK)   Author's Point of View = (APoV)   Author's Purpose = (AP)   Cause/Effect = (C/E)   Charts/Graphs/Diagrams/Visual Aids = (VA)

Classify and Categorize = (C+C)   Compare/Contrast = (C/C)   Determine Character Emotions, Motivation = (DCE)   Drawing Conclusions = (DC)   Drawing Inferences = (DI)

Fact and Opinion = (F/O)   Hypothesizing = (H)   Main Idea = (MI)   Making Connections = (MC)   Making Deductions = (MD)   Making Judgements = (MJ)

Narrative Elements = (NE)   Noting Details = (ND)   Predict = (P)   Reality/Fantasy = (R/F)   Recall Facts/Rules = (RF/R)   Retell = (R)   Sequence = (Seq)

Steps in a Process = (SP)   Story Structure = (SS)   Summarize = (Sum)   Understanding Dialogue = (UD)   Using Context to Confirm Meaning(s) = (UCCM)   Visualize = (V)

BEFORE READING

(Have students find lesson 96, part A, in their textbooks.)

Word Practice

1. Look at column 1.
- We're going to practice these words.

1. lawless	4. barely
2. idle	5. barley
3. suspender	

2. Word 1. Everybody, what word? (Signal.) *Lawless.*
- (Repeat this procedure for every word in the column.)
3. (Repeat the column until firm.)

New Vocabulary

1. Look at column 2.
- First we'll read the words in this column. Then we'll read their definitions.

1. juvenile	4. wistful
2. vulgar	5. doze
3. tick	6. lull

2. Word 1. Everybody, what word? (Signal.) *Juvenile.*
- (Repeat this procedure for every word in the column.)
3. (Repeat the column until firm.)

Vocabulary Definitions

1. Everybody, find part B. ✔
- These are definitions for the words you just read.
2. (For each word, call on a student to read the definition and the item. Then ask the student to complete the item.)

1. **juvenile**—A *juvenile* is a young person.
- What's another way of saying *Sharon was a young person who acted like an adult*?
- What's the answer? (Response: *Sharon was a juvenile who acted like an adult.*)

2. **vulgar**—*Vulgar* is another word for crude.
- What's another way of saying *His manners were crude*?
- What's the answer? (Response: *His manners were vulgar.*)

3. **tick**—A *tick* is an eight-legged bug that digs into your skin and sucks blood.
- What is a tick?
- What's the answer? (Idea: *An eight-legged bug that digs into your skin and sucks blood.*)

4. **wistful**—When you are *wistful,* you are full of longing.
- What's another way of saying *When they looked at the new car, they became full of longing*?
- What's the answer? (Response: *When they looked at the new car, they became wistful.*)

5. **doze**—When you *doze,* you sleep lightly.
- What's another way of saying *She slept lightly for a few moments*?
- What's the answer? (Response: *She dozed for a few moments.*)

6. **lull**—When something *lulls* you, it makes you sleepy or relaxed.
- What's another way of saying *The sound of the rain made her sleepy*?
- What's the answer? (Response: *The sound of the rain lulled her.*)

READING

Focus Question

1. Everybody, find part C. ✔
2. What's the focus question for today's lesson? (Response: *How did Huck and Tom think they could get rid of warts?*)

> **Note:** The "Reading Aloud" exercise is recommended for this lesson.

EXERCISE 5

Reading Aloud

1. We're going to read aloud to the diamond.
   - (Call on individual students to read several sentences each.)

Chapter 6
Huckleberry Finn

Focus Question: How did Huck and Tom think they could get rid of warts?

On his way to school that Monday morning, Tom came upon the juvenile outcast of the village—Huckleberry Finn, son of the town bum. Huckleberry was hated and dreaded by all the mothers of the town because he was idle, lawless, vulgar, and bad. They particularly hated him because all their children admired him, and delighted in his company, and wished they could be like him. Like the rest of the boys, Tom envied Huckleberry and was under strict orders not to play with him. So Tom played with him every time he got a chance.

Huckleberry was always dressed in old clothes that full-grown men had thrown away. His hat had a wide hole in it. His coat, when he wore one, hung nearly to his knees. His trousers were held up by only one suspender, and the legs of the trousers dragged in the dirt.

Huckleberry came and went as he pleased. He slept on doorsteps in fine weather and in empty barrels in wet weather. He did not have to go to school or church, nor did he have to obey anybody. He could go fishing or swimming when and where he chose and stay as long as it suited him. He could sit up as late as he pleased. He was always the first boy barefoot in the spring and the last to wear shoes in the fall. He never had to wash, nor put on clean clothes. Every boy in Saint Petersburg thought Huckleberry Finn had everything that makes life precious.

Tom hailed the outcast. "Hello, Huckleberry."

"Hello, yourself."

"What's that you got?"

"Dead rat."

"Lemme see him, Huck. My, he's pretty stiff. Where'd you get him?"

"Bought him off a boy."

"What did you give?"

"I give a blue marble."

"Where'd you get the blue marble?"

"Bought it off Ben Rogers two weeks ago for a lucky rabbit's foot."

"Say . . . what are dead rats good for, Huck?"

"Good for? You can cure warts with them."

"No—is that so? I know something that's better."

"I bet you don't. What is it, Tom?"

"Why, stump water."

"Stump water! I wouldn't give anything for stump water."

"You wouldn't, wouldn't you? Did you ever try it?"

"No, I haven't. But Bob Tanner did."

"Who told you so?" asked Tom.

"Why, he told Jeff Thatcher, and Jeff told Johnny Baker, and Johnny told Jim Hollis, and Jim told Ben Rogers, and Ben told me. So there!"

"Well, what of it? They'll all lie. Shucks! Now you tell me how Bob Tanner did it, Huck."

"Why, he dipped his hand in a rotten stump where the rainwater was."

"In the daytime?"

"Certainly."

"With his face to the stump?"

"Yes. Least I reckon so."

"Did he say anything?"

"I don't reckon he did, Tom."

"Aha! You can't cure warts with stump water in such a foolish way as that. Why, that ain't going to do any good. You got to go all by yourself, to the middle of the woods, where you know there's a stump with water in it. Just as it's midnight, you back up against the stump and jam your hand in and say:

> Barley-corn, barley-corn,
>   Injun-meal shorts,
> Stump water, stump water,
>   swallow these warts.

Then you walk away quick, eleven steps, with your eyes shut, and then turn around three times and walk home without speaking to anybody. Because if you speak, the charm's busted."

"Well, that sounds like a good way, but that ain't what Bob Tanner did," said Huck.

"No, sir, you can bet he didn't, because he's the wartiest boy in this town. He wouldn't have a wart on him if he knew how to work stump water. I've taken thousands of warts off my hands that way, Huck. I play with frogs so much that I've always got a lot of warts." ♦

EXERCISE 6

Silent Reading

1. Read the rest of the lesson to yourselves and be ready to answer some questions.

Tom paused and said, "Sometimes I take the warts off with a bean."

"Yes, beans are good," Huck agreed. "I've done that."

"Have you? What's your way?" asked Tom.

"You split the bean. You touch the wart with one part of the bean, and then you dig a hole and bury that part of the bean. You bury it about midnight at the crossroads in the dark of the moon. Then you burn up the rest of the bean."

"Yes, that's it, Huck—that's it; though when you're burying it if you say, 'Down bean, off wart, come no more to bother me!' it's better. That's the way Joe Harper does, and he's been nearly everywhere. But say—how do you cure warts with dead rats?"

"Why, you take your rat and go to the graveyard along about midnight when somebody that was wicked has been buried. And when it's midnight a devil will come, or maybe two or three, but you can't see 'em, you can only hear something like the wind, or maybe hear 'em talk. And when they're taking that dead feller away,

you heave your rat after 'em and say, 'Devil follow corpse, rat follow devil, warts follow rat, I'm done with you!' That'll get rid of any wart!"

"Sounds right. Did you ever try it, Huck?"

"No, but old Mother Hopkins told me."

"Well, I reckon it's so, then, because they say she's a witch. Say, Hucky, when you going to try that rat?"

"Tonight. I reckon the devils'll come after old Horse Williams tonight."

"But they buried him Saturday. Didn't the devils get him Saturday night?"

"No! How could devil charms work till midnight? And then it's a Sunday. Devils don't mess around much on Sunday, I don't reckon," said Huck. ★

"I never thought of that. That's so. Lemme go with you tonight."

"Of course—if you ain't afraid."

"Afraid!" Tom said. "It ain't likely. Will you come to my window and meow?"

"Yes—and you meow back, if you get a chance. Last time, you kept me a-meowing around till old Hays started throwing rocks at me and saying 'Darn that cat!' I heaved a brick through his window—but don't you tell."

"I won't. I couldn't meow that night because Auntie was watching me, but I'll meow this time."

Tom noticed that Huck had something else in his hands. Tom asked, "Say—what's that?"

"Nothing but a tick."

"Where'd you get him?"

"Out in the woods."

"What'll you take for him?"

"I don't know. I don't want to sell him."

"All right. It's a mighty small tick, anyway."

"Oh, I'm satisfied with it. It's a good enough tick for me."

"Sure, there's plenty of ticks. I could have a thousand of 'em if I wanted to," said Tom.

"Well, why don't you? Because you know mighty well you can't. This is a pretty early tick, I reckon. It's the first one I've seen this year."

"Say, Huck . . . I'll give you my tooth for him."

"Let's see it."

Tom got out a bit of paper and carefully unrolled his tooth. Huckleberry looked at it wistfully. The temptation was very strong. At last he said, "Is it genuine?"

Tom lifted his lip and showed the empty spot.

"Well, all right," said Huckleberry, "it's a trade."

Tom enclosed the tick in the little box that had once been the pinch bug's prison, and the boys separated, each feeling wealthier than before.

- How did Huck and Tom think they could get rid of warts? (Ideas: *By using stump water; by using a bean; by using a dead rat.*) (Sum)
- Describe Huckleberry Finn's clothing. (Ideas: *He wore clothes that men had thrown away; his hat had a hole; his coat hung to his knees; his trousers were held up by one suspender, and one leg dragged in the dirt.*) (V)
- Why did all the mothers of the town dread Huckleberry Finn? (Ideas: *Because he was idle, lawless, vulgar, and bad; because all their children admired him.*) (C/E)
- Why did all the children admire Huckleberry Finn? (Ideas: *Because he could do whatever he wanted; because he was free.*) (C/E)
- Do you think any of the boys' tricks will get rid of warts? Explain your answer. (Ideas: *No, because their tricks are just superstitions; yes, because they believe their tricks will work.*) (MJ)

EXERCISE 7

Paired Practice (Optional)

1. Now you'll read in pairs.
- Whoever read second the last time will read first today.
- Remember to start at the diamond and switch at the star.
2. (Observe students and answer questions as needed.)

AFTER READING

EXERCISE 8

Independent Work

1. Do all the items in your workbook and textbook for this lesson.
2. (The independent work in this lesson includes the following activities.)
- Story details
- Vocabulary
- Graphs
- Similes
- Character traits
- Vocabulary review
- Logic
- Irony
- Comprehension
- Writing

EXERCISE 9

Workcheck

1. (Using the Answer Key, read the questions and answers for the workbook.)
2. (Have students read their answers for the textbook activities.)
3. (Have two or three students read their writing assignments aloud. Comment on each assignment.)
4. (Have students correct and turn in their work.)

SPELLING

(Present Spelling lesson 96 after completing Reading lesson 96. See *Spelling Presentation Book.*)

BEFORE READING

(Have students find lesson 97, part A, in their textbooks.)

1. critical	4. scuffle
2. foolhardy	5. harass
3. scrawl	6. prod

EXERCISE 1

Hard Words

1. Look at column 1.
- These are hard words from your textbook stories.

1. critical	3. engaged
2. harass	4. chemistry

2. Word 1 is **critical.** Everybody, what word? (Signal.) *Critical.*
- (Repeat this procedure for every word in the column.)
3. Let's read the words again.
4. Word 1. Everybody, what word? (Signal.) *Critical.*
- (Repeat this procedure for every word in the column.)
5. (Repeat the column until firm.)

EXERCISE 2

Word Practice

1. Look at column 2.
- We're going to practice these words.

1. vacant	4. redden
2. tiptoe	5. reddened
3. tiptoeing	

2. Word 1. Everybody, what word? (Signal.) *Vacant.*
- (Repeat this procedure for every word in the column.)
3. (Repeat the column until firm.)

EXERCISE 3

New Vocabulary

1. Look at column 3.
- First we'll read the words in this column. Then we'll read their definitions.

2. Word 1. Everybody, what word? (Signal.) *Critical.*
- (Repeat this procedure for every word in the column.)
3. (Repeat the column until firm.)

EXERCISE 4

Vocabulary Definitions

1. Everybody, find part B. ✔
- These are definitions for the words you just read.
2. (For each word, call on a student to read the definition and the item. Then ask the student to complete the item.)

1. **critical**—When you are *critical* of something, you find fault with that thing. If you find fault with a meal, you are critical of that meal.
- What's another way of saying *She found fault with the painting*?

- What's the answer? (Response: *She was critical of the painting.*)

2. **foolhardy**—When you are *foolhardy,* you are foolishly bold.
- What's another way of saying *They made a foolishly bold trip into the desert*?

- What's the answer? (Response: *They made a foolhardy trip into the desert.*)

3. **scrawl**—When you *scrawl,* you write carelessly.
- What's another way of saying *She carelessly wrote her name on the sidewalk*?

- What's the answer? (Response: *She scrawled her name on the sidewalk.*)

4. **scuffle**—A *scuffle* is a small fight.
- What do we call a small fight?

- What's the answer? (Response: *A scuffle.*)

5. **harass**—When you *harass* somebody, you taunt and tease that person.
- What's another way of saying *They teased the new boy*?

- What's the answer? (Response: *They harassed the new boy.*)

6. **prod**—When you *prod* something, you poke it, usually with a pointed object.
- What's another way of saying *Al poked the beetle with a stick*?

- What's the answer? (Response: *Al prodded the beetle with a stick.*)

EXERCISE 5
Vocabulary Review

1. Everybody, find part C. ✔
- We're going to review these words.
2. (Call on a student to read the words in the box.)

wistful	**perplexed**
lulls	**tranquil**
unanimous	**vulgar**
juvenile	**gavel**
gingerly	**lapse**
aggravate	**considerable**
dozing	

3. (For each item, have a student read the item and say the answer.)

1. Another word for *crude* is ▇▇▇.

- What's the answer? (Response: *Vulgar.*)

2. When something makes you sleepy or relaxed, it ▇▇▇ you.

- What's the answer? (Response: *Lulls.*)

3. When you are sleeping lightly, you are ▇▇▇.

- What's the answer? (Response: *Dozing.*)

4. When you are full of desire, you are ▇▇▇.

- What's the answer? (Response: *Wistful.*)

5. A young person is a ▇▇▇.

- What's the answer? (Response: *Juvenile.*)

6. When you make something worse, you ▇▇▇ it.

- What's the answer? (Response: *Aggravate.*)

7. When you do something cautiously, you do it ▇▇▇.

- What's the answer? (Response: *Gingerly.*)

8. Another word for *large* or *great* is ▇▇▇.

- What's the answer? (Response: *Considerable.*)

9. Another word for *calm* is ▇▇▇.

- What's the answer? (Response: *Tranquil.*)

READING

EXERCISE 6
Story Background

1. Everybody, find part D. ✔
- (Call on individual students to read several sentences each.)
- (After each section, present the questions for that section.)

Schools in the 1840s

In the 1840s, schools were different from the schools of today. Some schools had students of all ages in the same classroom, which was run by a schoolmaster. The schoolmaster was often strict and punished students severely if they did not work or behave properly.

- How were some schools in the 1840s different from modern schools? (Ideas: *Students of all ages were in one classroom; the schoolmaster was often strict and punished students severely.*) Ⓒ/Ⓒ

Students usually sat on long benches. Each student had a desk, a slate, and chalk. When students were required to write, they wrote on their slates—small blackboards—with chalk. They would then erase their assignment with a cloth.

The classroom was often divided into two sections—one for the boys and one for the girls. Sometimes, the schoolmaster would punish a student who misbehaved by making that student sit on the other side of the room. If the misbehaving student was a boy, for example, he would have to sit with the girls.

- Why do you think students wrote their assignments on slates instead of paper? (Ideas: *Paper was expensive; paper was hard to find; slates and chalk were cheap.*) Ⓓ
- How did the schoolmaster sometimes punish misbehaving students? (Idea: *By making them sit in the other section.*) Ⓡ

EXERCISE 7

Focus Question

1. Everybody, find part E. ✔
2. What's the focus question for today's lesson? (Response: *How did Tom win Becky's heart?*)

EXERCISE 8

Reading Aloud (Optional)

1. We're going to read aloud to the diamond.
- (Call on individual students to read several sentences each.)

Chapter 7

Tom Meets Becky

Focus Question: How did Tom win Becky's heart?

When Tom reached the little frame schoolhouse that Monday morning, he walked in briskly. He hung his hat on a peg and flung himself into his seat. The schoolmaster was dozing in front of the class in his great wooden armchair. He had been lulled to sleep by the drowsy hum of study. Tom's entrance woke him.

"Thomas Sawyer!"

Tom knew that when his name was pronounced in full, it meant trouble.

"Sir!"

"Come up here. Why are you late again, as usual?"

Tom was about to lie when he saw two long tails of yellow hair hanging down a back that he recognized. It was the Adored Unknown Girl! And next to her was the only vacant place on the girl's side of the schoolhouse.

Tom instantly said, "I STOPPED TO TALK WITH HUCKLEBERRY FINN!"

The schoolmaster's heart stopped, and he stared helplessly. The buzz of study ceased. The pupils wondered if this foolhardy boy had lost his mind. The master said:

"You . . . did what?"

"Stopped to talk with Huckleberry Finn." There was no mistaking the words.

"Thomas Sawyer, this is the most astounding confession I have ever listened to. You will be punished for this."

Then the order followed: "Thomas Sawyer, I order you to go and sit with the girls! And let this be a warning to you."

The laughter that rippled around the room appeared to embarrass the boy. He sat down upon the end of the pine bench, and the Adored Unknown Girl moved away from him with a toss of her head. Nudges and winks and whispers crossed the room. But Tom sat still, with his arms upon the long, low desk before him, as he seemed to study his book.

By and by, the usual school murmur rose upon the dull air once more. Tom began to cast secret glances at the girl. She observed his glances and showed him the back of her head for about a minute. During this time, Tom placed a peach on her desk. She shoved it away. Tom gently put it back. She shoved it away again, but with less force. Tom patiently returned it to its place. She let the peach remain.

Tom scrawled on his slate, "Please take it—I got more." The girl glanced at the words but did not react. ◆

Silent Reading

1. Read the rest of the lesson to yourselves and be ready to answer some questions.

Now Tom began to draw something on the slate, hiding his work with his left hand. For a time the girl refused to notice, but her curiosity got the better of her. The boy worked on. The girl made an attempt to see it, but the boy did not show that he was aware of her attempt.

At last she gave in and whispered, "Let me see it."

Tom partly uncovered a dismal picture of a house with smoke coming from the chimney. Then the girl became interested in the drawing, and she soon forgot everything else. When it was finished, she gazed a moment, then whispered:

"It's nice—make a man."

The artist drew a man in the front yard. The man was so large that he could have stepped over the house. But the Adored Girl was not critical of the drawing. She was satisfied with the monster and whispered, "It's a beautiful man—now show me coming along."

Tom drew a rounded form with a round head and straw limbs.

The girl said, "It's ever so nice—I wish I could draw."

"It's easy," whispered Tom. "I'll teach you."

"Oh, will you? When?"

"At noon. Do you go home for lunch?"

"I'll stay if you will."

"Good. What's your name?"

"Becky Thatcher. What's yours? Oh, I know. It's Thomas Sawyer."

"That's my full name. You just call me Tom, will you?"

"Yes."

Now, Tom began to scrawl something on the slate, hiding the words from the girl. She was not shy this time. She begged to see.

Tom said, "Oh, it ain't anything."

"Yes, it is."

"No, it ain't. You don't want to see."

"Yes, I do, indeed I do. Please let me."

"You'll tell."

"No, I won't—indeed I won't."

"You won't tell anybody at all? Ever, so long as you live?"

"No, I won't ever tell anybody. Now let me see."

She put her small hand upon his, and a little scuffle followed. Tom pretended to resist but let his hand slip until these words on the slate were revealed: "I love you."

"Oh, you bad thing!" And she hit his hand, but reddened and looked pleased, nevertheless.

Just at this point the boy felt a slow, fateful grip closing on his ear, and a steady lifting force. The schoolmaster carried Tom across the room to his own seat in the boy's section. The whole school giggled. Then the schoolmaster stood over Tom during a few awful moments and finally moved away to his armchair without saying a word. Although Tom's ear tingled, his heart was joyful.

As the school quieted down, Tom made an honest effort to study, but the confusion within him was too great. The harder Tom tried to fasten his mind on his studies, the more his ideas wandered. At last, with a sigh and a yawn, he gave up. It seemed to him that noon would never come. The air was utterly dead. There was not a breath stirring. It was the sleepiest of sleepy days. The twenty-five studying scholars sent up a drowsy murmur. Away off in the flaming sunshine, Cardiff Hill lifted its soft green sides through the heat. A few birds floated high in the air. No other living thing was visible but some cows, and they were asleep. ★

Tom's heart ached to be free. His hand wandered into his shirt pocket, and his face lit up with a glow of gratitude. He slowly pulled out the small box with the tick in it. He released the tick and put him on the long flat desk. The tick probably glowed with gratitude, too, at this moment. But when he started to travel off, Tom turned him aside with a pin and made him take a new direction.

Tom's best friend sat next to him, suffering just as Tom had been. This friend was Joe Harper. He was deeply and gratefully interested in the tick. Joe took a pin out and began to assist in directing the tick. The sport grew more and more interesting. Soon Tom said that the two of them were interfering with each other. So he put Joe's slate on the desk and drew a line down the middle of it from top to bottom.

"Now," said Tom, "as long as he is on your side, you can stir him up, and I'll let him alone. But if you let him get away and get on my side, you're to leave him alone as long as I can keep him from crossing over."

"All right, go ahead. Start him up."

The tick escaped from Tom and crossed the line. Joe harassed him awhile, but then he got away and crossed back again. This change of sides occurred often. While one boy was prodding the tick with absorbing interest, the other would look on with equal interest. The two heads were bowed together over the slate, and the two minds ignored everything else.

At last, luck seemed to settle with Joe. Over and over, just as the tick was about to cross the line, Joe's pin would head him off, and Joe would keep the tick on his side. At last, Tom could stand it no longer. The temptation was too strong. He reached out and touched the tick with his pin while the tick was still on Joe's side. Joe was angry in a moment. He said:

"Tom, you let him alone."

"I only just want to stir him up a little, Joe."

"No, sir, it ain't fair. You just let him alone."

"Darn it, I ain't going to stir him up much."

"Let him alone, I tell you."

"I won't."

"You will—he's on my side of the line."

"Look here, Joe Harper, whose tick is that?"

"I don't care whose tick he is! He's on my side of the line, and you can't touch him!"

"Well, I'll just bet I will, though. He's my tick, and I'll do what I please with him or die!"

A tremendous whack from the schoolmaster's hand came down on Tom's shoulders and the same on Joe's. The boys had been too absorbed to notice the hush that had come upon the school a while before, when the schoolmaster came tiptoeing down the room and stood over them. He had seen a good part of the performance before putting an end to it.

- How did Tom win Becky's heart? (Ideas: *He gave her a peach; he made her a drawing; he told her he loved her.*) (Sum)
- The story says, "Tom knew when his name was pronounced in full, it meant trouble." Why do you think the schoolmaster pronounced Tom's name in full? (Ideas: *He wanted to get Tom's attention; he didn't want to be friendly with Tom; he wanted to treat Tom in a formal way.*) (DCE)
- Explain how Tom got to sit next to Becky. (Idea: *Tom saw there was an empty seat next to Becky, so he confessed that he had talked to Huck. As punishment, the schoolmaster made Tom sit next to Becky.*) (R)
- Why do you think Tom hid his work on the slate from Becky? (Ideas: *He wanted her to be interested in his work; he wanted to make the slate hard to get.*) (DCE)
- Why didn't Tom and Joe notice the schoolmaster creeping up on them? (Idea: *They were too busy with their game.*) (C/E)

> **EXERCISE 10**

Paired Practice (Optional)

1. Now you'll read in pairs.
- Whoever read second the last time will read first today.
- Remember to start at the diamond and switch at the star.
2. (Observe students and answer questions as needed.)

AFTER READING

> **EXERCISE 11**

Independent Work

1. Do all the items in your workbook and textbook for this lesson.
2. (The independent work in this lesson includes the following activities.)
- Story details
- Vocabulary
- Graphs
- Drawing conclusions
- Character traits
- Logic
- Comprehension
- Writing

EXERCISE 12

Workcheck

1. (Using the Answer Key, read the questions and answers for the workbook.)
2. (Have students read their answers for the textbook activities.)
3. (Have two or three students read their writing assignments aloud. Comment on each assignment.)
4. (Have students correct and turn in their work.)

SPELLING

(Present Spelling lesson 97 after completing Reading lesson 97. See *Spelling Presentation Book.*)

BEFORE READING

(Have students find lesson 98, part A, in their textbooks.)

EXERCISE 1

Word Practice

1. Look at column 1.
- We're going to practice these words.

1. research	**3. tiresome**
2. soothing	

2. Word 1. Everybody, what word? (Signal.) *Research.*
- (Repeat this procedure for every word in the column.)
3. (Repeat the column until firm.)

EXERCISE 2

New Vocabulary

1. Look at column 2.
- First we'll read the words in this column. Then we'll read their definitions.

1. engaged	**3. coffin**
2. blunder	**4. pathetic**

2. Word 1. Everybody, what word? (Signal.) *Engaged.*
- (Repeat this procedure for every word in the column.)
3. (Repeat the column until firm.)

EXERCISE 3

Vocabulary Definitions

1. Everybody, find part B. ✔
- These are definitions for the words you just read.
2. (For each word, call on a student to read the definition and the item. Then ask the student to complete the item.)

1. **engaged**—When you are *engaged,* you have agreed to marry somebody.
- What's another way of saying *Edward had agreed to marry Susan*?
- What's the answer? (Response: *Edward was engaged to Susan.*)

2. **blunder**—A *blunder* is a mistake.
- What's another way of saying *She made a mistake*?
- What's the answer? (Response: *She made a blunder.*)

3. **coffin**—A *coffin* is a large box that a dead person is placed in.
- What's a coffin?
- What's the answer? (Idea: *A large box that a dead person is placed in.*)

4. **pathetic**—*Pathetic* is another word for *sad.*
- What's another way of saying *The wet dog looked sad*?
- What's the answer? (Response: *The wet dog looked pathetic.*)

EXERCISE 4

Vocabulary Review

1. Everybody, find part C. ✔
- We're going to review these words.
2. (Call on a student to read the words in the box.)

scrawl	**harass**
critical	**lull**
vulgar	**scuffle**
prod	**juvenile**
wistful	

3. (For each item, have a student read the item and say the answer.)

1. When you find fault with something, you are ▮▮▮▮ of that thing.

- What's the answer? (Response: *Critical.*)

2. When you write carelessly, you ▮▮▮▮.

- What's the answer? (Response: *Scrawl.*)

3. When you taunt and tease somebody, you ▮▮▮▮ that person.

- What's the answer? (Response: *Harass.*)

4. When you poke something, you ▮▮▮▮ it.

- What's the answer? (Response: *Prod.*)

5. A small fight is a ▮▮▮▮.

- What's the answer? (Response: *Scuffle.*)

6. When you are full of desire, you are ▮▮▮▮.

- What's the answer? (Response: *Wistful.*)

EXERCISE 5

Logic

1. Everybody, turn to part E at the end of today's story. ✔
- (Call on individual students to read several sentences each.)
- (At the end of each section, present the questions for that section.)

Write the answers for items 1–3.

Here's a rule of logic: *Just because you know about a part doesn't mean you know about the whole thing.*

The following statement by a writer breaks the rule: "You should buy this car. As you can see, the tires are in really good condition. Since the tires are in such good condition, you can be certain that the rest of the car is also in good condition."

1. Which thing in the statement is the part?

- What's the answer? (Response: *The tires.*)

2. Which thing is the whole?

- What's the answer? (Response: *The car.*)

3. What does the writer conclude about the whole?

- What's the answer? (Idea: *That it's in good condition.*)
- You'll write the answers later.

READING

EXERCISE 6

Focus Question

1. Everybody, turn back to part D. ✔
2. What's the focus question for today's lesson? (Response: *Why did Becky's heart break?*)

EXERCISE 7

Reading Aloud (Optional)

1. We're going to read aloud to the diamond.
- (Call on individual students to read several sentences each.)

Chapter 8
A Heartbreak

Focus Question: Why did Becky's heart break?

When school broke up at noon, Tom flew to Becky Thatcher and whispered in her ear, "Put on your bonnet and pretend you're going home. When you get to the corner, give your friends the slip and come back to the school. I'll go the other way and do the same thing."

Becky went off with one group of scholars, and Tom with another. When the two met later at the school, they had it all to themselves. They sat together, with a slate in front of them. Tom gave Becky the chalk and guided her hand. Together, they drew another house. When their interest in art began to fade, the pair began talking.

Tom said, "Do you love rats?"

"No! I hate them!"

"Well, I do, too—live ones. But I mean dead ones, to swing around your head."

"No, I don't care for rats much, anyway. What I like is chewing gum."

"Oh, me, too. I wish I had some now."

"Do you? I've got some. I'll let you have a piece, but you must leave a piece for me."

That was agreeable, so they chewed gum and dangled their legs against the bench.

"Were you ever at a circus?" said Tom.

"Yes, and my pa's going to take me again sometime, if I'm good."

"I've been to the circus three or four times—lots of times. There's things going on at a circus all the time. I'm going to be a clown in a circus when I grow up."

"Oh, are you? That will be nice. They're so entertaining, all spotted up."

"Yes, that's so. And they get tons of money—almost a dollar a day, Ben Rogers says. Say, Becky, were you ever engaged?"

"What's that?"

"Why, engaged to be married."

"No."

"Would you like to be?"

"I reckon so. I don't know. What is it like?"

"Like? Why, it ain't like anything. You just tell a boy you won't ever date anybody but him, ever ever ever, and then you kiss and that's all. Anybody can do it."

"Kiss? What do you kiss for?"

"Why, that, you know, is to . . . well, they always do that."

"Everybody?"

"Why, yes, everybody that's in love with each other." Then Tom added, "Do you remember what I wrote on the slate?"

"Ye . . . yes."

"What was it?"

"I won't tell you."

"Do you want me to tell you?" Tom asked.

"Ye . . . yes—but some other time."

"No, now."

"No," Becky insisted, "tomorrow."

"Oh, no, now. Please, Becky—I'll whisper it. I'll whisper it ever so quietly."

Becky hesitated, but Tom passed his arm about her waist and whispered the words "I love you" ever so softly, with his mouth close to her ear. Then he added, "Now you whisper it to me—just the same."

She resisted for a while and then said, "You turn your face away so you can't see, and then I will. But you mustn't ever tell anybody—will you, Tom?"

"No, indeed, indeed I won't."

He turned his face away. She bent timidly around till her breath stirred his curls and whispered, "I . . . love . . . you!"

Then she sprang away and ran around and around the desks and benches. She sat back down at last, and as she giggled, she held her little white apron to her face. ♦

Silent Reading

1. Read the rest of the lesson to yourselves and be ready to answer some questions.

Tom said, "Now, Becky, it's all done—all over but the kiss. Don't you be afraid of that—it ain't anything at all." And he tugged at her apron and her hands.

She finally gave up, and let her hands drop. Her face was glowing. Tom kissed her red lips and said, "Now it's all done, Becky. And always after this, you know, you ain't ever to love anybody but me, and you ain't ever to marry anybody but me, never, never and forever. Will you?"

"No, I'll never love anybody but you, Tom, and I'll never marry anybody but you—and you ain't to ever marry anybody but me, either."

"Certainly. That's part of it. And when we're going home, you're to walk with me, when there isn't anybody looking."

"It's so nice. I never heard of it before."

"Oh, it's a lot of fun. Why, when me and Amy Lawrence were engaged . . ."

Becky's big eyes told Tom he had made a blunder. He stopped, confused.

"Oh, Tom! Then I ain't the first girl you've ever been engaged to!"

Becky began to cry.

Tom said, "Oh, don't cry, Becky. I don't care for her anymore."

"Yes, you do, Tom—you know you do."

Tom tried to put his arm around Becky, but she pushed him away and turned her face to the wall and went on crying. Tom tried again, with soothing words, and was pushed away again. Then his pride was hurt, and he walked away and went outside. Tom stood around, restless and uneasy, for a while. He glanced at the door every now and then, hoping she would come to find him. But she did not.

Tom began to feel bad and feared he had done something wrong. It was a hard struggle, but he finally got up the nerve to reenter the school. Becky was still standing in the corner, sobbing, with her face to the wall. Tom's heart ached. He went to her and stood a moment, not knowing exactly what to say.

Then he said hesitatingly, "Becky, I . . . I don't care for anybody but you."

No reply but sobs.

"Becky . . .," pleadingly. "Becky, won't you say something?"

More sobs.

Tom got out his most prized possession, which was a small brass doorknob. He passed it around Becky so that she could see it, and said, "Please, Becky, won't you take it?" ★

She threw it to the floor. Then Tom marched out of the schoolhouse and over the hills and far away. He did not return to school that day. Presently Becky began to get worried. She ran to the door; he was not in sight. She flew around to the play yard; he was not there.

Then she called, "Tom! Come back!"

She listened intently, but there was no answer. She had no companions but silence and loneliness. So she sat down to cry again. By this time, the scholars had begun to gather again, and Becky had to hide her grief and her broken heart. She suffered greatly during the long, dreary afternoon.

• • •

At half past nine that night, Tom and Sid were sent to bed, as usual. They said their prayers, and Sid was soon asleep. But Tom remembered the plans he had made with Huckleberry Finn. He lay awake and waited impatiently. When it seemed to him that it must be nearly daylight, he heard the clock strike ten! This was despair. He would have tossed around, but he was afraid he might wake Sid. So he lay still and stared up into the dark.

Everything was dismally still. By and by, out of the stillness, he began to hear little noises. The clock seemed to tick more loudly. The stairs creaked faintly. Evidently, spirits were wandering about. A snore came from Aunt Polly's room. And now the tiresome chirping of a cricket began. Then the howl of a far-off dog rose on the night air and was answered by a fainter howl from a farther distance.

Tom was in agony. At last he began to doze, in spite of himself. The clock chimed eleven, but he did not hear it. Then a cat began to meow loudly, but the meowing only mingled with Tom's dreams. The raising of a neighboring window disturbed Tom. The neighbor cried, "Scat! You devil!" and tossed an empty bucket into the yard. The sound of the bucket woke Tom completely.

One minute later, Tom was dressed and out the window and creeping along the roof on all fours. He meowed once or twice as he went. He jumped to the roof of the woodshed and then to the ground. Huckleberry Finn was there with his dead rat. The boys moved off and disappeared in the gloom. A half hour later, they were wading through the tall grass of the graveyard.

- Why did Becky's heart break? (Ideas: *Because she found out Tom had been engaged to Amy Lawrence; because she discovered Tom didn't keep his promise to Amy.*) (DCE)
- According to Tom, what does a person do when he or she is engaged to somebody? (Ideas: *Promises not to date anybody else; speaks of love; kisses the person; never marries anybody else; walks home with the other person.*) (R)
- How did Tom try to make up with Becky after his blunder? (Ideas: *Told her he didn't care for Amy any more; tried to put his arm around her; gave her his brass doorknob.*) (R)
- How do you think Becky felt about Tom after he left? Explain your answer. (Ideas: *She missed him, because she tried to find him; she was mad at him, because she threw his brass doorknob on the floor; she was confused, because she liked him but was mad at him, too.*) (DCE)
- Tom said he wanted to be a clown in a circus when he grew up. Do you think that's a good job for Tom? Explain your answer. (Ideas: *Yes, because he's always playing tricks on people; no, because he'll get more serious when he grows up.*) (MJ)

Paired Practice (Optional)

1. Now you'll read in pairs.
- Whoever read second the last time will read first today.
- Remember to start at the diamond and switch at the star.
2. (Observe students and answer questions as needed.)

AFTER READING

Independent Work

1. Do all the items in your workbook and textbook for this lesson.
2. (The independent work in this lesson includes the following activities.)
- Story details
- Vocabulary
- Maps
- Logic
- Comprehension
- Writing

Workcheck

1. (Using the Answer Key, read the questions and answers for the workbook.)
2. (Have students read their answers for the textbook activities.)
3. (Have two or three students read their writing assignments aloud. Comment on each assignment.)
4. (Have students correct and turn in their work.)

(Present Spelling lesson 98 after completing Reading lesson 98. See *Spelling Presentation Book.*)

BEFORE READING

(Have students find lesson 99, part A, in their textbooks.)

EXERCISE 1

Hard Words

1. Look at column 1.
- These are hard words from your textbook stories.

1. cemetery	**3. vague**
2. tannery	

2. Word 1 is **cemetery.** Everybody, what word? (Signal.) *Cemetery.*
- (Repeat this procedure for every word in the column.)
3. Let's read the words again.
4. Word 1. Everybody, what word? (Signal.) *Cemetery.*
- (Repeat this procedure for every word in the column.)
5. (Repeat the column until firm.)

EXERCISE 2

Word Practice

1. Look at column 2.
- We're going to practice these words.

1. gone	**3. blubbering**
2. goners	

2. Word 1. Everybody, what word? (Signal.) *Gone.*
- (Repeat this procedure for every word in the column.)
3. (Repeat the column until firm.)

EXERCISE 3

New Vocabulary

1. Look at column 3.
- First we'll read the words in this column. Then we'll read their definitions.

1. oath	**3. tannery**
2. swear	

2. Word 1. Everybody, what word? (Signal.) *Oath.*
- (Repeat this procedure for every word in the column.)
3. (Repeat the column until firm.)

EXERCISE 4

Vocabulary Definitions

1. Everybody, find part B. ✔
- These are definitions for the words you just read.
2. (For each word, call on a student to read the definition and the item. Then ask the student to complete the item.)

1. **oath**—An *oath* is a solemn promise.
- What's another way of saying *They made a solemn promise to keep quiet*?

- What's the answer? (Response: *They made an oath to keep quiet.*)

2. **swear**—When you *swear,* you make an oath. If you make an oath to tell the truth, you swear to tell the truth.
- What's another way of saying *She made an oath to be honest*?

- What's the answer? (Response: *She swore to be honest.*)

3. **tannery**—A *tannery* is a factory that makes leather.
- What is a tannery?

- What's the answer? (Idea: *A factory that makes leather.*)

EXERCISE 5

Vocabulary Review

1. Everybody, find part C. ✔
- We're going to review these words.

2. (Call on a student to read the words in the box.)

considerable	**blunder**
vulgar	**juvenile**
dozing	**pathetic**
lulls	**wistful**
critical	

3. (For each item, have a student read the item and say the answer.)

1. A mistake is a ▨▨▨▨.

- What's the answer? (Response: *Blunder.*)

2. When you find fault with something, you are ▨▨▨▨ of that thing.

- What's the answer? (Response: *Critical.*)

3. When something makes you sleepy, it ▨▨▨▨ you.

- What's the answer? (Response: *Lulls.*)

4. Another word for *great* is ▨▨▨▨.

- What's the answer? (Response: *Considerable.*)

5. A young person is a ▨▨▨▨.

- What's the answer? (Response: *Juvenile.*)

6. Another word for *sad* is ▨▨▨▨.

- What's the answer? (Response: *Pathetic.*)

EXERCISE 6

Logic

1. Everybody, turn to part E at the end of today's story. ✔
- (Call on individual students to read several sentences each.)
- (At the end of each section, present the questions for that section.)

Write the answers for items 1–3.

Here's a rule of logic: *Just because you know about a part doesn't mean you know about the whole thing.*

The following statement by a writer breaks the rule: "Mr. Williams works for the Ajax Company. Mr. Williams is very kind and careful. He also works very hard. Therefore, the Ajax Company must be a very kind and careful organization."

1. Which thing in the argument is the part?

- What's the answer? (Response: *Mr. Williams.*)

2. Which thing is the whole?

- What's the answer? (Response: *The Ajax Company.*)

3. What does the writer conclude about the whole?

- What's the answer? (Idea: *That it's a kind and careful organization.*)
- You'll write the answers later.

READING

EXERCISE 7

Focus Question

1. Everybody, find part D. ✔
2. What's the focus question for today's lesson? (Response: *What was the tragedy in the graveyard?*)

EXERCISE 8

Reading Aloud (Optional)

1. We're going to read aloud to the diamond.
- (Call on individual students to read several sentences each.)

Chapter 9

Tragedy in the Graveyard

Focus Question: What was the tragedy in the graveyard?

The graveyard was on a hill about a mile and a half from the village. It had a crazy board fence around it. The fence leaned inward in places and outward the rest of the time. Grass and weeds grew over the whole cemetery. All the old graves were sunken in, and round-topped, worm-eaten boards leaned over them. Once, words had been painted on the boards that marked the graves, but the words could no longer be seen.

A faint wind moaned through the trees. Tom feared it might be the spirits of the dead, complaining of being disturbed. The boys talked little, and only under their breath. The time and the place and the silence darkened their spirits. They found the new grave they were seeking, and they hid near three great elm trees that grew in a bunch within a few feet of the grave.

Then they waited in silence for what seemed a long time. The hooting of a distant owl was the only sound that troubled the dead stillness.

Tom said in a whisper, "Hucky, do you believe the dead people like it for us to be here?"

Huckleberry whispered, "I wish I knew. It's awful solemn, ain't it?"

"It sure is."

There was a considerable pause while the boys thought about the quiet.

Presently Tom seized his comrade's arm and said, "Sh!"

"What is it, Tom?" The two boys clung together with beating hearts.

"Sh! There it is again! Didn't you hear it?"

"Tom, I can hear the spirits coming! They're coming, sure. What'll we do?"

"I dunno. Think they'll see us?"

"Oh, Tom, they can see in the dark, same as cats. I wish I hadn't come."

"Oh, don't be afraid, Huck. I don't believe they'll bother us. We ain't doing any harm. If we keep perfectly still, maybe they won't notice us at all."

The boys bent their heads together and scarcely breathed. A muffled sound of voices floated up from the far end of the graveyard.

"Look! See there!" whispered Tom. "What is it?"

"It's devil-fire. Oh, Tom, this is awful."

Some vague figures approached through the gloom, swinging an old-fashioned tin lantern that lit up the ground with little patches of light. ◆

Silent Reading

1. Read the rest of the lesson to yourselves and be ready to answer some questions.

Presently Huckleberry whispered with a shudder, "It's the devils, sure enough. Three of 'em! Tom, we're goners! Can you pray?"

"I'll try, but don't be afraid. They ain't going to hurt us."

"Sh!"

"What is it, Huck?"

"They're humans! One of 'em is, anyway. One of 'em's old Muff Potter's voice."

"Say, Huck, I know another of those voices. It's Outlaw Joe."

"You're right! I'd rather they were devils. What can they be up to?"

The boys stopped whispering, now, for the three men had reached the grave and stood within a few feet of the boys' hiding place.

"Here it is," said the third voice, and the speaker held the lantern up. The light revealed the face of young Dr. Robinson.

Potter and Outlaw Joe were carrying shovels. They began to dig. The doctor put the lantern at the head of the grave and came and sat down with his back against one of the elm trees. He was so close the boys could have touched him.

"Hurry, men!" he said. "The moon might come out at any moment."

The other men went on digging. For some time there was no noise except the sound of the shovels working. Finally, a shovel struck the coffin with a dull thud, and within another minute the men had hoisted the coffin out onto the ground.

Then Outlaw Joe said, "Now the coffin's ready, Doctor. Give us another five dollars, or the coffin stays here."

"That's right!" said Muff Potter.

"Look here, what does this mean?" said the doctor. "You required your pay in advance, and I've paid you."

"Yes, and you done more than that," said Outlaw Joe, approaching the doctor, who was now standing. "Five years ago you drove me away from your father's kitchen one night, when I came to ask for something to eat. You said I wasn't any good. When I swore I'd get even with you, your father had me jailed. Did you think I'd forget? I've got you, and you've got to settle with me!"

By this time, Outlaw Joe was threatening the doctor, with his fist in the doctor's face. The doctor struck out suddenly and hit Outlaw Joe, who fell to the ground.

Potter exclaimed, "Here, now, don't you hit my partner!" The next moment, he was grappling with the doctor, and the two were trampling the grass and tearing the ground with their heels.

Outlaw Joe sprang to his feet. His eyes were flaming with rage. He went creeping around and around the fighters, looking for his chance. All at once the doctor broke free, seized a heavy board, and hit Potter over the head with it. In the same instant, Outlaw Joe hit the doctor square on the jaw. The doctor fell down, cracking his head against the edge of the coffin. ★

Suddenly, the clouds covered the moon. The two frightened boys sped away silently in the dark.

When the moon emerged again, Outlaw Joe was standing over the two bodies. The doctor murmured, gave a long gasp or two, and died.

Outlaw Joe muttered, "Now I'm even with him at last."

Then Joe sat down on the coffin. Three . . . four . . . five minutes passed, and then Potter began to stir and moan. At last he sat up and gazed at the doctor. He looked around in confusion, and his eyes met Joe's.

"What happened, Joe?" he said.

"It's a dirty business," said Joe, without moving. "Why did you have to kill him, Potter?"

"I? I never done it!"

"Look here! You can't fool me with that kind of talk!"

Potter trembled and grew pale.

"I can't recollect anything, hardly. Tell me, Joe—honest, now—did I do it? Joe, I never meant to—upon my honor—I never meant to, Joe. Tell me how it was, Joe. Oh, it's awful—and him so young."

"Why, you two were scuffling, and he hit you with the board, and then you hit him in the jaw, and he cracked his head on the coffin. Then you passed out. And here you've laid till now."

"Oh, I didn't know what I was a-doing. I wish I may die this minute if I did. It was all on account of the excitement, I reckon. I never hurt anybody in my life before, Joe." Potter grabbed Joe's coat and pleaded, "Joe, don't tell! Say you won't tell, Joe. I always liked you, Joe, and stood up for you, too. Don't you remember? You won't tell, will you, Joe?" And the poor creature dropped on his knees before Outlaw Joe and clasped his hands.

"No, you've always been fair and square with me, Muff Potter, and I won't go back on you."

"Oh, Joe, thank you!" Potter said as he began to cry.

"Come now, that's enough of that. This ain't any time for blubbering. You go off that way, and I'll go this way. Move, now, and don't leave any tracks behind you."

Potter started trotting away, then quickly broke into a run. Outlaw Joe stood looking after him.

He muttered, "If he's as stunned and confused as he looks, he won't remember what happened. And if he does, he'll be afraid to challenge me, the chicken!"

Two or three minutes later Joe had left the graveyard. Now, the dead man, the coffin, and the open grave were seen only by the moon. The stillness was complete again.

- What was the tragedy in the graveyard? (Idea: *The doctor's death.*) (MI)
- Describe the graveyard. (Ideas: *It was on a hill outside the village; it had a crazy board fence around it; grass and weeds were everywhere; graves were sunken in; wooden gravestones leaned over the graves; words on gravestones had worn off.*) (V)
- Explain what Tom and Huck planned to do in the graveyard. (Idea: *Get rid of their warts by throwing a rat at spirits who took away a dead person.*) (R)
- Why do you think the doctor wanted to dig up the dead person? (Ideas: *To study the body; to learn more about disease.*) (DCE)

- Explain how the doctor was killed. (Idea: *Outlaw Joe knocked over the doctor. When the doctor fell, he cracked his head against the edge of the coffin and died.*) Ⓡ
- What do you think Tom and Huck should do next? Explain your answer. (Ideas: *Tell the police what they saw because a crime had been committed; keep quiet because Outlaw Joe might hurt them.*) Ⓜ Ⓙ

EXERCISE 10
Paired Practice (Optional)

1. Now you'll read in pairs.
- Whoever read second the last time will read first today.
- Remember to start at the diamond and switch at the star.
2. (Observe students and answer questions as needed.)

AFTER READING

EXERCISE 11
Independent Work

1. Do all the items in your workbook and textbook for this lesson.
2. (The independent work in this lesson includes the following activities.)
- Story details
- Vocabulary
- Logic
- Sequencing
- Poem review
- Logic
- Comprehension
- Writing

EXERCISE 12
Workcheck

1. (Using the Answer Key, read the questions and answers for the workbook.)
2. (Have students read their answers for the textbook activities.)
3. (Have two or three students read their writing assignments aloud. Comment on each assignment.)
4. (Have students correct and turn in their work.)

SPELLING

(Present Spelling lesson 99 after completing Reading lesson 99. See *Spelling Presentation Book.*)

BEFORE READING

(Have students find lesson 100, part A, in their textbooks.)

EXERCISE 1

Word Practice

1. Look at column 1.
   - We're going to practice these words.

1. cemetery	**4.** gingerly
2. initials	**5.** superstitious
3. genuine	

2. Word 1. Everybody, what word? (Signal.) *Cemetery.*
   - (Repeat this procedure for every word in the column.)
3. (Repeat the column until firm.)

EXERCISE 2

Vocabulary Review

1. Everybody, find part B. ✔
   - We're going to review these words.
2. (Call on a student to read the words in the box.)

prod	**wistful**
plush	**droned**
scrawl	**considerable**
oath	**genuine**
vulgar	

3. (For each item, have a student read the item and say the answer.)

1. A solemn promise is an ▮▮▮▮▮.
   - What's the answer? (Response: *Oath.*)

2. When you are full of desire, you are ▮▮▮▮.
   - What's the answer? (Response: *Wistful.*)

3. When you poke something, you ▮▮▮▮ it.
   - What's the answer? (Response: *Prod.*)

4. Another word for *crude* is ▮▮▮▮.
   - What's the answer? (Response: *Vulgar.*)

5. Another word for *great* is ▮▮▮▮.
   - What's the answer? (Response: *Considerable.*)

6. When something is real, it is ▮▮▮▮.
   - What's the answer? (Response: *Genuine.*)

EXERCISE 3

Graphs

1. Everybody, turn to part D at the end of today's story. ✔
   - (Call on individual students to read several sentences each.)
   - (At the end of each section, present the questions for that section.)

APPLE PRODUCTION AT THE EDEN APPLE ORCHARDS

Assume the graph above is accurate. Examine the graph carefully and then read the statements in the next column. Some of the statements contradict what is shown on the graph. Write **contradictory** for those statements. If the statement does not contradict the graph, write **not contradictory.**

1. Seven thousand apples were produced in 1993.

- What's the answer? (Response: *Not contradictory.*)

2. Eight thousand bushels of apples were produced in 1998.

- What's the answer? (Response: *Contradictory.*)

3. Apple production went up from 1993 to 1995.

- What's the answer? (Response: *Contradictory.*)

4. More apples were produced in 1994 than in 1997.

- What's the answer? (Response: *Not contradictory.*)

5. The best year for apple production was 1998.

- What's the answer? (Response: *Contradictory.*)
- You'll write the answers later.

READING

EXERCISE 4

Focus Question

1. Everybody, turn back to part C. ✔
2. What's the focus question for today's lesson? (Response: *Why did the two boys decide to keep quiet about what they had seen?*)

EXERCISE 5

Reading Aloud (Optional)

1. We're going to read aloud to the diamond.
- (Call on individual students to read several sentences each.)

Chapter 10
The Howling Dog

Focus Question: Why did the two boys decide to keep quiet about what they had seen?

Huck and Tom ran toward the village, speechless with horror. They glanced backward over their shoulders from time to time, as if they feared they might be followed. Every stump that appeared in their path seemed to be an enemy and made them catch their breath. As they sped by some cottages near the village, the barking of the watchdogs seemed to give wings to their feet.

"If we can only get to the old tannery before we break down!" whispered Tom between breaths. "I can't stand it much longer."

Huckleberry's hard pantings were his only reply, and the boys fixed their eyes on their goal and continued running. They ran steadily towards the tannery. At last, they burst through the open door and fell exhausted on the floor.

By and by, their breathing slowed down, and Tom whispered, "Huckleberry, what do you reckon'll come of this?"

"If Dr. Robinson dies, I reckon there'll be a hanging."

"Do you?"

"Why, I know it, Tom."

Tom thought a while; then he said, "Who'll tell on Outlaw Joe? Will we tell?"

"What are you talking about? Suppose something happened, and Outlaw Joe didn't hang? Why, he'd kill us, just as sure as we're a-laying here."

"That's just what I was thinking to myself, Huck."

"If anybody tells, let Muff Potter do it, if he's fool enough."

Tom said nothing and went on thinking. Presently he whispered, "Huck, Muff Potter don't know what happened. How can he tell?"

"What's the reason he don't know it?"

"Because he was knocked out when Outlaw Joe hit the doctor, and besides, maybe Potter wasn't just knocked out. Maybe that whack killed him."

"No, it ain't likely, Tom. I could see that Potter was still alive." ♦

EXERCISE 6

Silent Reading

1. Read the rest of the lesson to yourselves and be ready to answer some questions.

After another silence, Tom said, "Huck, are you sure you can keep quiet about this?"

"Tom, we got to keep quiet. You know that. Outlaw Joe wouldn't think any more of drowning us than a couple of rats. Now look here, Tom, let's swear to one another—that's what we have to do—swear to keep quiet."

"I agree. Let's shake hands and swear that we . . ."

"Oh, no, Tom, that wouldn't do for this. That's good enough for common things, but not for a big thing like this. We have to write out our oath. And we have to sign it in blood."

Tom approved of Huck's idea. It was deep and dark and awful. The hour and the surroundings were in keeping with it. Tom picked up a clean pine board that lay in the moonlight, took a little fragment of pencil out of his pocket, turned so that the moonlight was on the board, and painfully scrawled this oath.

"Huck Finn and Tom Sawyer swears they will keep quiet about this, and they will drop down dead if they ever tell."

Huckleberry was filled with admiration for Tom's writing. He at once took a pin out, and then each boy pricked his thumb and squeezed out a drop of blood. After many squeezes, Tom managed to sign his initials, using his little finger for a pen. Then he showed Huckleberry how to make an H and an F, and the oath was complete. They buried the board close to the wall. Their tongues were sworn to silence.

A figure crept into the other end of the building, but the boys did not notice it.

"Tom," whispered Huckleberry, "does this keep us from ever telling—always?"

"Of course it does. It don't make any difference what happens, we got to keep quiet or we'll drop down dead."

"Yes, I reckon that's so." ★

They continued to whisper for a little while. Presently, a dog set up a long howl just outside—within ten feet of them. The boys clasped each other in an agony of fright.

A howling dog was a sure sign of trouble. Tom knew that if a stray dog howled at night and faced a person, that person was marked for death.

"Which of us is that dog after?" gasped Huckleberry.

"I dunno . . . peep through the crack. Quick!"

"No, you, Tom. Please, Tom. There it is again!"

Tom whispered, "I know his voice. It's Harbison's dog."

"Oh, that's good. I tell you, Tom, I was scared to death. I'd have bet anything it was a stray dog."

The dog howled again. The boys' hearts sank once more.

"Oh, my! That ain't Harbison's dog!" whispered Huckleberry. "Look, Tom!"

Tom, quaking with fear, put his eye to the crack. His whisper could hardly be heard when he said, "Oh, Huck, IT'S A STRAY DOG!"

"Quick, Tom! Who is he howling at?"

"Huck, he must be howling at both of us—we're right together."

"Oh, Tom, I reckon we're goners."

Tom moaned, "This comes from playing hooky and doing everything a feller's told not to do. I should have been good, like Sid." Tom began to sniffle a little.

Huckleberry began to sniffle, too. "Confound it, Tom Sawyer, you're an angel alongside of what I am. Oh, lordy, lordy, lordy, I wish I was half as good as you are."

Tom choked off and whispered, "Look, Huck, look! He's got his back to us!"

Huck looked, with joy in his heart, because the stray was not facing them.

"If he's not after us, who is he after?" Huck asked.

Suddenly the howling stopped. Tom pricked up his ears.

"Sh! What's that?" he whispered.

"Sounds like . . . like hogs grunting. No . . . it's somebody snoring, Tom."

"That's it! Whereabouts is it, Huck?"

"I believe it's down at the other end of this building. Sounds so, anyway. Pa used to sleep there sometimes, along with the hogs. But I reckon he ain't ever coming back to this town anymore."

The spirit of adventure rose in the boys once more.

"Huck, do you dare to go if I lead?"

"I don't like to, much. Tom, suppose it's Outlaw Joe!"

- Why did the two boys decide to keep quiet about what they had seen? (Idea: *They were afraid Outlaw Joe would kill them if he found out.*) (DCE)
- Why didn't Muff Potter know what had really happened to the doctor? (Idea: *Because he was knocked out when Outlaw Joe killed the doctor.*) (C/E)
- Why do you think Tom and Huck decided to write out their oath? (Ideas: *To make it official; to be sure they would keep it.*) (DCE)
- Do you think Tom will keep the oath? Explain your answer. (Ideas: *Yes, because he swore to keep the oath and signed it in blood; no, because Tom has already broken his engagement to Amy Lawrence.*) (P)
- Why were Tom and Huck frightened by the stray dog? (Idea: *Because they believed if a stray dog howled at night and faced a person, that person was marked for death.*) (DCE)

EXERCISE 7

Discussion

1. (Lead students in a general discussion about the boy's decision to keep quiet about the murder. Use the following questions as a guide.)
2. What did Tom and Huck think would happen if they told the police about the murder? (Idea: *Outlaw Joe would kill them.*) (DCE)
- What do you think would have happened if they had told the police? (Ideas: *The police would have protected them; the police would have put Outlaw Joe in jail.*) (MJ)
- Do you agree with the boys' decision to keep quiet? Explain your answer. (Ideas: *No, because you should always report a crime; yes, because Outlaw Joe might hurt them.*) (MJ)

EXERCISE 8

Paired Practice (Optional)

1. Now you'll read in pairs.
- Whoever read second the last time will read first today.
- Remember to start at the diamond and switch at the star.
2. (Observe students and answer questions as needed.)

AFTER READING

EXERCISE 9

Independent Work

1. Do all the items in your workbook and textbook for this lesson.
2. (The independent work in this lesson includes the following activities.)
- Story details
- Vocabulary
- Logic
- Character traits
- Graphs
- Comprehension
- Writing

EXERCISE 10

Workcheck

1. (Using the Answer Key, read the questions and answers for the workbook.)
2. (Have students read their answers for the textbook activities.)
3. (Have two or three students read their writing assignments aloud. Comment on each assignment.)
4. (Have students correct and turn in their work.)

MASTERY TEST

(The Lesson 100 Mastery Test should be administered after students complete lesson 100. See *Curriculum-Based Assessment and Fluency Teacher Handbook* for details.)

SPELLING

(Present Spelling lesson 100 after completing Reading lesson 100. See *Spelling Presentation Book*.)

ACTIVITIES ACROSS THE CURRICULUM

(Students should complete the appropriate project in *Activities across the Curriculum* after completing lesson 100. See *Activities across the Curriculum* book for details.)

Lessons 101–105 • Planning Page *Looking Ahead*

	Lesson 101	**Lesson 102**	**Lesson 103**	**Lesson 104**	**Lesson 105**
BEFORE READING	Hard words Word practice New vocabulary Vocabulary definitions Vocabulary review Graphs	Word practice New vocabulary Vocabulary definitions Vocabulary review Logic	Word practice New vocabulary Vocabulary definitions Vocabulary review	Hard words Word practice New vocabulary Vocabulary definitions	Word practice New vocabulary Vocabulary definitions Logic
NEW VOCABULARY	play hooky electrified ghastly	antic crestfallen independent random	indifferent flirt jealous spite	anatomy flustered proceedings folly sensation diary villain	stand trial atmosphere topic abuse lynch isolated
READING	*Tom Sawyer* (Chapter 11)	*Tom Sawyer* (Chapter 12)	*Tom Sawyer* (Chapter 13)	*Tom Sawyer* (Chapter 14)	*Tom Sawyer* (Chapter 15)
INDEPENDENT WORK	Story details Vocabulary Referents Character traits Logic Graphs Comprehension Writing	Story details Vocabulary Logic Sequencing Maps Character traits Inference Comprehension Writing	Story details Vocabulary Perspectives Following directions Logic Spoonerisms Comprehension Writing	Story details Vocabulary Perspectives Logic Combined sentences Vocabulary review Comprehension Writing	Story details Cause and effect Vocabulary Graphs Logic Settings Vocabulary review Comprehension Writing
SUPPLEMENTS	*Spelling*	*Spelling*	*Spelling*	*Spelling*	*Spelling* *Activities across the Curriculum*

Comprehension Questions Abbreviations Guide

Access Prior Knowledge = (APK)   Author's Point of View = (APoV)   Author's Purpose = (AP)   Cause/Effect = (C/E)   Charts/Graphs/Diagrams/Visual Aids = (VA)

Classify and Categorize = (C+C)   Compare/Contrast = (C/C)   Determine Character Emotions, Motivation = (DCE)   Drawing Conclusions = (DC)   Drawing Inferences = (DI)

Fact and Opinion = (F/O)   Hypothesizing = (H)   Main Idea = (MI)   Making Connections = (MC)   Making Deductions = (MD)   Making Judgements = (MJ)

Narrative Elements = (NE)   Noting Details = (ND)   Predict = (P)   Reality/Fantasy = (R/F)   Recall Facts/Rules = (RF/R)   Retell = (R)   Sequence = (Seq)

Steps in a Process = (SP)   Story Structure = (SS)   Summarize = (Sum)   Understanding Dialogue = (UD)   Using Context to Confirm Meaning(s) = (UCCM)   Visualize = (V)

BEFORE READING

(Have students find lesson 101, part A, in their textbooks.)

Hard Words

1. Look at column 1.
• These are hard words from your textbook stories.

> **1. pathetic** **4. jealousy**
> **2. ghastly** **5. randomly**
> **3. decomposer**

2. Word 1 is **pathetic.** Everybody, what word? (Signal.) *Pathetic.*
• (Repeat this procedure for every word in the column.)
3. Let's read the words again.
4. Word 1. Everybody, what word? (Signal.) *Pathetic.*
• (Repeat this procedure for every word in the column.)
5. (Repeat the column until firm.)

Word Practice

1. Look at column 2.
• We're going to practice these words.

> **1. tannery** **4. crestfallen**
> **2. fascination** **5. antics**
> **3. crest**

2. Word 1. Everybody, what word? (Signal.) *Tannery.*
• (Repeat this procedure for every word in the column.)
3. (Repeat the column until firm.)

New Vocabulary

1. Look at column 3.
• First we'll read the words in this column. Then we'll read their definitions.

> **1. play hooky** **3. ghastly**
> **2. electrified**

2. Line 1. Everybody, what words? (Signal.) *Play hooky.*
• (Repeat this procedure for every word in the column.)
3. (Repeat the column until firm.)

Vocabulary Definitions

1. Everybody, find part B. ✔
• These are definitions for the words you just read.
2. (For each word, call on a student to read the definition and the item. Then ask the student to complete the item.)

1. **play hooky**—When you *play hooky* from school, you don't go to school when you're supposed to.
• What does *play hooky* mean?

• What's the answer? (Idea: *Not going to school when you're supposed to.*)

2. **electrified**—When something is *electrified,* it becomes suddenly excited, as if electricity were surging through it.
• What's another way of saying *The village was suddenly excited by the news*?

• What's the answer? (Response: *The village was electrified by the news.*)

3. **ghastly**—When something is *ghastly*, it is horrible or shocking.
- What's another way of saying *The drapes were a horrible color?*

- What's the answer? (Response: *The drapes were a ghastly color.*)

EXERCISE 5
Vocabulary Review

1. Everybody, find part C. ✔
- We're going to review these words.
2. (Call on a student to read the words in the box.)

considerable	prod
blunder	genuine
casual	conscience
pathetic	lulls
harass	

3. (For each item, have a student read the item and say the answer.)

1. When something makes you sleepy, it ▮▮▮▮▮ you.

- What's the answer? (Response: *Lulls.*)

2. Another word for *great* is ▮▮▮▮.

- What's the answer? (Response: *Considerable.*)

3. A mistake is a ▮▮▮▮.

- What's the answer? (Response: *Blunder.*)

4. Another word for *sad* is ▮▮▮▮.

- What's the answer? (Response: *Pathetic.*)

5. When something is real, it is ▮▮▮▮.

- What's the answer? (Response: *Genuine.*)

6. When you taunt and tease somebody, you ▮▮▮▮ that person.

- What's the answer? (Response: *Harass.*)

EXERCISE 6
Graphs

1. Everybody, turn to part E at the end of today's story. ✔
- (Call on individual students to read several sentences each.)
- (At the end of each section, present the questions for that section.)

Assume the graph in the next column is accurate. Examine the graph carefully and then read the following statements. Some of the statements contradict what is shown on the graph. Write **contradictory** for those statements. If the statement does not contradict the graph, write **not contradictory.**

1. Seven inches of rain fell in April.

- What's the answer? (Response: *Contradictory.*)

2. Four inches of rain fell in June.

- What's the answer? (Response: *Not contradictory.*)

3. September was the rainiest month.

- What's the answer? (Response: *Contradictory.*)
- You'll write the answers later.

READING

EXERCISE 7
Focus Question

1. Everybody, turn back to part D. ✔
2. What's the focus question for today's lesson? (Response: *What was Muff Potter's confession?*)

> ***Note:*** The "Reading Aloud" exercise is recommended for this lesson.

Reading Aloud

1. We're going to read aloud to the diamond.
- (Call on individual students to read several sentences each.)

Chapter 11
Muff Potter's Confession

Focus Question: What was Muff Potter's confession?

For a moment, Tom and Huck were afraid of the snoring. But the boys soon agreed to see where the snoring came from, with the understanding that they would run off if the snoring stopped. So they went tiptoeing through the tannery. They were within five steps of the snorer's dark form when Tom stepped on a stick, which broke with a sharp snap. The man moaned and writhed a little. Then his face came into the moonlight. It was Muff Potter.

The boys' hearts had stood still, and their hopes, too, when the man moved; but their fears passed away now. They tiptoed out, through the broken wall, and stopped a little distance away to exchange a parting word. That long howl rose in the night air again! They turned and saw the strange dog standing within a few feet of Potter, facing him, with its nose pointing to the sky.

"The dog's after him!" exclaimed both boys in the same breath.

"Say, Tom . . . they say a stray dog came howling around Johnny Miller's house about midnight, two weeks ago. But there ain't anybody dead there yet."

"Well, I know that. And suppose there ain't. Didn't his wife Gracie fall in the kitchen fire and burn herself the very next Saturday?"

"Yes, but she ain't dead. And what's more, she's getting better, too."

"All right, you wait and see. She's a goner, just as sure as Muff Potter's a goner. A howling stray always means death, Huck."

Then the two boys separated. When Tom crept in at his bedroom window, the night was almost over. He undressed with caution and fell asleep thinking nobody knew what he had done. He was not aware that Sid was actually awake and had been so for an hour.

When Tom awoke later, Sid was dressed and gone. It was late in the morning. Tom was startled. Why hadn't he been called as usual? The thought filled him with fear. Within five minutes he was dressed and downstairs, feeling sore and drowsy. His aunt was still at the table, but she had finished breakfast. There was a silence that struck a chill to Tom's heart. He sat down and tried to seem happy, but it was hard work. He received no smile and no response. Tom lapsed into silence.

After breakfast, Aunt Polly took Tom aside. Tom thought he was going to be punished, but it was not so. His aunt wept over him for disobeying her and staying out all night. She asked him how he could go and break her old heart. Finally, she told him to go on and ruin himself and bring her gray hairs, for it was no use for her to try anymore. This was worse than any punishment, and Tom's heart was sorer now than his body. He cried, he pleaded for forgiveness, and over and over again he promised to reform. But his aunt only sent him away.

Tom moped to school gloomy and sad, and he took his punishment for playing hooky the afternoon before. Then he went to his seat and rested his elbows on his desk and his chin in his hands. He stared at the wall with the stony stare of suffering. His elbow was pressing against some hard substance. After a long time he slowly and sadly changed his position and took up the object with a sigh. The object was wrapped in a piece of paper, which Tom unrolled. A long sigh followed, and his heart broke. It was his brass doorknob! ♦

Silent Reading

1. Read the rest of the lesson to yourselves and be ready to answer some questions.

Around noon, the whole village was suddenly electrified with the ghastly news of the murder. The tale flew from person to person, from group to group, from house to house, with little less than the speed of light. Because of the news, the schoolmaster made that afternoon a holiday.

All the village was drifting toward the graveyard. Tom's heartbreak vanished as he joined the crowd. He would rather have gone just about anywhere else, but an awful fascination drew him on.

When Tom arrived at the dreadful place, he wormed his small body through the crowd and saw the dismal scene. It seemed to him that a year had passed since he was there before. Somebody pinched his arm. He turned, and his eyes met Huckleberry's. Then they both looked elsewhere at once and wondered if anybody had noticed them. But everybody was talking and looking at the terrible scene before them.

People were saying, "Poor fellow!" "Poor young fellow!" "This ought to be a lesson to grave robbers!" "Someone will hang for this!"

Now Tom shivered from head to heel, for his eye fell upon a face in the crowd. It was Outlaw Joe. At this moment, the crowd began to sway and struggle, and voices shouted, "Here comes the sheriff and someone else!"

"Who? Who?" from twenty voices.

"Muff Potter!"

The crowd fell apart, and the sheriff came through, leading Potter by the arm. Potter's face was solemn, and his eyes showed his fear. When he stood before the dead man, he shook, put his face in his hands, and burst into tears.

"I didn't do it, friends," he sobbed. "Upon my word and honor, I never done it!" ★

Potter lifted his face and looked around him with a pathetic hopelessness in his eyes. He saw Outlaw Joe and exclaimed, "Oh, Outlaw Joe, you promised me you'd never tell!"

A slight smile came into Joe's face as he stared at the shaking Potter. Potter would have fallen if they had not caught him and eased him to the ground.

Potter shuddered, then waved his hand and said in a weary voice, "It don't matter, Joe, it ain't any use anymore."

Then Huckleberry and Tom stared, and heard Outlaw Joe say that Potter had killed the doctor. Tom and Huck expected every moment that lightning would strike upon Joe's head for telling such a dreadful lie, and they were amazed the lightning never came.

When Joe had finished, he still stood alive and whole. The boys were afraid to break their oath and save poor Potter's life. It seemed that Joe had sold himself to the devil, and they did not dare to challenge the devil.

"Why didn't you leave the village?" somebody asked Potter.

"I couldn't help it . . . I couldn't help it," Potter moaned. "I wanted to run away, but I couldn't seem to go anywhere." And he started sobbing again.

Joe repeated his statement a few minutes afterward, under oath. The boys, seeing there was still no lightning, were firm in their belief that Joe had sold himself to the devil. He had now become, to them, the most horrid person they had ever looked upon, and they could not take their fascinated eyes from his face.

- What was Muff Potter's confession? (Idea: *He confessed to killing the doctor.*) Ⓡ
- Why do you think Outlaw Joe told the sheriff about Muff Potter? (Ideas: *Outlaw Joe didn't want to be charged with the murder; Outlaw Joe wanted somebody else to take the blame.*) ⒹⒾ
- When Aunt Polly cried about Tom's bad behavior, the story says, "This was worse than any punishment, and Tom's heart was sorer now than his body." Explain why Tom felt that way. (Ideas: *Tom loved his aunt, and he hated to make her cry; despite all his adventures, Tom really loved his aunt.*) ⒹⒾ
- Where do you think Tom and Huck get all their beliefs about stray dogs, dead rats, and warts? (Ideas: *From other kids; from hearing ghost stories; they make them up.*) ⓂⒿ
- Why do you think Becky returned Tom's doorknob? (Ideas: *She was still mad at Tom; she didn't want to be engaged anymore.*) ⒹⒸⒺ

EXERCISE 10

Paired Practice (Optional)

1. Now you'll read in pairs.
- Whoever read second the last time will read first today.
- Remember to start at the diamond and switch at the star.

2. (Observe students and answer questions as needed.)

AFTER READING

Independent Work

1. Do all the items in your workbook and textbook for this lesson.
2. (The independent work in this lesson includes the following activities.)

- Story details
- Vocabulary
- Referents
- Character traits
- Logic
- Graphs
- Comprehension
- Writing

Workcheck

1. (Using the Answer Key, read the questions and answers for the workbook.)
2. (Have students read their answers for the textbook activities.)
3. (Have two or three students read their writing assignments aloud. Comment on each assignment.)
4. (Have students correct and turn in their work.)

(Present Spelling lesson 101 after completing Reading lesson 101. See *Spelling Presentation Book.*)

BEFORE READING

(Have students find lesson 102, part A, in their textbooks.)

EXERCISE 1
Word Practice

1. Look at column 1.
• We're going to practice these words.

1. independent	**4. indifferent**
2. hero	**5. decomposer**
3. heroic	

2. Word 1. Everybody, what word? (Signal.) *Independent.*
• (Repeat this procedure for every word in the column.)
3. (Repeat the column until firm.)

EXERCISE 2
New Vocabulary

1. Look at column 2.
• First we'll read the words in this column. Then we'll read their definitions.

1. antic	**3. independent**
2. crestfallen	**4. random**

2. Word 1. Everybody, what word? (Signal.) *Antic.*
• (Repeat this procedure for every word in the column.)
3. (Repeat the column until firm.)

EXERCISE 3
Vocabulary Definitions

1. Everybody, find part B. ✔
• These are definitions for the words you just read.
2. (For each word, call on a student to read the definition and the item. Then ask the student to complete the item.)

1. **antic**—An *antic* is a playful act. Sometimes, people use antics to show off or to draw attention to themselves.
• What's another way of saying *Tom tried to impress her with his playful acts?*

• What's the answer? (Response: *Tom tried to impress her with his antics.*)

2. **crestfallen**—When you are *crestfallen,* you are ashamed or humiliated.
• What's another way of saying *Tara was ashamed after flunking the test?*

• What's the answer? (Response: *Tara was crestfallen after flunking the test.*)

3. **independent**—When somebody is *independent,* he or she is not controlled by other people.
• What is an independent person?

• What's the answer? (Idea: *A person who is not controlled by other people.*)

4. **random**—When something is *random,* it doesn't follow a plan or a pattern. Events that don't follow a pattern are random events.
• What's another way of saying *words that don't follow a plan?*

• What's the answer? (Response: *Random words.*)

EXERCISE 4
Vocabulary Review

1. Everybody, find part C. ✔
• We're going to review these words.
2. (Call on a student to read the words in the box.)

ghastly	**blunder**
harass	**electrified**
pathetic	**oath**

3. (For each item, have a student read the item and say the answer.)

1. When something is horrible or shocking, it is ▮▮▮▮▮.

- What's the answer? (Response: *Ghastly.*)

2. A solemn promise is an ▮▮▮▮▮.

- What's the answer? (Response: *Oath.*)

3. When something becomes suddenly excited, it is ▮▮▮▮▮.

- What's the answer? (Response: *Electrified.*)

EXERCISE 5

Logic

1. Everybody, turn to part E at the end of today's story. ✔
- (Call on individual students to read several sentences each.)
- (At the end of each section, present the questions for that section.)

Write the answers for items 1–4.

Here's a rule of logic: *Just because a person is an expert in one field doesn't mean the person is an expert in another field.*

The following statement by a writer breaks the rule: "Professor Jones teaches chemistry at the university. He knows all about chemistry and has won many prizes for his research. So when Professor Jones tells us we need a new airport, we should listen to what he says."

1. Who is the expert in the statement?

- What's the answer? (Response: *Professor Jones.*)

2. In which field is that person an expert?

- What's the answer? (Response: *Chemistry.*)

3. That person makes a statement about another field. What field?

- What's the answer? (Idea: *Airports.*)

4. Is the person an expert in the second field?

- What's the answer? (Idea: *We don't know.*)
- You'll write the answers later.

READING

EXERCISE 6

Focus Question

1. Everybody, turn back to part D. ✔
2. What's the focus question for today's lesson? (Response: *Why did Becky ignore Tom's antics?*)

EXERCISE 7

Reading Aloud (Optional)

1. We're going to read aloud to the diamond.
- (Call on individual students to read several sentences each.)

Chapter 12
Tom Longs for Becky
Focus Question: Why did Becky ignore Tom's antics?

Tom's fearful secret disturbed his sleep for as much as a week after he and Huck observed the murder.

At breakfast one morning Sid said, "Tom, you toss and turn and talk in your sleep so much that you keep me awake half the time."

Tom turned pale and dropped his eyes.

"It's a bad sign," said Aunt Polly gravely. "What's on your mind, Tom?"

"Nothing. Nothing that I know of." But the boy's hand shook so much that he spilled his milk.

"You do talk such stuff," Sid said. "Last night you said 'It's blood, it's blood, that's what it is!' You said that over and over. And you said, 'Don't torment me so—I'll tell.' Tell what? What is it you'll tell?"

Everything was swimming before Tom. Luckily, the concern passed out of Aunt Polly's face, and she came to Tom's relief.

She said, "Sho! It's that dreadful murder. I dream about it most every night myself. Sometimes I dream it's me that did it."

Sid seemed satisfied. Tom got out as quick as he could. After that, he complained of a toothache for a week, and he tied up his jaws every night so he wouldn't be able to talk in his sleep. ◆

EXERCISE 8
Silent Reading

1. Read the rest of the lesson to yourselves and be ready to answer some questions.

Every day or two, Tom visited the jail, which was an unguarded brick building that stood in a marsh at the edge of the village. Tom crept up to the little jail window and smuggled small gifts through to the "murderer," Muff Potter. These gifts helped to ease Tom's conscience.

Some of the villagers suspected that Outlaw Joe's story was not true. But Joe's character was so powerful that nobody could be found who was willing to challenge him.

After a while, Tom's mind drifted away from its secret troubles and found a new matter of interest—Becky Thatcher had stopped coming to school. Tom had struggled with his pride a few days, and he tried to forget about her but failed. He began to find himself hanging around her house at night and feeling very miserable. She was ill. What if she should die! There was misery in the thought. The charm of life was gone; there was nothing but dreariness left.

Tom began to arrive at school ahead of time. This strange event occurred every day. He hung around the gate of the schoolyard instead of playing with his comrades. He was sick, he said, and he looked it. He always seemed to be looking down the road.

When Jeff Thatcher came in sight, Tom's face lighted. He gazed a moment and then turned sorrowfully away. Tom talked to Jeff and slyly tried to get information about Becky, but Jeff never gave him any. ★

One day, Tom watched and watched, hoping it was Becky whenever a dress came in sight, and hating the owner of it as soon as he saw she was not the right one. At last, dresses ceased to appear that morning, and Tom dropped hopelessly into the dumps.

He entered the empty schoolhouse and sat down to suffer. Then one more dress passed in at the gate, and Tom's heart gave a great bound. The next instant he was out and carrying on like a madman: yelling, laughing, chasing boys, jumping over the fence at risk of life and limb, throwing handsprings, standing on his head. He did all the heroic things he could think of, and he kept an eye out, all the while, to see if Becky Thatcher was noticing. But she seemed to be unconscious of it all; she never looked.

Could it be possible that she was not aware of him? He carried his antics close to her. He came war-whooping around, snatched a boy's cap, hurled it to the roof of the schoolhouse, broke through a group of boys, tumbling them in every direction, and fell sprawling, himself, under Becky's nose, almost knocking her down. But she just turned away, with her nose in the air, and he heard her say, "Hmph! Some people think they're mighty smart . . . always showing off!"

Tom's cheeks burned. He gathered himself and sneaked off, crushed and crestfallen.

- Why did Becky ignore Tom's antics? (Ideas: *She was still mad at him; she didn't like show-offs.*) ⓄⒸⒺ
- How do you think Tom should have tried to make up with Becky? (Ideas: *Tell her he was sorry; ignore her; make her jealous by talking to other girls; send messages to her through Jeff.*) ⓂⒿ
- Why do you think Tom talked in his sleep? (Ideas: *He was worried about the murder; he knew he had done something wrong.*) ⓄⒸⒺ
- Explain how Tom solved the problem of talking in his sleep. (Idea: *He complained of a toothache and tied up his jaws so he wouldn't be able to talk in his sleep.*) Ⓡ
- The story says, "Joe's character was so powerful that nobody could be found who was willing to challenge him." Explain what that sentence means. (Idea: *Joe was such a strong person that people were afraid to contradict him.*) ⓊⒸⒸⓂ

EXERCISE 9
Paired Practice (Optional)

1. Now you'll read in pairs.
- Whoever read second the last time will read first today.

- Remember to start at the diamond and switch at the star.
2. (Observe students and answer questions as needed.)

AFTER READING

Independent Work

1. Do all the items in your workbook and textbook for this lesson.
2. (The independent work in this lesson includes the following activities.)
- Story details
- Vocabulary
- Logic
- Sequencing
- Maps
- Character traits
- Inference
- Comprehension
- Writing

Workcheck

1. (Using the Answer Key, read the questions and answers for the workbook.)
2. (Have students read their answers for the textbook activities.)
3. (Have two or three students read their writing assignments aloud. Comment on each assignment.)
4. (Have students correct and turn in their work.)

(Present Spelling lesson 102 after completing Reading lesson 102. See *Spelling Presentation Book*.)

BEFORE READING

(Have students find lesson 103, part A, in their textbooks.)

EXERCISE 1

Word Practice

1. Look at column 1.
- We're going to practice these words.

1. cozy	**3. folly**
2. cozily	**4. proceedings**

2. Word 1. Everybody, what word? (Signal.) *Cozy.*
- (Repeat this procedure for every word in the column.)
3. (Repeat the column until firm.)

EXERCISE 2

New Vocabulary

1. Look at column 2.
- First we'll read the words in this column. Then we'll read their definitions.

1. indifferent	**3. jealous**
2. flirt	**4. spite**

2. Word 1. Everybody, what word? (Signal.) *Indifferent.*
- (Repeat this procedure for every word in the column.)
3. (Repeat the column until firm.)

EXERCISE 3

Vocabulary Definitions

1. Everybody, find part B. ✔
- These are definitions for the words you just read.
2. (For each word, call on a student to read the definition and the item. Then ask the student to complete the item.)

1. **indifferent**—When you are *indifferent* about something, you don't care about that thing.
- What's another way of saying *They didn't care about the weather*?
- What's the answer? (Response: *They were indifferent about the weather.*)

2. **flirt**—When people *flirt,* they seem to take an affectionate interest in another person.
- What's another way of saying *The boys seemed to take an affectionate interest in the girls*?
- What's the answer? (Response: *The boys flirted with the girls.*)

3. **jealous**—When you are *jealous,* you are suspicious of other people. You feel jealousy toward them.
- What do you feel when you are suspicious of other people?
- What's the answer? (Response: *Jealousy.*)

4. **spite**—*Spite* is another word for hatred.
- What's another way of saying *He had great hatred for fools*?
- What's the answer? (Response: *He had great spite for fools.*)

EXERCISE 4

Vocabulary Review

1. Everybody, find part C. ✔
- We're going to review these words.
2. (Call on a student to read the words in the box.)

independent	**crestfallen**
antic	**wistful**
oath	**ghastly**
electrified	**random**

3. (For each item, have a student read the item and say the answer.)

1. A playful act is an ▭.

- What's the answer? (Response: *Antic.*)

2. When somebody is not controlled by other people, he or she is ▭.

- What's the answer? (Response: *Independent.*)

3. When you are ashamed or humiliated, you are ▭.

- What's the answer? (Response: *Crestfallen.*)

4. Events that follow no pattern are ▭ events.

- What's the answer? (Response: *Random.*)

5. When something is horrible or shocking, it is ▭.

- What's the answer? (Response: *Ghastly.*)

READING

EXERCISE 5

Focus Question

1. Everybody, find part D. ✔
2. What's the focus question for today's lesson? (Response: *How did Becky and Tom try to get even with each other?*)

EXERCISE 6

Reading Aloud (Optional)

1. We're going to read aloud to the diamond.

- (Call on individual students to read several sentences each.)

Chapter 13
The Spelling Book

Focus Question: How did Becky and Tom try to get even with each other?

Tom was crestfallen for only a little while. By the next day, he had decided to be independent of Becky Thatcher. If he seemed independent, maybe she would want to "make up." Well, let her—she would see that he could be as indifferent as some other people.

That day, Tom waited in front of the school. Presently Becky arrived.

Tom pretended not to see her. He moved away and joined a group of boys and girls and began to talk. Soon he observed that Becky was running merrily back and forth. She was pretending to be busy chasing schoolmates and screaming with laughter when she made a capture. But Tom noticed that Becky always made her captures near him, and that she was casting glances in his direction.

Presently Becky stopped running and moved randomly about. She sighed once or twice and glanced wistfully toward Tom. She observed that now Tom was talking to Amy Lawrence. Becky felt a sharp pang and grew disturbed and uneasy. She tried to go away, but her feet betrayed her and carried her toward Tom instead. Becky spoke to a girl almost at Tom's elbow. She said, "Why, Mary Austin! You bad girl, why didn't you come to Sunday school?"

"I did come. Didn't you see me?"

"Why, no! Did you? Where did you sit?"

"I was in Miss Peters's class, where I always go. I saw you."

"Did you? Why, it's funny I didn't see you. I wanted to tell you about the picnic."

"Oh, that's jolly! Who's going to give it?"

"My ma's going to let me have one."

"Oh, I hope she'll let me come!"

"Well, she will. The picnic's for me. She'll let anybody come that I want, and I want you."

"That's nice. When is it going to be?"

"By and by. Maybe after summer vacation starts."

"Oh, won't it be fun! Are you going to have all the girls and boys?"

"Yes, everyone that's friends with me— or wants to be," and she glanced quickly at

Tom, but he continued to talk to Amy Lawrence.

"Oh, may I come?" said Gracie Miller.

"Yes."

"And me?" said Sally Rogers.

"Yes."

"And me, too?" said Susy Harper. "And Joe?"

"Yes."

And so on, till all the group had begged for invitations but Tom and Amy. Then Tom turned coolly away, still talking, and took Amy with him. Becky's lips trembled and tears came to her eyes. She hid her sorrow and went on chattering, but the life had gone out of her plans. When the bell rang, Becky gave her pigtails a shake and resolved to get even with Tom. ◆

Silent Reading

1. Read the rest of the lesson to yourselves and be ready to answer some questions.

At recess, Tom continued to flirt with Amy. But he kept looking for Becky out of the corner of his eye. At last he saw her, and his blood suddenly ran cold. Becky was sitting cozily on a little bench looking at a picture book with Alfred Temple. They were so absorbed, and their heads were so close together over the book, that they did not seem to be aware of anything else in the world. Jealousy ran red-hot through Tom. He began to hate himself for throwing away the chance Becky had offered for making up. He called himself a fool and all the names he could think of. He wanted to yell with frustration.

Amy chatted happily along, as they walked, but Tom's tongue had lost its power. He did not hear what Amy was saying, and whenever she wanted an answer, Tom could only stammer. He kept drifting to the rear of the schoolhouse, again and again, to burn his eyeballs with the hateful scene there. He could not help it. It maddened him to see that Becky Thatcher never once seemed to take notice of him. But Becky did see Tom, and she knew she was winning the fight, too. She was glad to see Tom suffer as she had suffered.

Amy's happy jabbering became intolerable to Tom. Tom hinted at things he had to do—things that must be done. But the girl chirped on. Tom thought, "Oh, hang her, ain't I ever going to get rid of her?" At last she said she would be "around" when school let out, and Tom hurried away.

"I wouldn't mind any other boy," Tom thought, grating his teeth. "Any boy in the whole town but Alfred Temple! Oh, all right, I licked you the first day you ever saw this town, mister, and I'll lick you again! You just wait till I catch you out! I'll just take and . . ." ★

Tom began to thrash an imaginary boy—striking the air and kicking and flailing. "Oh, you do, do you? You holler 'nuff, do you? Now, then, let that learn you!"

Tom fled home at noon. He could not endure any more of Amy's chatter, and his jealousy could bear no more of the other problem. Becky resumed looking at pictures with Alfred. But as the minutes dragged along and no Tom came to suffer, her triumph began to cloud, and she lost interest. She became absent-minded and then melancholy. At last, she became entirely miserable and wished she hadn't carried her plan so far. When poor Alfred kept exclaiming, "Oh, here's a jolly picture! Look at this!" she lost patience at last and said, "Oh, don't bother me! I don't care for them!" and got up and walked away.

Alfred dropped alongside and was trying to comfort her, but she said, "Go away and leave me alone, can't you! I hate you!"

Alfred halted, wondering what he had done. Becky had said she would look at pictures all through lunch. Then Alfred went into the deserted schoolhouse. He was humiliated and angry. He easily guessed the truth—the girl had simply taken advantage of him to vent her spite upon Tom Sawyer. He hated Tom when this thought occurred to him. He wished there was some way to get Tom into trouble.

Tom's spelling book fell under Alfred's eye. Here was his opportunity. He gratefully opened to the lesson for the afternoon and poured ink on the page.

Becky was observing Alfred through a window. She saw the act and moved on without making a noise. She decided to find Tom and tell him. Tom would be thankful, and their troubles would be healed. Before she was halfway home, however, she changed her mind. She remembered how Tom had treated her when she was talking about her picnic. She resolved to let him get punished because of the damaged spelling book and to hate him forever.

- How did Becky and Tom try to get even with each other? (Ideas: *Tom started flirting with Amy Lawrence; Becky looked at pictures with Alfred Temple; Tom ignored Becky's invitation to the picnic; Becky decided not to tell Tom about the spelling book.*) (Sum)
- When Tom was flirting with Amy, the story says Becky "tried to go away, but her feet betrayed her and carried her toward Tom instead." Explain what "her feet betrayed her" means. (Idea: *Even though Becky wanted to go away, she couldn't help coming back toward Tom.*) (UCCM)
- When Tom saw Becky sitting with Alfred, the story says Tom "burned his eyeballs with the hateful scene." Explain what that phrase means. (Ideas: *Tom hated what he saw; the sight was painful to Tom.*) (UCCM)
- Explain how Tom first met Alfred Temple. (Idea: *At the beginning of the novel, Tom and Alfred got into a fight.*) (R)
- What do you think will happen with the spelling book? (Ideas: *The schoolmaster will punish Tom for ruining the book; Tom will guess that Alfred ruined the book and get into a fight with him; Becky will change her mind again and tell Tom what happened.*) (P)

Paired Practice (Optional)

1. Now you'll read in pairs.
- Whoever read second the last time will read first today.
- Remember to start at the diamond and switch at the star.

2. (Observe students and answer questions as needed.)

AFTER READING

Independent Work

1. Do all the items in your workbook and textbook for this lesson.
2. (The independent work in this lesson includes the following activities.)
- Story details
- Vocabulary
- Perspectives
- Following directions
- Logic
- Spoonerisms
- Comprehension
- Writing

Workcheck

1. (Using the Answer Key, read the questions and answers for the workbook.)
2. (Have students read their answers for the textbook activities.)
3. (Have two or three students read their writing assignments aloud. Comment on each assignment.)
4. (Have students correct and turn in their work.)

(Present Spelling lesson 103 after completing Reading lesson 103. See *Spelling Presentation Book*.)

BEFORE READING

(Have students find lesson 104, part A, in their textbooks.)

EXERCISE 1

Hard Words

1. Look at column 1.
- These are hard words from your textbook stories.

1. anatomy	**4. lynch**
2. isolated	**5. diary**
3. villain	

2. Word 1 is **anatomy.** Everybody, what word? (Signal.) *Anatomy.*
- (Repeat this procedure for every word in the column.)
3. Let's read the words again.
4. Word 1. Everybody, what word? (Signal.) *Anatomy.*
- (Repeat this procedure for every word in the column.)
5. (Repeat the column until firm.)

EXERCISE 2

Word Practice

1. Look at column 2.
- We're going to practice these words.

1. impatient	**4. topic**
2. sphere	**5. use**
3. atmosphere	**6. abuse**

2. Word 1. Everybody, what word? (Signal.) *Impatient.*
- (Repeat this procedure for every word in the column.)
3. (Repeat the column until firm.)

EXERCISE 3

New Vocabulary

1. Look at column 3.
- First we'll read the words in this column. Then we'll read their definitions.

1. anatomy	**5. sensation**
2. flustered	**6. diary**
3. proceedings	**7. villain**
4. folly	

2. Word 1. Everybody, what word? (Signal.) *Anatomy.*
- (Repeat this procedure for every word in the column.)
3. (Repeat the column until firm.)

EXERCISE 4

Vocabulary Definitions

1. Everybody, find part B. ✔
- These are definitions for the words you just read.
2. (For each word, call on a student to read the definition and the item. Then ask the student to complete the item.)

1. **anatomy**—*Anatomy* is the study of a body and its parts. *Human anatomy* is the study of the human body and its parts.
- What is anatomy?

- What's the answer? (Idea: *The study of a body and its parts.*)

2. **flustered**—*Flustered* is another word for confused.
- What's another way of saying *He was confused by her rude comments*?

- What's the answer? (Response: *He was flustered by her rude comments.*)

3. **proceedings**—*Proceedings* are events or activities. Events that happen during a trial are the proceedings of the trial.
   - What another way of saying *events that happen during a lesson*?

   - What's the answer? (Response: *The proceedings of a lesson.*)

4. **folly**—A *folly* is a foolish act.
   - What's another way of saying *The clown was known for his foolish acts*?

   - What's the answer? (Response: *The clown was known for his follies.*)

5. **sensation**—When something makes a *sensation,* it creates great excitement.
   - What's another way of saying *The circus created great excitement in the village*?

   - What's the answer? (Response: *The circus made a sensation in the village.*)

6. **diary**—A *diary* is a book where you write about your activities, thoughts, and feelings.
   - What is a diary?

   - What's the answer? (Idea: *A book where you write about your activities, thoughts, and feelings.*)

7. **villain**—A *villain* is a criminal or an evil person.
   - What's another way of saying *Many stories have an evil person*?

   - What's the answer? (Response: *Many stories have a villain.*)

READING

Focus Question

1. Everybody, find part C. ✔
2. What's the focus question for today's lesson? (Response: *Why did Tom take Becky's punishment?*)

Reading Aloud (Optional)

1. We're going to read aloud to the diamond.
   - (Call on individual students to read several sentences each.)

Chapter 14

Tom Takes Becky's Punishment

Focus Question: Why did Tom take Becky's punishment?

While Alfred was pouring ink over Tom's spelling book, Tom arrived home for lunch in a dreary mood. But there was something about Aunt Polly's manner during lunch that swept away his low spirits. And when she kissed him goodbye, he became lighthearted and happy again. He started to school and met Becky Thatcher in Meadow Lane.

Without a moment's hesitation, Tom ran to her and said, "I acted mighty mean today, Becky, and I'm so sorry. I won't ever, ever do that again, as long as ever I live. Please make up, won't you?"

The girl stopped and looked him scornfully in the face. "I'll never speak to you again, Mr. Thomas Sawyer."

She tossed her head and passed on. Tom was so stunned that he said nothing. But he was in a rage, nevertheless. He moped into the schoolyard. He soon saw Becky and delivered a stinging remark as he passed. Becky could hardly wait for school to begin, because she was so impatient to see Tom punished for the spelling book.

Poor girl, she did not know how fast she was nearing trouble herself. The schoolmaster, Mr. Dobbins, had always wanted to be a doctor. Every day, he took a mysterious book out of his desk and read it when the class was studying. He kept that book under lock and key. Every student in school was dying to have a glimpse of the book, but the chance never came.

Now, as Becky was passing by the desk, she noticed that the key was in the lock! It was a precious moment. She glanced around, found herself alone, and the next instant had the book in her hands. The title page—Anatomy—meant nothing to her, so she began to turn the pages.

She turned to a handsome picture of a man—completely naked.

At that moment, a shadow fell on the page. Tom Sawyer stepped in at the door and caught a glimpse of the picture. Becky snatched at the book to close it—and tore the picture right down the middle. She thrust the book into the desk, turned the key, and turned away with shame. ♦

EXERCISE 7

Silent Reading

1. Read the rest of the lesson to yourselves and be ready to answer some questions.

"Tom Sawyer, you are just as mean as you can be, to sneak up on a person and look at what they're looking at."

"How could I know you were looking at anything?"

"You ought to be ashamed of yourself, Tom Sawyer. You know you're going to tell on me, and oh, what shall I do, what shall I do? I'll be punished—and I've never been punished in school."

Then she stamped her foot and said, "Be so mean if you want to! I know something that's going to happen. You just wait and you'll see!" And she ran out of the school.

Tom stood still, rather flustered by this attack. Presently he said to himself, "So, Becky's never been punished in school! Shucks. Well, of course, I ain't going to tell old Dobbins, because there's other ways of getting even with her that ain't so mean. Old Dobbins will ask who tore his book. Nobody'll answer. Then he'll do what he always does—ask first one and then another, and when he comes to the right girl, he'll know it, without any telling. Well, it's a kind of tight place for Becky Thatcher, because there ain't any way out of it."

Tom joined the mob of scholars outside. In a few moments, the schoolmaster arrived and school began. The boy did not feel a strong interest in his studies. Every time he stole a glance at the girls' side of the room, Becky's face troubled him. Considering all things, he did not want to pity her, and yet he did feel pity.

Presently, the spelling book discovery was made, and Tom's mind was entirely full of his own matters for a while after that. Becky showed good interest in the proceedings. She did not expect that Tom could get out of his trouble by denying he spilled the ink on the book himself, and she was right. The denial only seemed to make the thing worse for Tom.

Becky tried to believe she was glad, but she found she was not. When Mr. Dobbins began to punish Tom, she had an impulse to get up and tell on Alfred Temple. But she made an effort and forced herself to keep still because, said she to herself, "He'll tell about me tearing the picture. I wouldn't say a word, not to save his life!"

Tom took his punishment and went back to his seat. He thought it was possible that he had upset the ink on the spelling book himself without knowing it. He had denied the crime because it was his custom. ★

A whole hour drifted by. The schoolmaster sat nodding in his chair, and the air was drowsy with the hum of study. By and by, Mr. Dobbins straightened himself, yawned, unlocked his desk, and reached for his book. But he did not know whether to take it out or leave it. Most of the pupils glanced up indifferently—but there were two that watched his movements with intent eyes.

Mr. Dobbins fingered his book absently for a while, then took it out and settled himself in his chair to read! Tom shot a glance at Becky. She looked like a hunted and helpless rabbit. Tom instantly forgot his quarrel with her. Quick—something must be done! Done in a flash, too! He had an inspiration! He would run and snatch the book, spring through the door, and run off!

But Tom waited for one little instant, and his chance was lost, for Mr. Dobbins opened the book. If Tom only had the chance back again! Too late. There was no help for Becky now, he thought. The next moment Mr. Dobbins faced the class. Every eye sank under his gaze, which even put fear in the innocent. There was silence for ten seconds while Mr. Dobbins gathered his anger.

Then he spoke. "Who tore this book?"

There was not a sound. One could have heard a pin drop. The stillness continued. Mr. Dobbins searched face after face for signs of guilt.

"Benjamin Rogers, did you tear this book?"

A denial. Another pause.

"Joseph Harper, did you?"

Another denial. Tom's uneasiness grew more and more intense under the slow torture of these proceedings. The schoolmaster scanned the ranks of boys, considered awhile, then turned to the girls.

"Amy Lawrence?"

A shake of the head.

"Gracie Miller?"

The same sign.

The next girl was Becky Thatcher. Tom was trembling from head to foot with excitement and a sense of the hopelessness of the situation.

"Becky Thatcher," (Tom glanced at her face—it was pale with terror) "did you tear . . . no, look me in the face," (her hands rose in appeal) "did you tear this book?"

A thought shot like lightning through Tom's brain. He sprang to his feet and shouted, "I done it!"

The class stared in amazement at Tom's incredible folly. Tom stood a moment to gather himself together and then stepped forward to receive his punishment. Surprise, gratitude, and admiration shone upon him out of poor Becky's eyes. Inspired by the greatness of his own act, he calmly received the cruel command to remain two hours after school. Tom knew that Becky would wait for him outside till his captivity was done, so the two hours would be well spent.

Tom went to bed that night planning revenge against Alfred Temple, for Becky had told him everything. But even the longing for revenge had to give way, soon, to more pleasant thoughts, and he fell asleep at last, with Becky's latest words lingering dreamily in his ear: "Tom, how could you be so noble!"

- Why did Tom take Becky's punishment? (Ideas: *He felt sorry for her; he knew she would forgive him if he took her punishment; he wanted to show her how brave he was.*) (DCE)
- Why did the schoolmaster have an anatomy book? (Ideas: *He had always wanted to be a doctor; he wanted to study anatomy.*) (DCE)
- Why was Becky particularly afraid of the schoolmaster's punishment? (Idea: *She had never been punished in school.*) (ND)
- When Tom was punished for the spelling book, why didn't Becky tell the schoolmaster what had really happened? (Idea: *She was afraid Tom would tell about her tearing the picture.*) (DCE)
- The story says Tom was "inspired by the greatness of his own act." What does that phrase mean? (Idea: *Tom was proud of himself for what he had done.*) (UCCM)

EXERCISE 8

Paired Practice (Optional)

1. Now you'll read in pairs.
- Whoever read second the last time will read first today.
- Remember to start at the diamond and switch at the star.
2. (Observe students and answer questions as needed.)

AFTER READING

EXERCISE 9

Independent Work

1. Do all the items in your workbook and textbook for this lesson.
2. (The independent work in this lesson includes the following activities.)
- Story details
- Vocabulary
- Perspectives
- Logic
- Combined sentences
- Vocabulary review
- Comprehension
- Writing

EXERCISE 10

Workcheck

1. (Using the Answer Key, read the questions and answers for the workbook.)
2. (Have students read their answers for the textbook activities.)
3. (Have two or three students read their writing assignments aloud. Comment on each assignment.)
4. (Have students correct and turn in their work.)

SPELLING

(Present Spelling lesson 104 after completing Reading lesson 104. See *Spelling Presentation Book*.)

BEFORE READING

(Have students find lesson 105, part A, in their textbooks.)

EXERCISE 1

Word Practice

1. Look at column 1.
- We're going to practice these words.

1. ceremonies	4. mortal
2. secure	5. immortal
3. insecure	

2. Word 1. Everybody, what word? (Signal.) *Ceremonies.*
- (Repeat this procedure for every word in the column.)
3. (Repeat the column until firm.)

EXERCISE 2

New Vocabulary

1. Look at column 2.
- First we'll read the words in this column. Then we'll read their definitions.

1. stand trial	4. abuse
2. atmosphere	5. lynch
3. topic	6. isolated

2. Line 1. Everybody, what words? (Signal.) *Stand trial.*
- (Repeat this procedure for every word in the column.)
3. (Repeat the column until firm.)

EXERCISE 3

Vocabulary Definitions

1. Everybody, find part B. ✔
- These are definitions for the words you just read.
2. (For each word, call on a student to read the definition and the item. Then ask the student to complete the item.)

1. **stand trial**—When somebody *stands trial,* that person is tried in court for a crime.
- What happens when somebody stands trial?

- What's the answer? (Idea: *That person is tried in court for a crime.*)

2. **atmosphere**—The *atmosphere* of a setting is the mood of that setting.
- What's another way of saying *The mood of the church was solemn*?

- What's the answer? (Response: *The atmosphere of the church was solemn.*)

3. **topic**—A *topic* is a subject that people discuss. If people discuss a trial, that trial is the *topic* of their discussion.
- What is a topic?

- What's the answer? (Idea: *A subject that people discuss.*)

4. **abuse**—When you *abuse* something, you treat it badly.
- What's another way of saying *He treated his bike badly*?

- What's the answer? (Response: *He abused his bike.*)

5. **lynch**—When a person is *lynched,* that person is hanged by a mob without receiving a trial.
- What happens to a person who is lynched?

- What's the answer? (Idea: *That person is hanged by a mob without a trial.*)

6. **isolated**—When something is *isolated,* it is all alone.
- What's another way of saying *The house was all alone on the hill*?

- What's the answer? (Response: *The house was isolated on the hill.*)

Logic

1. Everybody, turn to part D at the end of today's story. ✔
- (Call on individual students to read several sentences each.)
- (At the end of each section, present the questions for that section.)

Write the answers for items 1 and 2.

Here's a rule of logic: *Just because the writer presents some choices doesn't mean there are no other choices.*

The following statement by a writer breaks the rule. "Whenever there are fairs, the ground gets littered. People drop cups, popcorn, candy wrappers, and other types of litter onto the ground. We have to pay thousands of dollars to clean up this litter, and we can't afford it anymore. Either we go broke, or we close down all fairs."

1. Which two choices does the writer present?

- What's the answer? (Idea: *Going broke or closing down all fairs.*)

2. Name another choice that could be possible.

- What's the answer? (Ideas: *Prevent the litter; provide trash cans.*)
- You'll write the answers later.

READING

Focus Question

1. Everybody, turn back to part C. ✔
2. What's the focus question for today's lesson? (Response: *Why did the gossip about Muff Potter make Tom uncomfortable?*)

Reading Aloud (Optional)

1. We're going to read aloud to the diamond.
- (Call on individual students to read several sentences each.)

Chapter 15
Vacation at Last

Focus Question: Why did the gossip about Muff Potter make Tom uncomfortable?

Summer vacation finally came, and Tom's hopes were high. They soon crashed with disappointment.

He started to write a diary, but during three days nothing happened worth recording, so he abandoned it.

A minstrel show came to town and made a sensation, but only for two days.

A circus came. The boys played circus for three days afterward, in tents made of rag carpeting—admission: three pins for boys, two for girls—and then circusing was abandoned.

Even the Fourth of July was a failure, for it rained hard, and there was no parade.

There were some boys-and-girls' parties, but they were so few and so delightful that they only made the aching time between parties ache the harder.

Worst of all, Becky Thatcher had gone to stay with family friends during vacation, so there was no bright side to Tom's life anywhere.

Tom presently found that his wonderful vacation was beginning to drag on heavily.

At last the sleepy atmosphere was stirred—and vigorously. It was time for Muff Potter to stand trial. The trial immediately became the major topic of village talk. Tom could not get away from it. Every mention of the murder sent a shudder to his heart. No one suspected he knew anything about the murder, but the gossip made him uncomfortable. It kept him in a cold shiver all the time.

Tom took Huck to a lonely place to have a talk with him. It would be a relief to talk with another sufferer. He also wanted to make sure Huck had kept his oath. ♦

Silent Reading

1. Read the rest of the lesson to yourselves and be ready to answer some questions.

"Huck, have you ever told anybody about . . . that?"

"About what?"

"You know what."

"Oh . . . of course I haven't."

"Never a word?"

Huck replied, "Never a single word, so help me. What makes you ask?"

"Well, I was afraid."

"Why, Tom Sawyer, we wouldn't be alive two days if that got out! You know that."

Tom felt more comfortable. After a pause, he said, "Huck, nobody could get you to tell, could they?"

"Get me to tell? Why, if I wanted that outlaw devil to drown me, they could get me to tell. But that's the only way."

"Well, that's all right, then. I reckon we're safe as long as we keep quiet. But let's swear again, anyway."

"I'm agreed."

So they swore again with dread and solemn ceremonies.

"What is the talk that's going around, Huck?"

"Talk? Well, it's just Muff Potter, Muff Potter, Muff Potter all the time. It keeps me in a sweat constantly. I want to hide somewhere."

"That's just the same way I feel. I reckon he's a goner. Don't you feel sorry for him, sometimes?"

Huck said, "Almost always . . . almost always. He ain't any good, but then he ain't ever done anything to hurt anybody. Just fishes a little and loafs around. But we all do that—at least most of us. But he's kind of good—he gave me half a fish once, when there wasn't enough for two. And lots of times he's kind of stood by me when I was out of luck."

"Well, he's mended kites for me, Huck, and knitted hooks onto my fishing line. I wish we could get him out of prison."

"My! We couldn't get him out, Tom. Besides, it wouldn't do any good; they'd catch him again."

"Yes, so they would. But I hate to hear them abuse him so much when he never did . . . that."

"I hate it, too, Tom. I hear 'em say he's the bloodiest-looking villain in this country, and they wonder why he wasn't ever hung before."

"Yes, they talk like that, all the time. I've heard 'em say that if he was to get free, they'd lynch him."

"And they'd do it, too." ★

The boys had a long talk, but it brought them little comfort. As the twilight drew on, they found themselves hanging around the little isolated jail. They both hoped something would happen to clear away their difficulties. But nothing happened; there seemed to be no angels or fairies interested in Muff Potter.

The boys did something they had often done before. They went to the jail window and gave Potter some gifts. He was on the ground floor, and there were no guards.

His gratitude for their gifts had always made the boys feel bad before, and it cut deeper than ever this time. They felt cowardly and treacherous when Potter said, "You've been mighty good to me, boys, better than anybody else in this town. I don't forget it, I don't. Often I says to myself that I used to mend all the boys' kites and things and show 'em where the good fishin' places was and be a friend to 'em, and now they've all forgotten old Muff when he's in trouble. But Tom didn't, and Huck didn't—they didn't forget him. And I don't forget them."

"Well, boys," he continued, "I done an awful thing, and now I got to hang for it, and it's right. Right, and best, too, I reckon—hope so, anyway. Well, we won't talk about that. I don't want to make you feel bad; you've been my friends. Let's shake hands—your hands will come through the bars, but mine are too big. Little hands, and weak—but they've helped Muff Potter, and they'd help him more if they could."

- Why did the gossip about Muff Potter make Tom so uncomfortable? (Ideas: *Because Tom knew Muff Potter was innocent; because Tom knew he could save Muff Potter*.) (DCE)
- The story says, "There seemed to be no angels or fairies interested in Muff Potter." Explain what that means. (Ideas: *Muff Potter couldn't get any help from magic; nobody could help Muff Potter.*) (UCCM)
- Why didn't the boys tell anybody the truth about Muff Potter? (Idea: *They were afraid Outlaw Joe would kill them.*) (DCE)

- Why do you think the boys visited Muff Potter? (Ideas: *They wanted to make up for their silence; they felt bad about keeping quiet.*) (MJ)
- What do you think Tom will do when the trial begins? Explain your answer. (Ideas: *Keep quiet, because he and Huck have made an oath; tell what happened, because he'll decide to do the right thing.*) (P)

Paired Practice (Optional)

1. Now you'll read in pairs.
- Whoever read second the last time will read first today.
- Remember to start at the diamond and switch at the star.
2. (Observe students and answer questions as needed.)

AFTER READING

Independent Work

1. Do all the items in your workbook and textbook for this lesson.
2. (The independent work in this lesson includes the following activities.)
- Story details
- Cause and effect
- Vocabulary
- Graphs
- Logic
- Settings
- Vocabulary review
- Comprehension
- Writing

Workcheck

1. (Using the Answer Key, read the questions and answers for the workbook.)
2. (Have students read their answers for the textbook activities.)
3. (Have two or three students read their writing assignments aloud. Comment on each assignment.)
4. (Have students correct and turn in their work.)

ACTIVITIES ACROSS THE CURRICULUM

(Students should complete the appropriate project in *Activities across the Curriculum* after completing lesson 105. See *Activities across the Curriculum* book for details.)

SPELLING

(Present Spelling lesson 105 after completing Reading lesson 105. See *Spelling Presentation Book.*)

Lessons 106–110 • Planning Page   *Looking Ahead*

	Lesson 106	**Lesson 107**	**Lesson 108**	**Lesson 109**	**Lesson 110**
BEFORE READING	Hard words Word practice New vocabulary Vocabulary definitions Vocabulary review	Word practice New vocabulary Vocabulary definitions Vocabulary review	Hard words New vocabulary Vocabulary definitions Vocabulary review Logic	Hard words Word practice New vocabulary Vocabulary definitions Logic	Hard words New vocabulary Vocabulary definitions Logic
NEW VOCABULARY	verdict haggard climax trifle immortal insecure	confidential interfere pick	bay utterly intruder	mute distinct eternity unearth blissful	amid clutter slaughterhouse charter throng reflect
READING	*Tom Sawyer* (Chapter 16)	*Tom Sawyer* (Chapter 17)	*Tom Sawyer* (Chapter 18)	*Tom Sawyer* (Chapter 19)	*Tom Sawyer* (Chapter 20)
INDEPENDENT WORK	Story details Vocabulary Contradictions Logic Comprehension Writing	Story details Vocabulary Logic Metaphors Comparisons Comprehension Writing	Story details Vocabulary Logic Exaggeration Perspectives Story review Comprehension Writing	Story details Vocabulary Maps Logic Sequencing Vocabulary review Comprehension Writing	Story details Perspectives Vocabulary Conversations Logic Vocabulary review Comprehension Writing
SUPPLEMENTS	*Spelling*	*Spelling*	*Spelling*	*Spelling*	*Mastery Test* *Spelling* *Activities across the Curriculum*

Comprehension Questions Abbreviations Guide

Access Prior Knowledge = (APK)   Author's Point of View = (APoV)   Author's Purpose = (AP)   Cause/Effect = (C/E)   Charts/Graphs/Diagrams/Visual Aids = (VA)

Classify and Categorize = (C+C)   Compare/Contrast = (C/C)   Determine Character Emotions, Motivation = (DCE)   Drawing Conclusions = (DC)   Drawing Inferences = (DI)

Fact and Opinion = (F/O)   Hypothesizing = (H)   Main Idea = (MI)   Making Connections = (MC)   Making Deductions = (MD)   Making Judgements = (MJ)

Narrative Elements = (NE)   Noting Details = (ND)   Predict = (P)   Reality/Fantasy = (R/F)   Recall Facts/Rules = (RF/R)   Retell = (R)   Sequence = (Seq)

Steps in a Process = (SP)   Story Structure = (SS)   Summarize = (Sum)   Understanding Dialogue = (UD)   Using Context to Confirm Meaning(s) = (UCCM)   Visualize = (V)

LESSON 106

BEFORE READING

(Have students find lesson 106, part A, in their textbooks.)

EXERCISE 1

Hard Words

1. Look at column 1.
   - These are hard words from your textbook stories.

1. climax	4. verdict
2. haggard	5. confidentially
3. trifle	

2. Word 1 is **climax.** Everybody, what word? (Signal.) *Climax.*
   - (Repeat this procedure for every word in the column.)
3. Let's read the words again.
4. Word 1. Everybody, what word? (Signal.) *Climax.*
   - (Repeat this procedure for every word in the column.)
5. (Repeat the column until firm.)

EXERCISE 2

Word Practice

1. Look at column 2.
   - We're going to practice these words.

1. wretched	3. detective
2. wretchedness	4. interfere

2. Word 1. Everybody, what word? (Signal.) *Wretched.*
   - (Repeat this procedure for every word in the column.)
3. (Repeat the column until firm.)

EXERCISE 3

New Vocabulary

1. Look at column 3.
   - First we'll read the words in this column. Then we'll read their definitions.

1. verdict	4. trifle
2. haggard	5. immortal
3. climax	6. insecure

2. Word 1. Everybody, what word? (Signal.) *Verdict.*
   - (Repeat this procedure for every word in the column.)
3. (Repeat the column until firm.)

EXERCISE 4

Vocabulary Definitions

1. Everybody, find part B. ✔
   - These are definitions for the words you just read.
2. (For each word, call on a student to read the definition and the item. Then ask the student to complete the item.)

1. **verdict**—In a trial, a jury decides whether a person is guilty or innocent of a crime. The jury's decision is the *verdict.*
   - What is a verdict?

   - What's the answer? (Idea: *A jury's decision in a trial.*)

2. **haggard**—When something is *haggard,* it looks thin and worn out.
   - What's another way of saying *She looked thin and worn out after a week in the desert*?

   - What's the answer? (Response: *She looked haggard after a week in the desert.*)

3. **climax**—The *climax* of a story is the story's most important event or highest point.
   - What is the climax of a story?

   - What's the answer? (Idea: *The story's most important event or highest point.*)

4. **trifle**—A *trifle* is a slight amount. If someone is slightly faster, that person is a trifle faster.
   - What's another way of saying *She was slightly more talented*?
   - What's the answer? (Response: *She was a trifle more talented.*)

5. **immortal**—If something is *immortal*, it lives forever. A book that lives forever is an immortal book.
   - What's another way of saying *a song that lives forever*?
   - What's the answer? (Response: *An immortal song.*)

6. **insecure**—When you feel *insecure*, you feel uncertain or unsafe.
   - What's another way of saying *She felt uncertain during the earthquake*?
   - What's the answer? (Response: *She felt insecure during the earthquake.*)

EXERCISE 5
Vocabulary Review

1. Everybody, find part C. ✔
   - We're going to review these words.
2. (Call on a student to read the words in the box.)

topic	sensation
diary	flustered
atmosphere	abuse
isolated	indifferent
villain	

3. (For each item, have a student read the item and say the answer.)

1. When you treat something badly, you ▓▓▓▓ it.
   - What's the answer? (Response: *Abuse.*)

2. A subject that people discuss is a ▓▓▓▓.
   - What's the answer? (Response: *Topic.*)

3. The mood of a setting is the ▓▓▓▓ of that setting.
   - What's the answer? (Response: *Atmosphere.*)

4. When something is all alone, it is ▓▓▓▓.
   - What's the answer? (Response: *Isolated.*)

5. When you don't care about something, you are ▓▓▓▓ about that thing.
   - What's the answer? (Response: *Indifferent.*)

6. Another word for *confused* is ▓▓▓▓.
   - What's the answer? (Response: *Flustered.*)

READING

EXERCISE 6
Story Background

1. Everybody, find part D. ✔
   - We're going to read this passage aloud.
   - (Call on individual students to read several sentences each.)
   - (At the end of each section, present the questions for that section.)

Trials

Chapter 16 tells about Muff Potter's trial. The trial follows the same basic steps found in modern trials.

A lawyer from the government will try to prove that Potter is guilty. The lawyer will present evidence and have a person who witnessed the crime tell what he saw.

Potter's lawyer will try to prove that Potter is innocent. This lawyer will also present evidence and call witnesses.

As the lawyers present their arguments, a judge will make sure the arguments follow the rules. The judge can tell the lawyers to stop asking questions that break the rules.

- What will Potter's lawyer try to prove? (Idea: *That Potter is innocent.*) ©/©

- What will the government's lawyer try to prove? (Idea: *That Potter is guilty*.) Ⓒ/Ⓒ
- Who will make sure the lawyers follow the rules? (Response: *The judge*.) Ⓒ₊Ⓒ
- What might happen if a lawyer asks a question that breaks the rules? (Idea: *The judge will tell the lawyer to stop*.) Ⓟ

A jury will decide whether Muff Potter is guilty or innocent. The jury is made up of twelve people who will listen to the arguments presented by the lawyers. Then the jury will leave the room to make a decision, or *verdict*. All members of the jury must agree on the verdict.

If the jury decides Muff Potter is innocent, he will be freed. If the jury decides he is guilty, he will probably be sentenced to death by hanging.

- Who will decide whether Muff Potter is guilty or innocent? (Response: *The jury*.) Ⓒ₊Ⓒ
- How many people are on the jury? (Response: *Twelve*.) Ⓡ🅕/Ⓡ
- If the jury decides Potter is innocent, what will happen to him? (Idea: *He will go free*.) Ⓒ/Ⓔ
- If the jury decides Potter is guilty, what will happen to him? (Idea: *He will hang*.) Ⓒ/Ⓔ

EXERCISE 7

Focus Question

1. Everybody, find part E. ✔
2. What's the focus question for today's lesson? (Response: *Why did Tom decide to tell his story?*)

> *Note:* The "Reading Aloud" exercise is recommended for this lesson.

EXERCISE 8

Reading Aloud

1. We're going to read aloud to the diamond.
- (Call on individual students to read several sentences each.)

Chapter 16
Muff Potter's Rescue

Focus Question: Why did Tom decide to tell his story?

Tom went home miserable, and his dreams that night were full of horrors. Muff

Potter's trial began the next day. That day and the day after, Tom hung around the courtroom. He had a strong impulse to go in, but he forced himself to stay out.

Huck was having the same experience. The two boys carefully avoided each other. Each wandered away, from time to time, but the same dismal fascination always brought them back to the courtroom.

Tom kept his ears open when people came out of the courtroom. He always heard distressing news. It seemed that the rope was closing more and more tightly around poor Potter's neck. At the end of the second day, the gossipers said that Outlaw Joe had told his story. The evidence he gave was firm and unshaken. There was not the slightest question as to what the jury's verdict would be.

Tom was out late that night on a mission so secret that he could hardly bear to think of it. He came to bed through the window. He was in a tremendous state of excitement, and it was hours before he got to sleep.

The whole village flocked to the courthouse the next morning, for this was to be the great day—the day the jury would decide if Potter was to hang. After a long wait, the jury filed in and took their places. Shortly afterward, Potter, pale and haggard, timid and hopeless, was brought in, with chains on him. He was seated where all the curious eyes could stare at him. Outlaw Joe sat in a corner, grim as ever. There was another pause, and then the judge arrived, and the sheriff opened the court. The lawyers whispered to each other and gathered together their papers.

Several witnesses testified about Potter's guilty behavior when he was brought to the scene of the murder. But Potter's lawyer did not ask these witnesses any questions. The attorney for the government now said, "The evidence shows that this awful crime was committed by Muff Potter. We rest our case here." ◆

EXERCISE 9

Silent Reading

1. Read the rest of the lesson to yourselves and be ready to answer some questions.

A groan escaped from poor Potter. He put his face in his hands and rocked his body softly back and forth. Many people were moved, and some broke into tears.

Potter's lawyer rose and said, "Call Thomas Sawyer!"

The audience was amazed by this statement. Every eye fastened itself upon Tom as he rose and took his place on the stand. The boy looked terribly scared.

Muff Potter's lawyer said, "Thomas Sawyer, where were you on the seventeenth of June, about the hour of midnight?"

Tom glanced at Outlaw Joe's iron face. The boy's tongue could not move. The audience listened breathlessly, but the words refused to come. After a few moments, however, Tom got a little of his strength back.

In a soft voice, he said, "In the graveyard."

"A little bit louder, please. Don't be afraid. You were . . ."

"In the graveyard!"

A horrid smile flitted across Outlaw Joe's face.

"Were you anywhere near Horse Williams's grave?"

"Yes, sir."

"Speak up . . . just a trifle louder. How near were you?"

"Near as I am to you."

"Were you hidden, or not?"

"I was hid."

"Where?"

"Behind the elms on the edge of the grave."

Outlaw Joe gave a start.

"Anyone with you?"

"Yes, sir. I went there with . . ."

"Wait . . . wait a moment. Never mind mentioning your companion's name. We will produce him at the proper time. Did you carry anything there with you?"

Tom hesitated and looked confused.

"Speak out, my boy. What did you take there?"

"Only a . . . a . . . dead rat."

There was a ripple of laughter.

"We will produce the skeleton of that rat. Now, my boy, tell us everything that occurred—tell it in your own way—don't skip anything, and don't be afraid." ★

Tom began. He hesitated at first, but as he warmed up, his words flowed more and more easily. In a little while every sound in the courtroom ceased but his own voice. Every eye fixed itself upon him. With parted lips the audience hung upon his words, taking no note of time. They were all caught up in the ghastly tale. The strain reached its climax when the boy said, ". . . and as the doctor fetched the board around and Muff Potter fell, Outlaw Joe jumped at him and . . ."

Crash! All heads turned toward the corner of the courtroom where Outlaw Joe had been sitting. Quick as lightning, the outlaw sprang for a window, tore his way through the crowd, and was gone!

• • •

Tom was a glittering hero—the pet of the old, the envy of the young. His name even went into immortal print, for the village paper had a story about him the next day. There were some who believed he would be president, if he escaped hanging.

Tom's days were days of splendor, but his nights were seasons of horror. Outlaw Joe invaded all his dreams, always with doom in his eye. Hardly any temptation could persuade the boy to go out after nightfall. Poor Huck was in the same state of wretchedness and terror. Huck was afraid that Muff Potter's lawyer would tell what he knew.

Tom had told the whole story to the lawyer the night before the last day of the trial. Huck was sorely afraid that his share in the business might leak out yet. The lawyer had promised secrecy, but Huck wasn't sure he could be trusted. After all, Tom had broken their solemn oath—and the attorney might, too.

Muff Potter's gratitude made Tom glad he had spoken, but at night, Tom wished he had sealed his tongue. Half the time he was afraid Outlaw Joe would never be captured. During the other half, Tom was afraid he *would* be captured.

Rewards for Outlaw Joe were offered, and the country was searched, but no Outlaw Joe was found. A detective came up from Saint Louis, snooped around, shook his head, looked wise, and "found a clue." But you can't hang a "clue" for murder, and after the detective had gone home, Tom felt just as insecure as before.

The slow days drifted on.

- Why did Tom decide to tell his story? (Ideas: *He wanted to save Muff Potter's life; he wanted to do the right thing; he wanted Outlaw Joe to go to prison.*) ⓓⒸⒺ
- Before Tom told his story, why did it seem the jury would find Muff Potter guilty? (Ideas: *The evidence was against Muff Potter; Outlaw Joe said Muff Potter had committed the murder.*) ⓂⒿ
- On the last day of the trial, why didn't Muff Potter's lawyer ask the witnesses any questions? (Ideas: *Their testimony didn't matter; he only needed to ask Tom questions.*) ⓓⒸⒺ
- The story says, "Tom's days were days of splendor, but his nights were seasons of horror." Why do you think the writer used the word *seasons* to describe Tom's nights? (Idea: *To show that his nights seemed to last a long time.*) ⒶⓅ
- How do you think Huck feels about Tom's decision? Explain your answer. (Ideas: *He's unhappy with Tom, because Tom broke their oath; he's happy, because he knows Tom did the right thing; he's nervous, because people might find out he was involved, too.*) ⓂⒿ

EXERCISE 10
Paired Practice (Optional)

1. Now you'll read in pairs.
- Whoever read second the last time will read first today.
- Remember to start at the diamond and switch at the star.
2. (Observe students and answer questions as needed.)

AFTER READING

EXERCISE 11
Independent Work

1. Do all the items in your workbook and textbook for this lesson.
2. (The independent work in this lesson includes the following activities.)
- Story details
- Vocabulary
- Contradictions
- Logic
- Comprehension
- Writing

EXERCISE 12
Workcheck

1. (Using the Answer Key, read the questions and answers for the workbook.)
2. (Have students read their answers for the textbook activities.)
3. (Have two or three students read their writing assignments aloud. Comment on each assignment.)
4. (Have students correct and turn in their work.)

SPELLING

(Present Spelling lesson 106 after completing Reading lesson 106. See *Spelling Presentation Book.*)

BEFORE READING

(Have students find lesson 107, part A, in their textbooks.)

EXERCISE 1
Word Practice

1. Look at column 1.
- We're going to practice these words.

1. bay	3. baying
2. wretchedness	4. anatomy

2. Word 1. Everybody, what word? (Signal.) *Bay.*
- (Repeat this procedure for every word in the column.)
3. (Repeat the column until firm.)

EXERCISE 2
New Vocabulary

1. Look at column 2.
- First we'll read the words in this column. Then we'll read their definitions.

1. confidential	3. pick
2. interfere	

2. Word 1. Everybody, what word? (Signal.) *Confidential.*
- (Repeat this procedure for every word in the column.)
3. (Repeat the column until firm.)

EXERCISE 3
Vocabulary Definitions

1. Everybody, find part B. ✔
- These are definitions for the words you just read.
2. (For each word, call on a student to read the definition and the item. Then ask the student to complete the item.)

1. **confidential**—When something is *confidential*, it is private or secret. When you speak *confidentially,* you speak in private or in secret.
- What's another way of saying *Huck and Tom spoke in private*?
- What's the answer? (Response: *Huck and Tom spoke confidentially.*)

2. **interfere**—When something *interferes*, it gets in the way. If somebody gets in the way of your plans, that person interferes with your plans.
- What's another way of saying *Huck didn't want to get in the way of the trial*?
- What's the answer? (Response: *Huck didn't want to interfere with the trial.*)

3. **pick**—A *pick* is a large digging tool with a wooden handle and a pointed metal head.
- What is a pick?
- What's the answer? (Idea: *A large digging tool with a wooden handle and a pointed metal head.*)

EXERCISE 4
Vocabulary Review

1. Everybody, find part C. ✔
- We're going to review these words.
2. (Call on a student to read the words in the box.)

climax	immortal
verdict	trifle
insecure	flustered
haggard	

3. (For each item, have a student read the item and say the answer.)

1. A jury's decision is a ▇▇▇▇.

• What's the answer? (Response: *Verdict.*)

2. When you feel uncertain, you feel ▇▇▇▇.

• What's the answer? (Response: *Insecure.*)

3. The most important event in a story is the ▇▇▇▇ of the story.

• What's the answer? (Response: *Climax.*)

4. Another word for *confused* is ▇▇▇▇.

• What's the answer? (Response: *Flustered.*)

5. When somebody is thin and worn out, that person is ▇▇▇▇.

• What's the answer? (Response: *Haggard.*)

6. A slight amount is a ▇▇▇▇.

• What's the answer? (Response: *Trifle.*)

7. Something that lives forever is ▇▇▇▇.

• What's the answer? (Response: *Immortal.*)

READING

EXERCISE 5

Focus Question

1. Everybody, find part D. ✔
2. What's the focus question for today's lesson? (Response: *How were Huck's plans for the treasure different from Tom's?*)

EXERCISE 6

Reading Aloud (Optional)

1. We're going to read aloud to the diamond.
• (Call on individual students to read several sentences each.)

Chapter 17
Seeking the Buried Treasure

Focus Question: How were Huck's plans for the treasure different from Tom's?

There comes a time in every boy's life when he has a raging desire to go somewhere and dig for hidden treasure. This desire suddenly came upon Tom one day. He tried to find Joe Harper but failed. Next he sought Ben Rogers, but he had gone fishing. Presently he stumbled upon Huck Finn. Tom took him to a private place and talked to him confidentially. Huck was willing. Huck was always willing to take part in any project that offered entertainment and required no money.

"Where'll we dig for treasure?" said Huck.

"Oh, most anywhere."

"Why, is treasure hid all around?"

"No, indeed it ain't. It's hid in mighty particular places, Huck—sometimes on islands, sometimes in rotten chests under the end of a limb of an old dead tree, just where the shadow falls at midnight, but mostly under the floor in haunted houses."

"Who hides it?"

"Why, robbers, of course—who'd you reckon? Sunday school teachers?"

"I don't know. If it was mine, I reckon I wouldn't hide it. I'd spend it and have a good time."

"So would I. But robbers don't do it that way. They always hide it and leave it there. Then somebody finds an old yellow paper that tells how to find the place. The paper's got to be puzzled over for about a week because it's mostly written in a secret code."

"Have you got one of them papers?"

"No," said Tom.

"Well, then, how are you going to find the hiding place?"

"Look, Huck, robbers always bury it under a haunted house or on an island or under a dead tree that's got one limb sticking out. Well, we could try Jackson's Island sometime, and there's the old haunted house up Still Creek, and there's lots of dead-limb trees."

"How are you going to know which place to go for?"

"Go for all of 'em!"

"Why, Tom, it'll take all summer."

"Well, what of that? Suppose you find a brass pot with a hundred dollars in it, all rusty and gray, or a rotten chest full of diamonds. How's that?"

Huck's eyes glowed. "That's great," he said. "Plenty great enough for me. Just you gimme the hundred dollars, and I don't want no diamonds."

"All right. But I bet you I ain't going to refuse diamonds. Some of 'em's worth twenty dollars apiece."

"No! Is that so?"

"Certainly—anybody'll tell you so. Ain't you ever seen one, Huck?"

"Not as I remember."

"Oh, kings have tons of them."

"Well, I don't know no kings, Tom."

"I reckon you don't. But if you was to go to Europe, you'd see a bunch of 'em hopping around."

"Do they hop?"

"No!"

"Well, what did you say they did for?"

"I only meant you'd see 'em," Tom said.

"Where are you going to dig first?" Huck asked.

"Well, I don't know. Suppose we tackle that old dead-limb tree on the hill on the other side of Still Creek?"

"I'm agreed."

They got an old pick and a shovel and set out on their three-mile journey. They arrived hot and panting and threw themselves down in the shade of a neighboring elm to rest. ◆

Silent Reading

1. Read the rest of the lesson to yourselves and be ready to answer some questions.

"I like this," said Tom, as he looked at Still Creek and the large dead-limb tree.

"So do I."

"Say, Huck, if we find a treasure here, what are you going to do with your share?"

"Well, I'll have good food every day, and I'll go to every circus that comes along. I bet I'll have a great time."

"Well, ain't you going to save any of your share?"

"Save it? What for?"

"Why, so as to have something to live on, by and by."

"Oh, that ain't any use. Pa would come back to town someday and get his claws on it if I didn't spend it fast, and I tell you he'd clean it out pretty quick. What you going to do with yours, Tom?"

"I'm going to buy a new drum, and a red necktie and a puppy, and get married."

"Married!"

"That's it."

"Tom, you . . . why, you ain't in your right mind!"

"Wait, you'll see."

"Well, that's the foolishest thing you could do. Look at Pa and my mother. Fight! Why, they used to fight all the time. I remember, mighty well."

"That ain't anything. The girl I'm going to marry won't fight."

"Tom, I reckon they're all alike. Now you better think about this a while. I tell you, you better. What's the name of the gal?"

"It ain't a gal at all—it's a girl."

"It's all the same, I reckon—some says gal, some says girl—both are right. Anyway, what's her name, Tom?"

"I'll tell you sometime—not now."

"All right—that'll do. Only if you get married, I'll be more lonesome than ever."

"No, you won't. You'll come and live with me. Now let's stop talking and start digging."

They worked and sweated for half an hour. No result. They toiled another half hour. Still no result.

Huck said, "Do they always bury it as deep as this?" ★

"Sometimes—not always. Not generally. I reckon we haven't got the right place."

They chose a new spot near the dead-limb tree and began again. The labor dragged a little, but still they made progress. They dug away in silence for some time.

Finally, Huck leaned on his shovel, mopped the sweat from his brow, and said, "Where you going to dig next, after we finish this one?"

"I reckon maybe we'll tackle the old tree that's over yonder on Cardiff Hill back of the Widow Douglas's place."

"I reckon that'll be a good place. But won't the widow take our treasure away from us, Tom? It's on her land."

"She take it away! Maybe she'd like to try it once. Whoever finds one of these hidden treasures, it belongs to him. It don't make any difference whose land it's on."

Huck was satisfied with that. The work went on.

By and by, Huck said, "Blame it, we must be in the wrong place again. What do you think?"

"It is mighty curious, Huck. I don't understand it. Sometimes witches interfere. I reckon maybe that's the trouble now."

"Shucks, witches ain't got no power in the daytime."

"Well, that's so. I didn't think of that. Oh, I know what the matter is! What fools we are! You got to find out where the shadow of the limb falls at midnight, and that's where you dig!"

"Then confound it, we've fooled away all this work for nothing. We got to come back here in the night. It's an awful long way. Can you get out?"

"I bet I will. We've got to do it tonight, too, because if somebody sees these holes, they'll know in a minute what's here, and they'll go for it."

"Well, I'll come around and meow tonight."

"All right. Let's hide the tools in the bushes."

- How were Huck's plans for the treasure different from Tom's? (Ideas: *Huck wanted to eat well and go to the circus, but Tom wanted to buy a new drum, a red necktie, and a puppy and get married.*) Ⓒ/ⓒ
- Why didn't Huck want to save any of his money? (Idea: *He was afraid his father would come back to town and take it.*) ⒹⒸⒺ
- Why did Huck think Tom shouldn't get married? (Ideas: *He thought Tom and his wife would fight; he thought Tom wouldn't be his friend anymore.*) Ⓜ︎Ⓙ
- Name three places where Tom thought treasure is buried. (Ideas: *On islands; under dead limbs; in haunted houses.*) Ⓡ
- Do you think Tom and Huck will find buried treasure? Explain your answer. (Ideas: *No, because they don't have a map; no, because they're just digging at random; yes, because they've been lucky in the past; yes, because this is a story.*) Ⓟ

Paired Practice (Optional)

1. Now you'll read in pairs.
   - Whoever read second the last time will read first today.
   - Remember to start at the diamond and switch at the star.
2. (Observe students and answer questions as needed.)

AFTER READING

EXERCISE 9

Independent Work

1. Do all the items in your workbook and textbook for this lesson.
2. (The independent work in this lesson includes the following activities.)
- Story details
- Vocabulary
- Logic
- Metaphors
- Comparisons
- Comprehension
- Writing

EXERCISE 10

Workcheck

1. (Using the Answer Key, read the questions and answers for the workbook.)
2. (Have students read their answers for the textbook activities.)
3. (Have two or three students read their writing assignments aloud. Comment on each assignment.)
4. (Have students correct and turn in their work.)

SPELLING

(Present Spelling lesson 107 after completing Reading lesson 107. See *Spelling Presentation Book*.)

BEFORE READING

(Have students find lesson 108, part A, in their textbooks.)

EXERCISE 1

Hard Words

1. Look at column 1.
   - These are hard words from your textbook stories.

1. whiten	**3. mute**
2. whitening	**4. unearth**

2. Word 1 is **whiten.** Everybody, what word? (Signal.) *Whiten.*
   - (Repeat this procedure for every word in the column.)
3. Let's read the words again.
4. Word 1. Everybody, what word? (Signal.) *Whiten.*
   - (Repeat this procedure for every word in the column.)
5. (Repeat the column until firm.)

EXERCISE 2

New Vocabulary

1. Look at column 2.
   - First we'll read the words in this column. Then we'll read their definitions.

1. bay	**3. intruder**
2. utterly	

2. Word 1. Everybody, what word? (Signal.) *Bay.*
   - (Repeat this procedure for every word in the column.)
3. (Repeat the column until firm.)

EXERCISE 3

Vocabulary Definitions

1. Everybody, find part B. ✔
   - These are definitions for the words you just read.

2. (For each word, call on a student to read the definition and the item. Then ask the student to complete the item.)

1. **bay**—*Bay* is another word for *howl.*
   - What's another way of saying *The hounds howled at night*?
   - What's the answer? (Response: *The hounds bayed at night.*)

2. **utterly**—*Utterly* is another word for *completely.*
   - What's another way of saying *They were completely defeated by the other team*?
   - What's the answer? (Response: *They were utterly defeated by the other team.*)

3. **intruder**—An *intruder* is somebody who enters into something without permission or an invitation.
   - What is an intruder?
   - What's the answer? (Idea: *Somebody who enters into something without permission or an invitation.*)

EXERCISE 4

Vocabulary Review

1. Everybody, find part C. ✔
   - We're going to review these words.
2. (Call on a student to read the words in the box.)

immortal	haggard
pick	interferes
atmosphere	climax
confidential	isolated
trifle	

3. (For each item, have a student read the item and say the answer.)

1. When something gets in the way, it **▮▮▮▮**.

- What's the answer? (Response: *Interferes.*)

2. A digging tool with a pointed metal head is a **▮▮▮▮**.

- What's the answer? (Response: *Pick.*)

3. Things that are alone are **▮▮▮▮**.

- What's the answer? (Response: *Isolated.*)

4. Things that are private or secret are **▮▮▮▮**.

- What's the answer? (Response: *Confidential.*)

5. Something that lives forever is **▮▮▮▮**.

- What's the answer? (Response: *Immortal.*)

6. The mood of a setting is the **▮▮▮▮** of that setting.

- What's the answer? (Response: *Atmosphere.*)

EXERCISE 5

Logic

1. Everybody, turn to part E at the end of today's story. ✔
- (Call on individual students to read several sentences each.)
- (At the end of each section, present the questions for that section.)

Write the answers for items 1–3.

Here's a rule of logic: *Just because you know about the whole thing doesn't mean you know about every part.*

The following statement by a writer breaks the rule: "The Googblat Company is well known and highly respected. Their treasurer could not possibly be a crook."

1. Which is the whole in this statement?

- What's the answer? (Response: *The Googblat Company.*)

2. Which is the part?

- What's the answer? (Response: *The company's treasurer.*)

3. What conclusion does the writer draw about the part?

- What's the answer? (Idea: *That the treasurer is not a crook.*)
- You'll write the answers later.

READING

EXERCISE 6

Focus Question

1. Everybody, turn back to part D. ✔
2. What's the focus question for today's lesson? (Response: *What did the outside of the haunted house look like?*)

EXERCISE 7

Reading Aloud (Optional)

1. We're going to read aloud to the diamond.
- (Call on individual students to read several sentences each.)

Chapter 18
The Haunted House
Focus Question: What did the outside of the haunted house look like?

The boys were back at the dead-limb tree around midnight. They sat in the shadow waiting. It was a lonely place, and the hour was solemn. Spirits whispered in the rustling leaves; ghosts lurked in the gloomy shadows; the deep baying of a hound floated up out of the distance; an owl answered with his mysterious note. The boys were a bit frightened, and they talked little.

When they judged that midnight had come, they marked where the moonlit shadow of the limb fell and began to dig. Their hopes started to rise. Their interest grew stronger, and their labor kept pace with it. The hole deepened and still deepened. But every time they heard the pick strike upon something, they were disappointed. It was only a stone.

At last Tom said, "It ain't any use, Huck, we're wrong again."

"Well, but we can't be wrong. We marked the shadow exactly."

"I know it, but then there's another thing."

"What's that?"

"Why, we only guessed at the time. I might have been too late or too early."

Huck dropped his shovel.

"That's it," said he. "That's the very trouble. We got to give this spot up. We can't ever tell the right time. Besides, this kind of thing's too awful here this time of night with witches and ghosts a-fluttering around. I feel as if something's behind me all the time, and I'm afraid to turn around because maybe there are other ghosts in front. I've been creeping all over, ever since I got here."

"Well, me too, Huck. They most always put in a dead man when they bury a treasure under a tree, to look out for it."

"Lordy!"

"Yes, they do. I've always heard that."

"Tom, I don't like to fool around much where there's dead people. You're bound to get into trouble with 'em, sure."

Tom replied, "I don't like to stir 'em up, either. Suppose this one here was to stick his skull out and say something!"

"Don't, Tom! It's awful."

"Well, it just is. Huck, I don't feel comfortable a bit."

"Say, Tom, let's give this place up and try somewhere else."

"All right, I reckon we better."

"What'll it be?" ♦

EXERCISE 8

Silent Reading

1. Read the rest of the lesson to yourselves and be ready to answer some questions.

Tom considered a while and then said, "The haunted house. That's it!"

"Blame it, I don't like haunted houses, Tom. Why, they're a dern sight worse than dead people. Dead people might talk, maybe, but they aren't like ghosts that come around when you ain't looking and peep over your shoulder all of a sudden. I couldn't stand such a thing as that, Tom—nobody could."

"Yes, but Huck, ghosts travel around only at night. They won't hinder us from digging there in the daytime."

"Well, that's so. But you know mighty well people don't go near that haunted house in the day nor the night."

"Well," Tom said, "nothing's ever been seen around that house except in the night—just some blue lights slipping by the windows—no regular ghosts."

"Well, where you see one of them blue lights flickering around, Tom, you can bet there's a ghost mighty close behind it. It stands to reason. Because you know that only ghosts use blue lights."

"Yes, that's so. But anyway, they don't come around in the daytime, so what's the use of our being afraid?"

"Well, all right. We'll tackle the haunted house if you say so—but I reckon it's taking chances."

They had started down the hill by this time. There in the middle of the moonlit valley below them stood the haunted house. It was utterly isolated. Its fences had gone long ago. Huge weeds smothered the doorsteps, the chimney had crumbled to ruin, and a corner of the roof was caved in. The boys gazed at the house a while. They half expected to see a blue light flit past a window.

Then, talking in a low tone, they moved far off to the right. They walked home through the woods on the far side of Cardiff Hill.

About noon the next day, the boys arrived at the dead-limb tree. They had come for their tools. Tom was impatient to go to the haunted house.

But Huck suddenly said, "Look here, Tom, do you know what day it is?"

Tom ran over the days of the week and then quickly lifted his eyes with a startled look in them. "My! I never once thought of it, Huck!"

"Well, I didn't neither, but all at once it popped onto me that it was Friday."

"You can't be too careful, Huck. We might have got into an awful scrape, tackling such a thing on a Friday."

"Might! Better say we would! There's some lucky days, maybe, but Friday ain't."

"Any fool knows that. I don't reckon you was the first that found it out, Huck."

"Well, I never said I was, did I? And Friday ain't all, neither. I had a rotten bad dream last night—I dreamed about rats."

"No! Sure sign of trouble. Did they fight?"

"No."

"Well, that's good, Huck. When they don't fight, it's only a sign there's trouble around, you know. All we got to do is to look mighty sharp and keep out of trouble. We'll forget about digging today, and play. Do you know Robin Hood, Huck?" ★

"No. Who's Robin Hood?"

"Why, he was one of the greatest men that was ever in England—and the best. He was a robber."

"I wish I was. Who did he rob?"

"Only sheriffs and rich people and kings. But he never bothered the poor. He loved 'em. He always divided his money with 'em."

"Well, he must have been a great man."

"He was, Huck. Oh, he was the noblest man that ever was. They ain't any such men now, I can tell you. He could lick any man in England with one hand tied behind him, and he could take his bow and hit a ten-cent piece every time, a mile and a half away. We'll play Robin Hood—it's a lot of fun. I'll teach you."

"I'm agreed."

So they played Robin Hood all the afternoon. Now and then they looked down upon the haunted house and passed a remark about it. As the sun began to sink into the west, they walked home under the long shadows of the trees and were soon buried from sight in the forests of Cardiff Hill.

On Saturday, shortly after noon, the boys were at the dead tree again. They had a chat in the shade and then shouldered the tools and went to the haunted house.

When they reached the house, there was something so weird and ghastly about the dead silence that they were afraid, for a moment, to go in. Then they crept to the door and took a trembling peep. They saw a weed-grown, floorless room, an ancient fireplace, broken windows, and a ruined staircase. Ragged and abandoned cobwebs hung here, there, and everywhere.

The boys entered softly, talking in whispers. Their ears were alert to catch the slightest sound, and their muscles were ready for instant retreat.

In a little while their fears lessened, and they gave the downstairs a critical examination. They admired their own boldness, and wondered at it, too. Next they wanted to look upstairs. They agreed that if they went upstairs, it would be hard for them to escape from the house if an intruder came in. But they began to dare each other, and they soon threw their tools into a corner and climbed upstairs.

Up there were the same signs of decay. In one corner they found a closet that seemed mysterious, but there was nothing in it. Their courage was up now. They were about to go down and begin work when . . .

"Sh!" said Tom.

"What is it?" whispered Huck, whitening with fright.

"Sh! . . . There! . . . Hear it?"

"Yes!" Huck whispered, "Let's run!"

"Keep still! Don't you budge! They're coming right toward the door!"

The boys stretched themselves upon the floor. They pressed their faces against holes in the planking so they could look downstairs. They lay waiting in a misery of fear.

- What did the outside of the haunted house look like? (Ideas: *It was isolated; weeds smothered the doorsteps; the chimney was crumbled; a corner of the roof was caved in.*) Ⓡ
- Describe the inside of the haunted house. (Ideas: *It was floorless and weed-grown; it had an ancient fireplace, broken windows, and a ruined staircase; cobwebs were everywhere; it had a closet upstairs.*) Ⓡ
- Why do you think the boys could only guess at the time when they dug at night? (Ideas: *They had no watches; they had no radios.*) Ⓓⓘ
- Why did the boys think the haunted house would be safe during the day? (Idea: *Because ghosts travel around only at night.*) Ⓓⓒⓔ
- Why do you think Huck admired Robin Hood so much? (Idea: *Because Robin Hood stole from the rich and gave to the poor, and Huck was poor.*) Ⓜⓙ

EXERCISE 9

Paired Practice (Optional)

1. Now you'll read in pairs.
- Whoever read second the last time will read first today.
- Remember to start at the diamond and switch at the star.
2. (Observe students and answer questions as needed.)

AFTER READING

EXERCISE 10

Independent Work

1. Do all the items in your workbook and textbook for this lesson.
2. (The independent work in this lesson includes the following activities.)
- Story details
- Vocabulary
- Logic
- Exaggeration
- Perspectives
- Story review
- Comprehension
- Writing

EXERCISE 11

Workcheck

1. (Using the Answer Key, read the questions and answers for the workbook.)
2. (Have students read their answers for the textbook activities.)
3. (Have two or three students read their writing assignments aloud. Comment on each assignment.)
4. (Have students correct and turn in their work.)

SPELLING

(Present Spelling lesson 108 after completing Reading lesson 108. See *Spelling Presentation Book.*)

BEFORE READING

(Have students find lesson 109, part A, in their textbooks.)

EXERCISE 1
Hard Words

1. Look at column 1.
- These are hard words from your textbook stories.

1. eternity	3. amid
2. distinct	4. slaughter

2. Word 1 is **eternity.** Everybody, what word? (Signal.) *Eternity.*
- (Repeat this procedure for every word in the column.)
3. Let's read the words again.
4. Word 1. Everybody, what word? (Signal.) *Eternity.*
- (Repeat this procedure for every word in the column.)
5. (Repeat the column until firm.)

EXERCISE 2
Word Practice

1. Look at column 2.
- We're going to practice these words.

1. shanty	4. exaggeration
2. infernal	5. charter
3. hideous	

2. Word 1. Everybody, what word? (Signal.) *Shanty.*
- (Repeat this procedure for every word in the column.)
3. (Repeat the column until firm.)

EXERCISE 3
New Vocabulary

1. Look at column 3.
- First we'll read the words in this column. Then we'll read their definitions.

1. mute	4. unearth
2. distinct	5. blissful
3. eternity	

2. Word 1. Everybody, what word? (Signal.) *Mute.*
- (Repeat this procedure for every word in the column.)
3. (Repeat the column until firm.)

EXERCISE 4
Vocabulary Definitions

1. Everybody, find part B. ✔
- These are definitions for the words you just read.
2. (For each word, call on a student to read the definition and the item. Then ask the student to complete the item.)

1. **mute**—Someone who is *mute* is unable to speak.
- What's another way of saying *The deaf person was also unable to speak*?
- What's the answer? (Response: *The deaf person was also mute.*)

2. **distinct**—When something is *distinct,* it is easy to recognize.
- What's another way of saying *Her voice was easy to recognize*?
- What's the answer? (Response: *Her voice was distinct.*)

3. **eternity**—When something lasts for an *eternity,* it seems to last forever.
- What's another way of saying *The speech seemed to last forever*?
- What's the answer? (Response: *The speech lasted an eternity.*)

4. **unearth**—When you *unearth* something, you dig it up.
- What's another way of saying *They dug up the buried treasure*?

- What's the answer? (Response: *They unearthed the buried treasure.*)

5. **blissful**—*Blissful* is another word for *joyful*.
- What's another way of saying *a joyful feeling*?

- What's the answer? (Response: *A blissful feeling.*)

Logic

1. Everybody, turn to part D at the end of today's story. ✔
- (Call on individual students to read several sentences each.)
- (At the end of each section, present the questions for that section.)

Write the answers for items 1–3.
Here's a rule of logic: *Just because you know about the whole thing doesn't mean you know about every part.*

The following statement by a writer breaks the rule: "The soccer team took first place in a city-wide tournament. Ginny is on that team, so she must be the best soccer player in the city."
1. Which is the whole in this statement?

- What's the answer? (Response: *The soccer team.*)

2. Which is the part?

- What's the answer? (Response: *Ginny.*)

3. What conclusion does the writer draw about the part?

- What's the answer? (Idea: *That Ginny must be the best soccer player in the city.*)
- You'll write the answers later.

READING

Focus Question

1. Everybody, turn back to part C. ✔
2. What's the focus question for today's lesson? (Response: *Why were the men staying in the haunted house?*)

Reading Aloud (Optional)

1. We're going to read aloud to the diamond.
- (Call on individual students to read several sentences each.)

Chapter 19

Real Robbers Seize the Box of Gold
Focus Question: Why were the men staying in the haunted house?

Two men entered the house. One was the old deaf and mute man who had been around town once or twice lately. The boys had never seen the other man before. He was a ragged creature, with nothing pleasant in his face.

The deaf and mute man was wrapped in a cloak. He had bushy white whiskers. Long white hair flowed from under his hat, and he wore green spectacles.

When they came in, the other man was talking in a low voice. The two men sat down on the ground, facing the door, with their backs to the wall, and the stranger continued his remarks. His words became more distinct.

"No," said he, "I've thought it all over, and I don't like it. It's dangerous."

"Dangerous!" grunted the deaf and mute man, to the vast surprise of the boys. "You're a chicken!"

This voice made the boys gasp and quake. It was Outlaw Joe's!

There was more silence for some time.

Then Joe said, "It's no more dangerous than that job we did up the river. We never got caught for that one."

"That's different."

"Well, what's more dangerous than coming here in the daytime? Anybody would suspect us that saw us."

"I know that. But there wasn't any other place as handy after that last job. I want to stop using this shanty as our hideout. I wanted to yesterday, only it wasn't any use trying to leave with those infernal boys playing over there on the hill right in full view."

At this remark, the boys thought how lucky it was they had remembered it was Friday and decided to wait a day. They wished they had waited a year.

The two men got out some food and had lunch.

After a long and thoughtful silence, Joe said, "Look here, you go back up the river where you belong. Wait there till you hear from me. I'll take the chance on dropping into Saint Petersburg just once more, for a look. We'll do our 'dangerous' job in Saint Petersburg when the time is right. Then for Texas! We'll go there together!"

This was satisfactory. Both men presently started yawning, and Joe said, "I've got to sleep! It's your turn to watch." ◆

EXERCISE 8
Silent Reading

1. Read the rest of the lesson to yourselves and be ready to answer some questions.

Joe curled down in the dirt and soon began to snore. His comrade prodded him once or twice, and Joe stopped snoring. Presently Joe's comrade began to nod. His head drooped lower and lower, and both men began to snore.

The boys drew a long, grateful breath.

Tom whispered, "Now's our chance—come!"

Huck said, "I can't! I'd die if they woke up."

Tom urged—Huck held back. At last Tom rose slowly and softly and started home. But the first step he made brought such a hideous creak from the crazy floor that he sank down almost dead with fright. He never made a second attempt. The boys lay there counting the dragging moments till it seemed an eternity had gone by. They were grateful to note at last that the sun was setting.

Now one snore ceased. Outlaw Joe sat up and stared around. He smiled grimly upon his comrade, whose head was drooping upon his knees.

Joe woke the comrade with his foot and said, "You're a fine watchman, ain't you? All right, though, nothing's happened."

"My! Have I been asleep?"

"Oh, partly, partly. Nearly time for us to be moving. What'll we do with the loot we've got left?"

"I don't know—leave it here as we've always done, I reckon. No use to take it away till we start south for Texas. Six hundred and fifty in silver is a heavy load to carry."

"Well—all right—it won't matter if we come here once more."

"No, but I'd say come in the night as we used to do—it's better."

"Yes, but look here," said Joe. "It may be a good while before the time is right for that job in Saint Petersburg. The loot we've got is not in a very good place. We'll just bury it—and bury it deep."

"Good idea," said the comrade. He walked across the room, knelt down, and tilted up a wide, flat stone. Underneath was a bag that jingled pleasantly. He removed twenty or thirty dollars for himself and as much for Outlaw Joe. Then he passed the bag to Joe, who was on his knees in the corner now, digging with his knife.

The boys forgot all their fears and miseries in an instant. Good luck! It was beyond all imagination! Six hundred dollars was money enough to make half a dozen boys rich! Here was treasure hunting of the best kind—there would not be any doubt as to where to dig. They nudged each other every moment. These nudges were easily understood, for they simply meant "Now, ain't you glad we're here!"

Joe's knife struck something.

"What is it?" said his comrade. ★

"Half-rotten plank—no, it's a box, I believe. Here—give me a hand, and we'll see what it's here for. Never mind, I've got it."

He reached his hand in and drew it out—"Man, it's money!"

The two men examined the handful of coins. They were gold. The boys above were as excited as the men and as delighted.

Joe's comrade said, "It'll take us forever to get at all the treasure with that knife."

The comrade got up and looked around for something to dig with. His face lit with delight as he spotted the tools that Tom and Huck had left downstairs next to the fireplace.

"What luck, Joe!" the comrade announced. "Look what I found!"

He brought the boys' pick and shovel over to Joe. Outlaw Joe took the pick and looked it over critically. He shook his head, muttered something to himself, and then began to use the pick. The box was soon unearthed. It was not very large; it was iron and had been very strong before the slow years had rusted it. The men looked at the treasure a while in blissful silence.

"There's thousands of dollars here!" said Outlaw Joe.

"They say that Murrel's gang used to be around here one summer," the comrade observed.

"I know it," said Outlaw Joe, "and this looks like their treasure, I should say."

"Now you won't need to do that job."

Outlaw Joe frowned. Said he, "You don't know me. The job ain't robbery—it's *revenge!*"

A wicked light flamed in his eyes.

"I'll need your help in it. When it's finished—then Texas. Go home to your wife and kids and stand by till you hear from me."

"Well, if you say so. What'll we do with this—bury it again?"

"Yes," Joe said slowly—and the boys upstairs felt a surge of delight.

"No, wait . . . ," Joe continued—and the boys felt great distress.

Joe frowned and looked around. Then he said, "That pick had fresh earth on it!"

The boys were sick with terror.

"What business has a pick and a shovel here? What business with fresh earth on them? Who brought them here—and where have they gone? Have you heard anybody? Seen anybody? If we bury it again, they'll come and see the ground disturbed. We won't let that happen. We'll take the treasure to my den."

"Why, of course! Might have thought of that before. You mean hiding place Number One?"

"No—Number Two—under the cross. The other place is bad—too common."

"All right. It's nearly dark enough to start."

Outlaw Joe got up and went from window to window cautiously peeping out.

Presently he said, "Who could have brought those tools here? Do you reckon the owners can be upstairs?"

- Why were the men staying in the haunted house? (Idea: *They were using it as a hideout until they did their "dangerous" job.*) ⓓⒸⒺ
- What belief did Tom and Huck have about Friday? (Idea: *That is was an unlucky day.*) ⓓⒸⒺ
- How did that belief come true in this chapter? (Idea: *If they had come to the house on Friday, they would have run into Outlaw Joe.*) ⓂⒿ
- What other belief of Tom's came true in this chapter? (Idea: *The haunted house had buried treasure.*) Ⓒ⁄Ⓒ
- What do you think Outlaw Joe's "revenge" job might be? Explain your answer. (Ideas: *He wants to take revenge on Tom for testifying against him in court; he wants to take revenge on Muff Potter for going free.*) Ⓗ

EXERCISE 9

Paired Practice (Optional)

1. Now you'll read in pairs.
- Whoever read second the last time will read first today.
- Remember to start at the diamond and switch at the star.
2. (Observe students and answer questions as needed.)

AFTER READING

EXERCISE 10

Independent Work

1. Do all the items in your workbook and textbook for this lesson.

2. (The independent work in this lesson includes the following activities.)
- Story details
- Vocabulary
- Maps
- Logic
- Sequencing
- Vocabulary review
- Comprehension
- Writing

(Present Spelling lesson 109 after completing Reading lesson 109. See *Spelling Presentation Book.*)

EXERCISE 11
Workcheck

1. (Using the Answer Key, read the questions and answers for the workbook.)
2. (Have students read their answers for the textbook activities.)
3. (Have two or three students read their writing assignments aloud. Comment on each assignment.)
4. (Have students correct and turn in their work.)

BEFORE READING

(Have students find lesson 110, part A, in their textbooks.)

EXERCISE 1
Hard Words

1. Look at column 1.
- These are hard words from your textbook stories.

1. profound	4. rollick
2. resemble	5. throng
3. slaughterhouse	

2. Word 1 is **profound.** Everybody, what word? (Signal.) *Profound.*
- (Repeat this procedure for every word in the column.)
3. Let's read the words again.
4. Word 1. Everybody, what word? (Signal.) *Profound.*
- (Repeat this procedure for every word in the column.)
5. (Repeat the column until firm.)

EXERCISE 2
New Vocabulary

1. Look at column 2.
- First we'll read the words in this column. Then we'll read their definitions.

1. amid	4. charter
2. clutter	5. throng
3. slaughterhouse	6. reflect

2. Word 1. Everybody, what word? (Signal.) *Amid.*
- (Repeat this procedure for every word in the column.)
3. (Repeat the column until firm.)

EXERCISE 3
Vocabulary Definitions

1. Everybody, find part B. ✔
- These are definitions for the words you just read.
2. (For each word, call on a student to read the definition and the item. Then ask the student to complete the item.)

1. **amid**—*Amid* means "in the middle of."
- What's another way of saying *in the middle of her friends*?

- What's the answer? (Response: *Amid her friends.*)

2. **clutter**—*Clutter* is a confused mess.
- What's another way of saying *His desk was covered with a confused mess*?

- What's the answer? (Response: *His desk was covered with clutter.*)

3. **slaughterhouse**—A *slaughterhouse* is a place where people kill animals and cut them into pieces of meat.
- What is a slaughterhouse?

- What's the answer? (Idea: *A place where people kill animals and cut them into pieces of meat.*)

4. **charter**—When you *charter* a vehicle, you rent the vehicle for a group of people.
- What's another way of saying *They rented a boat for the party*?

- What's the answer? (Response: *They chartered a boat for the party.*)

5. **throng**—A *throng* is a large crowd of people.
- What's another way of saying *a large crowd of children*?

- What's the answer? (Response: *A throng of children.*)

6. **reflect**—When you *reflect,* you think quietly and calmly.
*   What's another way of saying *She thought quietly and calmly for a moment?*

*   What's the answer? (Response: *She reflected for a moment.*)

EXERCISE 4

Logic

1. Everybody, turn to part D at the end of today's story. ✔
*   (Call on individual students to read several sentences each.)
*   (At the end of each section, present the questions for that section.)

Write the answers for items 1 and 2.
Here are three rules about logic.
*   Rule 1: *Just because two events happen around the same time doesn't mean one event causes the other event.*
*   Rule 2: *Just because you know about a part doesn't mean you know about the whole thing.*
*   Rule 3: *Just because a person is an expert in one field doesn't mean the person is an expert in another field.*
The following statement by a writer breaks one of the rules: "We live on a farm, and the sun always rises after the rooster crows. But today our rooster got sick. I guess the sun won't rise tomorrow."
1. Which rule does the argument break?

*   What's the answer? (Response: *Rule 1.*)

The following statement by a writer breaks one of the rules: "Veronica James is a highly skilled banker. She knows all about the different accounts and how to figure interest payments. So when she tells me which car to buy, I listen."
2. Which rule does the argument break?

*   What's the answer? (Response: *Rule 3.*)
*   You'll write the answers later.

READING

EXERCISE 5

Focus Question

1. Everybody, find part C. ✔
2. What's the focus question for today's lesson? (Response: *Why did Tom think his adventure might be a dream?*)

EXERCISE 6

Reading Aloud (Optional)

1. We're going to read aloud to the diamond.
*   (Call on individual students to read several sentences each.)

Chapter 20
Trembling on the Trail
Focus Question: Why did Tom think his adventure might be a dream?

The boys' breath left them. Outlaw Joe put his hand on his knife, halted a moment, undecided, and then turned toward the stairway. The boys thought of the closet, but their strength was gone. Joe's steps came creaking up the stairs.

Suddenly, there was a crash of rotten timbers. Outlaw Joe fell through the rotten stair and landed on the ground amid the clutter of the ruined stairway.

He got up angry, and his comrade said, "Now what's the use of all that? If it's anybody, they would have gone through that stair the same way you did. It will be dark in fifteen minutes—and then let anybody try to follow us if they want to. In my opinion, whoever brought those things in here caught a sight of us and took us for ghosts or devils or something. I'll bet they're running yet."

Joe grumbled awhile; then he agreed with his friend that what daylight was left ought to be used in getting things ready for leaving. Shortly afterward they slipped out of the house in the deepening twilight and moved toward the river with their precious box.

Tom and Huck rose up, weak but vastly relieved, and stared after them through the cracks between the boards of the house. They were not interested in following the men. They were content to reach ground again without broken necks and head back to town.

They did not talk much. They were much too busy with hating themselves—hating the bad luck that made them take the shovel and the pick there. If they hadn't done that, Outlaw Joe never would have suspected them. He would have hidden the silver with the gold to wait there till his revenge was satisfied, and then he would have had the bad luck to find the money missing.

Tom and Huck remembered what the men had said about hiding place Number Two. They resolved to keep a lookout for that deaf and mute man and follow him to Number Two, wherever that might be. Then a ghastly thought occurred to Tom.

"Revenge? What if he wants to get us for revenge, Huck?"

"Oh, don't say that!" said Huck, nearly fainting.

Tom and Huck talked it over, and as they entered town, they agreed to believe that Joe's revenge might possibly be intended for somebody else. ◆

EXERCISE 7

Silent Reading

1. Read the rest of the lesson to yourselves and be ready to answer some questions.

The adventure of the day tormented Tom's dreams that night. Four times in his dream he had his hands on that rich treasure, and four times it slipped away. As he lay in the early morning, recalling his great adventure, he noticed that it seemed curiously far away—as if it had happened in another world or in a time long gone by.

Then it occurred to Tom that the great adventure itself must be a dream! There was one very strong argument in favor of this idea, namely, that the amount of cash he had seen was too vast to be real. He had never seen as much as fifty dollars in one mass before. Like all boys his age, he imagined that all references to "hundreds" and "thousands" were just exaggerations, and that such large sums did not really exist.

But the events of Tom's adventure grew sharper and clearer as he thought them over. He soon found himself thinking that the thing might not have been a dream after all. This uncertainty must be swept away. He decided to eat a hurried breakfast and find Huck.

Huck was sitting on a flatboat, dangling his feet in the water and looking very melancholy. Tom decided to let Huck bring up the subject. If he did not do it, that would prove the adventure had been only a dream.

"Hello, Huck."

"Hello, yourself."

Silence for a minute.

"Tom, if we'd left the blame tools at the dead tree, we'd have got the money. Oh, ain't it awful!"

"It ain't a dream, then, it ain't a dream! Somehow I almost wish it was. Dogged if I don't, Huck."

"What ain't a dream?"

"Oh, that thing yesterday. I been half thinking it was."

"Dream! If them stairs hadn't broke down, you'd have seen how much of a dream it was! I've had dreams enough all night—with that Outlaw Joe devil going for me all through 'em!"

"We've got to find him! Track the money!"

"Tom, we'll never find him. We had one chance for the money—and now we've lost it. I'd feel mighty shaky if I was to see him."

"Well, so would I. But I'd like to see him anyway—and track him out to his Number Two hiding place."

"Number Two. Yes, that's it. I been thinking about that, but I can't make nothing out of it. What do you reckon it is?"

"I dunno," Tom replied. "Say, Huck, maybe it's the number of a house!" ★

"No, Tom, that ain't it. If it is, it ain't in this one-horse town. There ain't no house numbers here."

"Well, that's so. Lemme think a minute. Here—it's the number of a room—in a hotel, you know!"

"Oh, that's the trick! There are only two hotels. We can find out quick."

"You stay here, Huck, till I come."

Tom was off at once. He was gone half an hour. He found out that in the best hotel, Number Two had long been occupied by a young lawyer and was still so occupied. In the less fancy hotel, Number Two was a mystery. The hotel-keeper's young son said it was kept locked all the time, and he never saw anybody go into it or come out of it except at night. He did not know any particular reason for this state of things, but he thought the room might be haunted. He had noticed a light in there the night before.

Tom reported everything he had found out. Then he added, "I reckon that's the very Number Two we're after."

"I reckon it is, Tom. Now what are you going to do?"

"Lemme think."

Tom thought a long time. Then he said, "I'll tell you. There's a back door to that Number Two that comes out into that little alley between the hotel and the old brick store. Now you get hold of all the door keys you can find, and I'll borrow all of Aunt Polly's, and the first dark night we'll go there and try the keys. And mind you, keep a lookout for Outlaw Joe, because he said he was going to drop into town and spy around once more for a chance to get his revenge. If you see him, you just follow him. If he don't go to that Number Two, that ain't the place."

"I don't want to follow him by myself!" Huck cried.

"Why, it'll be night when you follow him. He might not ever see you. And if he did, maybe he'd never think anything."

Huck said, "Well, if it's pretty dark, I reckon I'll track him. I dunno . . . I dunno. I'll try."

"You bet I'll follow him, if it's dark, Huck. Why, he might have found out he couldn't get his revenge and be going right after that money."

"All right, I'll follow him."

"Now you're talking! Don't you ever weaken, Huck, and I won't either."

- Why did Tom think his adventure might be a dream? (Ideas: *Because the treasure was so large; because the adventure seemed so far away.*) (DCE)
- How did Tom prove the adventure wasn't a dream? (Idea: *He waited for Huck to bring up the adventure, which Huck did.*) (MD)
- Why did Joe's comrade think there wasn't anybody upstairs? (Idea: *If they'd gone upstairs, they would have fallen through the stairs just as Joe did.*) (DCE)

- Do you think hiding place Number Two is the hotel room? Explain your answer. (Idea: *Yes, because the room has the same number as the hiding place; no, because Number Two could be any hiding place.*) (MJ)
- Explain Tom's plan for getting into hotel room Number Two. (Idea: *He and Huck would find several door keys. On the first dark night, they would go to the room and try the keys.*) (R)

<hr>

EXERCISE 8

Paired Practice (Optional)

1. Now you'll read in pairs.
- Whoever read second the last time will read first today.
- Remember to start at the diamond and switch at the star.
2. (Observe students and answer questions as needed.)

AFTER READING

EXERCISE 9

Independent Work

1. Do all the items in your workbook and textbook for this lesson.
2. (The independent work in this lesson includes the following activities.)
- Story details
- Perspectives
- Vocabulary
- Conversations
- Logic
- Vocabulary review
- Comprehension
- Writing

EXERCISE 10

Workcheck

1. (Using the Answer Key, read the questions and answers for the workbook.)
2. (Have students read their answers for the textbook activities.)
3. (Have two or three students read their writing assignments aloud. Comment on each assignment.)
4. (Have students correct and turn in their work.)

MASTERY TEST

(The Lesson 110 Mastery Test should be administered after students complete lesson 110. See *Curriculum-Based Assessment and Fluency Handbook* for details.)

ACTIVITIES ACROSS THE CURRICULUM

(Students should complete the appropriate project in *Activities across the Curriculum* after completing lesson 110. See *Activities across the Curriculum* book for details.)

SPELLING

(Present Spelling lesson 110 after completing Reading lesson 110. See *Spelling Presentation Book*.)

Lessons 111–115 • Planning Page *Looking Ahead*

	Lesson 111	Lesson 112	Lesson 113	Lesson 114	Lesson 115
BEFORE READING	Hard words Word practice New vocabulary Vocabulary definitions Logic	Word practice New vocabulary Vocabulary definitions Vocabulary review Logic	Hard words Word practice New vocabulary Vocabulary definitions Vocabulary review Logic	Hard words New vocabulary Vocabulary definitions Vocabulary review	Hard words Word practice New vocabulary Vocabulary definitions Vocabulary review
NEW VOCABULARY	resemble profound catastrophe sentry consent rollick	inlet romp intricate elude flinch	scoundrel deputy bore	lavish relic whiskey	stalactite stalagmite apprehensive revive
READING	*Tom Sawyer* (Chapter 21)	*Tom Sawyer* (Chapter 22)	*Tom Sawyer* (Chapter 23)	*Tom Sawyer* (Chapter 24)	*Tom Sawyer* (Chapter 25)
INDEPENDENT WORK	Story details Vocabulary Irony Logic Vocabulary review Comprehension Writing	Story details Vocabulary Logic Sequencing Comprehension Writing	Story details Vocabulary Logic Character traits Inference Comprehension Writing	Story details Vocabulary Following directions Settings Logic Comprehension Writing	Story details Combined sentences Vocabulary Graphs Poem review Logic Comprehension Writing
SUPPLEMENTS	*Spelling*	*Spelling*	*Spelling*	*Spelling*	*Spelling* *Activities across the Curriculum*

Comprehension Questions Abbreviations Guide

Access Prior Knowledge = (APK)   Author's Point of View = (APoV)   Author's Purpose = (AP)   Cause/Effect = (C/E)   Charts/Graphs/Diagrams/Visual Aids = (VA)

Classify and Categorize = (C+C)   Compare/Contrast = (C/C)   Determine Character Emotions, Motivation = (DCE)   Drawing Conclusions = (DC)   Drawing Inferences = (DI)

Fact and Opinion = (F/O)   Hypothesizing = (H)   Main Idea = (MI)   Making Connections = (MC)   Making Deductions = (MD)   Making Judgements = (MJ)

Narrative Elements = (NE)   Noting Details = (ND)   Predict = (P)   Reality/Fantasy = (R/F)   Recall Facts/Rules = (RF/R)   Retell = (R)   Sequence = (Seq)

Steps in a Process = (SP)   Story Structure = (SS)   Summarize = (Sum)   Understanding Dialogue = (UD)   Using Context to Confirm Meaning(s) = (UCCM)   Visualize = (V)

BEFORE READING

(Have students find lesson 111, part A, in their textbooks.)

Hard Words

1. Look at column 1.
- These are hard words from your textbook stories.

1. catastrophe	4. elude
2. sentry	5. tolerant
3. inlet	6. intricate

2. Word 1 is **catastrophe.** Everybody, what word? (Signal.) *Catastrophe.*
- (Repeat this procedure for every word in the column.)
3. Let's read the words again.
4. Word 1. Everybody, what word? (Signal.) *Catastrophe.*
- (Repeat this procedure for every word in the column.)
5. (Repeat the column until firm.)

Word Practice

1. Look at column 2.
- We're going to practice these words.

1. gravel	3. hayloft
2. outweigh	4. yield

2. Word 1. Everybody, what word? (Signal.) *Gravel.*
- (Repeat this procedure for every word in the column.)
3. (Repeat the column until firm.)

New Vocabulary

1. Look at column 3.
- First we'll read the words in this column. Then we'll read their definitions.

1. resemble	4. sentry
2. profound	5. consent
3. catastrophe	6. rollick

2. Word 1. Everybody, what word? (Signal.) *Resemble.*
- (Repeat this procedure for every word in the column.)
3. (Repeat the column until firm.)

Vocabulary Definitions

1. Everybody, find part B. ✔
- These are definitions for the words you just read.
2. (For each word, call on a student to read the definition and the item. Then ask the student to complete the item.)

1. **resemble**—When something *resembles* another thing, it is like that other thing. If Henry looks like John, Henry resembles John.
- What's another way of saying *The pictures did not look like each other*?
- What's the answer? (Response: *The pictures did not resemble each other.*)

2. **profound**—When something is *profound,* it is deep or serious.
- What's another way of saying *His thoughts were serious*?
- What's the answer? (Response: *His thoughts were profound.*)

3. **catastrophe**—*Catastrophe* is another word for *disaster.*
- What's another way of saying *The hurricane was a disaster*?
- What's the answer? (Response: *The hurricane was a catastrophe.*)

4. **sentry**—A *sentry* is a guard.
- What's another way of saying *There were four guards outside the gate*?

- What's the answer? (Response: *There were four sentries outside the gate.*)

5. **consent**—When you *consent* to do something, you agree to do it.
- What's another way of saying *He agreed to take his brother to the park*?

- What's the answer? (Response: *He consented to take his brother to the park.*)

6. **rollick**—When you *rollick,* you act in a carefree or joyful way.
- What's another way of saying *The children acted joyfully at the picnic*?

- What's the answer? (Response: *The children rollicked at the picnic.*)

EXERCISE 5

Logic

1. Everybody, turn to part D at the end of today's story. ✔
- (Call on individual students to read several sentences each.)
- (At the end of each section, present the questions for that section.)

Write the answers for items 1 and 2.
Here are three rules of logic:
- Rule 1: *Just because two events happen around the same time doesn't mean one event causes the other event.*
- Rule 2: *Just because a person is an expert in one field doesn't mean the person is an expert in another field.*
- Rule 3: *Just because you know about the whole thing doesn't mean you know about every part.*
The following statement breaks one of the rules: "The Bashers have the best basketball team in the league. They haven't lost a game all season. I'm sure they must have the best center in the league."
1. Which rule does the argument break?

- What's the answer? (Response: *Rule 3.*)

The following statement breaks one of the rules: "Sylvester Prince is one of the finest architects in the world. He has designed several skyscrapers and countless homes. He recommends using Pummel soap, so that's what I use."
2. Which rule does the argument break?

- What's the answer? (Response: *Rule 2.*)
- You'll write the answers later.

READING

EXERCISE 6

Focus Question

1. Everybody, turn back to part C. ✔
2. What's the focus question for today's lesson? (Response: *What was Tom and Huck's new plan for getting the treasure?*)

> *Note:* The "Reading Aloud" exercise is recommended for this lesson.

EXERCISE 7

Reading Aloud

1. We're going to read aloud to the diamond.
- (Call on individual students to read several sentences each.)

Chapter 21

In the Hideout of Outlaw Joe

Focus Question: What was Tom and Huck's new plan for getting the treasure?

That night, Tom and Huck hung around the neighborhood of the hotel until after nine. Tom watched the alley, and Huck watched the front door of the hotel. Nobody entered the alley or left it, and nobody resembling Outlaw Joe entered or left the front door of the hotel.

The night was too bright for secrecy, so Tom went home with the understanding that if real darkness came on, Huck was to come and meow. Then Tom would slip out and try the keys. But the night remained clear, so Huck ended his watch and retired to bed in an empty barrel about midnight.

Tuesday, the boys had the same ill luck. Also Wednesday. But Thursday night promised better. Tom slipped out with his aunt's old tin lantern and a large towel to cover it with. He hid the lantern in Huck's barrel, and the watch began.

An hour before midnight, the hotel closed and its lights (the only ones around there) were put out. No deaf and mute man had been seen. Nobody had entered or left the alley. Everything was right. The darkness was profound, and the perfect stillness was interrupted only by occasional distant thunder.

Tom got his lantern, lit it in Huck's barrel, and wrapped it in the towel. Then he removed the concealed lantern from the barrel. The two adventurers crept in the gloom toward the hotel. Huck stood sentry, and Tom felt his way into the alley. Then there was a long wait that weighed upon Huck's spirits like a mountain. He began to wish he could see a flash from the lantern—it would frighten him, but it would at least tell him that Tom was still alive. It seemed hours since Tom had disappeared. Surely he must have fainted; maybe he was dead; maybe his heart had burst under terror and excitement.

Huck found himself drawing closer and closer to the alley. He feared all sorts of dreadful things, and he expected some catastrophe to take his breath away. But there was not much breath to take away, for he seemed unable to inhale any breath. He suspected that his heart would soon wear itself out, the way it was beating.

Suddenly, there was a flash of light, and Tom came tearing by him.

"Run!" said he. "Run for your life!" ◆

EXERCISE 8
Silent Reading

1. Read the rest of the lesson to yourselves and be ready to answer some questions.

Huck was going thirty or forty miles an hour before Tom had finished speaking. The boys didn't stop till they reached the shed of a deserted slaughterhouse at the lower end of the village. Just as they got within the shed, the storm burst and the rain poured down.

As soon as Tom got his breath, he said, "Huck, it was awful! I tried two of the keys, just as soft as I could, but they seemed to make such a racket that I couldn't hardly get my breath, I was so scared. They wouldn't turn in the lock, either. Well, without noticing what I was doing, I took hold of the knob, and the door came open! It wasn't locked! I hopped in and took off the towel; it dropped to the floor and . . ."

"What—what'd you see, Tom?"

"Huck, I almost stepped on Outlaw Joe's hand!"

"No!"

"Yes! He was lying there, sound asleep on the floor, with his old patch on his eye and his arms spread out."

"Lordy, what did you do? Did he wake up?"

"No, never budged. I just picked up that towel and ran!"

"I'd never have thought of the towel, I bet!"

"Well, I would. My aunt would be mighty angry if I lost it."

"Say, Tom, did you see the treasure box?"

"Huck, I didn't wait to look around. I didn't see the box, and I didn't see the cross they hid the box under. I didn't see anything but Outlaw Joe."

"But say, Tom, now's a mighty good time to get that box, if Outlaw Joe's asleep."

"It is? You try it!"

Huck shuddered.

"Well, no—I reckon not."

There was a long pause. Then Tom said, "Let's not try that thing anymore till we know Joe's not in there. It's too scary. Now, if we watch every night, we'll be dead sure to see him go out, sometime or other, and then we'll snatch that box quicker than lightning!"

"Well, I'm agreed. I'll watch the whole night long, and I'll do it every night, too, if you'll snatch the box."

"All right, I will. All you got to do is to trot up Hooper Street a block and meow—and if I'm asleep, you throw some gravel at the window, and that'll wake me."

"I'm agreed."

"Now, Huck, the storm's over, and I'll go home. It'll begin to be daylight in a couple of hours. You go back and watch."

"I said I would, Tom, and I will. I'll haunt that hotel every night for a year! I'll sleep all day, and I'll stand watch all night."

"That's all right. Now, where are you going to sleep?"

"In Ben Rogers's hayloft. He lets me, and so does his servant, Uncle Jake. I fetch water for Uncle Jake whenever he wants me to, and anytime I ask him, he gives me a little something to eat if he can spare it. That's a mighty good man, Tom."

"Well, if I don't need you in the daytime, I'll let you sleep. I won't come bothering around. Anytime you see something's up in the night, just come around and meow." ★

• • •

The first thing Tom heard on Friday morning was a glad piece of news: Judge Thatcher's family had come back to town the night before. Both Outlaw Joe and the treasure sank in importance for a moment, and Becky took the chief place in Tom's interest. He saw her, and they had a good time playing with a crowd of their schoolmates. At the end of the day, Becky asked her mother to let them have a picnic on Saturday. Becky's mother consented. Becky was delighted, and so was Tom.

The invitations were sent out before sunset. The picnic would take place several miles south of town, near the cave. Tom's excitement over the picnic kept him awake until a pretty late hour. He had good hopes of hearing Huck's meow and of having his treasure to astonish Becky with. But he was disappointed. No signal came that night.

Saturday morning came, and by eleven o'clock a rollicking group of children was gathered at Judge Thatcher's. Everything was ready. It was not the custom for older people to ruin picnics with their presence. The children were considered safe enough under the watch of a few young ladies and gentlemen in their early twenties. The old steamboat was chartered for the occasion. Presently, the throng of children filed up the main street carrying baskets. Sid was sick and had to miss the fun.

The last thing Mrs. Thatcher said to Becky was, "You'll not get back till late. Perhaps you'd better stay all night with some of the girls that live near the steamboat landing."

"Then I'll stay with Susy Harper."

"Very well. Now you behave yourself and don't be any trouble."

Later, as they walked along, Tom said to Becky, "Say . . . I'll tell you what we'll do. Instead of going to Susy Harper's after the picnic, we'll climb right up the hill and spend the night at the Widow Douglas's. She'll have ice cream! She has it almost every day—loads of it. And she'll be awful glad for our company."

"Oh, that will be fun." Then Becky reflected a moment and said, "But what will Mamma say?"

"How'll she ever know?"

The girl turned the idea over in her mind and said reluctantly, "I reckon it's wrong . . . but . . ."

"But, shucks! Your mother won't know, so what's the harm? All she wants is that you'll be safe. I bet you she'd have said go to the widow's if she'd have thought of it. I know she would!"

The Widow Douglas's ice cream was a tempting bait, and it soon convinced Becky. They decided to say nothing to anybody about their plans for the night.

As Tom was making these plans, it occurred to him that maybe Huck might come that night and give the signal. The thought disturbed him. Still, he could not bear to give up the fun at the Widow Douglas's. Why should he give it up, he reasoned—the signal did not come the night before, so why should it be any more likely to come tonight? The sure fun of the evening outweighed the uncertain treasure. Tom decided to yield to the fun and not to think of the box of money anymore that day.

• What was Tom and Huck's new plan for getting the treasure? (Idea: *Huck would watch the hotel all night long. When Outlaw Joe left, Huck would get Tom, and then the boys would sneak into the room and grab the treasure box.*) Ⓡ

- Do you think the hotel room really is the hiding place? Explain your answer. (Ideas: *Yes, because it's Number Two and Outlaw Joe was sleeping there; no, because it's just a coincidence that the hotel room is Number Two.*) (MJ)
- Why didn't Tom and Huck use a flashlight when they went to the hotel? (Idea: *Because flashlights hadn't been invented yet.*) (DCE)
- Why did Tom decide to spend Saturday night at the Widow Douglas's? (Ideas: *Because she would have ice cream; because it would be fun; because he would be with Becky.*) (DCE)
- Do you agree with Tom's decision about the Widow Douglas? Explain your answer. (Ideas: *No, because Tom won't be able to help Huck; no, because Tom is letting Huck down; yes, because Huck probably won't come by.*) (MJ)

EXERCISE 9

Paired Practice (Optional)

1. Now you'll read in pairs.
- Whoever read second the last time will read first today.
- Remember to start at the diamond and switch at the star.
2. (Observe students and answer questions as needed.)

AFTER READING

EXERCISE 10

Independent Work

1. Do all the items in your workbook and textbook for this lesson.
2. (The independent work in this lesson includes the following activities.)
- Story details
- Vocabulary
- Irony
- Logic
- Vocabulary review
- Comprehension
- Writing

EXERCISE 11

Workcheck

1. (Using the Answer Key, read the questions and answers for the workbook.)
2. (Have students read their answers for the textbook activities.)
3. (Have two or three students read their writing assignments aloud. Comment on each assignment.)
4. (Have students correct and turn in their work.)

SPELLING

(Present Spelling lesson 111 after completing Reading lesson 111. See *Spelling Presentation Book.*)

BEFORE READING

(Have students find lesson 112, part A, in their textbooks.)

EXERCISE 1
Word Practice

1. Look at column 1.
- We're going to practice these words.

1. romantic	4. murder
2. estate	5. murderous
3. horsewhipped	6. scoundrel

2. Word 1. Everybody, what word? (Signal.) *Romantic.*
- (Repeat this procedure for every word in the column.)
3. (Repeat the column until firm.)

EXERCISE 2
New Vocabulary

1. Look at column 2.
- First we'll read the words in this column. Then we'll read their definitions.

1. inlet	4. elude
2. romp	5. flinch
3. intricate	

2. Word 1. Everybody, what word? (Signal.) *Inlet.*
- (Repeat this procedure for every word in the column.)
3. (Repeat the column until firm.)

EXERCISE 3
Vocabulary Definitions

1. Everybody, find part B. ✔
- These are definitions for the words you just read.
2. (For each word, call on a student to read the definition and the item. Then ask the student to complete the item.)

1. **inlet**—An *inlet* is a small bay.
- What is an inlet?

- What's the answer? (Idea: *A small bay.*)

2. **romp**—When you *romp,* you play actively.
- What's another way of saying *They played actively around the playground*?

- What's the answer? (Response: *They romped around the playground.*)

3. **intricate**—*Intricate* is another word for *complicated.*
- What's another way of saying *Computers are complicated machines*?

- What's the answer? (Response: *Computers are intricate machines.*)

4. **elude**—*Elude* is another word for *avoid.*
- What's another way of saying *They avoided the pirates*?

- What's the answer? (Response: *They eluded the pirates.*)

5. **flinch**—When you *flinch,* you tense up or wince.
- What's another way of saying *Ted winced when he caught the fastball*?

- What's the answer? (Response: *Ted flinched when he caught the fastball.*)

EXERCISE 4
Vocabulary Review

1. Everybody, find part C. ✔
- We're going to review these words.
2. (Call on a student to read the words in the box.)

catastrophe	verdict
resembles	profound
reflect	consent

3. (For each item, have a student read the item and say the answer.)

1. When something is like another thing, it ▨▨▨▨ that other thing.

• What's the answer? (Response: *Resembles.*)

2. When you agree to do something, you ▨▨▨▨ to do it.

• What's the answer? (Response: *Consent.*)

3. When you think quietly and calmly, you ▨▨▨▨.

• What's the answer? (Response: *Reflect.*)

4. Another word for *disaster* is ▨▨▨▨.

• What's the answer? (Response: *Catastrophe.*)

5. When something is deep or serious, it is ▨▨▨▨.

• What's the answer? (Response: *Profound.*)

EXERCISE 5

Logic

1. Everybody, turn to part E at the end of today's story. ✔
• (Call on individual students to read several sentences each.)
• (At the end of each section, present the questions for that section.)

Write the answers for items 1–3.
Here's a rule of logic: *Just because two words sound the same doesn't mean they have the same meaning.*

The following statement by a writer breaks the rule. "Bob said he would give me a ring on Thursday, and all he did was call me on the phone. I wonder if I should ever see him again."

1. Which word has two meanings in the statement?

• What's the answer? (Response: *Ring.*)

2. What does the writer think the word means?

• What's the answer? (Idea: *A piece of jewelry.*)

3. What is the word supposed to mean?

• What's the answer? (Idea: *A telephone call.*)
• You'll write the answers later.

READING

EXERCISE 6

Focus Question

1. Everybody, turn back to part D. ✔
2. What's the focus question for today's lesson? (Response: *What was Outlaw Joe's plan for revenge?*)

EXERCISE 7

Reading Aloud (Optional)

1. We're going to read aloud to the diamond.
• (Call on individual students to read several sentences each.)

Chapter 22

Huck Saves the Widow

Focus Question: What was Outlaw Joe's plan for revenge?

The steamboat was filled with the shouts and laughter of children on a holiday. Three miles south of town, the craft stopped at the mouth of a small inlet and tied up. The crowd swarmed ashore, and the forests and cliffs echoed far and near with shouting and laughter.

The children were soon hot and tired, and by and by they straggled back to camp with large appetites. After the feast, there was a refreshing rest and chatting in the shade of spreading oaks.

By and by somebody shouted, "Who's ready for McDougal's Cave?"

Everybody was. They grabbed some candles, and then there was a general scamper up the hill to the cave.

The mouth of the cave was shaped like the letter A. It had a massive oak door that stood open. Behind the door was a small chamber that was chilly as an icehouse and walled with solid limestone. It was romantic and mysterious to stand there in the deep gloom and look out upon the green valley shining in the sun.

The children soon began to romp again. If someone lighted a candle, the other children would try to put it out. A struggle would follow, but the candle was soon knocked down or blown out, and then there was a new chase.

The game soon ended. Then the children went filing down the steep path of the main cave. The flickering candles dimly revealed the lofty walls of rock that came together sixty feet overhead. The main path was about ten feet wide. Every few steps other paths branched out from it on both sides.

McDougal's Cave was a vast maze of crooked paths that ran into each other and out again and led nowhere. It was said that one might wander days and nights through the intricate network of paths and never find the end of the cave. It was also said that one could go down and down, and still down, into the earth, and it was just the same—maze underneath maze, and no end to any of them. No one "knew" the cave. That was an impossible thing. Most of the young men knew a part of it, and they did not venture beyond the part they knew. Tom knew as much of the cave as anyone.

The children moved along the main path for three-quarters of a mile, and then groups and couples began to slip aside into other corridors. They flew along the dismal paths, and they surprised each

other at points where the corridors joined again. Parties were able to elude each other for the space of half an hour without going beyond the familiar part of the cave.

By and by, one group after another came straggling back to the mouth of the cave, smeared from head to foot with candle drippings and clay and entirely delighted with the success of the picnic. Then they were astonished to find they had been taking no note of time and that it was almost night. The steamboat whistle had been calling for half an hour. However, when the steamboat pushed into the river with her wild freight, the only one who cared about wasted time was the captain of the craft. ◆

<hr>

EXERCISE 8
Silent Reading

1. Read the rest of the lesson to yourselves and be ready to answer some questions.

Huck had already begun his watch at the hotel when the steamboat's lights went past the wharf and toward the Saint Petersburg landing. He heard no noise on board, for the young people were nearly tired to death. He wondered what boat it was. Then he dropped it out of his mind and put his attention to his business.

The night was growing cloudy and dark. Ten o'clock came, and the noise of vehicles ceased. Scattered lights began to wink out, and the village began to slumber. Huck was left alone with the silence and the ghosts. Eleven o'clock came, and the hotel lights were put out. Darkness was everywhere now. Huck waited what seemed a long time, but nothing happened. His faith was weakening. Was there any use? Was there really any use? Why not give it up and turn in?

A noise fell upon his ear. He snapped to attention in an instant. The hotel door closed softly. Huck sprang to the corner of the brick store. The next moment two men brushed by him, and one seemed to have something under his arm. It must be that box! So they were going to remove the treasure. Why call Tom now? It would be absurd—the men would get away with the box and never be found again. No, he would follow them and hide in the darkness.

Huck stepped out and glided along behind the men, catlike, with bare feet, allowing them to keep far enough ahead that they were still in sight.

The men moved up River Street three blocks, then turned left. They went straight ahead until they came to the path that led up Cardiff Hill. They took the path. They passed by the old Welshman's house, halfway up the hill, and still climbed upward.

Good, thought Huck—they will bury the box in the old quarry. But they never stopped at the quarry. They passed on, up to the summit. They plunged into a narrow path between some tall bushes and were at once hidden in the gloom.

Huck came closer, now, for they would never be able to see him. He trotted along a while; then he slowed his pace. Then he stopped altogether. He listened—no sound, except for the beating of his own heart.

The hooting of an owl came from over the hill—dreadful sound! But no footsteps. He was about to spring away when a man cleared his throat not four feet from him!

Huck's heart shot into his throat, but he swallowed it again. He stood there shaking as if he had a fever. He was so weak he thought he would fall to the ground. But he knew where he was. He was within five steps of the gate that led to the Widow Douglas's estate. Very well, he thought, let them bury the box here. It wouldn't be hard to find.

Now there was a voice—a very low voice—Outlaw Joe's.

"Blast her, maybe she's got company—there's lights, late as it is."

"I can't see any."

This was that stranger's voice—the stranger of the haunted house. A deadly chill went to Huck's heart—this, then, was the revenge job! Huck wanted to run. Then he remembered that the Widow Douglas had been kind to him more than once, and maybe these men were going to murder her. He wished he could warn her. But he didn't dare—they might come and catch him. He thought all this and more in the moment between the stranger's remark and Outlaw Joe's next

remark, which was, "You can't see because the bush is in your way. Now—this way—now you see, don't you?" ★

"Yes. Well, there *is* company there, I reckon. Better give it up."

"Give it up? Give it up and maybe never have another chance? I tell you again, as I've told you before, I don't care for her money—you may have it. But her husband was rough on me—many times he was rough on me. He was a judge, and he had me horsewhipped!—horsewhipped in front of the jail!—with all the town looking on! HORSEWHIPPED! Do you understand? He was lucky enough to die. But I'll take it out on *her*."

"Oh, don't kill her! Don't do that!"

"Keep your opinion to yourself! It will be safer for you, my friend. You'll help in this thing—that's why you're here—I might not be able to do it alone. If you flinch, I'll kill you. Do you understand that?"

"Well, if it's got to be done, let's get at it. The quicker the better."

"Do it now? With company there? No—we'll wait till the lights are out—there's no hurry."

Huck felt that a silence was coming on. Silence was even more awful than any amount of murderous talk. He held his breath and gingerly stepped back. He planted his foot carefully and firmly. He took another step back, in the same way, then another and another and—a twig snapped under his foot!

Huck's breath stopped. There was no sound—the stillness was perfect. His gratitude was endless. Now he turned in his tracks, between the bushes—turned himself as carefully as if he were a ship—and then stepped quickly but cautiously along. When he came out at the quarry, he felt secure, and so he picked up his nimble heels and flew. Down he sped, till he reached the Welshman's house. He banged at the door, and presently the heads of the old man and his two sons came out at the window.

"What's the racket there? Who's banging? What do you want?"

"Let me in . . . quick! I'll tell everything!"

"Why, who are you?"

"Huckleberry Finn—quick, let me in!"

"Huckleberry Finn, indeed! It ain't a name to open many doors! But let him in, lads, and let's see what's the trouble."

"Please don't ever tell I told you" were Huck's first words when he got in. "Please don't—I'd be killed, sure—but the widow's been good friends to me sometimes, and I want to tell—I will tell if you'll promise you won't ever say it was me."

"By George, he has got something to tell, or he wouldn't act so!" exclaimed the old man. "Out with it and nobody here'll ever tell, lad."

Three minutes later the old man and his sons, well armed, went up the hill. They entered the path between the bushes on tiptoes, with their weapons in their hands. Huck accompanied them no farther. He hid behind a great boulder and listened. There was a lagging, anxious silence, and then all of a sudden there was an explosion of firearms and a cry.

Huck did not wait to find out the details. He sprang away and sped down the hill as fast as his legs could carry him.

- What was Outlaw Joe's plan for revenge? (Idea: *He wanted to kill the Widow Douglas because her husband had punished him.*) Ⓡ
- Why didn't Huck go to Tom's house when Outlaw Joe left the hotel? (Idea: *Huck thought Outlaw Joe was carrying the treasure box, so he followed Outlaw Joe instead.*) ⒹⒸⒺ
- The Welshman said Huckleberry Finn wasn't "a name to open many doors." Explain what the Welshman meant. (Ideas: *Most people wouldn't open the door if they knew it was Huck; most people didn't like Huck.*) ⓊⒸⒸⓂ
- Describe McDougal's Cave. (Ideas: *It was a huge, dark cave with a maze of passages; it was a huge cave that nobody had fully explored.*) Ⓥ
- Where do you think Tom was at the end of the chapter? Explain your answer. (Ideas: *At the Widow Douglas's, because she had company; at home, because he'd changed his mind about going to the Widow Douglas's; still at the cave, because he had missed the boat.*) Ⓜ Ⓙ

Paired Practice (Optional)

1. Now you'll read in pairs.
- Whoever read second the last time will read first today.
- Remember to start at the diamond and switch at the star.
2. (Observe students and answer questions as needed.)

AFTER READING

Independent Work

1. Do all the items in your workbook and textbook for this lesson.
2. (The independent work in this lesson includes the following activities.)
- Story details
- Vocabulary
- Logic
- Sequencing
- Comprehension
- Writing

Workcheck

1. (Using the Answer Key, read the questions and answers for the workbook.)
2. (Have students read their answers for the textbook activities.)
3. (Have two or three students read their writing assignments aloud. Comment on each assignment.)
4. (Have students correct and turn in their work.)

(Present Spelling lesson 112 after completing Reading lesson 112. See *Spelling Presentation Book.*)

BEFORE READING

(Have students find lesson 113, part A, in their textbooks.)

EXERCISE 1

Hard Words

1. Look at column 1.
- These are hard words from your textbook stories.

> 1. deputy   3. lavish
> 2. relic

2. Word 1 is **deputy.** Everybody, what word? (Signal.) *Deputy.*
- (Repeat this procedure for every word in the column.)
3. Let's read the words again.
4. Word 1. Everybody, what word? (Signal.) *Deputy.*
- (Repeat this procedure for every word in the column.)
5. (Repeat the column until firm.)

EXERCISE 2

Word Practice

1. Look at column 2.
- We're going to practice these words.

> 1. pleasant   4. tolerant
> 2. burglar   5. intolerant
> 3. murderous

2. Word 1. Everybody, what word? (Signal.) *Pleasant.*
- (Repeat this procedure for every word in the column.)
3. (Repeat the column until firm.)

EXERCISE 3

New Vocabulary

1. Look at column 3.
- First we'll read the words in this column. Then we'll read their definitions.

> 1. scoundrel   3. bore
> 2. deputy

2. Word 1. Everybody, what word? (Signal.) *Scoundrel.*
- (Repeat this procedure for every word in the column.)
3. (Repeat the column until firm.)

EXERCISE 4

Vocabulary Definitions

1. Everybody, find part B. ✔
- These are definitions for the words you just read.
2. (For each word, call on a student to read the definition and the item. Then ask the student to complete the item.)

1. **scoundrel**—A *scoundrel* is an evil or mean person.
- What's another way of saying *That evil person stole my backpack?*

- What's the answer? (Response: *That scoundrel stole my backpack.*)

2. **deputy**—A *deputy* is an assistant.
- What's another way of saying *an assistant sheriff?*

- What's the answer? (Response: *A deputy sheriff.*)

3. **bore**—When something *bores,* it makes a hole by drilling.
- What's another way of saying *The carpenter made a hole by drilling through the wall?*

- What's the answer? (Response: *The carpenter bored through the wall.*)

EXERCISE 5

Vocabulary Review

1. Everybody, find part C. ✔
- We're going to review these words.

2. (Call on a student to read the words in the box.)

intricate	consent
romp	baying
cluttered	elude
sentry	amid
profound	

3. (For each item, have a student read the item and say the answer.)

1. When something is in the middle, it is ▋▋▋.

- What's the answer? (Response: *Amid.*)

2. Another word for *complicated* is ▋▋▋.

- What's the answer? (Response: *Intricate.*)

3. Another word for *avoid* is ▋▋▋.

- What's the answer? (Response: *Elude.*)

4. When you play actively, you ▋▋▋.

- What's the answer? (Response: *Romp.*)

5. When something is deep or serious, it is ▋▋▋.

- What's the answer? (Response: *Profound.*)

6. When you agree to do something, you ▋▋▋ to do it.

- What's the answer? (Response: *Consent.*)

EXERCISE 6

Logic

1. Everybody, turn to part E at the end of today's story. ✔
- (Call on individual students to read several sentences each.)
- (At the end of each section, present the questions for that section.)

Write the answers for items 1–3.

Here's a rule of logic: *Just because two words sound the same doesn't mean they have the same meaning.*

The following statement by a writer breaks the rule: "The description of the robber said he was carrying arms. Since most people have arms, I don't think it was a very good description."

1. Which word has two meanings in this statement?

- What's the answer? (Response: *Arms.*)

2. What does the writer think the word means?

- What's the answer? (Idea: *Parts of the body.*)

3. What is the word supposed to mean?

- What's the answer? (Idea: *Weapons.*)
- You'll write the answers later.

READING

EXERCISE 7

Focus Question

1. Everybody, turn back to part D. ✔
2. What's the focus question for today's lesson? (Response: *Why was Huck glad at the end of the chapter?*)

EXERCISE 8

Reading Aloud (Optional)

1. We're going to read aloud to the diamond.
- (Call on individual students to read several sentences each.)

Chapter 23

Huck's Story

Focus Question: Why was Huck glad at the end of the chapter?

At the crack of dawn on Sunday morning, Huck came groping up the hill and rapped gently at the old Welshman's door. The residents were asleep, but it was a light sleep, on account of the excitement of the night before.

A call came from the window. "Who's there?"

Huck's scared voice answered in a low tone, "Please let me in! It's only Huck Finn!"

"It's a name that can open this door night or day, lad!—and welcome!"

These were strange words to the boy's ears and the most pleasant he had ever heard. The door was quickly unlocked, and Huck entered. He was given a seat while the old man and his sons speedily dressed themselves.

"Now, my boy, I hope you're good and hungry, because breakfast will be ready as soon as the sun's up, and we'll have a piping hot one, too. The boys and I hoped you'd turn up and stop here last night."

"I was awful scared," said Huck, "and I ran. I took off when the pistols went off, and I didn't stop for three miles. I've come now because I wanted to know about it, you know. I came at daylight because I didn't want to run across them devils, even if they was dead."

"Well, poor chap," the Welshman answered, "you do look as if you'd had a hard night—but there's a bed here for you when you've had your breakfast. No, they ain't dead, lad. You see, we knew right where to put our hands on them, thanks to you. So we crept along on tiptoes till we got within fifteen feet of the scoundrels—and just then I found I was going to sneeze. It was the meanest kind of luck! I tried to keep it back but no use—it was bound to come, and it did come! I was in the lead with my pistol raised, and when the sneeze came, those scoundrels tried to get out of the path. I cried out, 'Fire, boys!' and blazed away at the place where they were. So did the boys. But those villains were off in a jiffy, and we ran after them, down through the woods. I judge we never touched them."

The Welshman paused, then continued. "They fired a shot apiece as they started, but their bullets whizzed by and didn't do us any harm. As soon as we lost the sound of their feet, we quit chasing, and we went down and stirred up the sheriff. He got his deputies together and went off to guard the riverbank. As soon as it's light enough, they're going to look in the woods. My boys will be with them presently. I wish we had some sort of description of those scoundrels—it would

help a good deal. But you couldn't see what they were like in the dark, lad, I suppose?"

"Oh, yes, I saw them downtown and followed them."

"Splendid! Describe them—describe them, my boy!"

"One's the old deaf and mute man that's been around here once or twice, and the other's a mean-looking ragged . . ."

"That's enough, lad, we know the men! I came upon them in the woods back of the widow's one day, and they slunk away."

Then he turned to his sons and said, "Off with you, boys, and tell the sheriff— get your breakfast tomorrow morning!" ♦

EXERCISE 9

Silent Reading

1. Read the rest of the lesson to yourselves and be ready to answer some questions.

The Welshman's sons departed at once. As they were leaving the room, Huck sprang up and exclaimed, "Oh, please don't tell anybody it was me that told on them! Oh, please!"

"All right, if you say it, Huck, but you ought to have the credit for what you did."

"Oh, no, no! Please don't tell!"

When the young men were gone, the old Welshman said, "They won't tell—and I won't. But why don't you want it known?"

Huck would not explain, other than to say that he already knew too much about one of those men and that he would be killed for knowing it, sure.

The old man promised secrecy once more and said, "How did you come to follow those fellows, lad?"

Huck was silent while he thought of an answer. Then he said, "Well, you see, I've got a hard life—and sometimes I can't sleep much on account of thinking about it. That was the way it was last night. I couldn't sleep, and so I came along up the street about midnight. When I got to that old brick store by the hotel, I backed up against the wall to think. Well, just then along comes those two chaps slipping along close by me. One had something under his arm, and I reckoned they'd stole it. One was a-smoking, and the other wanted a light; so they stopped right before me, and the cigars lit up their faces, and I see that the big one was the deaf and mute man, and the other one was a rusty, ragged-looking devil."

"Could you see the rags by the light of the cigars?"

This question staggered Huck for a moment. Then he said, "Well, I don't know—but somehow it seems as if I did. Then they went on, and I followed 'em . . . yes. That was it. I wanted to see what was up. I followed 'em to the widow's gate and stood in the dark and heard the ragged one beg to spare the widow's life and the deaf and mute man swear he'd kill her just as I told you and your two . . ."

"What? The deaf and mute man said all that?"

Huck had made another terrible mistake! He was trying his best to keep the old man from getting the faintest hint of who the deaf and mute man might be. But his tongue seemed to get him into trouble in spite of all he could do. He made several efforts to get out of his lie; but the old man's eyes were upon him, and Huck made blunder after blunder. ★

Presently, the Welshman said, "My boy, don't be afraid of me. I wouldn't hurt a hair of your head for all the world. No—I'd protect you—I'd protect you. This man is not deaf and mute. You've let that slip without intending it. You can't cover that up now. You know something about that man that you want to keep secret. Now trust me—tell me what it is and trust me— I won't betray you."

Huck looked into the old man's honest eyes a moment, then bent over and whispered in his ear, "It ain't a deaf and mute man—it's Outlaw Joe!"

The Welshman almost jumped out of his chair. In a moment he said, "It's all plain enough, now. Outlaw Joe wants revenge."

During breakfast the talk went on. The old man said that the last thing he and his sons had done before going to bed was to get a lantern and examine the area near the gate for marks of blood. They found none, but they captured a bulky bundle of . . .

"Of WHAT?" asked Huck.

If the words had been lightning, they could not have leaped more quickly from Huck's lips. His eyes were staring wide, now, and his breath was held—waiting for the answer. The Welshman stared in return—three seconds—five seconds— then he replied, "Of burglar's tools. Why, what's the matter with you?"

Huck sank back, panting gently, but deeply grateful. The Welshman eyed him gravely, curiously, and presently said, "Yes, burglar's tools. That appears to relieve you a good deal. But what were you expecting we'd found?"

Huck was in trouble now—the Welshman's eyes were upon him. He would have given anything for a good answer, but he could think of nothing. The Welshman's eyes were boring deeper and deeper. Huck thought of a reply and uttered it feebly: "I thought there might be Sunday school books in that bundle."

Poor Huck was too distressed to smile, but the old man laughed loud and joyously. He shook from head to foot. Then he said, "Poor old chap, you're pale—you ain't well a bit—no wonder you're a little off balance. But you'll come out of it. Rest and sleep will fix you up all right, I hope."

Huck was irritated to think he had betrayed his secret. He now knew that the parcel brought from the hotel was not the treasure. But on the whole he felt glad. The treasure was still in the hotel, and so his mind was at rest. In fact, everything seemed to be drifting just in the right direction, now. The treasure must still be in Number Two, the men would be captured and jailed that day, and he and Tom could seize the gold that night without any trouble.

- Why was Huck glad at the end of the chapter? (Idea: *He thought the treasure was still in Number Two and the men would be captured so that he and Tom could get the treasure.*) ⒹⒸⒺ
- Explain what happened when the Welshman and his sons sneaked up on Outlaw Joe. (Idea: *As they were sneaking up, the Welshman sneezed. Outlaw Joe and his companion fled. The Welshman and his sons fired at them but missed.*) Ⓡ
- Why do you think Huck had such a hard time making up a story? (Ideas: *He wasn't a good liar; he didn't know how to tell stories.*) ⓂⒿ

- Do you think Tom would have told a better story if he had been in Huck's place? Explain your answer. (Idea: *Probably, because Tom had a good imagination and was always lying and exaggerating.*) (MJ)
- Why did Huck think the treasure was still in Number Two? (Idea: *Because the men were just carrying burglars' tools, not the treasure.*) (C/E)

EXERCISE 10
Paired Practice (Optional)

1. Now you'll read in pairs.
- Whoever read second the last time will read first today.
- Remember to start at the diamond and switch at the star.
2. (Observe students and answer questions as needed.)

AFTER READING

EXERCISE 11
Independent Work

1. Do all the items in your workbook and textbook for this lesson.
2. (The independent work in this lesson includes the following activities.)
- Story details
- Vocabulary
- Logic
- Character traits
- Inference
- Comprehension
- Writing

EXERCISE 12
Workcheck

1. (Using the Answer Key, read the questions and answers for the workbook.)
2. (Have students read their answers for the textbook activities.)
3. (Have two or three students read their writing assignments aloud. Comment on each assignment.)
4. (Have students correct and turn in their work.)

SPELLING

(Present Spelling lesson 113 after completing Reading lesson 113. See *Spelling Presentation Book.*)

BEFORE READING

(Have students find lesson 114, part A, in their textbooks.)

EXERCISE 1
Hard Words

1. Look at column 1.
   - These are hard words from your textbook stories.

1. crazed	**3. revive**
2. homeward	

2. Word 1 is **crazed.** Everybody, what word? (Signal.) *Crazed.*
   - (Repeat this procedure for every word in the column.)
3. Let's read the words again.
4. Word 1. Everybody, what word? (Signal.) *Crazed.*
   - (Repeat this procedure for every word in the column.)
5. (Repeat the column until firm.)

EXERCISE 2
New Vocabulary

1. Look at column 2.
   - First we'll read the words in this column. Then we'll read their definitions.

1. lavish	**3. whiskey**
2. relic	

2. Word 1. Everybody, what word? (Signal.) *Lavish.*
   - (Repeat this procedure for every word in the column.)
3. (Repeat the column until firm.)

EXERCISE 3
Vocabulary Definitions

1. Everybody, find part B. ✔
   - These are definitions for the words you just read.

2. (For each word, call on a student to read the definition and the item. Then ask the student to complete the item.)

1. **lavish**—When something is *lavish,* it's considerable or excessive.
   - What's another way of saying *a considerable amount of praise*?
   - What's the answer? (Response: *A lavish amount of praise.*)

2. *relic*—A *relic* is something left over from the past.
   - What's another way of saying *These arrowheads are left over from the past*?
   - What's the answer? (Response: *These arrowheads are relics.*)

3. **whiskey**—*Whiskey* is a strong alcoholic drink.
   - What is whiskey?
   - What's the answer? (Idea: *A strong alcoholic drink.*)

EXERCISE 4
Vocabulary Review

1. Everybody, find part C. ✔
   - We're going to review these words.
2. (Call on a student to read the words in the box.)

bore	lull
sentry	catastrophe
scoundrel	resembles
consent	intricate
profound	

3. (For each item, have a student read the item and say the answer.)

1. When you make a hole by drilling, you ▬▬▬.
   - What's the answer? (Response: *Bore.*)

2. A mean or evil person is a ▮▮▮▮▮.

- What's the answer? (Response: *Scoundrel.*)

3. When something is deep or serious, it is ▮▮▮▮.

- What's the answer? (Response: *Profound.*)

4. When you agree to do something, you ▮▮▮▮▮ to do it.

- What's the answer? (Response: *Consent.*)

5. Another word for *complicated* is ▮▮▮▮.

- What's the answer? (Response: *Intricate.*)

6. When something looks like another thing, it ▮▮▮▮ that thing.

- What's the answer? (Response: *Resembles.*)

READING

EXERCISE 5

Focus Question

1. Everybody, find part D. ✔
2. What's the focus question for today's lesson? (Response: *What did Huck learn about the hotel?*)

EXERCISE 6

Reading Aloud (Optional)

1. We're going to read aloud to the diamond.
- (Call on individual students to read several sentences each.)

Chapter 24
Sound the Alarm!

Focus Question: What did Huck learn about the hotel?

Just as Huck completed breakfast at the Welshman's house, there was a knock at the door. The boy jumped for a hiding place because he did not want to be connected even remotely with the events at the Widow Douglas's house. Several ladies and gentlemen were at the door. The Widow Douglas was among them. Groups of citizens were climbing up the hill to stare at the gate. The news had spread.

The Welshman had to tell part of the story of the night to the visitors. The widow's gratitude was lavish, but the Welshman said, "Don't say a word about it, Madam. There's another person you should be more thankful to than you are to me and my boys. But he won't allow me to tell his name. We wouldn't have been there if it hadn't been for him."

Of course, this statement excited curiosity—but the Welshman refused to part with his secret. Then the Widow Douglas said, "I went to sleep reading in bed and slept straight through all that noise. Why didn't you come and wake me?"

"We judged it wasn't worthwhile. Those fellows weren't likely to come again—they hadn't any tools left to work with, and what was the use of waking you up and scaring you to death? One of my boys stood guard all the rest of the night."

More visitors came, and the story had to be told and retold for a couple of hours. ♦

EXERCISE 7

Silent Reading

1. Read the rest of the lesson to yourselves and be ready to answer some questions.

Everybody was early at church that Sunday. The stirring events of the previous night were discussed a great deal. News came that not a sign of the two villains had yet been discovered.

When the sermon was finished, Judge Thatcher's wife came up to Mrs. Harper and said, "Is my Becky going to sleep all day? She must be tired to death!"

"Your Becky?"

"Yes," Mrs. Thatcher said, with a startled look, "didn't she stay with you last night?"

"Why, no."

Mrs. Thatcher turned pale and sank down just as Aunt Polly passed by.

Aunt Polly said, "Good morning, Mrs. Thatcher. Good morning, Mrs. Harper. Tom is missing. I reckon he stayed at one of your houses last night, and now he's afraid to come to church. I've got to settle with him."

Mrs. Thatcher shook her head feebly and turned paler than ever.

"He didn't stay with us," said Mrs. Harper, beginning to look uneasy. Anxiety came into Aunt Polly's face.

"Joe Harper, have you seen my Tom this morning?"

"No, Ma'am."

"When did you see him last?"

Joe tried to remember but was not sure he could say. The people had stopped moving out of the church. Whispers passed along, and uneasiness came into every face. Children were anxiously questioned. They all said they had not noticed whether Tom and Becky were on board the steamboat on the homeward trip. It was dark, and no one had thought of asking if anyone was missing. One young man finally blurted out his fear that they were still in the cave! Mrs. Thatcher nearly fainted, and Aunt Polly started wringing her hands.

The alarm swept from lip to lip, from group to group, from street to street. Within five minutes, the church bells were wildly clanging, and the whole town was up! The burglars were forgotten, horses were saddled, skiffs were manned, and the steamboat was ordered out. Before the news was half an hour old, two hundred men were pouring down roads and river toward the cave.

All the long afternoon the village seemed empty and dead. Many women visited Aunt Polly and Mrs. Thatcher and tried to comfort them. The day dragged on and turned into night. The town waited for news; but when the next morning dawned at last, all the word that came was, "Send more candles— and send food." Mrs. Thatcher was almost crazed, and Aunt Polly also. Judge Thatcher sent messages of hope and encouragement from the cave, but they carried no real cheer. ★

The old Welshman came home toward daylight, spattered with candle wax, smeared with clay, and almost worn out. He found Huck still in the bed that had been provided for him, and sick with fever. The doctors were all at the cave, so the Widow Douglas came and took charge of the patient. She did not tell Huck what had happened to Tom Sawyer.

By late Monday morning, parties of men began to straggle into the village, but the strongest of the citizens continued searching. The only news was that the searchers were exploring parts of the cave that had never been explored before. Every corner of the cave was going to be thoroughly searched. In one place, far from the main section, the names "BECKY AND TOM" had been found traced upon the rocky wall with candle smoke. A grease-soiled bit of ribbon had also been found. Mrs. Thatcher recognized the ribbon and cried over it. She said it was the last relic she should ever have of her child.

Some said that now and then, in the cave, a faraway speck of light would glimmer. At those times, the searchers would shout and go trooping down the passage. But a sickening disappointment always followed. The children were not there; it was only a searcher's light.

Three dreadful days and nights dragged their hours along, and the village sank into a hopeless state. No one had heart for anything.

Meanwhile, the Widow Douglas continued to take care of Huck. At one point, Huck feebly led up to the subject of hotels and finally asked—dimly dreading the worst—if anything had been discovered at the hotel since he had been ill.

"Yes," said the widow.

Huck started up in bed, wild-eyed. "What? What was it?"

"Illegal whiskey. And because of that, the hotel has been closed down. Lie down, child—what a turn you did give me!"

"Only tell me just one thing—only just one—please! Was it Tom Sawyer that found it?"

The widow burst into tears. "Hush, hush, child, hush! I've told you before, you must not talk. You are very, very sick!"

Then nothing but illegal whiskey had been found. There would have been a great stir if it had been the gold. So the treasure was gone forever—gone forever! But what could the widow be crying about? Curious that she should cry.

These thoughts worked their dim way through Huck's mind, and he soon fell asleep.

The widow said to herself, "There—he's asleep, poor wreck. And he wants to know if Tom Sawyer found that whiskey. If only somebody could find Tom Sawyer! Ah, there ain't many left, now, that's got hope enough, or strength enough, to go on searching."

- What did Huck learn about the hotel? (Ideas: *That illegal whiskey had been found there; that the treasure wasn't there.*) (Sum)
- Why didn't Mrs. Thatcher notice that Becky was missing until Sunday? (Idea: *Because Becky was supposed to spend the night at the Harpers' house.*) (C/E)
- Why didn't Aunt Polly telephone the sheriff when Tom didn't come home? (Idea: *Because telephones hadn't been invented yet.*) (DCE)
- How did the news about Tom and Becky spread? (Ideas: *People told each other on the street; the church bells clanged.*) (R)
- What evidence of Tom and Becky did the searchers find? (Ideas: *The searchers found Tom's and Becky's names on the wall; they found Becky's ribbon.*) (ND)

EXERCISE 8

Paired Practice (Optional)

1. Now you'll read in pairs.
- Whoever read second the last time will read first today.
- Remember to start at the diamond and switch at the star.
2. (Observe students and answer questions as needed.)

AFTER READING

EXERCISE 9

Independent Work

1. Do all the items in your workbook and textbook for this lesson.
2. (The independent work in this lesson includes the following activities.)
- Story details
- Vocabulary
- Following directions
- Settings
- Logic
- Comprehension
- Writing

EXERCISE 10

Workcheck

1. (Using the Answer Key, read the questions and answers for the workbook.)
2. (Have students read their answers for the textbook activities.)
3. (Have two or three students read their writing assignments aloud. Comment on each assignment.)
4. (Have students correct and turn in their work.)

SPELLING

(Present Spelling lesson 114 after completing Reading lesson 114. See *Spelling Presentation Book*.)

BEFORE READING

(Have students find lesson 115, part A, in their textbooks.)

EXERCISE 1

Hard Words

1. Look at column 1.
- These are hard words from your textbook stories.

1. stalagmite	3. apprehensive
2. stalactite	4. paralyze

2. Word 1 is **stalagmite.** Everybody, what word? (Signal.) *Stalagmite.*
- (Repeat this procedure for every word in the column.)
3. Let's read the words again.
4. Word 1. Everybody, what word? (Signal.) *Stalagmite.*
- (Repeat this procedure for every word in the column.)
5. (Repeat the column until firm.)

EXERCISE 2

Word Practice

1. Look at column 2.
- We're going to practice these words.

1. reference	4. clam
2. bygone	5. clammy
3. famished	

2. Word 1. Everybody, what word? (Signal.) *Reference.*
- (Repeat this procedure for every word in the column.)
3. (Repeat the column until firm.)

EXERCISE 3

New Vocabulary

1. Look at column 3.
- First we'll read the words in this column. Then we'll read their definitions.

1. stalactite	3. apprehensive
2. stalagmite	4. revive

2. Word 1. Everybody, what word? (Signal.) *Stalactite.*
- (Repeat this procedure for every word in the column.)
3. (Repeat the column until firm.)

EXERCISE 4

Vocabulary Definitions

1. Everybody, find part B. ✔
- These are definitions for the words you just read.
2. (For each word, call on a student to read the definition and the item. Then ask the student to complete the item.)

1. **stalactite**—A *stalactite* is a type of rock that hangs from the ceiling of a cave. Stalactites look like icicles.
- What is a stalactite?

- What's the answer? (Idea: *A type of rock that hangs from the ceiling of a cave.*)

2. **stalagmite**—A *stalagmite* is a type of rock that forms on the floor of a cave. Stalagmites look like jagged towers.
- What is a stalagmite?

- What's the answer? (Idea: *A type of rock that forms on the floor of a cave.*)

3. **apprehensive**—When you're *apprehensive,* you're uncertain and afraid.
- What's another way of saying *Becky grew uncertain and afraid around midnight?*

- What's the answer? (Response: *Becky grew apprehensive around midnight.*)

4. **revive**—When something *revives,* it comes back to life or to health.
- What's another way of saying *The plant came back to life?*

- What's the answer? (Response: *The plant revived.*)

Vocabulary Review

1. Everybody, find part C. ✔
- We're going to review these words.
2. (Call on a student to read the words in the box.)

throng	**intricate**
haggard	**elude**
lavish	

3. (For each item, have a student read the item and say the answer.)

1. Another word for *complicated* is ▮▮▮▮.

- What's the answer? (Response: *Intricate.*)

2. Another word for *avoid* is ▮▮▮▮.

- What's the answer? (Response: *Elude.*)

3. A large crowd of people is a ▮▮▮▮.

- What's the answer? (Response: *Throng.*)

4. When something is considerable or excessive, it is ▮▮▮▮.

- What's the answer? (Response: *Lavish.*)

READING

Focus Question

1. Everybody, find part D. ✔
2. What's the focus question for today's lesson? (Response: *Why did Tom and Becky get lost in the cave?*)

Reading Aloud (Optional)

1. We're going to read aloud to the diamond.
- (Call on individual students to read several sentences each.)

Chapter 25
Tom and Becky in the Cave

Focus Question: Why did Tom and Becky get lost in the cave?

Now let us return to Tom and Becky's part in the picnic. They walked along the dark aisles with the rest of the children and visited the familiar wonders of the cave. Presently, a hide-and-seek game began, and Tom and Becky took part in it until they grew tired. Then they wandered down a curving path. They held their candles up and read the names, dates, addresses, and notes that had been written on the rocky walls with candle smoke. They drifted along and scarcely noticed that they were now in a part of the cave without any writing on the walls. They wrote their own names under an overhanging shelf and moved on.

Presently they came to a small waterfall. Tom squeezed his small body behind the waterfall and found a sort of steep natural stairway enclosed between narrow walls. At once, he wanted to explore this new area. Becky responded to his call, and they made a smoke mark for future reference.

They wound this way and that, far down into the secret depths of the cave, made another mark, and branched off in search of curiosities to tell the upper world about. In one place they found a spacious cavern. Shining stalactites as big as a man's leg hung from the ceiling. They walked all around the cavern, wondering and admiring. Then they left the cavern by one of the numerous passages that came into it.

This passage soon brought them to an enchanting spring whose bottom was covered with glittering crystals. The spring was in a cavern where stalactites and stalagmites joined together to form pillars.

Under the roof of the cavern, vast knots of bats had packed themselves together, thousands in a bunch. The light disturbed the creatures, and they came flocking down by hundreds, squeaking and darting furiously at the candles. Tom knew about bats and how dangerous they could be. He seized Becky's hand and hurried with her into the first corridor they found. And none too soon, for a bat struck Becky's light out with its wing while she was passing out of the cavern. The bats chased the children a good distance; but the children plunged into every new passage they found, and at last they were free of the bats. ◆

EXERCISE 8

Silent Reading

1. Read the rest of the lesson to yourselves and be ready to answer some questions.

Tom soon found an underground lake, which stretched away until its shape was lost in the shadows. He wanted to explore its borders but concluded it would be best to sit down and rest awhile. Now, for the first time, the deep stillness of the place laid a clammy hand upon the spirits of the children.

Becky said, "Why, I didn't notice, but it seems ever so long since I heard any of the others."

"Come to think of it, Becky, we are way down below them—and I don't know how far away to the north or south or east or whichever direction they are. We couldn't hear them here."

Becky grew apprehensive. "I wonder how long we've been down here, Tom. We better start back."

"Yes, I reckon we better. Perhaps we better."

"Can you find the way, Tom? It's all mixed up to me."

"I reckon I could find it—but then there's the bats. If they put both our candles out, it will be an awful fix. Let's try some other way so we can avoid the bats."

"Well, all right. But I hope we won't get lost. It would be so awful!" The girl shuddered at the dreadful possibilities.

Tom and Becky started through a passage, and they walked in silence a long way. They glanced at each new opening to see if there was anything familiar about it, but every one was strange. Every time Tom made an examination, Becky would watch his face for an encouraging sign, and he would say cheerily, "Oh, it's all right. This ain't the one, but we'll come to it right away!"

Tom felt less and less hopeful with each failure. He soon began to turn off into passages at random, in the desperate hope of finding the one he wanted. He continued to say it was "all right," but the words had lost their ring and sounded just as if he had said, "All is lost!"

At last Becky said, "Oh, Tom, never mind the bats. Let's go back that way! We seem to get worse and worse off all the time."

Tom stopped. "Listen!" he said.

Profound silence, silence so deep that their breathing was the loudest sound. Tom shouted. The call went echoing down the empty aisles and died out in the distance in a faint sound that resembled laughter. ★

"Oh, don't yell again, Tom. It is too horrid," said Becky.

"It is horrid, but I better, Becky. They might hear us, you know," and he shouted again.

The "might" was even more horrible than the ghostly laughter of the echoes. The two children stood still and listened, but they heard nothing. Tom turned around at once and hurried back. But he could not find his way back!

Becky said, "Oh, Tom, you didn't make any marks!"

"Becky, I was such a fool! Such a fool! I never thought we might want to come back! No—I can't find the way. It's all mixed up."

"Tom, Tom, we're lost! We're lost! We never can get out of this awful place! Oh, why did we ever leave the others!"

Tom and Becky moved on again—aimlessly—simply at random. All they could do was to move, to keep moving. For a little while, their hope revived, but only for a while.

By and by, Tom took Becky's candle and blew it out. Words were not needed. Becky understood, and her hope died again. She knew that Tom had a whole candle and three or four pieces in his pockets—yet he must save them.

By and by, the children grew tired. It was dreadful to think of sitting down when time was so precious. Moving, in some direction, in any direction, was at least progress, but to sit down was to invite death.

At last they sat down. They talked of home, and friends there, and the comfortable beds, and, above all, the light! Becky soon drowsed off to sleep. Tom sat looking into her worried face and saw it grow smooth and natural under the influence of pleasant dreams.

By and by, a smile dawned on Becky's face. This smile brought peace and healing to Tom's spirit, and his thoughts wandered away to bygone times and dreamy memories. While Tom was deep in his thoughts, Becky woke up with a breezy little laugh—but the laugh died on her lips, and a groan followed it.

"I'm glad you've slept, Becky; you'll feel rested, now, and we'll find the way out."

"We can try, Tom, but I've seen such a beautiful country in my dream. I reckon we are going there if we die."

"Maybe not, maybe not. Cheer up, Becky, and let's keep on trying."

- Why did Tom and Becky get lost in the cave? (Ideas: *Because they didn't make any marks to show where they'd been; because they wandered about aimlessly.*) Ⓒ/ⓔ
- The story says, "The deep stillness of the place laid a clammy hand upon the spirits of the children." Explain what that sentence means. (Idea: *The profound quiet of the cave deadened the children's hopes.*) ⓊⒸⒸⓂ
- Do you think it was wise of Tom to avoid the bats when he and Becky started back? Explain your answer. (Ideas: *No, because it would be better to fight off the bats than to get lost; yes, because the bats could have blown out their candles.*) Ⓜⓙ
- Tom says the other children might hear his yells. Then the story says, "The 'might' was even more horrible than the ghostly laughter of the echoes." Explain what that sentence means. (Idea: *Being lost was worse than the creepy sounds.*) ⓊⒸⒸⓂ
- Why do you think Becky dreamed about a beautiful country? (Ideas: *She thought they were going to die and go to heaven; she wanted to be somewhere else.*) Ⓜⓙ

EXERCISE 9
Paired Practice (Optional)

1. Now you'll read in pairs.
- Whoever read second the last time will read first today.
- Remember to start at the diamond and switch at the star.
2. (Observe students and answer questions as needed.)

AFTER READING

EXERCISE 10
Independent Work

1. Do all the items in your workbook and textbook for this lesson.
2. (The independent work in this lesson includes the following activities.)
- Story details
- Combined sentences
- Vocabulary
- Graphs
- Poem review
- Logic
- Comprehension
- Writing

EXERCISE 11
Workcheck

1. (Using the Answer Key, read the questions and answers for the workbook.)
2. (Have students read their answers for the textbook activities.)
3. (Have two or three students read their writing assignments aloud. Comment on each assignment.)
4. (Have students correct and turn in their work.)

SPELLING

(Present Spelling lesson 115 after completing Reading lesson 115. See *Spelling Presentation Book*.)

ACTIVITIES ACROSS THE CURRICULUM

(Students should complete the appropriate project in *Activities across the Curriculum* after completing lesson 115. See *Activities across the Curriculum* book for details.)

Lessons 116–120 • Planning Page   *Looking Ahead*

	Lesson 116	**Lesson 117**	**Lesson 118**	**Lesson 119**	**Lesson 120**
BEFORE READING	Hard words Word practice New vocabulary Vocabulary definitions Vocabulary review Logic	Word practice New vocabulary Vocabulary definitions Logic	Word practice New vocabulary Vocabulary definitions	Hard words Word practice Vocabulary review	Word practice Vocabulary review
NEW VOCABULARY	estimate pitfall famished tedious	peal clad hamlet provisions fret bluff	gloat loft foundry adopt impact quench furnish	(none)	(none)
READING	*Tom Sawyer* *(Chapter 26)*	*Tom Sawyer* *(Chapter 27)*	*Tom Sawyer* *(Chapter 28)*	*Tom Sawyer* *(Chapter 29)*	*Tom Sawyer* *(Chapter 30)*
INDEPENDENT WORK	Story details Perspectives Vocabulary Logic Outlining Comprehension Writing	Story details Sequencing Vocabulary Logic Character traits Settings Vocabulary review Comprehension Writing	Story details Comparisons Vocabulary Logic Literary forms Vocabulary review Comprehension Writing	Story details Vocabulary Perspectives Logic Comprehension Writing	Story details Vocabulary Logic Perspectives Outlining Comprehension Writing
SUPPLEMENTS	*Spelling*	*Spelling*	*Spelling*	*Spelling*	*Mastery Test* *Spelling* *Activities across the Curriculum*

Comprehension Questions Abbreviations Guide

Access Prior Knowledge = (APK)   Author's Point of View = (APoV)   Author's Purpose = (AP)   Cause/Effect = (C/E)   Charts/Graphs/Diagrams/Visual Aids = (VA)

Classify and Categorize = (C+C)   Compare/Contrast = (C/C)   Determine Character Emotions, Motivation = (DCE)   Drawing Conclusions = (DC)   Drawing Inferences = (DI)

Fact and Opinion = (F/O)   Hypothesizing = (H)   Main Idea = (MI)   Making Connections = (MC)   Making Deductions = (MD)   Making Judgements = (MJ)

Narrative Elements = (NE)   Noting Details = (ND)   Predict = (P)   Reality/Fantasy = (R/F)   Recall Facts/Rules = (RF/R)   Retell = (R)   Sequence = (Seq)

Steps in a Process = (SP)   Story Structure = (SS)   Summarize = (Sum)   Understanding Dialogue = (UD)   Using Context to Confirm Meaning(s) = (UCCM)   Visualize = (V)

BEFORE READING

(Have students find lesson 116, part A, in their textbooks.)

EXERCISE 1

Hard Words

1. Look at column 1.
- These are hard words from your textbook stories.

1. estimate	3. funeral
2. tedious	4. foundry

2. Word 1 is **estimate** [es tuh MATE]. Everybody, what word? (Signal.) *Estimate.*
- (Repeat this procedure for every word in the column.)
3. Let's read the words again.
4. Word 1. Everybody, what word? (Signal.) *Estimate.*
- (Repeat this procedure for every word in the column.)
5. (Repeat the column until firm.)

EXERCISE 2

Word Practice

1. Look at column 2.
- We're going to practice these words.

1. portion	3. provisions
2. paralyzed	

2. Word 1. Everybody, what word? (Signal.) *Portion.*
- (Repeat this procedure for every word in the column.)
3. (Repeat the column until firm.)

EXERCISE 3

New Vocabulary

1. Look at column 3.
- First we'll read the words in this column. Then we'll read their definitions.

1. estimate	3. famished
2. pitfall	4. tedious

2. Word 1. Everybody, what word? (Signal.) *Estimate.*
- (Repeat this procedure for every word in the column.)
3. (Repeat the column until firm.)

EXERCISE 4

Vocabulary Definitions

1. Everybody, find part B. ✔
- These are definitions for the words you just read.
2. (For each word, call on a student to read the definition and the item. Then ask the student to complete the item.)

1. **estimate**—When you *estimate* something, you try to determine its size or value.
- What's another way of saying *He tried to determine the value of the painting*?

- What's the answer? (Response: *He estimated the value of the painting.*)

2. **pitfall**—A *pitfall* is a deep hole in the ground.
- What is a pitfall?

- What's the answer? (Response: *A deep hole in the ground.*)

3. **famished**—When you are *famished,* you are very hungry.
- What's another way of saying *Because Mark hadn't eaten all day, he was very hungry*?

- What's the answer? (Response: *Because Mark hadn't eaten all day, he was famished.*)

4. **tedious**—When something is *tedious,* it is boring or tiresome.
- What's another way of saying *Watching television is boring*?

- What's the answer? (Response: *Watching television is tedious.*)

Vocabulary Review

1. Everybody, find part C. ✔
- We're going to review these words.
2. (Call on a student to read the words in the box.)

revives	resembles
amid	apprehensive
bore	sentry

3. (For each item, have a student read the item and say the answer.)

1. When you're uncertain and afraid, you are _____.

- What's the answer? (Response: *Apprehensive.*)

2. When something comes back to life or to a healthy state, it _____.

- What's the answer? (Response: *Revives.*)

3. A guard is a _____.

- What's the answer? (Response: *Sentry.*)

4. When you make a hole by drilling, you _____.

- What's the answer? (Response: *Bore.*)

Logic

1. Everybody, turn to part E at the end of today's story. ✔
- (Call on individual students to read several sentences each.)
- (At the end of each section, present the questions for that section.)

Write the answers for items 1–5.

Here's a rule of logic: *Just because you know about one part doesn't mean you know about another part.*

The following statement by a writer breaks the rule. "I can prove this bicycle has the best handlebars of any bike on the road. Here's the proof. This bike has the very best seat available. So you know the handlebars must be the best."

1. What is the whole?

- What's the answer? (Response: *The bicycle.*)

2. What are the two parts?

- What's the answer? (Idea: *The handlebars and the seat.*)

3. Which part do you know something about?

- What's the answer? (Response: *The seat.*)

4. Which part does the writer draw a conclusion about?

- What's the answer? (Response: *The handlebars.*)

5. What does the writer conclude about that part?

- What's the answer? (Idea: *That they're the best.*)
- You'll write the answers later.

READING

Focus Question

1. Everybody, turn back to part D. ✔
2. What's the focus question for today's lesson? (Response: *Why did Tom tie a string to a rock?*)

Note: The "Reading Aloud" exercise is recommended for this lesson.

Reading Aloud

1. We're going to read aloud to the diamond.

- (Call on individual students to read several sentences each.)

Chapter 26
Found and Lost Again

Focus Question: Why did Tom tie a string to a rock?

Tom and Becky rose and wandered along, hand in hand and hopeless. They tried to estimate how long they had been in the cave, but all they knew was that it seemed days and weeks. Yet it was plain that this could not be, for their candles were not gone yet.

A long time after this—they could not tell how long—Tom said they must go softly and listen for dripping water—they must find a spring. They found one presently, and Tom said it was time to rest again. Both children were cruelly tired, yet Becky said she thought she could go on a little farther. She was surprised to hear Tom disagree. She could not understand it. They sat down, and Tom fastened his candle to the wall in front of them with some clay. Nothing was said for some time.

Then Becky broke the silence. "Tom, I am so hungry!"

Tom took something out of his pocket. "Do you remember this?" he said.

Becky almost smiled. "It's cake from the picnic, Tom."

"Yes, and I wish it was as big as a barrel, for it's all we've got."

Tom divided the cake. Becky ate with good appetite while Tom nibbled at a piece. There was plenty of cold water to finish the feast with. By and by, Becky suggested they move on. Tom was silent a moment.

Then he said, "Becky, can you bear it if I tell you something?"

Becky's face paled, but she thought she could.

"Well, then, Becky, we must stay here, where there's water to drink. That little piece is our last candle!"

Becky sat in silence for a while. At last she said, "Tom!"

"What, Becky?"

"They'll miss us and hunt for us!"

"Yes, they will! Certainly they will!"

"Maybe they're hunting for us now, Tom."

"Why, I reckon maybe they are. I hope they are."

"When would they miss us, Tom?"

"When they get back to the boat, I reckon."

"Tom, it might be dark then—would they notice we hadn't come?"

"I don't know. But your mother would miss you as soon as they got home."

A frightened look in Becky's face brought Tom to his senses. He saw that he had made a blunder. Becky was not expected to come home that night! The children became silent and thoughtful. In a moment, a worried look from Becky showed Tom they were thinking the same thing—Sunday morning might be half spent before Mrs. Thatcher discovered Becky was missing.

The children fastened their eyes upon their bit of candle and watched it melt slowly and pitilessly away. They saw the half inch of wick stand alone at last. They saw the feeble flame rise and fall, climb the thin column of smoke, linger at its top a moment, and then—the horror of utter darkness surrounded them! ♦

Silent Reading

1. Read the rest of the lesson to yourselves and be ready to answer some questions.

The children went to sleep. After what seemed a long stretch of time, both awoke and resumed their miseries once more. Tom said it might be Sunday, now—maybe Monday. He tried to get Becky to talk, but all her hopes were gone. Tom said the search was probably going on by now. He would shout, and maybe someone would come. He tried it, but the distant echoes sounded so hideous in the darkness that he did not shout anymore.

The hours wasted away, and hunger came to torment the captives again. A portion of Tom's cake was left. They divided it and ate it, but they seemed hungrier than before.

By and by Tom said, "Sh! Did you hear that?"

Both held their breath and listened. There was a sound like the faintest, far-off shout. Instantly, Tom answered it. Leading Becky by the hand, he started groping down the corridor in its direction.

Presently he listened again. Again the sound was heard, and apparently a little nearer.

"It's them!" said Tom. "They're coming! Come along, Becky, we're all right now!"

The joy of the prisoners was almost overwhelming. Their speed was slow, however, because pitfalls were common. They shortly came to a pitfall and had to stop. It might be three feet deep, it might be a hundred—there was no passing it, at any rate. Tom got down on his chest and reached as far as he could. No bottom. They must stay there and wait until the searchers came.

As they listened, the distant shouting grew more distant. A moment or two more and it was gone altogether. The heartsinking misery of it! Tom whooped until he was hoarse, but it was no use. He talked hopefully to Becky, but an age of anxious waiting passed, and no sounds came.

The children groped their way back to the spring. The weary time dragged on. They slept again and awoke famished. Tom believed it must be Tuesday by this time.

Now an idea struck him. There were some side passages near at hand. It would be better to explore some of these than to remain at the spring. He took a string from his pocket and tied it to a rock. Then he and Becky started down a passage. Tom was in the lead and unwound the line as he groped along. ★

At the end of twenty steps, the corridor ended in a "jumping-off place." Tom got down on his knees and felt below, and then as far around the corner as he could reach with his hands. He made an effort to stretch yet a little farther to the right, and at that moment, not twenty yards away, a human hand, holding a candle, appeared from behind a rock! Tom let out a glorious shout, and instantly that hand was followed by the body it belonged to—Outlaw Joe's!

Tom was paralyzed—he could not move. He was vastly relieved to see the outlaw take to his heels and get himself out of sight. He was amazed that Joe had not recognized his voice and come over and killed him for testifying in court. But the echoes must have disguised his voice.

Tom's fright weakened every muscle in his body. He said to himself that if he had strength enough to get back to the spring, he would stay there, and nothing would tempt him to run the risk of meeting Outlaw Joe again. He was careful not to tell Becky what he had seen. He told her he had only shouted "for luck."

But hunger is greater than fear. Another tedious wait at the spring and another long sleep brought changes. The children awoke tortured with a raging hunger. Tom believed it must be Wednesday or Thursday or even Friday or Saturday now and that the search had been given up.

Tom proposed to explore another passage. He felt willing to risk Outlaw Joe and all the other terrors. But Becky was very sick. She said she would wait, now, where she was, and die—it would not be long. She told Tom to go with the string and explore if he chose. But she begged him to come back every little while and speak to her. She made him promise that when the awful time came for her to die, he would stay by her and hold her hand until all was over.

Tom kissed her, with a choking feeling in his throat. Then he took the string in his hand and went groping down one of the passages on his hands and knees, distressed with hunger and sick with a sense of coming doom.

- Why did Tom tie a string to a rock? (Idea: *So he wouldn't get lost when he explored the cave in the dark.*) Ⓓ🄲🄴
- How did the children find the spring? (Idea: *They listened for dripping water.*) 🄲/🄴
- Why did it take so long for the search to get started? (Ideas: *Because nobody noticed Tom and Becky were missing when the steamboat left; because Mrs. Thatcher wasn't expecting Becky until Sunday.*) 🄲/🄴

- Explain why pitfalls were such a problem for Tom and Becky. (Ideas: *After their candles burned out, they couldn't see the pitfalls, which are deep holes in the ground; when they came to a pitfall, they had to stop because they didn't know how deep or wide it was.*) Ⓡ
- What do you think Outlaw Joe was doing in the cave? (Ideas: *Hiding from the sheriff; taking the treasure to his hiding place; living there.*) Ⓗ

EXERCISE 10

Paired Practice (Optional)

1. Now you'll read in pairs.
- Whoever read second the last time will read first today.
- Remember to start at the diamond and switch at the star.
2. (Observe students and answer questions as needed.)

AFTER READING

EXERCISE 11

Independent Work

1. Do all the items in your workbook and textbook for this lesson.
2. (The independent work in this lesson includes the following activities.)
- Story details
- Perspectives
- Vocabulary
- Logic
- Outlining
- Comprehension
- Writing

EXERCISE 12

Workcheck

1. (Using the Answer Key, read the questions and answers for the workbook.)
2. (Have students read their answers for the textbook activities.)
3. (Have two or three students read their writing assignments aloud. Comment on each assignment.)
4. (Have students correct and turn in their work.)

SPELLING

(Present Spelling lesson 116 after completing Reading lesson 116. See *Spelling Presentation Book.*)

BEFORE READING

(Have students find lesson 117, part A, in their textbooks.)

EXERCISE 1

Word Practice

1. Look at column 1.
- We're going to practice these words.

1. secure	4. foundry
2. security	5. groped
3. stalagmite	6. stalactite

2. Word 1. Everybody, what word? (Signal.) *Secure.*
- (Repeat this procedure for every word in the column.)
3. (Repeat the column until firm.)

EXERCISE 2

New Vocabulary

1. Look at column 2.
- First we'll read the words in this column. Then we'll read their definitions.

1. peal	4. provisions
2. clad	5. fret
3. hamlet	6. bluff

2. Word 1. Everybody, what word? (Signal.) *Peal.*
- (Repeat this procedure for every word in the column.)
3. (Repeat the column until firm.)

EXERCISE 3

Vocabulary Definitions

1. Everybody, find part B. ✔
- These are definitions for the words you just read.
2. (For each word, call on a student to read the definition and the item. Then ask the student to complete the item.)

1. **peal**—When bells *peal,* they ring loudly.
- What's another way of saying *The bells rang loudly on New Year's Day*?
- What's the answer? (Response: *The bells pealed on New Year's Day.*)

2. **clad**—*Clad* means "dressed."
- What's another way of saying *He was dressed in a swimsuit*?
- What's the answer? (Response: *He was clad in a swimsuit.*)

3. **hamlet**—A *hamlet* is a small village.
- What's another way of saying *Only a few people lived in the small village*?
- What's the answer? (Response: *Only a few people lived in the hamlet.*)

4. **provisions**—*Provisions* is another word for *food.*
- What's another way of saying *They took lots of food on their trip*?
- What's the answer? (Response: *They took lots of provisions on their trip.*)

5. **fret**—*Fret* is another word for *worry.*
- What's another way of saying *He worried about his appearance*?
- What's the answer? (Response: *He fretted about his appearance.*)

6. **bluff**—A *bluff* is a high, steep riverbank or cliff.
- What's another way of saying *The water flowed beside the high, steep riverbanks*?
- What's the answer? (Response: *The water flowed beside the bluffs.*)

Logic

1. Everybody, turn to part D at the end of today's story. ✔
- (Call on individual students to read several sentences each.)
- (At the end of each section, present the questions for that section.)

Write the answers for items 1–5.

Here's a rule of logic: *Just because you know about one part doesn't mean you know about another part.*

The following statement by a writer breaks the rule: "My friend Manuel is very honest. He belongs to the Star Society, which meets twice a week. Yesterday I met a girl named Rosa. She also belongs to the Star Society. She must be very honest, too."

1. What is the whole?

- What's the answer? (Response: *The Star Society.*)

2. What are the two parts?

- What's the answer? (Idea: *Manuel and Rosa.*)

3. Which part do you know something about?

- What's the answer? (Response: *Manuel.*)

4. Which part does the writer draw a conclusion about?

- What's the answer? (Response: *Rosa.*)

5. What does the writer conclude about that part?

- What's the answer? (Idea: *That she is honest.*)
- You'll write the answers later.

READING

Focus Question

1. Everybody, turn back to part C. ✔
2. What's the focus question for today's lesson? (Response: *How did Tom and Becky escape from the cave?*)

Reading Aloud (Optional)

1. We're going to read aloud to the diamond.
- (Call on individual students to read several sentences each.)

Chapter 27
They're Found!

Focus Question: How did Tom and Becky escape from the cave?

Tuesday afternoon came. The village of Saint Petersburg still mourned. The lost children had not been found. Public prayers had been offered up for them and also many private prayers. But still no good news came from the cave. The majority of the searchers had given up the search and gone back to their jobs, saying it was plain the children could never be found.

Mrs. Thatcher was very ill and almost insane with grief. People said it was heartbreaking to hear her call her child. She would raise her head and listen a whole minute at a time and then lay her head wearily down again with a moan. Aunt Polly had dropped into melancholy, and her gray hair had grown almost white. The village went to bed on Tuesday night, sad and forlorn.

Away in the middle of the night, a wild peal burst from the village bells, and in a moment the streets were swarming with frantic half-clad people, who shouted, "They're found! They're found!" Tin pans and horns were added to the noise. People moved toward the river and met the children, who were riding in an open carriage drawn by shouting citizens. They thronged around the carriage, joined its homeward march, and swept magnificently up the main street roaring hurrah after hurrah!

The village was all lit up. Nobody went back to bed—it was the greatest night the little town had ever seen. During the first half hour, dozens of villagers filed through Judge Thatcher's house, seized the children and kissed them, squeezed Mrs. Thatcher's hand, tried to speak but couldn't—and drifted out raining tears all over the place.

Aunt Polly's happiness was complete, and Mrs. Thatcher's nearly so. It would be complete, however, as soon as a messenger got the great news to her husband at the cave. Tom lay upon a sofa with an eager audience around him and told the history of the wonderful adventure. He did not mention Outlaw Joe. ◆

EXERCISE 7

Silent Reading

1. Read the rest of the lesson to yourselves and be ready to answer some questions.

Here is the last part of what Tom's audience heard:

Tom left Becky and went exploring. He followed two passages as far as his string would reach. He followed a third passage to the end of his string and was about to turn back when he glimpsed a far-off speck that looked like daylight. He dropped the line and groped toward the speck. He pushed his head and shoulders through a small hole and saw the broad Mississippi River rolling by! And if it had happened at night, he would not have seen that speck of daylight and would not have explored that passage any farther!

Tom went back for Becky and broke the good news. She almost died for joy when she had groped to where she actually saw the blue speck of daylight. Tom pushed his way out of the hole and then helped her out. They sat there and cried for gladness.

Some men came along in a skiff. Tom hailed them and told them their situation. The men didn't believe the wild tale at first. They said, "You are five miles down the river below the valley the cave entrance is in!"

Then the men took the children aboard, rowed to a house, gave them supper, made them rest till two or three hours after dark, and brought them home.

Before dawn, Judge Thatcher and the handful of searchers with him were tracked down in the cave, and they were informed of the great news.

Three days and nights of toil and hunger in the cave could not be shaken off at once, as Tom and Becky soon discovered. They had to rest in bed all of Wednesday and Thursday, and they seemed to grow more and more tired and worn all the time.

Tom got around a little on Thursday, was downtown Friday, and nearly completely well by Saturday. But Becky did not leave her room until Sunday, and then she looked as if she had passed through a serious illness.

Tom learned of Huck's sickness and went to see him on Saturday, but he could not be admitted to Huck's bedroom. Neither could he on Sunday. He was finally admitted on Monday.

The Widow Douglas warned Tom to keep still about his adventure and to introduce no exciting topic. And the widow stayed by to see that Tom obeyed. Tom had already learned of the events at the widow's gate. He also found out that the body of Outlaw Joe's companion had been discovered in the river near the steamboat landing—perhaps the companion had drowned while trying to escape.

• • •

About two weeks after Tom's rescue from the cave, he started off to visit Huck, who had grown strong enough, now, to hear exciting talk. Tom had some that would interest him, he thought.

Judge Thatcher's house was on Tom's way, so the boy stopped to see Becky. The judge and some friends talked with Tom. One asked Tom if he would like to go to the cave again. Tom said he wouldn't mind it. ★

The judge said, "Well, there are others just like you, Tom. But we have taken care of that. Nobody will get lost in that cave ever again."

"Why?"

"Because we've closed the cave. I had its big door lined with iron when we finished the search and triple locked—and I've got the keys."

Tom turned as white as a sheet.

"What's the matter, boy? Here, run, somebody! Fetch a glass of water!"

The water was brought and thrown into Tom's face.

"Ah, now you're all right. What was the matter with you, Tom?"

"Oh, Judge, Outlaw Joe's in the cave!"

Within a few minutes, the news had spread, and a dozen boatloads of men were on their way to McDougal's Cave. Tom Sawyer was in a boat with Judge Thatcher.

When the cave door was unlocked, a sorrowful sight could be seen in the dim twilight of the place. Outlaw Joe lay stretched upon the ground, dead, with his face close to the crack of the door. His eyes had been fixed, to the last moment, on the light and the cheer of the free world outside. Tom was touched, for he knew from his own experience how Joe had suffered. Tom pitied Outlaw Joe, but still he felt an immense sense of relief and security now. A vast weight had been lying upon him since the day he testified against the bloody-minded outlaw.

Joe's knife lay close by, its blade broken in two. The lower part of the door had been chipped and hacked through, with much labor. It was useless labor, too, for there was still a rock sill behind that part of the door. The knife had had no effect on the rock—the only damage was to the knife itself.

Even if there were no rock, the labor would still have been useless. Joe could not have squeezed his body under the door, and he knew it. So he had only hacked that place in order to be doing something—in order to pass the weary time—in order to keep himself busy.

Ordinarily, one could find half a dozen bits of candle in this part of the cave. But there were none now. The prisoner had searched them out and eaten them. He had also caught a few bats, and these, also, he had eaten, leaving only their claws. The poor man had starved to death.

In one place near at hand, a stalagmite had been slowly growing up from the ground, formed by the water-drip from a stalactite overhead. The captive had broken off the stalagmite and scooped a shallow hole to catch the precious drop of water that fell once every three minutes. There was only a spoonful of water in a whole day.

Outlaw Joe was buried near the mouth of the cave. People flocked to the funeral in boats and wagons from the town and from all the farms and hamlets for seven miles around. They brought their children, and all sorts of provisions, and they confessed they had a satisfactory time.

- How did Tom and Becky escape from the cave? (Idea: *They crawled through the opening Tom had found.*) Ⓡ
- Why was the time of day so important for the children's escape? (Idea: *If Tom had gone exploring at night, he wouldn't have seen the speck of daylight.*) ⓂⒹ
- Why did Judge Thatcher lock the door of the cave? (Idea: *He didn't want anybody to get lost in the cave ever again.*) ⒹⒸⒺ
- When do you think Outlaw Joe entered the cave? Explain your answer. (Idea: *Probably between the time Huck saw him on Saturday night and the time the search party began on Sunday. If he'd entered later, the searchers would probably have seen him.*) Ⓗ
- Do you think Outlaw Joe knew about Tom's secret entrance to the cave? Explain your answer. (Idea: *No, because he would have escaped from the cave that way if he had known.*) ⓂⒿ

EXERCISE 8
Paired Practice (Optional)

1. Now you'll read in pairs.
- Whoever read second the last time will read first today.
- Remember to start at the diamond and switch at the star.
2. (Observe students and answer questions as needed.)

AFTER READING

EXERCISE 9
Independent Work

1. Do all the items in your workbook and textbook for this lesson.
2. (The independent work in this lesson includes the following activities.)
- Story details
- Sequencing
- Vocabulary
- Logic
- Character traits
- Settings
- Vocabulary review
- Comprehension
- Writing

Workcheck

1. (Using the Answer Key, read the questions and answers for the workbook.)

2. (Have students read their answers for the textbook activities.)

3. (Have two or three students read their writing assignments aloud. Comment on each assignment.)

4. (Have students correct and turn in their work.)

(Present Spelling lesson 117 after completing Reading lesson 117. See *Spelling Presentation Book.*)

BEFORE READING

(Have students find lesson 118, part A, in their textbooks.)

EXERCISE 1
Word Practice

1. Look at column 1.
- We're going to practice these words.

1. landslide	3. adopt
2. ransom	4. furnish

2. Word 1. Everybody, what word? (Signal.) *Landslide.*
- (Repeat this procedure for every word in the column.)
3. (Repeat the column until firm.)

EXERCISE 2
New Vocabulary

1. Look at column 2.
- First we'll read the words in this column. Then we'll read their definitions.

1. gloat	5. impact
2. loft	6. quench
3. foundry	7. furnish
4. adopt	

2. Word 1. Everybody, what word? (Signal.) *Gloat.*
- (Repeat this procedure for every word in the column.)
3. (Repeat the column until firm.)

EXERCISE 3
Vocabulary Definitions

1. Everybody, find part B. ✔
- These are definitions for the words you just read.
2. (For each word, call on a student to read the definition and the item. Then ask the student to complete the item.)

1. **gloat**—When you *gloat*, you feel delight or satisfaction.
- What's another way of saying *She felt delight over her victory*?

- What's the answer? (Response: *She gloated over her victory.*)

2. **loft**—A *loft* is an attic or an upper floor of a building.
- What is a loft?

- What's the answer? (Idea: *An attic or an upper floor of a building.*)

3. **foundry**—A *foundry* is a factory that melts metal and pours it into molds.
- What is a foundry?

- What's the answer? (Idea: *A factory that melts metal and pours it into molds.*)

4. **adopt**—When people *adopt* a child, they agree to raise that child as their own.
- What's another way of saying *The Ross family agreed to raise the abandoned child as their own*?

- What's the answer? (Response: *The Ross family agreed to adopt the abandoned child.*)

5. **impact**—*Impact* is another word for *effect*.
- What's another way of saying *The experience had a great effect on me*?

- What's the answer? (Response: *The experience had a great impact on me.*)

6. **quench**—When you *quench* something, you put it out.
- What's another way of saying *He put out the fire*?

- What's the answer? (Response: *He quenched the fire.*)

7. **furnish**—When you *furnish* something, you supply it.
- What's another way of saying *Rhonda supplied tools to the carpenter?*
- What's the answer? (Response: *Rhonda furnished tools to the carpenter.*)

READING

EXERCISE 4

Focus Question

1. Everybody, find part C. ✔
2. What's the focus question for today's lesson? (Response: *Why did Tom and Huck go back to the cave?*)

EXERCISE 5

Reading Aloud (Optional)

1. We're going to read aloud to the diamond.
- (Call on individual students to read several sentences each.)

Chapter 28
Back to the Cave

Focus Question: Why did Tom and Huck go back to the cave?

The morning after Outlaw Joe's funeral, Tom took Huck to a private place to have an important talk. Huck had learned about Tom's adventure from the Welshman and the Widow Douglas. But Tom said he reckoned there was one thing they had not told Huck. That thing was what he wanted to talk about now.

Huck's face saddened. He said to Tom, "I know what it is. They never found anything but illegal whiskey at that hotel. I knew you didn't have the money because you'd have let me know some way or other. Tom, something's always told me we'd never get a hold of that treasure."

"Well, Huck, think back to the Saturday I went to the picnic. Did you watch the hotel that night?"

"Oh, yes! Why, it seems about a year ago. It was that very night that I followed Outlaw Joe to the widow's place."

"You followed him?"

"Yes—but you keep quiet. I reckon Outlaw Joe's left friends behind him, and I don't want them doing me mean tricks. If it hadn't been for me, he'd be down in Texas now, all right."

Then Huck told his entire adventure to Tom, who had only heard part of it before.

"Well," said Huck, presently, coming back to the main question, "whoever found the whiskey in Number Two found the money, too, I reckon—anyways, it's a goner for us, Tom."

"Huck, that money wasn't ever in Number Two!"

"What!" Huck searched his comrade's face. "Tom, have you got on the track of that money again?"

"Huck, it's in the cave!"

Huck's eyes blazed.

"Say it again, Tom."

"The money's in the cave!"

"Tom—honest, now—are you making fun?"

"I'm serious, Huck—just as serious as I ever was in my life. Will you go in there with me and help get it out?"

"I bet I will! I will if it's where we can blaze our way to it and not get lost."

"Huck, we can do that without the least little bit of trouble in the world."

"Good as gold! What makes you think the money's . . ."

"Huck, you just wait till we get in there. If we don't find it, I'll agree to give you my drum and everything I've got in the world."

"All right. When do we leave?"

"Right now, if you say it. Are you strong enough?"

"Is it far inside the cave? I've been on my feet a little, three or four days now, but I can't walk more than a mile, Tom—least I don't think I could."

"It's about five miles into there the way anybody but me would go, Huck. But there's a mighty shortcut. I'll take you right to it in a skiff. I'll float the skiff down there, and I'll row it back again all by myself. You needn't lift a finger."

"Let's start right off, Tom."

"All right. We'll need some bread and meat and a little bag or two and two or three kite strings and some candles." ♦

Silent Reading

1. Read the rest of the lesson to yourselves and be ready to answer some questions.

Shortly after noon, the boys borrowed a small skiff and got under way at once. When they were several miles below Cave Hollow, Tom pointed to a bluff and said, "Now, you see this bluff here looks all alike—no houses, no woods, bushes all alike. But do you see that white place up yonder where there's been a landslide? Well, that's the landmark we're going to. We'll get ashore now."

They landed.

"Now, Huck, where we're a-standing you could touch that hole I got out of with a fishing pole. See if you can find it."

Huck searched all over and found nothing. Tom proudly marched into a thick clump of bushes and said, "Here you are! Here it is, Huck. It's the snuggest hole in this country. You just keep quiet about it. All along I've been wanting to find the right place to play robbers. We've got it now, and we'll keep it quiet. We'll only let Joe Harper and Ben Rogers in. Of course, there's got to be a robbers' gang, or else there wouldn't be any style about it. Tom Sawyer's Gang—it sounds splendid, don't it, Huck?"

"Well, it does, Tom. And who'll we pretend to rob?"

"Oh, most anybody."

"And then what?"

"Then we hide them in the cave till they pay a ransom."

"What's a ransom?"

"Money! You make them raise all they can, off their friends. After you've kept them a year and it ain't raised, then you kill them. That's the general way. Only you don't kill the women. They're always beautiful and rich. You take their watches and things, but you always take your hat off and talk polite. There ain't anybody as polite as robbers—you'll see that in any book. Well, the women get to liking you, and after they've been in the cave a week or two weeks, you can't get them to leave. If you drove them out, they'd turn right around and come back. It's so in all the books."

"Why, it's great, Tom. I believe it's better than being a pirate."

"Yes, it's better in some ways, because it's close to home and circuses and all that."

By this time everything was ready. The boys entered the hole, Tom in the lead. They walked to the end of the tunnel. Then they tied their strings and moved on. A few steps brought them to the spring. ★

Tom felt a shudder quiver all through him. He showed Huck the fragment of candle perched on a lump of clay against the wall and described how he and Becky had watched the flame struggle and die.

The boys began to quiet down to whispers, now, for the stillness and gloom of the place dampened their spirits. They went on. Presently they entered and followed Tom's other corridor until they reached the "jumping-off place." The candles revealed the fact that it was not really a cliff, but only a steep clay hill twenty or thirty feet high.

Tom whispered, "Now I'll show you something, Huck."

He held his candle up and said, "Look as far around the corner as you can. Do you see that? There—on the big rock over yonder—done with candle smoke."

"Tom, it's a cross!"

"Yes. Now think back, Huck, to the time we were in the haunted house. When Outlaw Joe and that other fellow talked about hiding place Number Two, where did they say it was?"

Huck's expression was blank for a moment. Then his face brightened, and he said, "Under the cross! Number Two is under the cross!"

"Under that cross, Huck. Right there. That's where I saw Outlaw Joe poke up his candle, Huck!"

Huck stared at the cross a while, and then he said with a shaky voice, "Tom, let's git out of here!"

"What! And leave the treasure?"

"Yes—leave it. Outlaw Joe's ghost is round about here, certain."

"No, it ain't, Huck, no, it ain't. It would haunt the place where he died—away out at the mouth of the cave—five miles from here."

> "No, Tom, it wouldn't. It would hang around the money. I know the ways of ghosts, and so do you."
>
> Tom began to fear that Huck was right. But presently an idea occurred to him.
>
> "Looky-here, Huck, what fools we're making of ourselves! Outlaw Joe's ghost ain't a-going to come around where there's a cross!"
>
> The point was well taken. It had its effect.
>
> "Tom, I didn't think of that. But that's so. It's luck for us, that cross is. I reckon we'll climb down there and hunt for that box."

- Why did Tom and Huck go back to the cave? (Idea: *To look for the treasure.*) ⓓⒸⒺ
- Why did Tom think the treasure was located in the cave? (Ideas: *He saw the cross on the cave wall; he saw Outlaw Joe near the cross.*) Ⓒ⁄Ⓔ
- What did Tom plan to do with Tom Sawyer's Gang? (Idea: *Kidnap people and hold them for ransom.*) Ⓝ�Ⓓ
- Do you think Tom Sawyer's Gang would really commit crimes? Explain your answer. (Ideas: *No, because Tom and Huck are just pretending; yes, because Tom and Huck might become criminals when they grow up.*) ⓂⒿ
- Do you think Outlaw Joe's ghost would come to a place with a cross? Explain your answer. (Ideas: *No, because a cross is a sign of goodness, and Outlaw Joe was evil; no, because there's no such thing as ghosts; yes, because Outlaw Joe wouldn't be scared of a cross.*) ⓂⒿ

EXERCISE 7

Paired Practice (Optional)

1. Now you'll read in pairs.
- Whoever read second the last time will read first today.
- Remember to start at the diamond and switch at the star.
2. (Observe students and answer questions as needed.)

AFTER READING

EXERCISE 8

Independent Work

1. Do all the items in your workbook and textbook for this lesson.
2. (The independent work in this lesson includes the following activities.)
- Story details
- Comparisons
- Vocabulary
- Logic
- Literary forms
- Vocabulary review
- Comprehension
- Writing

EXERCISE 9

Workcheck

1. (Using the Answer Key, read the questions and answers for the workbook.)
2. (Have students read their answers for the textbook activities.)
3. (Have two or three students read their writing assignments aloud. Comment on each assignment.)
4. (Have students correct and turn in their work.)

SPELLING

(Present Spelling lesson 118 after completing Reading lesson 118. See *Spelling Presentation Book.*)

BEFORE READING

(Have students find lesson 119, part A, in their textbooks.)

EXERCISE 1
Hard Words

1. Look at column 1.
* These are hard words from your textbook stories.

1. initiation	**3. moccasins**
2. rind	**4. biographical**

2. Word 1 is **initiation.** Everybody, what word? (Signal.) *Initiation.*
* (Repeat this procedure for every word in the column.)
3. Let's read the words again.
4. Word 1. Everybody, what word? (Signal.) *Initiation.*
* (Repeat this procedure for every word in the column.)
5. (Repeat the column until firm.)

EXERCISE 2
Word Practice

1. Look at column 2.
* We're going to practice these words.

1. gnawed	**4. editor**
2. rubbish	**5. quench**
3. edit	

2. Word 1. Everybody, what word? (Signal.) *Gnawed.*
* (Repeat this procedure for every word in the column.)
3. (Repeat the column until firm.)

EXERCISE 3
Vocabulary Review

1. Everybody, find part B. ✔
* We're going to review these words.

2. (Call on a student to read the words in the box.)

fret	**gloat**
revives	**tedious**
impact	**clad**
furnish	**quench**
lavish	**famished**

3. (For each item, have a student read the item and say the answer.)

1. When you supply something, you �a▬▬▬ it.
* What's the answer? (Response: *Furnish.*)

2. When you worry about something, you ▬▬▬▬ about that thing.
* What's the answer? (Response: *Fret.*)

3. When you are very hungry, you are ▬▬▬▬.
* What's the answer? (Response: *Famished.*)

4. When something is boring or tiresome, it is ▬▬▬▬.
* What's the answer? (Response: *Tedious.*)

5. When you put something out, you ▬▬▬▬ it.
* What's the answer? (Response: *Quench.*)

6. Another word for *effect* is ▬▬▬▬.
* What's the answer? (Response: *Impact.*)

7. When you feel delight or satisfaction, you ▬▬▬▬.
* What's the answer? (Response: *Gloat.*)

READING

EXERCISE 4

Focus Question

1. Everybody, find part C. ✔
2. What's the focus question for today's lesson? (Response: *How did Tom and Huck surprise the adults?*)

EXERCISE 5

Reading Aloud (Optional)

1. We're going to read aloud to the diamond.
- (Call on individual students to read several sentences each.)

Chapter 29

Floods of Gold

Focus Question: How did Tom and Huck surprise the adults?

Tom went first, cutting crude steps in the clay hill as he descended. Huck followed. The boys found some blankets spread near the rock. They also found an old suspender, some bacon rind, and the well-gnawed bones of two or three birds. But there was no money box. The lads searched all around, but in vain.

Tom said, "He said under the cross. It can't be under the rock itself, because that rock sits solidly on the ground."

They searched everywhere once more and then sat down discouraged. Huck could suggest nothing.

By and by Tom said, "Looky-here, Huck, there's footprints and some candle grease on the clay on one side of the rock, but not on the other sides. Now, what's that for? I bet you the money is under the rock. I'm going to dig in the clay."

"That ain't a bad idea, Tom!" said Huck.

Tom's knife was out at once, and he had not dug four inches before he struck wood.

"Hey, Huck! You hear that?"

Huck began to dig and scratch now. Some boards were soon uncovered and removed. The boards had concealed a passage that led under the rock. Tom got into this passage and held his candle as far under the rock as he could, but he could not see to the end of the passage. He proposed to explore.

The narrow passage descended gradually. Tom followed its winding course, first to the right, then to the left, with Huck at his heels. Tom turned a short curve, by and by, and exclaimed, "My goodness, Huck, looky-here!"

It was the treasure box, sure enough, occupying a snug little cavern, along with an empty powder keg, a couple of guns in leather cases, two or three pairs of old shoes, a leather belt, and some other rubbish well soaked with water.

"Got it at last!" said Huck, plowing among the coins with his hand. "My, but we're rich, Tom!"

"Huck, I always reckoned we'd get it. It's just too good to believe, but we have got it! Say—let's not fool around here. Let's drag it out. Lemme see if I can lift the box."

It weighed about fifty pounds. Tom could lift it, but he could not carry it.

"I thought so," he said. "They carried it like it was heavy that day at the haunted house. I noticed that. I reckon I was right to think of bringing these little bags along."

The money was soon in the bags, and the boys took it up to the rock with the cross.

"Now let's fetch the guns and things," said Huck.

"No, Huck, leave them there. They're just the things to have when we go robbing. We'll keep them there all the time, and we'll hold our parties there, too. It's an awful snug place for parties."

"What parties?"

"I dunno. But robbers always have parties, and of course we've got to have them, too. Come along, Huck, we've been in here a long time. It's getting late, I reckon. I'm hungry, too. We'll eat when we get to the skiff." ♦

EXERCISE 6

Silent Reading

1. Read the rest of the lesson to yourselves and be ready to answer some questions.

Tom and Huck soon came out behind the clump of bushes, looked out, found the coast clear, and began descending to the skiff. As the sun dipped toward the horizon, they pushed out and got under way. Tom skimmed up the shore through the long twilight, chatting cheerily with Huck, and they landed shortly after dark.

"Now, Huck," said Tom, "we'll hide the money in the loft of the widow's woodshed. I'll come up in the morning, and we'll count it and divide it. Then we'll hunt up a place out in the woods to hide it. Just you lay quiet here and watch the stuff till I run and grab Benny Taylor's little wagon. I won't be gone a minute."

Tom disappeared and presently returned with the wagon. The boys put the two small sacks into the wagon, threw some old rags on top of them, and started off, dragging the wagon behind them. When they reached the Welshman's house, they stopped to rest.

Just as they were about to move on, the Welshman stepped out and said, "Hello, who's that?"

"Huck and Tom."

"Good! Come along with me, boys; you are keeping everybody waiting. Here— hurry up, trot ahead—I'll haul the wagon for you. Why, it's not as light as it looks. Got bricks in it or old metal?"

"Old metal," said Tom.

"I judged so. The boys in this town will take more trouble and fool away more time hunting up a dollar's worth of old iron to sell to the foundry. But that's human nature—hurry along, hurry along!"

The boys wanted to know what the hurry was about.

"Never mind, you'll see when we get to the Widow Douglas's."

Huck said with some worry, "Mr. Jones, we haven't been doing nothing bad."

The Welshman laughed. "Well, I don't know, Huck. I don't know about that. Ain't you and the widow good friends?"

"Yes. Well, she's been good friends to me, always."

"All right, then. What do you want to be afraid for?"

That question was not answered in Huck's mind before he found himself pushed, along with Tom, into Mrs. Douglas's living room. Mr. Jones left the wagon near the door and followed.

The place was grandly lighted, and everybody of any importance in the village was there. The Thatchers were there, the Harpers, the Rogers family, Aunt Polly, Sid, the minister, the editor, and a great many more, and they were all dressed in their best clothes.

The widow received the boys as heartily as anyone could receive two ragged beings. The boys were covered with clay and candle wax. Aunt Polly blushed, and she frowned and shook her head at Tom. Nobody suffered half as much as the two boys did, however.

The Welshman said, "Tom wasn't at home yet, so I gave up; but I stumbled on him and Huck right at my door, and so I just brought them along in a hurry."

"And you did just right," said the widow. "Come with me, boys."

She took them to a bedroom and said, "Now wash and dress yourselves. Here are two new suits of clothes—shirts, socks, everything complete. They belong to Huck—I bought one suit, and the Welshman bought the other. But they'll fit both of you. Get into them. We'll wait. Come down when you are slicked up enough." ★

Then the widow left.

Huck said, "Tom, we can run off, if we can find a rope. The window ain't high from the ground."

"Shucks, what do you want to run off for?"

"Well, I ain't used to that kind of a crowd. I can't stand it. I ain't going down there, Tom."

"Oh, it ain't anything. I don't mind it a bit. I'll take care of you."

Sid appeared. "Tom," he said, "Auntie has been waiting for you all afternoon. She got your Sunday clothes ready, and everybody's been fretting about you. Say—ain't this grease and clay on your clothes?"

"Now, Mr. Siddy, you just tend to your own business. What's all this about?"

"It's one of the widow's parties that she's always having. Seems she's going to make some kind of announcement about Huck. I don't know what it's all about."

Some minutes later the widow's guests were at the supper table. A dozen children were propped up at little side tables in the same room. The guests began to eat. At the proper time, the Widow Douglas rose up to make her announcement.

The widow said, "As you know, I have been taking care of Huck for the past few weeks. I have become very fond of him, and I have decided to adopt him."

Huck's jaw dropped. He could say nothing. The other guests were excited by this news.

The widow continued to speak. She heaped so many compliments upon Huck that he almost forgot the discomfort of his new clothes in the discomfort of her praise.

The widow said she meant to give Huck a home under her roof and have him educated. When she could spare the money, she would start him in business in a modest way. Tom's chance had come.

Tom said, "Huck don't need any money. Huck's rich!"

Nothing but the good manners of the company kept back a laugh at this pleasant joke. But the silence was a little awkward. Tom broke it.

"Huck's got money. Maybe you don't believe it, but he's got lots of it. Oh, you needn't smile—I reckon I can show you. You just wait a minute."

Tom ran out. The company looked at each other with a perplexed interest.

"Sid, what ails Tom?" said Aunt Polly. "He—well, I can't ever figure that boy out. I never . . ."

Tom entered, struggling with the weight of the sacks, and Aunt Polly did not finish her sentence.

Tom poured the mass of yellow coins onto the table and said, "There . . . what did I tell you? Half of it's Huck's, and half of it's mine!"

The scene took everybody's breath away. All gazed, and nobody spoke for a moment. Then there was a general call for an explanation. Tom said he could furnish it, and he did. The tale was long but full of interest. There was not a single interruption to break its flow.

When Tom had finished, the Widow Douglas said, "I thought I had fixed up a little surprise for this occasion, but this surprise makes mine seem mighty small."

The money was counted. The sum amounted to a little over twelve thousand dollars. It was more than anyone present had ever seen at one time before.

- How did Tom and Huck surprise the adults? (Idea: *Tom and Huck showed the adults the treasure.*) Ⓝ Ⓓ
- How did Tom figure out where to dig for the treasure in the cave? (Idea: *He saw footprints and candle grease on one side of the rock under the cross.*) Ⓒ/Ⓔ
- At first, why did the Welshman think the treasure was just a pile of old metal? (Ideas: *Because the boys were hauling it around in sacks; because he didn't expect the boys to be hauling treasure.*) Ⓓ Ⓒ Ⓔ
- Why did the Widow Douglas want to adopt Huck? (Ideas: *She had grown fond of him; she wanted to do him a favor; she wanted a child of her own.*) Ⓓ Ⓒ Ⓔ
- Do you think Huck will like living with the Widow Douglas? Explain your answer. (Ideas: *No, because she'll tell him what to do and he won't be free anymore; yes, because he'll be living in comfort.*) Ⓟ

Paired Practice (Optional)

1. Now you'll read in pairs.
- Whoever read second the last time will read first today.
- Remember to start at the diamond and switch at the star.
2. (Observe students and answer questions as needed.)

AFTER READING

Independent Work

1. Do all the items in your workbook and textbook for this lesson.

2. (The independent work in this lesson includes the following activities.)
- Story details
- Vocabulary
- Perspectives
- Logic
- Comprehension
- Writing

(Present Spelling lesson 119 after completing Reading lesson 119. See *Spelling Presentation Book*.)

EXERCISE 9

Workcheck

1. (Using the Answer Key, read the questions and answers for the workbook.)
2. (Have students read their answers for the textbook activities.)
3. (Have two or three students read their writing assignments aloud. Comment on each assignment.)
4. (Have students correct and turn in their work.)

BEFORE READING

(Have students find lesson 120, part A, in their textbooks.)

EXERCISE 1
Word Practice

1. Look at column 1.
- We're going to practice these words.

1. glorified	**4. respectable**
2. initiation	**5. biography**
3. tranquil	**6. biographical**

2. Word 1. Everybody, what word? (Signal.) *Glorified.*
- (Repeat this procedure for every word in the column.)
3. (Repeat the column until firm.)

EXERCISE 2
Vocabulary Review

1. Everybody, find part B. ✔
- We're going to review these words.
2. (Call on a student to read the words in the box.)

impact	quenched
tedious	gloat
fret	peal
clad	

3. (For each item, have a student read the item and say the answer.)

1. When you feel delight or satisfaction, you ▊▊▊.
- What's the answer? (Response: *Gloat.*)

2. Another word for *effect* is ▊▊▊.
- What's the answer? (Response: *Impact.*)

3. When bells ring loudly, they ▊▊▊.
- What's the answer? (Response: *Peal.*)

4. When something is put out, it is ▊▊▊.
- What's the answer? (Response: *Quenched.*)

READING

EXERCISE 3
Focus Question

1. Everybody, find part C. ✔
2. What's the focus question for today's lesson? (Response: *How did Tom convince Huck to be respectable?*)

Note: The "Reading Aloud" exercise is recommended for this lesson.

EXERCISE 4
Reading Aloud

1. We're going to read aloud to the diamond.
- (Call on individual students to read several sentences each.)

Chapter 30

Respectable Huck Joins the Gang

Focus Question: How did Tom convince Huck to be respectable?

Tom and Huck's fortune made a mighty stir in the poor little village of Saint Petersburg. So vast a sum, all in actual cash, seemed next to incredible. It was talked about, gloated over, and glorified. Every "haunted" house in the village and the neighboring villages was taken apart plank by plank and its foundations dug up and searched for hidden treasure—and not by boys, but by men.

Wherever Tom and Huck appeared, they were courted, admired, stared at. The boys could not remember that their remarks had had any impact before. But now their sayings were treasured and repeated. Everything they did seemed somehow remarkable, and they had evidently lost the power of doing common things. The village paper even published biographical sketches of them.

The Widow Douglas put Huck's money in the bank, and Aunt Polly did the same for Tom. Each lad had an income, now, that was simply amazing—a dollar for every day of the year. It was just what the minister got. A dollar and a quarter a week would board, lodge, and school a boy in those old simple days—and clothe him and wash him, too, for that matter.

Judge Thatcher had a high opinion of Tom. He said no common boy would ever have got his daughter out of the cave. When Becky told her father how Tom had taken her punishment at school, the judge was visibly moved. He hoped Tom would become a great lawyer someday. He said Tom should be admitted to the best law school in the country.

The Widow Douglas introduced Huck into society—no, dragged him into society, hurled him into society—and his sufferings were almost more than he could bear. The widow's servants kept him clean and neat, combed and brushed. They put him to bed nightly in sheets that had not one little spot or wrinkle. He had to eat with a knife and a fork; he had to use a napkin, a cup, and a plate; he had to learn to read the Bible; and he had to go to church. He had to talk so properly that speech became ridiculous in his mouth. Wherever he turned, civilization shut him in and bound him hand and foot. ♦

EXERCISE 5

Silent Reading

1. Read the rest of the lesson to yourselves and be ready to answer some questions.

Huck bravely endured his miseries for three weeks, and then one day he turned up missing. For forty-eight hours the widow hunted for him everywhere in great distress. The public were profoundly concerned; they searched high and low; they dragged the river for his body.

Early the third morning, Tom Sawyer wisely went poking among some old empty barrels down behind the slaughterhouse, and he found Huck in one of them. Huck had slept there. He had just breakfasted upon some stolen odds and ends of food and was resting, now, in comfort. He was unwashed, uncombed, and clad in the same old ruin of rags that he had in the days when he was free and happy.

Tom told him the trouble he had been causing and urged him to go home. Huck's face lost its tranquil look.

Huck said, "Don't talk about it, Tom. I've tried it, and it don't work; it don't work, Tom. It ain't for me. I ain't used to it. The widow's good to me, and friendly, but I can't stand her ways. She makes me get up just at the same time every morning. She makes me wash, and the servants comb me all to thunder. She won't let me sleep in the woodshed. I got to wear them blamed clothes that just smothers me, Tom. They don't seem to let any air get through 'em, somehow. And they're so rotten nice that I can't sit down nor lay down nor roll around anywhere. I ain't slid on a hill for . . . well, it appears to be years. I got to go to church and sweat and sweat—I hate them endless sermons! I can't catch a fly in there. I got to wear shoes all Sunday. The widow eats by a bell; she goes to bed by a bell; she gets up by a bell—everything's so awful regular a body can't stand it!"

"Well, everybody does it that way, Huck."

"Tom, it don't make no difference. I ain't everybody, and I can't stand it. It's awful to be tied up so. And food comes too easy—I don't take no interest in food that way. I got to ask to go a-fishing; I got to ask to go in a-swimming—darned if I ain't got to ask to do everything. The widow wouldn't let me yell nor stretch nor scratch before folks. I never see such a woman! I had to leave, Tom, I just had to. And besides, that school's going to open, and I'd have to go to it—well, I wouldn't stand that, Tom."

Huck continued. "Looky-here, Tom, being rich ain't what it's cracked up to be. It's just worry and worry and sweat and sweat and a-wishing you was dead all the time. Now these clothes suits me, and this barrel suits me, and I ain't ever going to shake them anymore. Tom, I wouldn't ever have got into all this trouble if it hadn't been for that money. You just take my share of it along with yours, and gimme a dime sometimes—and you go apologize to the widow for me." ★

"Oh, Huck, you know I can't do that. It ain't fair; and besides, if you'll try this thing just a while longer, you'll come to like it."

"Like it! Yes . . . the way I'd like a hot stove if I was to sit on it long enough. No, Tom, I won't be rich, and I won't live in them cussed houses. I like the woods and the river and the barrels, and I'll stick to them, too. Blame it all! Just when we'd got guns and a cave and all just fixed to rob, here this darn foolishness has got to come up and spoil it all!"

Tom saw his opportunity. "Looky-here, Huck, being rich ain't going to keep me back from turning robber."

"No! Are you serious, Tom?"

"Just as serious as I'm sitting here. But, Huck, we can't let you into the gang if you ain't respectable, you know."

Huck's joy was quenched.

"Can't let me in, Tom? Tom, ain't you always been friendly to me? You wouldn't shut me out, would you, Tom? You wouldn't do that, now, would you, Tom?"

"Huck, I wouldn't want to, and I don't want to but what would people say? Why, they'd say, 'Humph! Tom Sawyer's Gang! Pretty low characters in it!' They'd mean you, Huck. You wouldn't like that, and I wouldn't."

Huck was silent for some time. He was engaged in a mental struggle. Finally he said, "Well, I'll go back to the widow for a month and tackle it and see if I can come to stand it, if you'll let me belong to the gang, Tom."

"All right, Huck, it's a deal! Come along, and I'll ask the widow to go easy on you, Huck."

"Will you, Tom—now will you? That's good. I hope she'll go easy on some of the roughest things. When are you going to start the gang and turn robbers?"

"Oh, right away. We'll get the boys together and have the initiation tonight, maybe."

"Have the which?"

"Have the initiation."

"What's that?"

"It's to swear to stand by one another and never tell the gang's secrets, even if you're chopped to bits, and stick up for all the members of the gang."

"That's great—that's great, Tom, I tell you."

"Well, I bet it is. And all that swearing's got to be done at midnight, in the lonesomest, awfulest place you can find— a haunted house is the best, but they're all ripped up, now."

"Well, midnight's good, anyway, Tom."

"Yes, so it is. And you've got to swear on a coffin and sign it with blood."

"Now, that's more like it! Why, it's a million times better than pirating. I'll stay with the widow till I rot, Tom; and if I get to be a famous robber, and everybody talking about me, I reckon she'll be proud she snaked me in out of the wet!"

- How did Tom convince Huck to become respectable? (Idea: *Tom said Huck couldn't join the gang unless Huck was respectable.*) Ⓢⓤⓜ
- Why do you think people treasured and repeated the boys' comments? (Idea: *Because the boys were rich.*) ⒹⒸⒺ
- Why did Huck run away from the Widow Douglas? (Ideas: *She took away his freedom; she tried to civilize him; she tried to tell him what to do.*) ⒹⒸⒺ
- The story says that when Huck stayed with the Widow Douglas "civilization shut him in and bound him hand and foot." Explain what that statement means. (Ideas: *Huck was a prisoner of civilization; Huck couldn't control his own life; Huck had no freedom.*) Ⓤ ⒸⒸⓂ
- Do you think Tom would ever run away from Aunt Polly? Explain your answer. (Ideas: *No, because Tom likes being civilized and just likes to break rules once in a while; yes, because Tom might decide he wants to be as free as Huck.*) Ⓟ

Interpretation

1. (Lead students in a general discussion of the novel, focusing on the characters of Tom and Huck and on the power of imagination. Use the following questions as a guide.)

2. Why did Huck have such a hard time living with the Widow Douglas? (Idea: *Because she tried to civilize him; because she took away his freedom; because he wasn't used to rules.*) (DCE)

• When Huck runs away, the story says he was "clad in the same old ruin of rags that he had in the days when he was free and happy." Do you think Huck was really free and happy before he moved in with the widow? Explain your answer. (Ideas: *Yes, because he could do whatever he wanted; no, because he had no money.*) (MJ)

• Do you think Tom would have a hard time living with the Widow Douglas? Explain your answer. (Ideas: *No, because he knows about civilization from living with Aunt Polly; yes, because the Widow Douglas is stricter than Aunt Polly.*) (MJ)

3. In what ways are Tom and Huck alike? (Ideas: *Both are superstitious; both collect things; both love playing games; both are full of adventure.*) (C/C)

• In what ways are Tom and Huck different? (Ideas: *Tom is civilized, but Huck isn't; Tom is a good liar, but Huck isn't; Tom likes girls, but Huck doesn't.*) (C/C)

• Which character do you admire more? Why? (Ideas: *Huck, because he's free and honest; Tom, because he's smart and imaginative.*) (MJ)

4. Why do you think the boys had so many superstitions? (Ideas: *Because they were young; because they believed the world was filled with magic; because superstitions are more fun than facts.*) (MJ)

• Many of the boys' beliefs about buried treasure and ghosts seemed to come true. Why do you think they came true? (Ideas: *Because beliefs do come true; because anything can happen in a story; because of luck.*) (MJ)

• How are the grown-ups in the novel different from the children? (Ideas: *The grown-ups set the rules, but the children break them; the grown-ups are civilized, but the children want to be free; some of the grown-ups are evil, but all the children are good; the children have lots of imagination, but the grown-ups don't have any; the children have fun, but the grown-ups just work.*) (C/C)

Paired Practice (Optional)

1. Now you'll read in pairs.
• Whoever read second the last time will read first today.
• Remember to start at the diamond and switch at the star.
2. (Observe students and answer questions as needed.)

AFTER READING

Independent Work

1. Do all the items in your workbook and textbook for this lesson.
2. (The independent work in this lesson includes the following activities.)
• Story details
• Vocabulary
• Logic
• Perspectives
• Outlining
• Comprehension
• Writing

Workcheck

1. (Using the Answer Key, read the questions and answers for the workbook.)
2. (Have students read their answers for the textbook activities.)
3. (Have two or three students read their writing assignments aloud. Comment on each assignment.)
4. (Have students correct and turn in their work.)

(The Lesson 120 Mastery Test should be administered after students complete lesson 120. See *Curriculum-Based Assessment and Fluency Teacher Handbook* for details.)

(Present Spelling lesson 120 after completing Reading lesson 120. See *Spelling Presentation Book.*)

ACTIVITIES ACROSS THE CURRICULUM

(Students should complete the appropriate project in *Activities across the Curriculum* after completing lesson 120. See *Activities across the Curriculum* book for details.)

Grade 5 Reading

Curriculum Map

	1	2	3	4	5
Word Attack/Vocabulary					
Word Attack/Word Analysis					
Modeled Words	3, 4	1, 2	1, 2	1	1
Words with endings: *ed, ly, er, y, ing, s*					
Compound Words					
Mixed Words/Review	5	3	3	2, 3	2, 3
Vocabulary					
New Vocabulary	6, 7	4, 5	4, 5	4, 5	4, 5
Vocabulary Preview					
Vocabulary from Context					
Vocabulary Review	IW	IW	IW	IW	IW
Fluency Read wordlists accurately, fluently	3, 4, 5, 6	1, 2, 3, 4	1, 2, 3, 4	1, 2, 3, 4	1, 2, 3, 4
Story Reading/Comprehension					
Read/reread decodable text	8, 9, 10	6, 7	6, 7	6, 7	6, 7
Teacher models fluency/expression					
Comprehension					
Predict/Confirm Prediction		6.3			
Recall facts/rules	8, 9, 10, IW	6, 7, IW	6, 7, IW	6, 7, IW	6, 7, IW
Note details	8, 9, 10, 12, IW	6, 7, 9, IW	6, 7, IW	6, 7, IW	6, 7, IW
Visualize					
Make Connections	8.3, 12		9	9	7
Draw inferences	9.2, 9.3, 9.4	7	6		7
Draw conclusions	10, IW	6.4, IW	8, 9		7
Activate Prior Knowledge	8.2, 9.2, 9.4	6.3, 9	6.1, 6.3	6	7, 9
Identify Cause/Effect			7, IW		IW
Determine Character, Emotion, Motivation	9.3, 10, IW	IW	7, IW	7, IW	7
Compare/Contrast				IW	
Make Judgments	10, IW	6.4	7, 9	9	7, 9, IW
Main Idea	8				
Sequencing	IW	6.2, IW	IW		
Study Skills					
Interpret chart/graph/visual aid			IW	6, IW	6, IW
Informal Assessment					
Ongoing comprehension check	8, 9, 10, IW	6, 7, IW	6, 7, IW	6, 7	6, 7
Ongoing decoding accuracy	8, 9	6	6	6	6
Spelling					
Phonograms					
Word Families					
Multisyllabic Words		1	1, 2	1, 2	
Word Parts	2	1	1	1	1
Spelling Rules					
Homonyms					
Antonyms					
Synonyms	7	5	5	5	5
Morphemic Analysis	4	2	2		1
Spelling Strategies					
Word Origins					
Review	5	3	3	2, 3	2, 3
Paired Practice for Fluency					
Ongoing practice to build fluency	11	8	8	8	8
Independent Work / Workcheck					
Ongoing Informal Assessment	14, 15	11, 12	11	11	11
Formal Assessment					
Individual Fluency Checkout					
Mastery Test					
Spelling Test					

Key: (for Teachers)   Ex 2.1 = Exercise 2, Column 1   IT = Individual Turns   IW = Independent Work

	6	7	8	9	10
Word Attack/Vocabulary					
Word Attack/Word Analysis					
Modeled Words	1	1	1	1	1
Words with endings: *ed, ly, er, y, ing, s*					
Compound Words					
Mixed Words/Review	2	2	2		2
Vocabulary					
New Vocabulary	3, 4	3, 4	3, 4	2, 3	3, 4
Vocabulary Preview					
Vocabulary from Context					
Vocabulary Review	IW	IW	IW	IW	IW
Fluency Read wordlists accurately, fluently	1, 2, 3	1, 2, 3	1, 2, 3	1, 2	1, 2, 3
Story Reading/Comprehension					
Read/reread decodable text	5, 6	5, 6	5, 6	4, 5	5, 6
Teacher models fluency/expression					
Comprehension					
Predict/Confirm Prediction		5, 6, IW		4, 5	
Recall facts/rules	5, 6, IW	5, 6, IW	5, 6, IW	4, 5, IW	5, 6, IW
Note details	5, 6, IW	5, 6, IW	5, 6, IW	4, 5, IW	5, 6, IW
Visualize				IW	
Make Connections	8	8	5, 8	7, IW	8
Draw inferences	5.3	6	5, 6, 8		5.2, 6
Draw conclusions			6, 8	4.3, 5	6
Activate Prior Knowledge	6	6	5.2, 6	IW	8
Identify Cause/Effect		6			
Determine Character, Emotion, Motivation	8, IW	5.2, 5.3, IW	8, IW		5, 6
Compare/Contrast					
Make Judgments	5.3, IW	5.2	6, 8, IW	4, 5, IW	5, 6, IW
Main Idea					
Sequencing		IW	IW		
Figurative Language			5		
Study Skills					
Interpret chart/graph/visual aid	5, IW	5.1	5.3, IW	IW	IW
Informal Assessment					
Ongoing comprehension check	5, 6, IW	5, 6, IW	5, 6, IW	4, 5, IW	5, 6, IW
Ongoing decoding accuracy	5	5	5	4	5
Spelling					
Phonograms					
Word Families					
Multisyllabic Words					
Word Parts	1	1, 2	1	2	1
Spelling Rules					
Homonyms					
Antonyms					
Synonyms	4	3	4	3	4
Morphemic Analysis			1	1	
Spelling Strategies					
Word Origins					
Review	2	2	2		2
Paired Practice for Fluency					
Ongoing practice to build fluency	7	7	7	6	7
Independent Work / Workcheck					
Ongoing Informal Assessment	10	10	10	9	10
Formal Assessment					
Individual Fluency Checkout					Lesson 10 Mastery Test
Mastery Test					Lesson 10 Mastery Test
Spelling Test					Lesson 10 Test

Key: (for Teachers)   Ex 2.1 = Exercise 2, Column 1   IT = Individual Turns   IW = Independent Work

	11	12	13	14	15
Word Attack/Vocabulary					
Word Attack/Word Analysis					
Modeled Words	1		1	1	1
Words with endings: *ed, ly, er, y, ing, s*	1, 3	1, 2	1	2, 3	
Compound Words		1			
Mixed Words/Review	2	1	2	2	2
Vocabulary					
New Vocabulary	3, 4	2, 3	3, 4	3, 4	3, 4
Vocabulary Preview					
Vocabulary from Context					
Vocabulary Review	IW	IW	IW	IW	IW
Fluency Read wordlists accurately, fluently	1, 2, 3	1, 2	1, 2, 3	1, 2, 3	1, 2, 3
Story Reading/Comprehension					
Read/reread decodable text	5, 6	4, 5	5, 6	5, 6	6, 7
Teacher models fluency/expression					
Comprehension					
Predict/Confirm Prediction		4.2			7
Recall facts/rules	5, 6, IW	4, 5, IW	5, 6, IW	5, 6, IW	6, 7, IW
Note details	5, 6, IW	4, 5, IW	5, 6, IW	5, 6, IW	6, 7, IW
Visualize					
Make Connections	IW				
Draw inferences	6	4.2, 5	5, 6	5.2	6, 7
Draw conclusions			IW	5.2	5.1
Activate Prior Knowledge	6, IW	5	5, 6, IW	6	
Identify Cause/Effect					
Determine Character, Emotion, Motivation	IW	5, IW	5, 6, IW	IW	IW
Compare/Contrast	5, IW			5.3, 6	6.2, IW
Make Judgments	6, IW	4, 5, IW	5, 6, IW	5.3	6, IW
Main Idea					5
Sequencing	IW		5.1	IW	5
Study Skills					
Interpret chart/graph/visual aid		IW	IW		IW
Informal Assessment					
Ongoing comprehension check	5, 6, IW	4, 5, IW	5, 6, IW	5, 6, IW	6, 7, IW
Ongoing decoding accuracy	5	4	5	5	6
Spelling					
Phonograms					
Word Families					
Multisyllabic Words	1, 3	3	3	4	4
Word Parts			1	1	1
Spelling Rules		1	2	2	2
Homonyms					
Antonyms					
Synonyms	4	3	4	4	4
Morphemic Analysis					1
Spelling Strategies					
Word Origins					
Review	2	1	2	2	2
Paired Practice for Fluency					
Ongoing practice to build fluency	7	6	7	7	8
Independent Work / Workcheck					
Ongoing Informal Assessment	9	8	9	9	10
Formal Assessment					
Individual Fluency Checkout					
Mastery Test					
Spelling Test					

	16	17	18	19	20
Word Attack/Vocabulary					
Word Attack/Word Analysis					
Modeled Words	1				
Words with endings: *ed, ly, er, y, ing, s*	2, 3				
Compound Words			1		
Mixed Words/Review	2	1	1	1	
Vocabulary					
New Vocabulary	3, 4	2, 3, 4	2	2, 3	
Vocabulary Preview					
Vocabulary from Context					
Vocabulary Review	IW	IW	IW	4, IW	
Fluency Read wordlists accurately, fluently	1, 2, 3	1, 2	1	1, 2, 3	
Story Reading/Comprehension					
Read/reread decodable text	6, 7	5, 6	3, 4	6, 7	2, 3
Teacher models fluency/expression					
Comprehension					
Predict/Confirm Prediction		5.1		6	
Recall facts/rules	6, 7, IW	5, 6, IW	3, 4, IW	6, 7, IW	2, 3, IW
Note details	6, 7, IW	6, IW	3, 4, IW	6, 7, IW	2, 3, IW
Visualize					
Make Connections					3.5, IW
Draw inferences		6.4, IW		7	
Draw conclusions	6.1, 7	5, 6.5	3, 4	6.2, 7	2
Activate Prior Knowledge	6.1	4, 6.4	2, 3		
Identify Cause/Effect			4		
Determine Character, Emotion, Motivation	6, 7, IW	5.2	3	IW	3.5, IW
Compare/Contrast	6.2, IW	6.5	3	7	
Make Judgments	6.2, 7, IW	6.4, IW	IW	7, IW	2, 3.4
Main Idea	5, IW	IW	IW	IW	IW
Sequencing	5, IW	IW			IW
Study Skills					
Interpret chart/graph/visual aid			IW		
Outlining				5, IW	1, IW
Informal Assessment					
Ongoing comprehension check	6, 7, IW	5, 6, IW	3, 4, IW	6, 7, IW	2, 3, IW
Ongoing decoding accuracy	6	5	3	6	2
Spelling					
Phonograms					
Word Families					
Multisyllabic Words	1				
Word Parts					
Spelling Rules				2	
Homonyms					
Antonyms					
Synonyms	4	3		3, 4	
Morphemic Analysis					
Spelling Strategies					
Word Origins					
Review	2		1	3	
Paired Practice for Fluency					
Ongoing practice to build fluency	8	7	5	8	4
Independent Work / Workcheck					
Ongoing Informal Assessment	10	9	7	10	6
Formal Assessment					
Individual Fluency Checkout					Lesson 20 Mastery Test
Mastery Test					Lesson 20 Mastery Test
Spelling Test					Lesson 20 Test

290 Lessons 16–20   Key: (for Teachers)   Ex 2.1 = Exercise 2, Column 1   IT = Individual Turns   IW = Independent Work

	21	22	23	24	25
Word Attack/Vocabulary					
Word Attack/Word Analysis					
Modeled Words	1, 3		1		1, 2
Words with endings: *ed, ly, er, y, ing, s*		2	1		
Compound Words	1, 2	1	1		
Mixed Words/Review	2	1	1	1	
Vocabulary					
New Vocabulary		2, 3	2, 3	2, 3	3, 4
Vocabulary Preview					
Vocabulary from Context					
Vocabulary Review		IW	IW	IW	IW
Fluency Read wordlists accurately, fluently	1, 2, 3	1, 2	1, 2	1, 2	1, 2, 3
Story Reading/Comprehension					
Read/reread decodable text	6, 7	4, 5	5, 6	4, 5	6, 7
Teacher models fluency/expression					
Comprehension					
Predict/Confirm Prediction		5, IIW		5, IW	
Recall facts/rules	5, 6, 7, IW	5, IW	4, 6, IW	5, IW	7, IW
Note details	6, 7, IW	5, IW	6, IW	5, IW	7, IW
Visualize				IW	
Make Connections	6.1, IW		IW		8, IW
Draw inferences	6.3	5	6	5	7, 8
Draw conclusions	6.3	5	6	5	
Activate Prior Knowledge	6.1, IW	IW	6, IW		IW
Identify Cause/Effect					
Determine Character, Emotion, Motivation	IW	IW	IW	5, IW	
Compare/Contrast	6.3, 7				7, 8
Make Judgments	6.3, IW	5, IW	6, IW	5	7, 8, IW
Main Idea			IW	IW	
Sequencing	7		IW		
Identify relevant information	5, IW	IW	4, IW	IW	5, IW
Contradictions					
Make deductions	7				8
Study Skills					
Interpret chart/graph/visual aid	3, 4		IW		
Outlining	IW	IW			IW
Informal Assessment					
Ongoing comprehension check	5, 6, 7, IW	5, IW	6, IW	5, IW	7, 8
Ongoing decoding accuracy	6	4	5	4	6
Spelling					
Phonograms					
Word Families					
Multisyllabic Words	1		3	3	2, 3
Word Parts	1	1	1, 2	1, 2	1, 2
Spelling Rules			3	3	
Homonyms					
Antonyms					
Synonyms		3	3	3	4
Morphemic Analysis		12			1
Spelling Strategies					
Word Origins					
Review	2	1	1	1	1
Paired Practice for Fluency					
Ongoing practice to build fluency	8	6	7	6	9
Independent Work / Workcheck					
Ongoing Informal Assessment	10	8	9	8	11
Formal Assessment					
Individual Fluency Checkout					
Mastery Test					
Spelling Test					

	26	27	28	29	30
Word Attack/Vocabulary					
Word Attack/Word Analysis					
Modeled Words	1	1	1	1	1
Words with endings: *ed, ly, er, y, ing, s*			2		
Compound Words					
Mixed Words/Review	2	2	2	2	
Vocabulary					
New Vocabulary	3, 4	3, 4	3, 4	3, 4	2, 3
Vocabulary Preview					
Vocabulary from Context					
Vocabulary Review	IW	IW	IW	IW	IW
Fluency Read wordlists accurately, fluently	1, 2, 3	1, 2, 3	1, 2, 3	1, 2, 3	1, 2
Story Reading/Comprehension					
Read/reread decodable text	5, 7, 8	7, 8	6, 7	5, 7, 8	6, 7
Teacher models fluency/expression					
Comprehension					
Predict/Confirm Prediction	8, IW	IW		IW	
Recall facts/rules	5, 6, 8, IW	5, 6, 8, IW	5, 7, IW	5, 6, 7, 8, IW	4, 7, IW
Note details	5, 6, 8, IW	6, 8, IW	7, IW	5, 6, 7, 8, IW	4, 7, IW
Visualize					
Make Connections	IW	IW		IW	
Draw inferences	8			7	7, IW
Draw conclusions	8			7	7
Activate Prior Knowledge			IW	5	
Identify Cause/Effect				7	
Determine Character, Emotion, Motivation		IW	IW	7, IW	
Compare/Contrast			7		5, IW
Make Judgments		8, IW	IW	7, IW	IW
Main Idea		IW	9, IW		
Sequencing					
Identify Relevant Information	IW	5, IW	9, IW	IW	IW
Contradictions					
Make Deductions					
Study Skills					
Interpret chart/graph/visual aid	5, IW			5	
Outlining	IW				IW
Informal Assessment					
Ongoing comprehension check	5, 8, IW	8, IW	7, IW	5, 7, 8, IW	7, IW
Ongoing decoding accuracy	7	7	6	7	6
Spelling					
Phonograms					
Word Families					
Multisyllabic Words	2, 3	2	2	1, 2	1, 2
Word Parts	1, 2	1, 2	1, 2	1, 2	1
Spelling Rules		1			
Homonyms					
Antonyms					
Synonyms	4	4	4	4	4
Morphemic Analysis	1, 2	1, 2	1, 2	1	1
Spelling Strategies					
Word Origins					
Review					
Paired Practice for Fluency					
Ongoing practice to build fluency	9	9	8	9	8
Independent Work / Workcheck					
Ongoing Informal Assessment	11	11	10	11	10
Formal Assessment					
Fluency: Rate/Accuracy					Lesson 30 Mastery Test
Mastery Test					Lesson 30 Mastery Test
Spelling Test					Lesson 30 Test

292 Lessons 26–30   Key: (for Teachers)   Ex 2.1 = Exercise 2, Column 1   IT = Individual Turns   IW = Independent Work

	31	32	33	34	35
Word Attack/Vocabulary					
Word Attack/Word Analysis					
Modeled Words	1	1	1	1	1
Words with endings: *ed, ly, er, y, ing, s*			1		2
Compound Words	2				
Mixed Words/Review	2	2	2		
Vocabulary					
New Vocabulary	3, 4	3, 4	3, 4	2, 3	2, 3
Vocabulary Preview					
Vocabulary from Context					
Vocabulary Review	IW	IW	IW	IW	IW
Fluency Read wordlists accurately, fluently	1, 2, 3	1, 2, 3	1, 2, 3	1, 2	1, 2
Story Reading/Comprehension					
Read/reread decodable text	5, 7, 8	7, 8	7, 8	6, 7	5, 7, 8
Teacher models fluency/expression					
Comprehension					
Predict/Confirm Prediction	8				
Recall facts/rules	5, 6, IW	6, 8, IW	6, 8, IW	5, 7, IW	5, 6, 8
Note details	5, 6, IW	8, IW	6, 8, IW	5, 7, IW	5, 6, 8
Visualize					
Make Connections	IW	IW			5
Draw inferences		IW	8	7	
Draw conclusions					8
Activate Prior Knowledge	IW	IW	IW	IW	5, IW
Identify Cause/Effect					
Determine Character, Emotion, Motivation	IW	IW		7, IW	
Compare/Contrast			8, IW		IW
Make Judgments	8.2, IW		IW		
Main Idea		IW			IW
Sequencing				IW	IW
Identify relevant information			IW		IW
Contradictions		5, IW	5, IW	4, IW	4, IW
Make Deductions	8.2				
Figurative Language			8		
Study Skills					
Interpret chart/graph/visual aid					
Outlining	IW			IW	
Informal Assessment					
Ongoing comprehension check	5, 8, IW	8, IW	8, IW	7, IW	5, 8, IW
Ongoing decoding accuracy	7	7	7	6	5, 60
Spelling					
Phonograms					
Word Families					
Multisyllabic Words	3	1, 3	1	1, 2	
Word Parts	1	1, 3	1	1, 2	
Spelling Rules		1			1
Homonyms					
Antonyms					
Synonyms	4	4	4	4	4
Morphemic Analysis	1	2	1, 2	2	2
Spelling Strategies					
Word Origins					
Review					
Paired Practice for Fluency					
Ongoing practice to build fluency	9	9	9	8	9
Independent Work / Workcheck					
Ongoing Informal Assessment	11	11	11	10	11
Formal Assessment					
Individual Fluency Checkout (name?)					
Mastery Test					
Spelling Test					

Key: (for Teachers)   Ex 2.1 = Exercise 2, Column 1   IT = Individual Turns   IW = Independent Work

	36	37	38	39	40
Word Attack/Vocabulary					
Word Attack/Word Analysis					
Modeled Words	1	1	1	1	1
Words with endings: *ed, ly, er, y, ing, s*					
Compound Words	1, 2	2		2	
Mixed Words/Review	2				
Vocabulary					
New Vocabulary	3, 4	2, 3	2, 3	2, 3	2, 3
Vocabulary Preview					
Vocabulary from Context					
Vocabulary Review	IW	IW	IW	IW	IW
Fluency Read wordlists accurately, fluently	1, 2, 3	1, 2	1, 2	1, 2	1, 2
Story Reading/Comprehension					
Read/reread decodable text	7, 8	5, 7, 8	6, 7	6, 7	6, 7
Teacher models fluency/expression					
Comprehension					
Predict/Confirm Prediction					
Recall facts/rules	6, 8, IW	5, 6, 8, IW	5, 7, IW	5, 7, IW	5, 7, IW
Note details	8, IW	5, 6, 8, IW	5, 7, IW	5, 7, IW	5, 7, IW
Visualize					
Make Connections		IW		7, IW	IW
Draw inferences	8	8	7		
Draw conclusions	8	8	7	7	7
Activate Prior Knowledge	8, IW	5, 6		IW	IW
Identify Cause/Effect				IW	
Determine Character, Emotion, Motivation		8, IW	7, IW	7, IW	7, IW
Compare/Contrast		5, IW		4	4, 7, IW
Make Judgments	8, IW		7, IW	7, IW	7, IW
Main Idea					
Sequencing			IW		
Identify relevant information			IW		
Contradictions	5, IW	4, IW	4, IW	IW	IW
Make Deductions					
Figurative Language				4	4
Study Skills					
Interpret chart/graph/visual aid	IW	6			
Outlining			IW		
Informal Assessment					
Ongoing comprehension check	8, IW	5, 8, IW	7, IW	7, IW	7, IW
Ongoing decoding accuracy	7	7	6	6	6
Spelling					
Phonograms					
Word Families					
Multisyllabic Words	1, 2	1		1,2	1, 2
Word Parts		2	2	2	2
Spelling Rules					
Homonyms					
Antonyms					
Synonyms	4	3	3	3	3
Morphemic Analysis					
Spelling Strategies					
Word Origins					
Review					
Paired Practice for Fluency					
Ongoing practice to build fluency	9	9	8	8	8
Independent Work / Workcheck					
Ongoing Informal Assessment	11	11	10	10	10
Formal Assessment					
Individual Fluency Checkout (name?)					Lesson 40 Mastery Test
Mastery Test					Lesson 40 Mastery Test
Spelling Test					Lesson 40 Test

Key: (for Teachers)   Ex 2.1 = Exercise 2, Column 1   IT = Individual Turns   IW = Independent Work

	41	42	43	44	45
Word Attack/Vocabulary					
Word Attack/Word Analysis					
Modeled Words			1		1
Words with endings: *ed, ly, er, y, ing, s*	1		3	2	
Compound Words					
Mixed Words/Review	1	1	2	1	
Vocabulary					
New Vocabulary		2, 3	3, 4	2, 3	2, 3
Vocabulary Preview					
Vocabulary from Context					
Vocabulary Review	2, IW	IW	IW	IW	IW
Fluency Read wordlists accurately, fluently	1, 2	1, 2	1, 2, 3	1, 2	1, 2
Story Reading/Comprehension					
Read/reread decodable text	4, 5	5, 6	7, 8	5, 6	6, 7
Teacher models fluency/expression					
Comprehension					
Predict/Confirm Prediction					7, IW
Recall facts/rules	3, 5, IW	4, 6, IW	6, 8, IW	6, IW	5, 7, IW
Note details	3, 5, IW	4, 6, IW	6, 8, IW	6, IW	5, 7, IW
Visualize					
Make Connections	IW	6, IW	8, IW	6, IW	IW
Draw inferences	5	6, IW	8, IW	6, IW	7
Draw conclusions	5				
Activate Prior Knowledge			8		
Identify Cause/Effect					
Determine Character, Emotion, Motivation	5, IW	6, IW	8, IW	6, IW	7, IW
Compare/Contrast			8, IW	6, IW	7, IW
Make Judgments	5, IW	6, IW	6, 8	6, IW	7, IW
Main Idea	IW				
Sequencing					
Identify relevant information			IW		
Contradictions	IW	IW			IW
Make Deductions					
Figurative Language	IW	IW	5, IW	IW	4, IW
Study Skills					
Interpret chart/graph/visual aid					
Outlining					
Informal Assessment					
Ongoing comprehension check	5, IW	6, IW	8, IW	6, IW	7, IW
Ongoing decoding accuracy	4	5	7	5	6
Spelling					
Phonograms					
Word Families					
Multisyllabic Words	2	2	1	1	1, 2
Word Parts	1	1	1	1	1, 2
Spelling Rules					
Homonyms					
Antonyms					
Synonyms	2	3	4	3	3
Morphemic Analysis				1, 2	
Spelling Strategies					2
Word Origins					
Review	2			3	
Paired Practice for Fluency					
Ongoing practice to build fluency	6	7	9	7	8
Independent Work / Workcheck					
Ongoing Informal Assessment	8	9	11	9	10
Formal Assessment					
Individual Fluency Checkout					
Mastery Test					
Spelling Test					

Key: (for Teachers)   Ex 2.1 = Exercise 2, Column 1   IT = Individual Turns   IW = Independent Work

	46	47	48	49	50
Word Attack/Vocabulary					
Word Attack/Word Analysis					
Modeled Words		1			
Words with endings: *ed, ly, er, y, ing, s*					
Compound Words					
Mixed Words/Review	1		1	1	1
Vocabulary					
New Vocabulary	2, 3	2, 3	2, 3		2, 3
Vocabulary Preview					
Vocabulary from Context					
Vocabulary Review	IW	IW	IW	2, IW	IW
Fluency Read wordlists accurately, fluently	1, 2	1, 2	1, 2	1, 2	1, 2
Story Reading/Comprehension					
Read/reread decodable text	6, 7	6, 7	6, 7	5, 6	6, 7
Teacher models fluency/expression					
Comprehension					
Predict/Confirm Prediction	7, IW		IW	6, IW	
Recall facts/rules	5, 7, IW	5, 7, IW	5, 7, IW	4, 6, IW	5, 7, IW
Note details	5, 7, IW	5, 7, IW	5, 7, IW	4, 6, IW	5, 7, IW
Visualize					
Make Connections	IW	IW	7, IW		7, IW
Draw inferences	7, IW	7, IW	7, IW	6, IW	7, IW
Draw conclusions					8, IW
Activate Prior Knowledge					
Identify Cause/Effect					8
Determine Character, Emotion, Motivation	IW	7, IW	7, IW	6, IW	7, 8, IW
Compare/Contrast					
Make Judgments	7, IW	7, IW	7, IW	IW	7, 8
Main Idea				IW	
Sequencing	IW				
Identify relevant information		IW			
Contradictions					
Make Deductions		IW			8
Figurative Language	4, IW	4, IW	4, IW	3, IW	4, IW
Study Skills					
Interpret chart/graph/visual aid					
Outlining	IW				
Informal Assessment					
Ongoing comprehension check	7, IW	7, IW	7, IW	6, IW	7, 8, IW
Ongoing decoding accuracy	6	6	6	5	6
Spelling					
Phonograms					
Word Families					
Multisyllabic Words	1	1	2	2	
Word Parts	1	1	1, 2	2	2
Spelling Rules					
Homonyms					
Antonyms					
Synonyms	3	3	3	2	3
Morphemic Analysis	1	1	1		
Spelling Strategies				2	
Word Origins					
Review				1, 2	
Paired Practice for Fluency					
Ongoing practice to build fluency	8	8	8	7	9
Independent Work / Workcheck					
Ongoing Informal Assessment	10	10	10	9	11
Formal Assessment					
Individual Fluency Checkout					Lesson 50 Mastery Test
Mastery Test					Lesson 50 Mastery Test
Spelling Test					Lesson 50 Test

   Key: (for Teachers)   Ex 2.1 = Exercise 2, Column 1   IT = Individual Turns   IW = Independent Work

	51	52	53	54	55
Word Attack/Vocabulary					
Word Attack/Word Analysis					
Modeled Words		1	1		1
Words with endings: *ed, ly, er, y, ing, s*					2
Compound Words					
Mixed Words/Review	1		2	1	2
Vocabulary					
New Vocabulary	2, 3	2, 3	3, 4	2, 3	3, 4
Vocabulary Preview					
Vocabulary from Context					
Vocabulary Review	IW	IW	IW	IW	IW
Fluency Read wordlists accurately, fluently	1, 2	1, 2	1, 2, 3	1, 2	1, 2, 3
Story Reading/Comprehension					
Read/reread decodable text	5	6, 8, 9	6, 7	6, 7	7, 8
Teacher models fluency/expression					
Comprehension					
Predict/Confirm Prediction			7, IW	7, IW	7.3, 8, IW
Recall facts/rules	5	7, 6, 9, IW	5, 7, IW	5, 7, IW	6, 7, 8, IW
Note details		7, 6, 9, IW	5, 7, IW	5, 7, IW	6, 7, 8, IW
Visualize	IW				
Make Connections	6	6, 9, IW	7	IW	
Draw inferences	5, 6, IW	9	7	7, IW	7, 8
Draw conclusions	6		7, IW	4	5
Activate Prior Knowledge	5	6, IW		IW	7.3, IW
Identify Cause/Effect					
Determine Character, Emotion, Motivation	6	9, IW	7	7, IW	8, IW
Compare/Contrast	5, 6, IW	6, IW		IW	8, IW
Make Judgments	5, 6, IW	9, IW	7, IW	7, IW	8
Main Idea					
Sequencing					
Identify relevant information					7.2
Contradictions					
Make Deductions				4	5, IW
Figurative Language	4, 5, 6, IW	4, IW	IW	IW	IW
Study Skills					
Interpret chart/graph/visual aid					7.2
Outlining					
Informal Assessment					
Ongoing comprehension check	5, 6, IW	6, 9, IW	7, IW	7, IW	7, 8, IW
Ongoing decoding accuracy	5	8	6	6	7
Spelling					
Phonograms					
Word Families					
Multisyllabic Words		1	1	2	1
Word Parts		1	1	2	1
Spelling Rules					
Homonyms					
Antonyms					
Synonyms	3	3	3	3	4
Morphemic Analysis		1			1
Spelling Strategies					2
Word Origins					
Review					
Paired Practice for Fluency					
Ongoing practice to build fluency		10	8	8	9
Independent Work / Workcheck					
Ongoing Informal Assessment	9	12	10	10	11
Formal Assessment					
Individual Fluency Checkout					
Mastery Test					
Spelling Test					

	56	57	58	59	60
Word Attack/Vocabulary					
Word Attack/Word Analysis					
Modeled Words	1	1		1	
Words with endings: *ed, ly, er, y, ing, s*			1		1
Compound Words					1
Mixed Words/Review	2	2	1	1	1
Vocabulary					
New Vocabulary	3, 4	3, 4	2, 3	2, 3	2, 3
Vocabulary Preview					
Vocabulary from Context					
Vocabulary Review	IW	IW	IW	IW	IW
Fluency Read wordlists accurately, fluently	1, 2, 3	1, 2, 3	1, 2	1, 2	1, 2
Story Reading/Comprehension					
Read/reread decodable text	8, 9	7, 8	6, 7	6, 7	5
Teacher models fluency/expression					
Comprehension					
Predict/Confirm Prediction		8, IW			5.1
Recall facts/rules	7, 9, IW	6, 8, IW	5, 7, IW	5, 7, 8	
Note details	7, 9, IW	6, 8, IW	5, 7, IW	5, 7, 8	5, 6
Visualize					
Make Connections		IW	IW	8, IW	IW
Draw inferences	6, 9, IW	5, IW	IW	6, 7, IW	5.2, 8, IW
Draw conclusions	5		4		IW
Activate Prior Knowledge				IW	5, 6
Identify Cause/Effect			IW		
Determine Character, Emotion, Motivation	9, IW	8, IW	7, 8, IW	7, IW	5.2
Compare/Contrast	9, IW	IW		7, 8	6, IW
Make Judgments	9, IW		7, IW	7, IW	5.2, 6, IW
Main Idea					
Sequencing	IW				
Identify relevant information					
Contradictions					4
Make Deductions	5, 6, IW	5, IW	4, IW		
Figurative Language		IW	IW	4, 7, IW	4, 5, 6, IW
Study Skills					
Interpret chart/graph/visual aid					
Outlining			IW		
Informal Assessment					
Ongoing comprehension check	9, IW	8, IW	7, IW	7, 8, IW	5, 6, IW
Ongoing decoding accuracy	8	7	6	6	5
Spelling					
Phonograms					
Word Families					
Multisyllabic Words	1		1		1
Word Parts	1		1		
Spelling Rules					
Homonyms					
Antonyms					
Synonyms	4	4	4	3	3
Morphemic Analysis					
Spelling Strategies					
Word Origins					3
Review					
Paired Practice for Fluency					
Ongoing practice to build fluency	10	9	8	9	
Independent Work / Workcheck					
Ongoing Informal Assessment	12	11	10	11	8
Formal Assessment					
Individual Fluency Checkout					Lesson 60 Mastery Test
Mastery Test					Lesson 60 Mastery Test
Spelling Test					Lesson 60 Test

Key: (for Teachers)   Ex 2.1 = Exercise 2, Column 1   IT = Individual Turns   IW = Independent Work

	61	62	63	64	65
Word Attack/Vocabulary					
Word Attack/Word Analysis					
Modeled Words	1	1			
Words with endings: *ed, ly, er, y, ing, s*				1	1
Compound Words					1
Mixed Words/Review	2		1	1	1
Vocabulary					
New Vocabulary	3, 4	2, 3	2, 3	2, 3	2, 3
Vocabulary Preview					
Vocabulary from Context					
Vocabulary Review		IW	IW	IW	IW
Fluency Read wordlists accurately, fluently	1, 2, 3	1, 2	1, 2	1, 2	1, 2
Story Reading/Comprehension					
Read/reread decodable text	5, 7, 8	5, 6	5, 6	5, 7, 8	4, 6, 7
Teacher models fluency/expression					
Comprehension					
Predict/Confirm Prediction		6, IW			
Recall facts/rules	6, 7, 8, IW	4, 6, IW	4, 6, IW	6, 5, 8, IW	5, 7, IW
Note details	6, 7, 8, IW	4, 6, IW	4, 6, IW	6, 5, 8, IW	5, 7, IW
Visualize					
Make Connections	7.1, 8			IW	IW
Draw inferences		6	6, IW		7, IW
Draw conclusions	7.2		IW	4, 8	7
Activate Prior Knowledge	7.1	IW	IW	IW	
Identify Cause/Effect				IW	
Determine Character, Emotion, Motivation	7.2, 8, IW	6	6, IW	8, IW	7
Compare/Contrast			IW		
Make Judgments	8	IW	6, IW	IW	7, IW
Main Idea				IW	
Sequencing					
Identify relevant information	IW				4
Contradictions					7, IW
Make Deductions	IW	IW		4, IW	
Figurative Language	IW	IW	IW		
Study Skills					
Interpret chart/graph/visual aid	7.2, 7.3, IW			5	
Outlining					
Informal Assessment					
Ongoing comprehension check	7, 8, IW	6, IW	6, IW	5, 8, IW	7, IW
Ongoing decoding accuracy	5, 7	5	5	5, 7	4, 6
Spelling					
Phonograms	1				
Word Families					
Multisyllabic Words	2			1, 2	1
Word Parts	1	1			
Spelling Rules			1	1	
Homonyms				2	
Antonyms					
Synonyms	4	3	3	3	3
Morphemic Analysis	1	1			2
Spelling Strategies			2		
Word Origins					
Review	4			3	3
Paired Practice for Fluency					
Ongoing practice to build fluency	9	7	7	9	8
Independent Work / Workcheck					
Ongoing Informal Assessment	11	9	9	11	10
Formal Assessment					
Individual Fluency Checkout					
Mastery Test					
Spelling Test					

	66	67	68	69	70
Word Attack/Vocabulary					
Word Attack/Word Analysis					
Modeled Words					
Words with endings, *ed,,ly, er, y, ing, s*					
Compound Words					
Mixed Words/Review					
Vocabulary					
New Vocabulary	1	1	1	1	1
Vocabulary Preview					
Vocabulary from Context	2	2	2	2	2
Vocabulary Review	2, IW	2, IW	2, IW	2, IW	2, IW
Fluency Read wordlists accurately, fluently	2	2	2	2	2
Story Reading/Comprehension					
Read/reread decodable text	3, 5, 6	4, 5	4, 5	3, 5, 6	3, 5, 6
Teacher models fluency/expression					
Comprehension					
Predict/Confirm Prediction	6			6	IW
Recall facts/rules	4, 6, IW	3, 5, IW	3, 5, IW	4, 6, IW	4, 6, IW
Note details	4, 6, IW	3, 5, IW	3, 5, IW	4, 6, IW	4, 6, IW
Visualize					
Make Connections	3, IW				
Draw inferences	6, IW	5, IW	5, IW		6, IW
Draw conclusions					6
Activate Prior Knowledge	6, IW		IW	6	IW
Identify Cause/Effect					
Determine Character, Emotion, Motivation	6, IW	5, IW	5, IW	6, IW	6, IW
Compare/Contrast		5, IW	5, IW		6
Make Judgments	6, IW	5	5, IW	6, IW	IW
Main Idea					
Sequencing					
Identify relevant information				3	3
Contradictions					
Make Deductions					
Figurative Language		IW		IW	6, IW
Study Skills					
Interpret chart/graph/visual aid	IW				IW
Outlining					
Informal Assessment					
Ongoing comprehension check	6, IW	5, IW	5, IW	6, IW	6, IW
Ongoing decoding accuracy	3, 5	4	4	3, 5	3, 5
Spelling					
Phonograms					
Word Families					
Multisyllabic Words					
Word Parts					
Spelling Rules					
Homonyms					
Antonyms					
Synonyms	1, 2	1, 2	1, 2	1, 2	1, 2
Morphemic Analysis				2	
Spelling Strategies			2		
Word Origins					
Review	2	2	2	2	2
Paired Practice for Fluency					
Ongoing practice to build fluency	7	6	6	7	7
Independent Work / Workcheck					
Ongoing Informal Assessment	9	8	8	9	9
Formal Assessment					
Individual Fluency Checkout					Lesson 7 Mastery Test
Mastery Test					Lesson 70 Mastery Test
Spelling Test					Lesson 70 Test

Key: (for Teachers)   Ex 2.1 = Exercise 2, Column 1   IT = Individual Turns   IW = Independent Work

	71	72	73	74	75
Word Attack/Vocabulary					
Word Attack/Word Analysis					
Modeled Words				1	1
Words with endings: *ed, ly, er, y, ing, s*	2	2			
Compound Words					
Mixed Words/Review				2	2
Vocabulary					
New Vocabulary	1	1	1	3	3
Vocabulary Preview					
Vocabulary from Context	2	2	2	4	5
Vocabulary Review	2, IW	2, IW	2, IW	IW	4, IW
Fluency Read wordlists accurately, fluently	2	2	2	1, 2	1, 2, 4
Story Reading/Comprehension					
Read/reread decodable text	3, 5, 6	3, 5, 6	4, 5	4, 5, 6, 7	5, 6, 7
Teacher models fluency/expression				6	7, 8
Comprehension					
Predict/Confirm Prediction			5, IW		6
Recall facts/rules	6, IW	6, IW	5, IW	5, 6, IW	6, IW
Note details	6, IW	6, IW	5, IW	5, 6, IW	7, IW
Visualize					
Make Connections	3, IW	3, IW		IW	
Draw inferences	6, IW	6, IW		5, IW	6, 7, IW
Draw conclusions	6		5, IW	6	IW
Activate Prior Knowledge		IW	5.1	IW	IW
Identify Cause/Effect					
Determine Character, Emotion, Motivation	6, IW		5	6, IW	7
Compare/Contrast			5, IW		7, IW
Make Judgments		6, IW	5, IW	6.3	6, 7, IW
Main Idea	3	3			
Sequencing	IW				IW
Identify relevant information				6, IW	
Contradictions		IW			
Make Deductions					
Figurative Language	IW	IW		5, 6, 7, IW	6, 7, IW
Study Skills					
Interpret chart/graph/visual aid			IW	IW	
Outlining					
Informal Assessment					
Ongoing comprehension check	6, IW	6, IW	5, IW	5, 6, IW	6, 7, IW
Ongoing decoding accuracy	3, 5	3, 5	4	4, 5, 6, 7	5, 6, 7
Spelling					
Phonograms					
Word Families					
Multisyllabic Words					
Word Parts				1	1
Spelling Rules					
Homonyms					
Antonyms					
Synonyms	1, 2	1, 2	1, 2	3	3, 4
Morphemic Analysis				1	1
Spelling Strategies					2
Word Origins					
Review					
Paired Practice for Fluency					
Ongoing practice to build fluency	7	7	6	8	9
Independent Work / Workcheck					
Ongoing Informal Assessment	9	9	8	10	11
Formal Assessment					
Individual Fluency Checkout					
Mastery Test					
Spelling Test					

Key: (for Teachers)   Ex 2.1 = Exercise 2, Column 1   IT = Individual Turns   IW = Independent Work

	76	77	78	79	80
Word Attack/Vocabulary					
Word Attack/Word Analysis					
Modeled Words	1	1			
Words with endings: *ed, ly, er, y, ing, s*	1	2			
Compound Words					
Mixed Words/Review	2	2			
Vocabulary					
New Vocabulary	3	3			
Vocabulary Preview					
Vocabulary from Context	4	4		1	
Vocabulary Review	IW	4		IW	IW
Fluency Read wordlists accurately, fluently	1, 2	1, 2, 4			
Story Reading/Comprehension					
Read/reread decodable text	4, 6, 8, 9	6, 7	1, 2	1, 3, 4	1, 3, 4
Teacher models fluency/expression	5				
Comprehension					
Predict/Confirm Prediction		7.2		4, IW	
Recall facts/rules	7, 6, 9, IW	5, 7, IW	1, 2, IW	2, 4, IW	2, 4, IW
Note details	7, 6, 9, IW	5, 7, IW	1, 2, IW	2, 4, IW	1, 2, 4, IW
Visualize					
Make Connections	6				IW
Draw inferences	6, 9, IW	7, IW	2, IW		
Draw conclusions	6	7	2	4	4.1
Activate Prior Knowledge	6			IW	
Identify Cause/Effect					
Determine Character, Emotion, Motivation	6, 9, IW		2, IW	4, IW	4, IW
Compare/Contrast	9, IW				
Make Judgments		IW	2, IW	4, IW	4, IW
Main Idea					1
Sequencing					
Identify relevant information	9	IW			
Contradictions					
Make Deductions					
Figurative Language		IW	IW		
Study Skills					
Interpret chart/graph/visual aid	6, IW		IW	IW	IW
Outlining					1
Informal Assessment					
Ongoing comprehension check	6, 9, IW	7, IW	2, IW	4, IW	4, IW
Ongoing decoding accuracy	4, 8	6	1	1, 3	3, 3
Spelling					
Phonograms					
Word Families					
Multisyllabic Words	1				
Word Parts	1	1			
Spelling Rules					
Homonyms					
Antonyms					
Synonyms					
Morphemic Analysis	3	3, 4			
Spelling Strategies					
Word Origins					
Review		4			
Paired Practice for Fluency					
Ongoing practice to build fluency	10	8	3	5	5
Independent Work / Workcheck					
Ongoing Informal Assessment	12	10	5	7	7
Formal Assessment					
Individual Fluency Checkout (name?)					Lesson 80 Mastery Test
Mastery Test					Lesson 80 Mastery Test
Spelling Test					Lesson 80 Test

302 Lessons 76–80 | Key: (for Teachers) | Ex 2.1 = Exercise 2, Column 1 | IT = Individual Turns | IW = Independent Work

	81	82	83	84	85
Word Attack/Vocabulary					
Word Attack/Word Analysis					
Modeled Words	1	1	1	1	
Words with endings: *ed, ly, er, y, ing, s*	3	2	1	1, 2, 3	1
Compound Words					
Mixed Words/Review				2	1
Vocabulary					
New Vocabulary	3, 4	2, 3	2, 3	3, 4	
Vocabulary Preview					
Vocabulary from Context					2
Vocabulary Review		IW	IW	IW	2, IW
Fluency Read wordlists accurately, fluently	1, 2, 3	1, 2	1, 2	1, 2, 3	1, 2
Story Reading/Comprehension					
Read/reread decodable text	5, 7, 8	4, 6, 7	5, 7	5, 7	3, 4
Teacher models fluency/expression					
Comprehension					
Predict/Confirm Prediction					
Recall facts/rules	5, 6, 8, IW	4, 7, 8, IW	4, 5, 6, IW	5, 6, IW	3, 4, 5, IW
Note details	6, 8, IW	4, 5, 7, 8, IW	4, 5, 6, IW	5, 6, IW	4, 5, IW
Visualize					
Make Connections	IW	8, IW			IW
Draw inferences	8, IW	7, IW			
Draw conclusions		8	6	6	5
Activate Prior Knowledge					IW
Identify Cause/Effect					
Determine Character, Emotion, Motivation	8, IW	7, IW	6, IW	6	5, IW
Compare/Contrast					
Make Judgments		7, 8, IW	6, IW	6, IW	5, 6, IW
Main Idea					
Sequencing	8, IW	IW	IW	IW	
Identify relevant information					
Contradictions					IW
Make Deductions				6, IW	
Figurative Language	8			IW	
Study Skills					
Interpret chart/graph/visual aid					
Outlining	IW	IW	IW	IW	
Informal Assessment					
Ongoing comprehension check	8, IW	7, 8, IW	6, IW	6, IW	5, IW
Ongoing decoding accuracy	5, 7	4, 6	5, 7	5, 7	3, 4
Spelling					
Phonograms					
Word Families					
Multisyllabic Words	2, 3	2	1	2, 3	1
Word Parts	1	1	1	1	
Spelling Rules					
Homonyms					
Antonyms					
Synonyms	4	3	3	4	2
Morphemic Analysis					
Spelling Strategies					
Word Origins					
Review	4				
Paired Practice for Fluency					
Ongoing practice to build fluency	9	9			
Independent Work / Workcheck					
Ongoing Informal Assessment	11	11	9	9	8
Formal Assessment					
Individual Fluency Checkout					
Mastery Test					
Spelling Test					

Key: (for Teachers)   Ex 2.1 = Exercise 2, Column 1   IT = Individual Turns   IW = Independent Work

	86	87	88	89	90
Word Attack/Vocabulary					
Word Attack/Word Analysis					
Modeled Words	1	1	1	1	1
Words with endings: *ed, ly, er, y, ing, s*					
Compound Words				1	2
Mixed Words/Review					
Vocabulary					
New Vocabulary	2, 3	3, 4	2, 3	2, 3	2, 3
Vocabulary Preview					
Vocabulary from Context	4	5	4	4	4
Vocabulary Review	4, IW	5, IW	4, IW	4, IW	4, IW
Fluency Read wordlists accurately, fluently	1, 2, 4	1, 2, 3, 5	1, 2, 4	1, 2, 4	1, 2, 4
Story Reading/Comprehension					
Read/reread decodable text	5, 6	6, 7	5, 7, 8	5, 6, 7	5, 7, 8
Teacher models fluency/expression	6.4, 6.5				
Comprehension					
Predict/Confirm Prediction		7			
Recall facts/rules	5, 6	7, 8, IW	6, 8, IW	6, 7, IW	6, 8, IW
Note details	6	7, 8, IW	6, 8, IW	6, 7, IW	6, 8, IW
Visualize					
Make Connections	IW		IW	IW	IW
Draw inferences	6, IW				
Draw conclusions		8		6	
Activate Prior Knowledge	IW	7, 8, IW	IW	6, IW	
Identify Cause/Effect				6	
Determine Character, Emotion, Motivation				IW	
Compare/Contrast		8, IW	8, IW	6, 7, IW	8, IW
Make Judgments	6	7, 8, IW	8, IW	6, 7, IW	8, IW
Main Idea					
Sequencing		IW			
Identify relevant information					
Contradictions					
Make Deductions					
Figurative Language	6, IW		IW		
Literary Devices			5, IW	5, IW	5, IW
Study Skills					
Interpret chart/graph/visual aid		6, 7, IW	IW	6, IW	IW
Outlining					
Informal Assessment					
Ongoing comprehension check	6, IW	7, 8, IW	8, IW	6, 7, IW	8, IW
Ongoing decoding accuracy	5, 6	6, 7	5, 7	5, 6	5, 7
Spelling					
Phonograms					
Word Families					
Multisyllabic Words	1	1	1		1, 2
Word Parts	1	1	1	1	1
Spelling Rules					
Homonyms					
Antonyms					
Synonyms	3, 4	4	3	3	3
Morphemic Analysis					
Spelling Strategies	2				
Word Origins					
Review					
Paired Practice for Fluency					
Ongoing practice to build fluency	7	9	9	8	9
Independent Work / Workcheck					
Ongoing Informal Assessment	9	11	11	10	11
Formal Assessment					
Individual Fluency Checkout (name?)					Lesson 90 Mastery Test
Mastery Test					Lesson 90 Mastery Test
Spelling Assessment					Lesson 90 Test

Key: (for Teachers)   Ex 2.1 = Exercise 2, Column 1   IT = Individual Turns   IW = Independent Work

	91	92	93	94	95
Word Attack/Vocabulary					
Word Attack/Word Analysis					
Modeled Words	1	1	1	1	1
Words with endings: *ed, ly, er, y, ing, s*				2	
Compound Words				2	2
Mixed Words/Review	2	2	2	2	2
Vocabulary					
New Vocabulary	3, 4	3, 4	3, 4	3, 4	3, 4
Vocabulary Preview					
Vocabulary from Context		5			
Vocabulary Review	IW	5, IW	IW	IW	IW
Fluency Read wordlists accurately, fluently	1, 2, 3	1, 2, 3, 5	1, 2, 3	1, 2, 3	1, 2, 3
Story Reading/Comprehension					
Read/reread decodable text	5, 8, 9	6, 7, 9, 10	5, 7, 8	5, 7, 8	5, 7, 8
Teacher models fluency/expression					
Comprehension					
Predict/Confirm Prediction					
Recall facts/rules	7, 9, IW	8, 7, 10, IW	6, 8, IW	6, 8, IW	6, 8, IW
Note details	7, 9, IW	8, 7, 10, IW	6, 8, IW	6, 8, IW	6, 8, IW
Visualize					
Make Connections				IW	
Draw inferences	9			8	8
Draw conclusions	9	7.1	8	8	8
Activate Prior Knowledge	IW				
Identify Cause/Effect					
Determine Character Emotion, Motivation	9, IW	10	8, IW	8, IW	8, IW
Compare/Contrast		7.2, 10			
Make Judgments	9, IW	7.1	8, IW	8, IW	IW
Main Idea					
Sequencing					
Identify relevant information					
Contradictions	5				
Make Deductions					
Figurative Language	IW			8, IW	
Literary Devices			IW		
Logic				5, IW	5, IW
Study Skills					
Interpret chart/graph/visual aid	5, 6, IW	6, IW	5, IW	IW	IW
Outlining					
Informal Assessment					
Ongoing comprehension check	9, IW	7, 10, IW	8, IW	8, IW	8, IW
Ongoing decoding accuracy	5, 8	6, 7, 9	5, 7	5, 7	5, 7
Spelling					
Phonograms					
Word Families					
Multisyllabic Words	2	1	2	3	3
Word Parts	1	1	1	1	1
Spelling Rules					
Homonyms					
Antonyms					
Synonyms	4	4, 5	4	4	4
Morphemic Analysis					
Spelling Strategies					
Word Origins					
Review					
Paired Practice for Fluency					
Ongoing practice to build fluency	10	11	9	9	9
Independent Work / Workcheck					
Ongoing Informal Assessment	12	13	11	11	11
Formal Assessment					
Individual Fluency Checkout					
Mastery Test					
Spelling Test					

Key: (for Teachers)   Ex 2.1 = Exercise 2, Column 1   IT = Individual Turns   IW = Independent Work

	96	97	98	99	100
Word Attack/Vocabulary					
Word Attack/Word Analysis					
Modeled Words		1		1	
Words with endings: *ed, ly, er, y, ing, s*	1	2	1, 2	2	
Compound Words					
Mixed Words/Review	1	2	1	2	1
Vocabulary					
New Vocabulary	2, 3	3, 4	2, 3	3, 4	
Vocabulary Preview					
Vocabulary from Context		5	4	5	5
Vocabulary Review	IW	5, IW	4, IW	5, IW	2, IW
Fluency Read wordlists accurately, fluently	1, 2	1, 2, 3, 5	1, 2, 4	1, 2, 3, 5	1, 2
Story Reading/Comprehension					
Read/reread decodable text	5, 6	6, 8, 9	5, 7, 8	5, 8, 9	3, 5, 6
Teacher models fluency/expression					
Comprehension					
Predict/Confirm Prediction					7
Recall facts/rules	4, 6, IW	7, 6, 9, IW	6, 8, IW	7, 9, IW	4, 6, 7, IW
Note details	4, 6, IW	7, 6, 9, IW	6, 8, IW	7, 9, IW	4, 6, 7, IW
Visualize					
Make Connections	IW				
Draw inferences					
Draw conclusions	6	9, IW	5, 8	5, 9	6, 7, 8
Activate Prior Knowledge				IW	
Identify Cause/Effect					
Determine Character, Emotion, Motivation	6, IW	9, IW	8, IW	9	6, IW
Compare/Contrast		6			
Make Judgments	6, IW	6, 9, IW	8, IW	9, IW	6, 7, IW
Main Idea					
Sequencing				IW	
Identify relevant information					
Contradictions					3
Make Deductions					
Figurative Language	IW			IW	
Literary Devices	IW				
Logic	IW	IW	5, IW	6, IW	IW
Study Skills					
Interpret chart/graph/visual aid	IW	IW	IW		3, IW
Outlining					
Informal Assessment					
Ongoing comprehension check	6, IW	6, 9, IW	8, IW	9, IW	6, 7, IW
Ongoing decoding accuracy	5	6, 8	5, 7	5, 8	3, 5
Spelling					
Phonograms					
Word Families					
Multisyllabic Words	1	1	1, 2		
Word Parts	1	1	1	1	
Spelling Rules					
Homonyms					
Antonyms					
Synonyms	3	3, 5	3, 4	4, 5.3	2.3
Morphemic Analysis		2			
Spelling Strategies					
Word Origins					
Review					
Paired Practice for Fluency					
Ongoing practice to build fluency	7	10	9	10	8
Independent Work / Workcheck					
Ongoing Informal Assessment	9	12	11	12	10
Formal Assessment					
Individual Fluency Checkout					Lesson 100 Mastery Test
Mastery Test					Lesson 100 Mastery Test
Spelling Test					Lesson 100 Test

Key: (for Teachers) Ex 2.1 = Exercise 2, Column 1 IT = Individual Turns IW = Independent Work

	101	102	103	104	105
Word Attack/Vocabulary					
Word Attack/Word Analysis					
Modeled Words	1			1	
Words with endings: *ed, ly, er, y, ing, s*	1				
Compound Words		2			
Mixed Words/Review	2	1	1	2	1
Vocabulary					
New Vocabulary	3, 4	2, 3	2, 3	3, 4	2, 3
Vocabulary Preview					
Vocabulary from Context	5	4	4		
Vocabulary Review	5, IW	4, IW	4, IW	IW	IW
Fluency Read wordlists accurately, fluently	1, 2, 3, 5	1, 2, 4	1, 2, 4	1, 2, 3	1, 2
Story Reading/Comprehension					
Read/reread decodable text	6, 8, 9	5, 7, 8	6, 7	6, 7	4, 6, 7
Teacher models fluency/expression					
Comprehension					
Predict/Confirm Prediction			7, IW		7, IW
Recall facts/rules	7, 9, IW	6, 8, IW	5, 7, IW	5, 7, IW	5, 7, IW
Note details	7, 9, IW	6, 8, IW	5, 7, IW	5, 7, IW	5, 7, IW
Visualize					
Make Connections		IW			IW
Draw inferences		8, IW	7, IW	7, IW	7, IW
Draw conclusions	9, IW	5, 8			
Activate Prior Knowledge		IW	7, IW		
Identify Cause/Effect					4, IW
Determine Character, Emotion, Motivation	9, IW	8, IW		7, IW	7, IW
Compare/Contrast					
Make Judgments	9, IW	8, IW	IW	IW	4
Main Idea					
Sequencing		IW	IW		
Identify relevant information					
Contradictions	6				
Make Deductions					
Figurative Language			7, IW	7, IW	7, IW
Literary Devices			IW		
Logic	IW	5, IW	IW	IW	4, IW
Study Skills					
Interpret chart/graph/visual aid	6, IW	IW			IW
Outlining					
Informal Assessment					
Ongoing comprehension check	9, IW	8, IW	7, IW	7, IW	7, IW
Ongoing decoding accuracy	6, 8	5, 7	6	6	4, 6
Spelling					
Phonograms					
Word Families					
Multisyllabic Words	1	1	1	1, 2	1, 2
Word Parts	1	1, 2	1	1, 2	1, 2
Spelling Rules			1	1	1
Homonyms					
Antonyms					
Synonyms	3, 5	3, 4	4	4	3
Morphemic Analysis		1			
Spelling Strategies					
Word Origins					
Review					
Paired Practice for Fluency					
Ongoing practice to build fluency	10	9	8	8	8
Independent Work / Workcheck					
Ongoing Informal Assessment	12	11	10	10	10
Formal Assessment					
Individual Fluency Checkout					
Mastery Test					
Spelling Test					

	106	107	108	109	110
Word Attack/Vocabulary					
Word Attack/Word Analysis					
Modeled Words	1		1	1	1
Words with endings: *ed, ly, er, y, ing, s*	1, 2		1, 2		
Compound Words					1
Mixed Words/Review	2	1		2	
Vocabulary					
New Vocabulary	3, 4	2, 3	2, 3	3, 4	2, 3
Vocabulary Preview					
Vocabulary from Context	5	4	4		
Vocabulary Review	5, IW	4, IW	4, IW	IW	IW
Fluency Read wordlists accurately, fluently	1, 2, 3, 5	1, 2, 4	1, 2, 4	1, 2, 3	1, 2
Story Reading/Comprehension					
Read/reread decodable text	6, 8, 9	6, 7	5, 7, 8	5, 7, 8	4, 6, 7
Teacher models fluency/expression					
Comprehension					
Predict/Confirm Prediction	6.2	7			
Recall facts/rules	7, 6, 9, IW	5, 7, IW	6, 8, IW	6, 8, IW	5, 7, IW
Note details	7, 6, 9, IW	5, 7, IW	6, 8, IW	6, 8, IW	5, 7, IW
Visualize					
Make Connections	IW	IW	IW		IW
Draw inferences				8, IW	
Draw conclusions	9		5, 8	5, 8	4, 7
Activate Prior Knowledge					
Identify Cause/Effect					
Determine Character, Emotion, Motivation	9, IW	7, IW	8		
Compare/Contrast	9	7, IW			
Make Judgments		7, IW	8, IW		4, 7, IW
Main Idea					
Sequencing				IW	7
Identify relevant information					
Contradictions	IW				
Make Deductions					
Figurative Language	9	IW	IW		
Literary Devices			IW		
Logic	IW	IW	5, IW	5, IW	4, IW
Study Skills					
Interpret chart/graph/visual aid				IW	
Outlining					
Informal Assessment					
Ongoing comprehension check	6, 9, IW	7, IW	8, IW	8, IW	7, IW
Ongoing decoding accuracy	6, 8	6	5, 7	5, 7	4, 6
Spelling					
Phonograms					
Word Families					
Multisyllabic Words	1, 2	1, 2	1, 2		1
Word Parts	1, 2	1, 2	1, 2	1, 2	
Spelling Rules					
Homonyms					
Antonyms					
Synonyms	4, 5	3, 4	3, 4	4	3
Morphemic Analysis					
Spelling Strategies					
Word Origins					
Review					
Paired Practice for Fluency					
Ongoing practice to build fluency	10	8	9	9	8
Independent Work / Workcheck					
Ongoing Informal Assessment	12	10	11	11	10
Formal Assessment					
Individual Fluency Checkout					Lesson 110 Mastery Test
Mastery Test					Lesson 110 Mastery Test
Spelling Test					Lesson 110 Test

	111	112	113	114	115
Word Attack/Vocabulary					
Word Attack/Word Analysis					
Modeled Words	1		1	1	1
Words with endings: *ed, ly, er, y, ing, s*					
Compound Words		1		1	2
Mixed Words/Review	2	1	2		2
Vocabulary					
New Vocabulary	3, 4	2, 3	3, 4	2, 3	3, 4
Vocabulary Preview					
Vocabulary from Context		4, 5	6	4	5
Vocabulary Review	IW	4, IW	5, IW	4, IW	5, IW
Fluency Read wordlists accurately, fluently	1, 2, 3	1, 2, 4	1, 2, 3, 5	1, 2, 4	1, 2, 3, 5
Story Reading/Comprehension					
Read/reread decodable text	5, 7, 8	5, 7, 8	6, 8, 9	6, 7	7, 8
Teacher models fluency/expression					
Comprehension					
Predict/Confirm Prediction		8, IW			
Recall facts/rules	6, 8, IW	6, 8, IW	7, 9, IW	5, 7, IW	6, 8, IW
Note details	6, 8, IW	6, 8, IW	7, 9, IW	5, 7, IW	6, 8, IW
Visualize					
Make Connections	8, IW				IW
Draw inferences	8	8, IW	IW		8, IW
Draw conclusions	5, 8	8	6		8
Activate Prior Knowledge	8			7, IW	IW
Identify Cause/Effect					
Determine Character, Emotion, Motivation	8, IW	8, IW	9, IW	7, IW	8, IW
Compare/Contrast					
Make Judgments	5, 8, IW	8, IW	9, IW		8, IW
Main Idea					
Sequencing		IW	9	IW	
Identify relevant information					
Contradictions					
Make Deductions					
Figurative Language					8, IW
Literary Devices	IW				
Logic	5, IW	5, IW	6, IW	IW	IW
Study Skills					
Interpret chart/graph/visual aid					IW
Outlining					
Informal Assessment					
Ongoing comprehension check	8, IW	8, IW	9, IW	7, IW	8, IW
Ongoing decoding accuracy	5, 7	5, 7	6, 8	6	7
Spelling					
Phonograms					
Word Families					
Multisyllabic Words	1	1	2	2	1
Word Parts	1	1	2	2	
Spelling Rules					
Homonyms					
Antonyms					
Synonyms	4	3, 4	4, 5	3, 4	4, 5
Morphemic Analysis					2
Spelling Strategies					
Word Origins					
Review			5	4	5
Paired Practice for Fluency					
Ongoing practice to build fluency	9	9	10	8	9
Independent Work / Workcheck					
Ongoing Informal Assessment	11	11	12	10	11
Formal Assessment					
Individual Fluency Checkout					
Mastery Test					
Spelling Test					

	116	117	118	119	120
Word Attack/Vocabulary					
Word Attack/Word Analysis					
Modeled Words	1			1	
Words with endings: *ed, ly, er, y, ing, s*	2				
Compound Words			1		
Mixed Words/Review	2	1	1	2	1
Vocabulary					
New Vocabulary	3, 4	2, 3	2, 3		
Vocabulary Preview					
Vocabulary from Context	5			3	2
Vocabulary Review	5, IW	IW	IW	3, IW	2, IW
Fluency Read wordlists accurately, fluently	1, 2, 3, 5	1, 2	1, 2	1, 2, 3	1, 2
Story Reading/Comprehension					
Read/reread decodable text	6, 8, 9	4, 6, 7	5, 6	5, 6	4, 5
Teacher models fluency/expression					
Comprehension					
Predict/Confirm Prediction				6	5, 6, IW
Recall facts/rules	7, 9, IW	5, 7, IW	4, 6, IW	4, 6, IW	3, 5, 6, IW
Note details	7, 9, IW	5, 7, IW	4, 6, IW	4, 6, IW	3, 5, 6, IW
Visualize					
Make Connections	IW				6
Draw inferences	9, IW	7, IW			5, IW
Draw conclusions	6, 9	4, 7	6	6	5, 6
Activate Prior Knowledge		IW	IW		
Identify Cause/Effect					
Determine Character, Emotion, Motivation	9, IW	7, IW	6, IW	6, IW	6, IW
Compare/Contrast			IW		6
Make Judgments	IW	7, IW	6, IW	6, IW	5, 6, IW
Main Idea					
Sequencing		IW			
Identify relevant information					
Contradictions					
Make Deductions					
Figurative Language					5, IW
Literary Devices			IW		
Logic	6, IW	4, IW	IW	IW	IW
Study Skills					
Interpret chart/graph/visual aid					
Outlining	IW				IW
Informal Assessment					
Ongoing comprehension check	9, IW	7, IW	6, IW	6, IW	5, 6, IW
Ongoing decoding accuracy	6, 8	4, 6	5	5	4
Spelling					
Phonograms					
Word Families					
Multisyllabic Words	1	1		1	1
Word Parts	1	1		1	1
Spelling Rules					
Homonyms					
Antonyms					
Synonyms	4, 5	3	3	3	2
Morphemic Analysis					
Spelling Strategies					
Word Origins					
Review					2
Paired Practice for Fluency					
Ongoing practice to build fluency	10	8	7	7	7
Independent Work / Workcheck					
Ongoing Informal Assessment	12	10	9	9	9
Formal Assessment					
Individual Fluency Checkout (name?)					Lesson 120 Mastery Test
Mastery Test					Lesson 120 Mastery Test
Spelling Test					Lesson 120 Test

Key: (for Teachers) Ex 2.1 = Exercise 2, Column 1 IT = Individual Turns IW = Independent Work